"This is a sophisticated and practically important body of work that I think will interest a cross-section of scholars, bureaucrats, and anyone interested in the migration and asylum seeker regime. It deserves to be read and analysed by others."

Afshin Akhtar-Khavari, *Professor of International Law, Queensland University of Technology, Australia.*

Sovereignty, Migration and the Law

This book examines how states justify the creation of physical, policy and legislative barriers of entry for migrants by drawing on a concept of sovereignty.

The movement of people across the world in search of refuge from persecution, war and poverty is accelerating. And as states confronted with this movement create physical, policy and legislative barriers to entry, they justify this exclusion by drawing on concepts of sovereignty. This book interrogates that justification in an historical and theoretical context using the case study of Australian law and policy since 1900, as well as instances from other Western countries that have routinely copied from Australia. But just as Australian migration polices are being replicated in the US, Britain and Europe, so, this book argues, is their employment of an anachronistic concept of sovereignty: one that is reasserted precisely because of its waning power in the face of globalisation.

This book will be an important resource for law and political science scholars, researchers and students in the fields of migration and refugee law and policy, as well as to professional policy makers, government institutions, lawyers and international agencies with a particular focus on those fields.

Patricia Rushton is a barrister and solicitor of the Supreme Court of South Australia and of the High Court of Australia and practices law at Beena Rezaee Legal and Migration. She is also an occasional lecturer at the College of Business Government and Law, Flinders University, Australia.

Sovereignty, Migration and the Law

The Exclusion of Non-Citizens

Patricia Rushton

Routledge
Taylor & Francis Group
a GlassHouse Book

First published 2025
by Routledge
4 Park Square, Milton Park, Abingdon, Oxon OX14 4RN

and by Routledge
605 Third Avenue, New York, NY 10158

Routledge is an imprint of the Taylor & Francis Group, an informa business

A GlassHouse book

British Library Cataloguing-in-Publication Data
A catalogue record for this book is available from the British Library

Library of Congress Cataloging-in-Publication Data
Names: Rushton, Patricia, author.
Title: Sovereignty, migration, and the law : the exclusion of non-citizens / Patricia Rushton.
Description: Abingdon, Oxon [UK] ; New York, NY : Routledge, 2025. | Includes bibliographical references and index.
Identifiers: LCCN 2024043675 (print) | LCCN 2024043676 (ebook) | ISBN 9781032849676 (hardback) | ISBN 9781032849690 (paperback) | ISBN 9781003515852 (ebook)
Subjects: LCSH: Noncitizens. | Emigration and immigration law. | Emigration and immigration law—Australia. | Refugees—Legal status, laws, etc. | Sovereignty.
Classification: LCC K3275 .R87 2025 (print) | LCC K3275 (ebook) | DDC 342.08/2—dc23/eng/20240918
LC record available at https://lccn.loc.gov/2024043675
LC ebook record available at https://lccn.loc.gov/2024043676

ISBN: 978-1-032-84967-6 (hbk)
ISBN: 978-1-032-84969-0 (pbk)
ISBN: 978-1-003-51585-2 (ebk)

DOI: 10.4324/9781003515852

Typeset in Sabon
by Apex CoVantage, LLC

I dedicate this book to the members of the Circles of Friends for Refugees and to Besmellah Rezaee and his team at Beena Rezaee Legal and Migration whose work and dedication to asylum seekers has inspired me.

. . . and to the Rushtons and Beggs and a Murphy and a Forster, human and animal, with us or a memory, for their love and support.

Contents

Foreword

Migration and human mobility are amongst the most discussed concepts in many areas of scholarship and practice, including social science, humanities and law. Since the emergence of the Westphalian system in the 17th century, the principle of the nation-state and the international law concept of 'sovereignty' became the fundamentals of international relations and international law. This means states have the sovereign power to regulate migration and exclude migrants and noncitizens. In recent decades, as the global movement of people increases, migration has impacted not only law but also diplomatic relations, security, trade, international aid, human rights and even national elections.

Since its federation in 1901, Australia has been fundamentally shaped by migration and it continues to impact the law, policies and politics of this country. Two of the first pieces of legislation, alongside the constitution of Australia, enacted, in 1901, at the start of the establishment of the Australian Federation, were concerned with foreign labour and restricting immigration. According to the most recent census (2021), almost half of Australians have a parent who is born overseas.

Beginning from almost one hundred years after the enactment of the Immigration Restriction Act 1901 (Cth), Dr Patricia Rushton has investigated and examined changes in legislation from 2000 to 2020 to interrogate Australia's restrictive immigration law and policies based on the international principle of sovereignty and security. The author, skilfully, investigates the historical background, political consideration and intended policies of changing law for a two-decade period which shows the importance of migration policies in shaping Australia's political landscape of dealing with noncitizens. She investigates and examines various parliamentary documents, discussions, legislative provisions and judicial decisions to discover how the executive branch of government employs the international concept of sovereignty to exclude noncitizens and regulate and shape immigration and refugee laws and policies.

The book is based on the author's PhD book, completed at Flinders University Discipline of Law, in 2023. The author's decades of experiences as a senior executive in the Commonwealth of Australia, along with several years of research and scholarly work at Flinders College of Business, Government and Law College and her legal practice in Australia has enabled her to produce a thesis, now a book, which significantly contributes to knowledge and demonstrates the significance of Australia's experience to the rest of the world.

I had the privilege, and the pleasure, of acting as a supervisor of Dr Rushton's PhD thesis at Flinders Law, College of Business Government and Law at Flinders University in Adelaide, Australia. I am now privileged to introduce her excellent work to the fields of social sciences, humanities, legal scholarship, human rights, national and international legal practice, government and policy and international institutions. The author should be congratulated for such important, timely and excellent work.

Dr Hossein Esmaeili
Associate Professor of Law
College of Government, Business and Law
Flinders University, Adelaide, Australia
August 2024

Preface

After a successful and eye-opening career as a senior executive in Australia's Commonwealth Government, at times working closely with government ministers, I left to more directly follow my passion for social justice. I established the presence of the children's charity the Smith Family in the Northern Territory. Adapting the Smith Family's models, I introduced a 'school at the centre' approach, using partnerships with the school as a scaffold of business and philanthropic support for disadvantaged students. My same passion for social justice sparked my engagement with community efforts to support asylum seekers and refugees and this led to engaging in the study of law and a second career as a lawyer, a teacher of law and researcher.

This book is informed by that firsthand knowledge of the machinations of government and of the complex circumstances of those fleeing discrimination, war, poverty, racism, sexism and prejudice arriving in a country that is not always what they expect. It is based on my doctoral thesis completed in October 2022.

Acknowledgements

I am most grateful for the depth of wisdom, guidance, encouragement and wonderful sense of humour of my guide and supporter Associate Professor Hossein Esmaeili. I also thank Dr Rowan Nicholson whose knowledge and expertise have added to my capability to complete this work.

Part One

The Theoretical, International and Historical Context

Chapter 1

Introduction

I Rationale

In 1901 a group of British colonies joined together to become an Australian Federation, a dominion of the British Empire. The order of business for the first Federal Parliament of Australia included two of the most nation-defining pieces of legislation.[1] This legislation aimed to exclude unwanted migrants.[2] It was justified by the policy imperative of achieving a white Australia.[3] The Federation Parliament's power to pass this exclusionary legislation derived from Britain's 'essential prerogative of a sovereign State to determine who shall be allowed to come within its dominions'.[4]

Almost one hundred years later Australia had been an independent sovereign state in its own right for many decades and as such, alongside other Western liberal democracies, had committed to international human rights conventions. From 2000 to 2020 the Australian Parliament passed many pieces of migration legislation that were designed to exclude, using this 'essential prerogative of a sovereign State' but without the policy purpose of a white Australia so clearly articulated and agreed upon in 1901.[5] Instead, amendments to the *Migration Act 1958* (Cth) (the Act) made between 2000 and 2020 were justified as a protection or assertion of sovereignty. This book interrogates that justification in an historical and international context.

The implications of this interrogation go beyond Australia's border. The movement of people across the world in search of refuge from persecution, war and poverty is accelerating. So too is the market for talent and

1 *Immigration Restriction Act 1901* (Cth); Myra Willard, *History of the White Australia Policy to 1920* (Melbourne University Press, 1923); *Pacific Island Labourers Act 1901* (Cth).
2 *Immigration Restriction Act 1901* (Cth); Myra Willard, *History of the White Australia Policy to 1920* (Melbourne University Press, 1923); *Pacific Island Labourers Act 1901* (Cth); Gwenda Tavan, *The Long, Slow Death of White Australia* (Scribe Publications, 2005).
3 See discussion of the 1901 parliamentary debates in Chapter 4.
4 *Robtelmes v Brenan* (1906) 4 CLR 395, 401.
5 *Robtelmes v Brenan* (1906) 4 CLR 395, 401.

DOI: 10.4324/9781003515852-2

opportunity. This movement of people is driven and facilitated by the globalised neoliberal values of the market and the interconnectedness that modern communication provides. Some European and North American countries have already drawn inspiration from the Australian experience.[6]

In 2017 Professor Juss advised from King's College London, 'we should take Australia seriously quite simply because what Australia does in border controls today, the rest of the world might do tomorrow. We ignore it at our peril'.[7] In the same year Australian prime minister Malcolm Turnbull received dubious praise from US president Donald Trump. Trump praised Australia's asylum seeker policies saying 'you are worse than I am'.[8] Two years later, in June 2019, Trump tweeted further praise for Australian migration policies. 'Much can be learned' he said, alongside pictures of Australian warnings to asylum seekers such as "NO WAY-You will not make Australia home'.[9] In March 2023 the British prime minister, Rishi Sunak, borrowed Australian prime minister Tony Abbott's 2014 election winning promise to 'Stop the Boats'.[10] Sunak passed legislation to deport asylum seekers to Rwanda with an apparent replica of Australian policy. His Home Secretary argued there was no comparison to the Australian policy. However, during the UK parliament's consideration of the Safety of Rwanda Bill 2023 (UK) Australia was held up in the second reading speech and debate as a model that such a policy of deterrence works and that we had solved the problem of unregulated immigrant boat arrivals.[11]

The Australian experience, a model for the world or a cautionary tale, is detailed here in its historical and an international context.

6 Sasha Polakow-Suransky, 'How Europe Fell in Love with Australia's Immigration Policy', *The Guardian* (12 October 2017) <www.theguardian.com/world/2017/oct/12/how-europes-far-right-fell-in-love-with-australias-immigration-policy>.

7 Satvinder Juss, 'Detention and Delusion in Australia's Kafkaesque Refugee Law' (2017) 36 *Refugee Survey Quarterly* 146, 161. Professor Juss is a leading academic at Dickson Poon School of Law, King's College London.

8 This was revealed in a transcript of a conversation between Trump and Turnbull concerning the US taking offshore asylum seekers from Australia. Turnbull said 'Even if we think you are the best person in the world, even if you are a Nobel Prize-winning genius, we will not let you in', Mr Turnbull said, according to the transcript. Mr Trump replied: 'That is a good idea. We should do that too. You are worse than I am'. Quoted in *SBS News* (4 August 2017) < www.sbs.com.au/news/article/you-are-worse-than-i-am-transcript-reveals-turnbull-told-trump-he-could-decide-not-to-take-asylum-seekers/pasw4h0t7>.

9 Jason Wilson, 'The USA Is Imprisoning People It Finds Undesirable. Australia Has Already Lived This Nightmare,' *The Guardian* (27 June 2019).

10 'PM Statement on the Stop the Boats Bill: 7 March 2023', *GOV.UK* <www.gov.uk>.

11 Madeline Gleeson and Theodore Konstadinides, 'The UK's Rwanda Policy and Lessons from Australia', *UHCLA* (14 March 2024) <https://ukconstitutionallaw.org>.

II Content

In Part One the book sets out three elements of context. It begins the interrogation of sovereignty as a justification for exclusion, by surveying the international historical development of concepts of sovereignty, their underlying values and the diverse functions of this concept used by the West in colonisation. From this history the book identifies the nature and function of the concept of sovereignty that is being used in the 21st century to justify exclusion.

Paired with this analysis of sovereignty the book examines phenomena of globalisation and the extent to which globalisation is a threat to sovereignty. The book asks whether today's phenomena of globalisation are in essence anything new: can 21st century globalisation be related to the earliest emergence of concepts of sovereignty and the ebbs and flows of international connectedness and interdependence? The book draws on the theoretical work of philosopher Wendy Brown and the legal research of Catherine Dauvergne, among others, to place the inquiry in a theoretical context.[12] The book tests a theory: that migration law is being used to express what Brown terms 'hypersovereignty': a demonstration of sovereign power that simultaneously signals the waning capacity to wield Westphalian sovereignty challenged by globalisation. It is an expression of sovereign authority when such expressions in other areas are thwarted:[13] The book argues that neoliberalism, the dominant value of globalisation, has ironically driven this harnessing of sovereignty as a justification to continue to exclude.

The third element of context for the 21st century migration policy and lawmaking, which is the focus of the book, is the history of Australian migration law and its international context. This history provides a benchmark. It can help answer the question regarding to what extent migration policy and law in the 21st century can be seen as what Brown terms hypersovereignty, a response to new challenges of globalisation.[14] Or alternatively is this exclusionary legislation, its techniques and goals, a continuum of past practice? In 1901 Australia's exclusionary policies and legislation were made under the rule of the global British Empire and limited by the strategies the empire employed to retain control of relationships with non-white subjects of the empire, such as those in India, and with countries outside the empire, such as

12 Wendy Brown, *Walled States, Waning Sovereignty* (Zone Books, 2010) ('*Walled States*'); Wendy Brown, *Undoing the Demos: Neo Liberalism's Stealth Revolution* (Zone Books, 2015) 9–10 ('*Undoing the Demos*'); Catherine Dauvergne, 'Sovereignty, Migration, and the Rule of Law in Global Times' (2004) 67(4) *Modern Law Review* 588 ('Sovereignty, Migration'); Catherine Dauvergne, *Making People Illegal: What Globalization Means for Migration Law* (Cambridge University Press, 2008) 30 ('*Making People Illegal*').

13 Brown, *Walled States* (n 12) 76–9.

14 Brown, *Walled States* (n 12) 76–9.

the Japanese.[15] By 1958, a new migration act was passed severing ties to the old legislation, but the policy imperative of a white Australia remained.[16] It was not until the late 20th century that the migration policy imperative of a white Australia was no longer espoused.[17] Sovereignty, the power to exclude, became the espoused justification to exclude.[18]

Within this context, Part 2 of this book examines the elements of the justification of sovereignty: its clash with the neoliberal value that underpins globalisation; its techniques of exclusion; and the extent of its consistency with the espoused values of Australian lawmakers. The clash of sovereignty and neoliberalism is illustrated with an examination of the amendments to the highly lucrative international student visa program. The rhetoric, parliamentary debates and legislative techniques of exclusion include instances of 'keeping out', 'kicking out' and exclusion from the community in immigration detention.[19] The values apparent in the legislation aimed to exclude are compared with values enacted in the regulations to the *Migration Act 1958* (Cth) as the Australian Values Statement.

In Part 3, the book examines the implications of this use of sovereignty for the primary liberal democratic, and espoused and enacted Australian value of the rule of law. The book argues that the sovereignty espoused to justify exclusion is an anachronistic concept that is indicative of a failure to face up to the challenges posed by globalisation and a betrayal of the espoused values enacted in Australian law as well as those common to western liberal democracies.

The conclusion summarises what has been uncovered about the justification of sovereignty to exclude the unwanted migrant: about its relationship to globalisation and to Australian history, about its underlying values, its implications for people subject to the legislation it justifies and about its impact on the rule of law.

III Key Relevant Historical Events in the Period 2000–20

The time period in focus spans two decades in Australia when migration policy became a central domestic political concern, arguably rivalling international

15 Commonwealth, Parliamentary Debates, House of Representatives, 5 June 1901, 692 (Langdon Bonython).

16 Commonwealth, *Parliamentary Debates*, House of Representatives, 1 May 1958, 1396 (Alexander Downer).

17 Commonwealth, *Parliamentary Debates*, House of Representatives, 28 February 1973, 53 (Al Grassby).

18 Commonwealth, *Parliamentary Debates*, House of Representatives, 7 June 1978, 3153 (Michael Mackellar).

19 Scott Morrison, 'Until the Bell Rings', *Prime Minister Media Centre* (Speech, Menzies Research Centre, 6 September 2018) <pm.gov.au/media>; Commonwealth, Parliamentary Debates, House of Representatives, 30 May 2011, 5045 (Scott Morrison).

terrorism, the issue of climate change and the vulnerability of Australia's economy to international financial markets. The latter was demonstrated by the 2008 Global Financial Crisis which was assessed in 2018 as one of the 'largest economic shocks to Australia for generations'.[20] Within two years of this assessment the world experienced a pandemic which had significant economic impact. Yet despite these international challenges migration policy continued its social, political and legal significance. The economic importance of migration also continued to be recognised, and the international student market developed to become Australia's fourth largest export industry.

Internationally the vulnerabilities as well as the opportunities of new technologies were demonstrated. The attack by Al-Qaeda on the twin towers in New York in September 2001, known as 9/11, heightened international fear of terrorism.[21] Ironically the technologies that amplified the 9/11 attack beyond its spatial reality were the computer-based technologies of the new millennium that have facilitated globalisation: 'TV channels, the Web, videotapes and audiotapes, and their producers'.[22] Economic globalisation also accelerated and with it the continued climate change concerns and the globalised movement of people. The Australian prime minister at the beginning of these two decades was John Howard, Coalition Prime Minister 1996–2007. He was quick to label the 9/11 attack an 'act of war'.[23] He committed Australia to join President Bush's prosecution of what Bush called a 'War on Terror'.[24]

Concurrent with these global events which impacted Australia, two significant events occurred near the Australian border. The first happened just days before the 9/11 attack, the second just a month after. The first event occurred in August 2001 when Australian troops were directed to board the

20 Malcolm Turnbull, 'Press Conference, Australian Embassy, Washington DC, USA', *PM Transcripts* (Speech, 7 March 2018) <https://pmtranscripts.pmc.gov.au/release/transcript-41489>.

21 See, e.g., Adrian Cherney and Kristina Murphy, 'Being a "Suspect Community" in a Post 9/11 World – The Impact of the War on Terror on Muslim Communities in Australia' (2016) 49(4) *Australian & New Zealand Journal of Criminology* 480.

22 Karin Knorr Cetina, 'Microglobalization', in Ino Rossi (ed), *Frontiers of Globalization Research: Theoretical and Methodological Approaches* (Springer Science and Business Media, 2007) 65, 82.

23 John Howard, 'Press Conference, Australian Embassy, Washington DC, USA', *PM Transcripts* (Press Conference, 11 September 2001) <https://pmtranscripts.pmc.gov.au/release/transcript-11783>.

24 Matthew L Sandgren, 'War Redefined in the Wake of September 11: Were the Attacks against Iraq Justified' (2003) 12(1) *Michigan State University Journal of International Law* 1; Brennan Tyler Brooks, 'Doctrines without Borders: Territorial Jurisdiction and the Force of International Law in the Wake of Rasul v. Bush' (2006) 39(1) *Vanderbilt Journal of Transnational Law* 161; Thomas McDonnell, *The United States, International Law, and the Struggle Against Terrorism* (Routledge, 2010) 1–36; Benjamin Wittes, 'Introduction', in Benjamin Wittes (ed), *Legislating the War on Terror: An Agenda for Reform* (Brookings Institution Press, 2009) 1.

Norwegian freighter *MV Tampa* off Christmas Island.[25] The Howard government had refused to allow the *MV Tampa* to approach Christmas Island to disembark asylum seekers and had called on the navy to intervene. After this unprecedented action the government passed the *Border Protection Act 2001* (Cth), which retrospectively gave legislative authority for the actions taken to stop the *MV Tampa* docking. The *MV Tampa* incident and the government's response are seen by some as the catalyst for Australia's policy pivot to border protection from that time.[26]

The second event occurred just one month after 9/11 and a month before a federal election. The prime minister had purportedly received advice that asylum seekers on a sinking vessel had thrown their children overboard.[27] During an interview on commercial radio his interviewer suggested that this showed, at least, the asylum seekers' desperation.[28] The prime minster rebuffed this interpretation: 'I don't want in Australia people who would throw their own children into the sea, I don't and I don't think any Australian does'.[29] Later enquiries found no evidence that children had been thrown overboard and also found that ministers in the Howard Coalition Government had been briefed within hours of the initial claim that the report was unreliable.[30] Both these events concerning asylum seekers were critical to the Howard Government's unexpected re-election.[31]

Across the two decades following, 2000 to 2020, the issue of excluding the unwanted migrant has remained a significant legal and political issue in Australia.[32] For example, 'Australia can't afford to lose on border protection'

25 David Marr and Marian Wilkinson, *Dark Victory* (Allen and Unwin, 2003); Peter Mares, *Borderline: Australia's Response to Refugees and Asylum Seekers in the Wake of the Tampa* (UNSW Press, 2nd ed, 2002); National Museum of Australia, *Tampa Affair* (Web Page, 13 July 2022) <www.nma.gov.au/defining-moments/resources/tampa-affair>.
26 Marr and Wilkinson (n 25).
27 John Howard, 'Interview with Phillip Clarke, Radio 2GB', *PM Transcripts* (Interview, 8 October 2001) <https://pmtranscripts.pmc.gov.au/release/transcript-12107>.
28 John Howard, 'Interview with Phillip Clarke, Radio 2GB', *PM Transcripts* (Interview, 8 October 2001) <https://pmtranscripts.pmc.gov.au/release/transcript-12107>.
29 John Howard, 'Interview with Phillip Clarke, Radio 2GB', *PM Transcripts* (Interview, 8 October 2001) <https://pmtranscripts.pmc.gov.au/release/transcript-12107>.
30 John Harrison, 'Appointed Public Officials and Public Relations Practice: Accountability, Ethics and Professionalism in the "Children Overboard" Affair' (2004) 5(1) *Asia Pacific Public Relations Journal* 1, 1–3; Senate, *Senate Select Committee on the Scrafton Evidence* (Report, 2004) <www.aph.gov.au/Parliamentary_Business/Committees/Senate/Former_Committees/scrafton/report/inde x>.
31 Katharine Betts, 'Boat People and the 2001 Election' (2002) 10(3) *People and Place* 36; Gwenda Tavan, 'Issues That Swung Elections: Tampa and the National Security Election of 2001', *The Conversation* (online, 3 May 2019) <https://theconversation.com/issues-that-swung-elections-tampa-and-the-national-security-election-of-2001-115143>.
32 Eg Kate Walton, '"Dark Day": Australia Repeals Medical Evacuation for Refugees', *Aljazeera* (online, 19 December 2019) <www.aljazeera.com/news/2019/12/4/dark-day-australia-repeals-medical-evacuation-for-refugees>; Australian Human Rights Commission, *Lives on Hold: Refugees and Asylum Seekers in the 'Legacy Caseload'* (Report,

is how, in October 2019, Scott Morrison, Coalition Prime Minister 2018–22, positioned his argument for repealing laws passed by the cross bench and the Opposition prioritising health assessment for refugee medical transfers to Australia from offshore immigration detention.[33]

Internationally by 2016 migration was recognised as a growing problem that needed a global response.[34] In 2018, the UN supported the adoption of the Global Compact for Migration.[35] This compact, together with the Global Compact on Refugees, aimed to address the 'moral and humanitarian' challenge of the 'growing global phenomenon of large movements of refugees and migrants' in 'unprecedented' numbers.[36]

The US opposed the Global Compact for Migration. It objected to the 'effort by the United Nations to advance global governance at the expense of the sovereign right of States to manage their immigration systems in accordance with their national laws, policies, and interests'.[37] Along with the US, Australia cited a threat to sovereignty in its reason for not supporting the compact.[38] The responsible minister, Peter Dutton, Minister for Home Affairs, 2017 to 2021 in the Turnbull/Morrison Coalition Government, explained: 'We're not going to surrender our sovereignty – I'm not going to allow unelected bodies dictate to us, to the Australian people'.[39]

2019); John Flannery and Maria Hawthorne, 'Asylum Seeker Death Was Preventable', *Australian Medicine* (online, 13 August 2018) 8.

33 Daniel McCulloch. 'Morrison Berates Border Security "Naivety"', *The NewDaily* (online, 18 October 2019) <https://thenewdaily.com.au/news/national/2019/10/18/scott-morrison-berates-border-security-naivety/>.

34 *New York Declaration for Refugees and Migrants*, UN Doc A/RES/71/1 (3 October 2016) ('*New York Declaration*') especially 1–4.

35 *Global Compact for Safe, Orderly and Regular Migration*, GA/RES/73/195(19 December 2018).

36 *New York Declaration* (n 34) 2, para 10.

37 United States Mission to the United Nations, 'National Statement of the United States of America on the Adoption of the Global Compact for Safe, Orderly, and Regular Migration' (Media Release, 7 December 2018).

38 United States Mission to the United Nations, 'National Statement of the United States of America on the Adoption of the Global Compact for Safe, Orderly, and Regular Migration' (Media Release, 7 December 2018); Amy Remeikis and Ben Doherty, 'Dutton Says Australia Won't "Surrender Our Sovereignty" by Signing UN Migration Deal', *The Guardian* (online, 25 July 2018) <www.theguardian.com/australia-news/2018/jul/25/dutton-says-australia-wont-surrender-our-sovereignty-by-signing-un-migration-deal>.

39 United States Mission to the United Nations, 'National Statement of the United States of America on the Adoption of the Global Compact for Safe, Orderly, and Regular Migration' (Media Release, 7 December 2018); Amy Remeikis and Ben Doherty, 'Dutton Says Australia Won't "Surrender Our Sovereignty" by Signing UN Migration Deal', *The Guardian* (online, 25 July 2018) <www.theguardian.com/australia-news/2018/jul/25/dutton-says-australia-wont-surrender-our-sovereignty-by-signing-un-migration-deal>. See also Scott Morrison, 'Global Compact for Migration' (Press release, Department of Prime Minister and Cabinet, 21 November 2018) <https://pmtranscripts.pmc.gov.au/release/transcript-41981>.

IV Literature Review

Literature on the 20th-century history of migration law and policy and the migration law of this 2000–20 period is plentiful. Examples of the most relevant literature are addressed in this review. A significant body of this literature describes the inconsistency between Australia's legislation and international commitments to human rights law.[40] Another group questions the origins of a claim to a sovereign right to exclude unwanted migrants.[41] A third group concerns the ongoing debate on the appropriate limits of executive power in migration decisions made under s 61 or s 51 of the Australian Constitution. Another focus is the legislation regulating the migrant as an economic asset. The final area of relevance is the discussion of values.

The historical research that describes the rise and demise of the White Australia policy in official migration policy but questions its broader demise is included for completeness. This review does not include literature concerning the definitions of globalisation and sovereignty which is dealt with in the first two contextual chapters. Nor does it include theoretical work on the rule of law which is addressed in Chapter 8.

40 *International Convention on the Elimination of All Forms of Racial Discrimination*, opened for signature 21 December 1965, 660 UNTS 195 (entered into force 4 January 1969); *International Covenant on Civil and Political Rights*, opened for signature 16 December 1965, 999 UNTS 171 (entered into force 3 March 1976); *Optional Protocol to the International Covenant on Civil and Political Rights*, opened for signature 16 December 1966, 999 UNTS 171 (entered into force 23 March 1976); *Second Optional Protocol to the International Covenant on Civil and Political Rights*, opened for signature 15 December 1989 (entered into force 15 December 1989); *International Covenant on Economic, Social and Cultural Rights*, opened for signature 16 December 1966, 993 UNTS 3 (entered into force 3 January 1976); *Convention on the Elimination of All Forms of Discrimination against Women*, opened for signature 18 December 1979, 1249 UNTS 13 (entered into force 3 September 1981); *Convention against Torture and Other Cruel, Inhuman or Degrading Treatment or Punishment*, opened for signature 10 December 1984, 1465 UNTS 85 (entered into force 26 June 1987); *Convention on the Rights of the Child*, opened for signature 20 November 1989, 1577 UNTS 3 (entered into force 2 September 1990); *International Convention on the Protection of the Rights of All Migrant Workers and Members of Their Families*, opened for signature 18 December 1990, (entered into force 18 December 1990); *International Convention for the Protection of All Persons from Enforced Disappearance*, opened for signature20 December 2006 (entered into force 23 December 2010); *Convention on the Rights of Persons with Disabilities*, opened for signature 24 January 2007 (entered into force 3 May 2008); *Convention relating to the Status of Refugees*, opened for signature 28 July 1951, 189 UNTS 150 (entered into force 22 April 1954); *United Nations Declaration on the Rights of Indigenous Peoples*, opened for signature 13 September 2007 (entered into force 13 September 2007) arts 3–5.

41 *Robtelmes v Brenan* (1906) 4 CLR 395, 401–3; *Ah Yin v Christie* (1907) 4 CLR 1428, 1431.

A *Migration Law and Human Rights*

A major focus of commentary relevant to Australia's migration law has been the gap between Australia's practices and international human rights obligations. Much of this focuses on refugee law.[42]

James C Hathaway covers the interpretation of international law regarding refugees and others draw from his work.[43] He argues that, while the definition of lawful presence in a state is left to states, this discretion is not unlimited.[44] States are obliged to comply with the 'normative requirements of the Refugee Convention'.[45] In essence he argues for an implied expectation that states abide by the spirit not just the letter of the UN Convention Relating to the Status of Refugees 1951 (Refugee Convention) and the Protocol Relating to the Status of Refugees 1967 (Refugee Protocol).[46] Jane McAdam addresses the history in international law of the right to emigrate.[47] She describes how this is now embedded in human rights law and is an enabler of other rights.[48] She notes that right is not yet reconciled with states' right to

42 James C Hathaway, *The Rights of Refugees under International Law* (Cambridge University Press, 2005). For a critique of international refugee law and practice see Patricia Tuitt, *False Images: Law's Construction of the Refugee* (Pluto Press, 1996); Michelle Foster, *International Refugee Law and Socio-Economic Rights: Refuge from Deprivation* (Cambridge University Press, 2007); Natalie Klein, 'Assessing Australia's Push Back the Boats Policy under International Law: Legality and Accountability for Maritime Interceptions of Irregular Migrants' (2014) 15 *Melbourne Journal of International Law* 414; Susan Kneebone (ed), *Refugees, Asylum Seekers and the Rule of Law: Comparative Perspectives* (Cambridge University Press, 2009). Penelope Mathews assesses the legislation arising from the *MV Tampa* incident against international law and finds it wanting in Penelope Mathews, 'Australian Refugee Protection in the Wake of the Tampa' (2002) 96(3) *American Journal of International Law* 661, 665–76. Chantal Bostok also comments on the neglect of international customary law in the management of the *MV Tampa* issue in Chantal Marie-Jeanne Bostock, 'The International Legal Obligations Owed to the Asylum Seekers on the MV Tampa' (2002) 14(2–3) *International Journal of Refugee Law* 279, 294–7. Mary Crock suggests political, not legal, considerations drove the legislative changes. Mary Crock, 'In the Wake of the Tampa: Conflicting Visions of International Refugee Law in the Management of Refugee Flows' (2003) 12(1) *Pacific Rim Law & Policy Journal* 49, 53.

43 Hathaway (n 42).

44 Hathaway (n 42).

45 Hathaway (n 42) 171. See also 172–4.

46 Hathaway (n 42) 171.

47 Jane McAdam, 'An Intellectual History of Freedom of Movement in International Law: The Right to Leave as a Personal Liberty', in Mary Crock and Tom D Campbell (eds), *Refugees and Rights* (Taylor & Francis Group, 2015) 3.

48 Jane McAdam, 'An Intellectual History of Freedom of Movement in International Law: The Right to Leave as a Personal Liberty', in Mary Crock and Tom D Campbell (eds), *Refugees and Rights* (Taylor & Francis Group, 2015) 3.

restrict entry.[49] She echoes Oppenheim.[50] He stated: 'the Law of nations does not, as yet, grant a right of emigration to every individual, although it is frequently maintained that it is a "natural" right of every individual to emigrate from his own State'.[51] He goes on to state: 'it is a moral right which could fittingly find a place in any international recognition of the Rights of man'.[52] McAdam and Chong provide an overview of refugee law in Australia up to 2014.[53] They argue that Australia's breaches of the Refugee Convention and the Refugee Protocol are severe but rectifying this lies only within the power of the Australian government.[54] The legality in international law of Australia's efforts to stop asylum seekers arriving on shore has been questioned by a number of writers.[55] Dauvergne argues that states create illegality through the assertion of sovereignty and calls for a reimagining of this paradigm but offers no concrete path forward.[56]

The experience of immigration detention is also a focus in the literature. Sharon Pickering and Leanne Weber comment on the narrow focus on deterrence of asylum seekers and unwelcome migrants rather than rights under international law.[57] Tania Penovic and Azadeh Dastyari document the history of offshore detention and the issues of cost, humanitarian concerns

49 Jane McAdam, 'An Intellectual History of Freedom of Movement in International Law: The Right to Leave as a Personal Liberty', in Mary Crock and Tom D Campbell (eds), *Refugees and Rights* (Taylor & Francis Group, 2015) 3.

50 L Oppenheim, *International Law: A Treatise*, ed H. Lauterpact (David Mckay Company, 8th ed, 1955) 647–8.

51 L Oppenheim, *International Law: A Treatise*, ed H. Lauterpact (David Mckay Company, 8th ed, 1955) 647–8.

52 L Oppenheim, *International Law: A Treatise*, ed H. Lauterpact (David Mckay Company, 8th ed, 1955) 647–8.

53 Jane McAdam and Fiona Chong, *Refugees: Why Seeking Asylum Is Legal, and Australia's Policies Are Not* (UNSW Press, 2014) especially 9–36, 170–80.

54 Jane McAdam and Fiona Chong, *Refugees: Why Seeking Asylum Is Legal, and Australia's Policies Are Not* (UNSW Press, 2014) 179. For an overview of significant cases and analysis of the relationship between international law and Australian municipal law see Donald R Rothwell, Stuart Kaye, Afshin Akhtar-Khavari, Ruth Davis and Imogen Saunders, *International Law: Cases and Materials with Australian Perspectives* (Cambridge University Press, 3rd ed, 2018) 173–233. Note especially at 216–33 materials on the status and influence of treaties on court decisions.

55 Joyce Chia, Jane McAdam and Kate Purcell, 'Asylum in Australia: "Operation Sovereign Borders" and International Law' (2014) 32 *Australian Year Book of International Law* 33; Azadeh Dastyari and Asher Hirsch, 'The Ring of Steel: Extraterritorial Migration Controls in Indonesia and Libya and the Complicity of Australia and Italy' (2019) 19 *Human Rights Law Review* 435. See Patrick Emerton and Maria O'Sullivan's discussion of the characterisation of asylum seekers as a border security issue in Patrick Emerton and Maria O'Sullivan, 'Rethinking Asylum Seeker Detention at Sea: The Power to Detain Asylum Seekers at Sea under the *Maritime Powers Act 2013* (Cth)' (2020) 38(2) *UNSW Law Journal* 695, 695–6.

56 Dauvergne, *Making People Illegal* (n 12).

57 Sharon Pickering and Leanne Weber, 'New Deterrence Scripts in Australia's Rejuvenated Offshore Detention Regime for Asylum Seekers' (2014) 39(4) *Law & Social Inquiry* 1006, 1007.

and breaches of international obligations.[58] Azadeh Dastyari and Maria O'Sullivan critique the physical and psychological conditions of offshore detainees and their ambivalent legal status.[59] Penovic and Sifris lament the lack of incorporation of the *Convention on the Rights of the Child* into Australian legislation and the consequential vulnerability of asylum seeker children to immigration detention.[60] Marinella Marmo examines the degrading treatment of detainees in Australian immigration detention.[61] Ghezelbash makes a comparison of US and Australian policies of mandatory detention, maritime interdiction and boat turn backs of asylum seekers and he warns that if this example is followed 'it will be inflicting a mortal wound on the universal principle of asylum and the international refugee protection regime'.[62] Dauvergne describes Australia post-Tampa as 'the global leader in the refugee law race to the bottom'.[63] Juss compares the implementation of Australia's security assessment of refugees to the 17th-century drowning test for witches, a test where the suspect always loses.[64] Zagor critiques the narrative process employed to establish refugee status and its uncomfortable fit with the lived experience of an asylum seeker.[65] Brennan sees human rights as something to be 'balanced with the national interest', 'compassion versus realism', but he fails to define what might constitute a legitimate national interest.[66] Jane McAdam optimistically characterises the codification of complementary protection as the beginning of a nondiscretionary humanitarian approach to asylum seekers that incorporates human rights into the act.[67]

58 Tania Penovic and Azadeh Dastyari, 'Boatloads of Incongruity: The Evolution of Australia's Offshore Processing Regime' (2007) 13(1) *Australian Journal of Human Rights* 33.

59 Azadeh Dastyari and Maria O'Sullivan, 'Not For Export: The Failure of Australia's Extraterritorial Processing Regime in Papua New Guinea and the Decision of the PNG Supreme Court in Namah' (2016) 42(2) *Monash University Law Review* 308.

60 Tania Penovic and Adiva Sifris, 'Children's Rights Through the Lens of Immigration Detention' (2006) 20 *Australian Journal of Family Law* 12. See also Susanna Dechent, Sharmin Tania and Jackie Mapulanga-Hulston, 'Asylum Seeker Children in Nauru: Australia's International Human Rights Obligations and Operational Realities' (2019) 31(1) *International Journal of Refugee Law* 83.

61 Marinella Marmo, 'Strip Searching: Seeking the Truth "in" and "on" the Regular Migrant's Body', in Peter Billings (ed), *Crimmigation in Australia* (Springer, 2019) 197.

62 Daniel Ghezelbash, *Refugee Lost: Asylum Law in an Interdependent World* (Cambridge University Press, 2018) 186.

63 Dauvergne, *Making People Illegal* (n 12) 51.

64 Juss (n 7) 146, 161.

65 Matthew Zagor, 'Recognition and Narrative Identities: Is Refugee Law Redeemable?', in Fiona Jenkins, Mark Nolan and Kim Rubenstein (eds), *Allegiance and Identity in a Globalised World* (Cambridge University Press, 2014) 311.

66 Frank Brennan, 'Human Rights and the National Interest: The Case Study of Asylum, Migration, and National Border Protection' (2016) 39 *Boston College International & Comparative Law Review* 47, 84.

67 Jane McAdam, 'From Humanitarian Discretion to Complementary Protection – Reflections on the Emergence of Human Rights-Based Refugee Protection in Australia' (2011) 18 *Australian International Law Journal* 53, 54.

In contrast to these approaches Eve Lester, in her analysis of migration law and policy, declined to frame her argument around human rights.[68] She notes correctly that in Australia international law cannot be enforced unless it is specifically transformed into legislation.[69] While it remains true that in statutory interpretation the judiciary presumes that Parliament would not intend to breach international law, that presumption cannot stand against specific legislation.[70]

B Sovereign Right To Exclude the Unwanted Migrant

Eve Lester, Kim Rubenstein and Anthony Anghie interrogate and contest the legitimacy of sovereignty as a justification for exclusion.[71] Lester makes a fundamental challenge to the legitimacy of the use of the concept that she terms absolute sovereignty to support the treatment of asylum seekers.[72] She makes this argument through a sweeping historical genealogy of the concept of absolute sovereignty. Asking 'how the laws and policies . . . [of mandatory detention and limiting the capacity of asylum seekers to work] have become thinkable', she traces the development of a common law doctrine of absolute sovereignty and demonstrates how this doctrine became integral to contemporary Australian migration law and policy.[73] She concludes that the 'putative authority of "absolute sovereignty" to exclude' that is now embodied in Australian migration jurisprudence, is a 'rationalisation for the political-economic desire of certain white settler societies to have complete power in the regulation of race and labour'.[74] She argues that Australia's relationship to the foreigner has been shaped by the concept of absolute sovereignty so that contemporary lawmakers, the politicians and judiciary, cannot think beyond the concept to address 'the barbarity and cruelty' that the concept is used to legitimate.[75] Antony Anghie similarly traces the origins of sovereignty as a tool for colonisation and a justification for excluding Indigenous people from the

68 Eve Lester, *Making Migration Law: The Foreigner, Sovereignty and the Case of Australia* (Cambridge University Press, 2018) 18–21.

69 Eve Lester, *Making Migration Law: The Foreigner, Sovereignty and the Case of Australia* (Cambridge University Press, 2018) 18–21.

70 Eve Lester, *Making Migration Law: The Foreigner, Sovereignty and the Case of Australia* (Cambridge University Press, 2018) 18–21.

71 Eve Lester, *Making Migration Law: The Foreigner, Sovereignty and the Case of Australia* (Cambridge University Press, 2018) 18–21; Antony Anghie, *Imperialism, Sovereignty and the Making of International Law* (Cambridge University Press, 2004) 13–114; Kim Rubenstein, 'Citizenship, Sovereignty and Migration: Australia's Exclusive Approach to Membership of the Community' (2002) 13(2) *Public Law Review* 102, 104.

72 Lester (n 68).

73 Lester (n 68) 21.

74 Lester (n 68) 109.

75 Lester (n 68) 288–9.

protection of international legal norms.[76] Kim Rubenstein contests the legitimacy of the use of the concept of a sovereign right as the justification of the use of executive power in the *MV Tampa* incident.[77] Irene Watson also challenges the claim of the Australian state to an exclusive sovereignty, exposing as Anghie does the ethnocentric roots of the claim.[78]

C Executive Power and Legitimacy

The issue of executive power in migration matters has been discussed in the literature. In particular, commentators have been critical of the use of the *Constitution* s 61 executive power, a power outside of statutory power, and the final court decision in *Ruddock v Vadarlis*.[79] Michael Head warns that the High Court's reversal of the original decision in the case gave licence to unfettered executive power and arbitrary detention.[80] Some commentators have questioned the legal reasoning and constitutional interpretation in the majority judgment.[81] Bradley Selway concludes that s 61 executive power is still subject to legislative and judicial restraint.[82] However, Peta Stephenson concludes that, even where there is comprehensive statutory coverage of a matter, the power under s 61 survives.[83]

The implications of executive power given in a statute made under s 51 of the Constitution are also a subject of debate. Michelle Foster traces the increase of executive power under the character test to exclude any non-citizen.[84] Chantal Bostok describes the power of the Immigration Minister

76 Anghie (n 71).
77 Rubenstein (n 71).
78 Irene Watson, 'Re-Centring Indigenous Knowledge and Places in a Terra Nullius Space' (2014) 10(5) *AlternNative* 508; Anghie (n 71).
79 (2001) FCA 1329 ('*MV Tampa Case*'); *Constitution* s 61 states: 'The executive power of the Commonwealth is vested in the Queen and is exercisable by the Governor-General as the Queen's representative, and extends to the execution and maintenance of this Constitution, and of the laws of the Commonwealth'. The majority decision in the *MV Tampa Case* held, in summary, that the government had executive power to prevent entry and that this was not extinguished by a statute 'absent of clear words or inescapable implications', that this was the Parliament's intention. *MV Tampa Case* [185]. Black CJ dissented.
80 Michael Head, 'The High Court and the Tampa Refugees' (2002) 11(1) *Griffith Law Review* 23, 32.
81 Bradley Selway, 'All At Sea – Constitutional Assumptions and "the Executive Power of the Commonwealth"' (2003) 31 *Federal Law Review* 495, 506; Zagor (n 65).
82 Bradley Selway, 'All At Sea – Constitutional Assumptions and "the Executive Power of the Commonwealth"' (2003) 31 *Federal Law Review* 495, 506; Zagor (n 65).
83 Peta Stephenson, 'Statutory Displacement of the Prerogative in Australia', in Janina Boughey and Lisa Burton Crawford (eds), *Interpreting Executive Power* (Federation Press, 2020) 203.
84 Michelle Foster, 'An "Alien" by the Barest of Threads: The Legality of the Deportation of Long Term Residents from Australia' (2009) 33 *Melbourne University Law Review* 483, 484–5 ('An Alien'). See also Chapter 8 on the character test in *Migration Act 1958* (Cth) s 501.

under s 499 of the act to direct the Administrative Appeal Tribunals and its implications for merits review.[85] Maria O'Sullivan suggests there is a conflict of interest in the Immigration Minister's roles as guardian and deporter of children and she notes the uneasy fit of this treatment of children with comparable countries' practice and with the *Convention on the Rights of the Child*.[86] Samuel C Duckett White, and Lauren Bull, Elizabeth Colliver, Emily Fischer, Shawn Rajanayagam and Edmund Simpson[87] explain the breadth of the executive power given to the Immigration Minister under the character test, s 501 of the Act.[88] Susan Rimmer describes the personal cost of the Immigration Minister's discretion under s 501 of the act in the case of *Minister for Immigration & Citizenship v Haneef*.[89] In that case the Full Federal Court dismissed the minister's appeal against a single judge who found jurisdictional error on the grounds that the minister's construction of 'association' in s 501(6)(b) exceeded the limits of the statute.[90] However the minister was still able to act against Mr Haneef. The limits of judicial power to constrain executive power provided in the statute is itself an issue of debate. For example, Alan Freckelton argues that legislative attempts to constrain judicial review have been largely ineffectual as the court has retained its power of legislative and constitutional interpretation.[91] However Lisa Burton Crawford argues that judicial interpretation is constrained by legislation.[92] Dominique Dalla-Pozza and Greg Weeks and others argue similarly.[93]

85 Chantal Bostok, 'The Effect of Ministerial Directions on Tribunal Independence' (2011) 66 *AIAL Forum* 33. Section 499 gives power to the Minister to make binding directions to 'persons or bodies' exercising power under the *Migration Act 1958* (Cth).

86 Maria O'Sullivan, 'The "Best Interests" of Asylum-Seeker Children: Who's Guarding the Guardian?' (2013) 38(4) *Alternative Law Journal* 224; see especially 227.

87 Samuel C Duckett White, 'God-Like Powers: The Character Test and Unfettered Ministerial Discretion' (2020) 41 *Adelaide Law Review* 1; Lauren Bull et al, Rights Advocacy Project, *Playing God: The Immigration Minister's Unrestrained Power* (Report, Liberty Victoria, 2017).

88 Section 501 gives the minister power to refuse or cancel any visa on character grounds.

89 (2007) FCAFC 203. See Susan Harris Rimmer, 'The Dangers of Character Tests: Dr Haneef and Other Cautionary Tales' (Discussion Paper No 101, Australia Institute, 2008).

90 *Haneef v Minister for Immigration and Citizenship* (2007) FCA 1273, [256]–[260].

91 Alan Freckelton, *Administrative Decision Making in Australian Migration Law* (ANU Press, 2015) 228.

92 Lisa Burton Crawford, 'The Entrenched Minimum Provision of Judicial Review and the Limits of "Law"' (2017) 45 *Federal Law Review* 569, 574.

93 Dominique Dalla-Pozza and Greg Weeks, 'A Statutory Shield of the Executive: To What Extent Does Legislation Help Administrative Action Evade Judicial Scrutiny?' in Janina Boughey and Lisa Crawford (eds), *Interpreting Executive Power* (Federation Press, 2020) 184. See also Mathew Groves, 'The Return of the Almost Absolute Statutory Discretion', in Janina Boughey and Lisa Crawford (eds), *Interpreting Executive Power* (Federation Press, 2020) 129, 136–47.

Several writers have dealt with this issue by trying to identify the content and limits of judicial review.[94]

D The Migrant as an Economic Asset

There is also literature on the migrant as an economic asset. Brown's theorising that neoliberal philosophy transforms humans into 'an intensely constructed and governed bit of human capital tasked with improving and leveraging its competitive positioning' has resonance here.[95] Saskia Sassen's description of a globalised neoliberal logic that values the individual exclusively as an economic entity to be measured according to their skill and productivity also resonates.[96] Researchers have critiqued the market-based philosophy and economic objectives of some provisions of migration law and policy, such as temporary skilled worker provisions and the student visa conditions, on the basis of their human cost.[97]

After the murder of an Indian accountancy student who was stabbed by a teenager in Melbourne, Gail Mason responded by arguing for intercultural respect, noting Australia's tarnished image in India and that Australia must 'acknowledge that cultural intolerance and chauvinism do exist in this country'.[98] Both Sudrishti Reich and Sanmati Verma discuss the impact of the Australian government's migration policy aimed at a share of the global market

94 Jeremy Kirk, 'The Entrenched Minimum Provision of Judicial Review' (2004) 12(1) *Australian Journal of Administrative Law* 64; Leighton McDonald, 'The Entrenched Minimum Provision of Judicial Review and the Rule of Law' (2010) 21(1) *Public Law Review* 14; Will Bateman, 'The Constitution and the Substantive Principles of Judicial Review: The Full Scope of The Entrenched Minimum Provision of Judicial Review' (2011) 39(3) *Federal Law Review* 463; Grant Hooper, 'Three Decades of Tension: From the Codification of Migration Decision-Making to an Overarching Framework for Judicial Review' (2020) 48(3) *Federal Law Review* 401; Greg Weeks and Matthew Groves, 'Legislative Limitations on Judicial Review: The High Court in Graham' (2018) 24 *Australian Journal of Administrative Law* 209. See also discussion in Chapter 8.

95 Brown, *Undoing the Demos* (n 12).

96 Saskia Sassen, *Expulsions: Brutality and Complexity in the Global Economy* (Harvard University Press, 2014) 213–16. See also Brown, *Undoing the Demos* (n 12) 9–10.

97 See Joanna Howe, Andrew Stewart and Rosemary Owens, 'Temporary Migrant Labour and Unpaid Work in Australia' (2018) 40 *Sydney Law Review* 183; Alexander Reilly, 'The Ethics of Seasonal Labour Migration' (2011) 20(1) *Griffith Law Review* 127; Yao-Tai Li and Katherine Whitworth, 'When the State Becomes Part of the Exploitation: Migrants' Agency within the Institutional Constraints in Australia' (2016) 54(6) *International Migration* 138.

98 Gail Mason, 'Violence Against Indian Students in Australia: A Question of Dignity' (2010) 21(3) *Current Issues in Criminal Justice* 461, 464. See also Australian High Commission, 'Australian Authorities Condemn Attack on Nitin Garg' (Press release PA0110, 4 January 2010); ABC, 'Boy Gets 13 Years for Stabbing Indian National', *ABC News* (online, 22 December 2011) <www.abc.net.au/news/2011-12-22/boy-gets-13-years-for-stabbing-indian-national/3743888>.

for international students, the promise in the policy that a student visa would be a pathway to permanent residency and the negative impact on students when this pathway was cut off.[99] Verma recounts how changes in migration law from 2009 with the stated goal of 're-establishing the integrity of Australian international education' had the impact of bolstering the sustainability of the industry while creating 'a sizable class of permanently provisional or overtly illegal migrants'.[100] She notes that these changes to law and policy aimed to increase the profitability of the sector and she implies that the characterisation in entry criteria of an applicant as a 'genuine student' was a way of cancelling the visas of TAFE students who were predominantly poorer Indian and Chinese students.[101] Her concern is the impact of a growing body of illegal migrants living in the community outside the social and health safety net.[102] Reich provides a detailed analysis of the policies and the impact on students 'whose legitimate expectations . . . were sacrificed' for the 'national economic interest'.[103]

Shanthi Robertson discusses the impact of the expansion of the temporary graduate (subclass 485) and working holiday (subclass 417) visa programs.[104] She argues that, while they boost the value of the tourism and education market, they also give the economy access to 'a cheap and exploitable workforce with no access to social welfare and limited access to rights'.[105] Wright and Clibborn make a similar point, arguing that student and working holiday visas allow the entry of low-skilled workers despite the emphasis of government policy on skilled migration.[106]

Alexander Reilly argues that for both ethical and economic reasons seasonal guest workers, such as those who come under the Pacific Seasonal

99 Sanmati Verma, 'Pathways to Illegality, or What became of the International Students', in Marianne Dickie, Dorota Gozdecka and Sudrishti Reich (eds), *Unintended Consequences: The Impact of Migration Law and Policy* (ANU Press, 2016) 9; Sudrishti Reich, 'Great Expectations and the Twilight Zone: The Human Consequences of the Linking of Australia's International Student and Skilled Migration Programs and the Dismantling of That Scheme', in Marianne Dickie, Dorota Gozdecka and Sudrishti Reich (eds), *Unintended Consequences: The Impact of Migration Law and Policy* (ANU Press, 2016) 31.

100 Verma (n 99) 10.

101 Verma (n 99) 14.

102 Verma (n 99) 26.

103 Sudrishti (n 99) 48.

104 Shanthi Robertson, 'Intertwined Mobilities of Education, Tourism and Labour: The Consequences of 417 and 485 Visas in Australia', in Marianne Dickie, Dorota Gozdecka and Sudrishti Reich (eds), *Unintended Consequences: The Impact of Migration Law and Policy* (ANU Press, 2016) 53.

105 Shanthi Robertson, 'Intertwined Mobilities of Education, Tourism and Labour: The Consequences of 417 and 485 Visas in Australia', in Marianne Dickie, Dorota Gozdecka and Sudrishti Reich (eds), *Unintended Consequences: The Impact of Migration Law and Policy* (ANU Press, 2016) 74.

106 Chris F Wright and Stephen Clibborn, 'Back Door, Side Door, or Front Door: An Emerging De-Factor Low-Skilled Immigration Policy in Australia' (2017) 39 *Comparative Labour Law and Policy Journal* 165.

Workers scheme, should be provided with an opportunity for permanent migration.[107] His ethical argument accepts that it is a historical reality that sovereignty gives a right to exclude but he questions the criteria that exclude people who are already de facto productive members of the community.[108] Foster argues similarly, critiquing the exclusion of long-term residents who fail the character test.[109] Judy Fudge and Joo-Cheong Tham, commenting on the Canadian experience, offer an analysis from a different perspective. They examine how welfare and social policies, and labour regulatory frameworks create a domestic labour shortage and employer demand for certain workers. In this way Fudge and Tham see the state as the creator of the precarity of temporary migrant workers.[110]

Citing Philip Pettit and John Rawls, Reilly constructs an argument that the liberal political community is diminished by the exclusion of seasonal workers.[111] He concludes that economic gain should not be pursued at the cost of 'exacerbating a power differential between migrants and citizens'.[112] This power differential under the law is taken up by Marie Segrave, Helen Forbes-Mewett and Chloe Ke who make a similar argument to Reilly about international students.[113] Citing Reilly, they describe international students as occupying a 'hybrid' status and detail how this is created.[114] They suggest that these students are both economically attractive temporary migrants but also noncitizens whose presence in Australia is highly controlled.[115] Mary Crock and Laura Berg make a similar point.[116]

107 Reilly (n 97) 149.
108 Reilly (n 97) 141–2.
109 Foster, 'An Alien' (n 84).
110 Judy Fudge and Joo-Cheong Tham, 'Dishing Up Migrant Workers for the Canadian Food Services Sector: Labor Law and the Demand for Migrant Workers' (2017) 39 *Comparative Labor Law and Policy Journal* 1.
111 Reilly (n 97) 142.
112 Reilly (n 97) 149.
113 Marie Segrave, Helen Forbes-Mewett and Chloe Keel, 'Migration Review Tribunal Decisions in Student Visa Cancellation Appeals: Sympathy, Hardship and Exceptional Circumstances' (2017) 29 *Current Issues in Criminal Justice* 1.
114 Marie Segrave, Helen Forbes-Mewett and Chloe Keel, 'Migration Review Tribunal Decisions in Student Visa Cancellation Appeals: Sympathy, Hardship and Exceptional Circumstances' (2017) 29 *Current Issues in Criminal Justice* 2, citing Alexander Reilly, 'Protecting Vulnerable Migrant Workers: The Case of International Students' (2012) 25(3) *Australian Journal of Labour Law* 181.
115 Marie Segrave, Helen Forbes-Mewett and Chloe Keel, 'Migration Review Tribunal Decisions in Student Visa Cancellation Appeals: Sympathy, Hardship and Exceptional Circumstances' (2017) 29 *Current Issues in Criminal Justice* 13–14.
116 Mary Crock and Laura Berg, *Immigration, Refugees and Forced Migration* (Federation Press, 2011) 299–318.

E History

Many of the historical accounts of Australia's migration policy focus on the role of racial discrimination. Writing in 1935, Lyng gives an analysis of the composition of Australia's population.[117] He analyses what mixture of people is needed for Australia to develop successfully and recommends 'to make life worth living . . . the blending of a multitude of colours into a harmonic whole . . . even coloured people if assimilation' is possible.[118] Writing in 1970, London concludes that Australians must learn tolerance of others.[119] In 1979 Andrew Markus traced the history of the exclusion of Chinese people based on economic and racial concerns.[120] Gwenda Tavan, writing in 2005, traces the origin and formal end of the White Australia policy but argues that race remains both an influence on migration policy makers and a powerful tool to influence political support.[121] She gives as examples contemporary public statements that identify non-Europeans as a threat to sovereignty and quotes anthropologist Hage's observation that race and cultural heritage can be believed to give one group an entitlement to make a 'governmental/managerial' statement about the nation and the place of 'lesser' groups.[122] Mark Finnane and Andy Kaladelfos trace the history of Australia's linking of immigration and criminal law administration from 1901 to the 1950s.[123] They argue that this link was forged as early as 1901 when the immigration law was implemented by police and continued in the link between commission of a crime and deportation.[124] They conclude that the legal mechanisms to link crime and immigration were in place by the 1950s in Australia.[125]

117 J Lyng, *Non-Britishers in Australia: Influence on Population and Progress* (Melbourne University Press, 1935).

118 J Lyng, *Non-Britishers in Australia: Influence on Population and Progress* (Melbourne University Press, 1935) 288.

119 HI London, *Non-White Immigration and the 'White Australia' Policy* (Sydney University Press, 1970) 265.

120 Andrew Markus, *Fear and Hatred: Purifying Australia and California 1850–1901* (Hale and Iremonger, 1979).

121 Tavan (n 2) 239.

122 Tavan (n 2) 222.

123 Mark Finnane and Andy Kaladelfos, 'Australia's Long History of Immigration, Policing and the Criminal Law', in Peter Billings (ed), *Crimmigration in Australia Law, Politics and Society* (Springer, 2019) 19.

124 Mark Finnane and Andy Kaladelfos, 'Australia's Long History of Immigration, Policing and the Criminal Law', in Peter Billings (ed), *Crimmigration in Australia Law, Politics and Society* (Springer, 2019) 25–9.

125 Mark Finnane and Andy Kaladelfos, 'Australia's Long History of Immigration, Policing and the Criminal Law', in Peter Billings (ed), *Crimmigration in Australia Law, Politics and Society* (Springer, 2019) 30–3.

F Evaluating Values

One focus of this extensive available literature on the evaluation of values is the globalised value assigned to neoliberalism.[126] Wendy Brown characterises neoliberalism as destructive of democracy.[127] She argues that globalisation 'displaces legal and political principles (especially liberal commitments to universal inclusion, equality, liberty, and the rule of law) with market criteria'.[128] Martin Krygier and Paul O'Connell make similar arguments.[129] There is also a range of literature theorising the expression of Australian values in public life.[130] Dauvergne argues that states that identify as liberal democracies espouse the value of humanitarianism.[131] Danielle Every and Martha Augoustinos analyse the discourses of racism in the parliamentary debate on the Border Protection Bill 2001.[132] Stephano Gulmanelli demonstrates how during John Howard's ten years in office he reinterpreted multiculturalism as diminishing the importance of ethnic identities other than the Anglo-Celtic identity of the original colonisers.[133]

G Sovereignty as the Australian Parliament's Justification To Exclude

This extensive available literature covers many aspects of Australian migration law. However there is no major work specifically covering how the

126 Martin Krygier, 'Transformations of the Rule of Law: Legal, Liberal and Neo', in Ben Golder and Daniel McLoughlin (eds), *The Politics of Legality in a Neoliberal Age* (Routledge, 2018) 19, 27–31.
127 Brown, *Undoing the Demos* (n 12).
128 Brown, *Walled States* (n 12) 34. See also discussion of the student visa in Chapter 5.
129 See discussion in Chapter 3 Section II D. See also Krygier (n 126) 19; Paul O'Connell, 'On Reconciling Irreconcilables: Neo-Liberal Globalisation and Human Rights' (2007) 7 *Human Rights Law Review* 483, 485; Samuel Moyn, 'A Powerless Companion: Human Rights in the Age of Neoliberalism' (2014) 77 *Law and Contemporary Problems* 147, 148.
130 See, e.g., Maria Chisari, 'Testing Citizen Identities: Australian Migrants and the Australian Values Debate' (2015) 21(6) *Social Identities* 573; Stefano Gulmanelli, 'John Howard and the "Anglospherist" Reshaping of Australia' (2014) 49(4) *Australian Journal of Political Science* 581; Mary Walsh and Alexander C Karolis, 'Being Australian, Australian Nationalism and Australian Values' (2008) 43(4) *Australian Journal of Political Science* 719; Christian Joppke, 'Through the European Looking Glass: Citizenship Tests in the USA, Australia, and Canada' (2013) 17(1) *Citizenship Studies* 1, 6–7. For a discussion on the values of humanitarianism in migration law see Catherine Dauvergne, *Humanitarianism, Identity and Nation: Migration Laws in Canada and Australia* (ProQuest Ebook Central, 2004) 7.
131 Dauvergne, *Humanitarianism, Identity and Nation* (n 130) 7.
132 Danielle Every, 'A Reasonable, Practical and Moderate Humanitarianism: The Co-option of Humanitarianism in the Australian Asylum Seeker Debates' (2008) 21(2) *Journal of Refugee Studies* 210.
133 Gulmanelli (n 130).

concept of sovereignty has been used and developed to justify amendments to the *Migration Act 1958* (Cth) in the period 2000 to 2020. Eve Lester has argued that contemporary lawmakers, the politicians and judiciary, cannot think beyond the concept of sovereignty as the absolute right to exclude, in order to address 'the barbarity and cruelty' that the concept is used to legitimate.[134] This book acknowledges the gap between the commitment to international human rights norms and conventions and the adherence to these, in spirit if not letter, and that this has been well documented and commented upon. This book examines the function of the assertion of sovereignty to justify the amendments to the act and assesses the amendments against the norms espoused and enacted as Australian values, not against international norms, nor using a moral assessment of their barbarity and cruelty. This contributes to an understanding of the rationale, consequences and values of Australian migration legislation made in the period 2000–20 by testing it as a response to the nexus of state sovereignty and the phenomenon of globalisation.

V Conclusion

This book describes how successive 21st century Australian governments have used sovereignty in an era of globalisation, to justify exclusion of the unwanted migrant. The world has taken note. In 2008 Dauvergne described Australia post-Tampa as 'the global leader in the refugee law race to the bottom'.[135] In 2017 Professor Juss, from King's College London, advised 'we should take Australia seriously quite simply because what Australia does in border controls today, the rest of the world might do tomorrow. We ignore it at our peril'.[136] And the UK government did not ignore it.[137] By 2018 Ghezelbash made a comparison of US and Australian policies of mandatory detention, maritime interdiction and boat turn backs of asylum seekers and he warned that if this example is followed 'it will be inflicting a mortal wound on the universal principle of asylum and the international refugee protection regime'.[138] He and others have proved prescient.[139]

This book is a description of the Australian law and policy to which they refer and an interrogation of its justification. The reader can decide whether it is an inspirational or cautionary tale.

134 Lester (n 68) 288–9.
135 Dauvergne, *Making People Illegal* (n 12) 51.
136 Juss (n 7) 153. Professor Juss is a leading academic at Dickson Poon School of Law, King's College London.
137 Gleeson and Konstadinides (n 11).
138 Ghezelbash (n 62) 186.
139 Wilson (n 9); *GOV.UK* (n 10).

Chapter 2

Defining Sovereignty at the Nexus of Globalisation and Migration

I Introduction

Wendy Brown and Catherine Dauvergne have proposed a theory that sits at the nexus of sovereignty, globalisation and migration law.[1] The theory is that state sovereignty is under challenge and that states compensate for this waning sovereignty, experienced in areas such as the economy, technology, security and migration pressure, by expressing their sovereignty as the power to exclude unwanted migrants at the territorial border.[2] Brown describes the construction of border walls as 'hypersovereignty' responding to 'waning' sovereignty.[3] Dauvergne proposes that migration law is the 'new last bastion of sovereignty' in a globalising world.[4] To test the explanatory power of this theory for Australian migration policy and law that has emerged in the 20th century legislative processes (the parliamentary debates, policy positions and legislative amendments to the Migration Act 1958 (Cth)) during the period 2000–20,[5] it is first necessary to define what is meant by sovereignty. That is the purpose of this chapter.

At the core of sovereignty is the idea of the supreme power of the state,[6] but the exact nature of this power and the function it has played historically are contested. This has resulted in a concept that is widely regarded as

1 Wendy Brown, *Walled States, Waning Sovereignty* (Zone Books, 2010); Catherine Dauvergne, 'Sovereignty, Migration and the Rule of Law in Global Times' (2004) 67(4) *Modern Law Review* 588, 588.
2 Wendy Brown, *Walled States, Waning Sovereignty* (Zone Books, 2010); Catherine Dauvergne, 'Sovereignty, Migration and the Rule of Law in Global Times' (2004) 67(4) *Modern Law Review* 588, 588.
3 Brown (n 1) 67, 107.
4 Dauvergne (n 1) 588.
5 The period from 2000 was chosen because of the significant number and impact of amendments made to the *Australian Migration Act 1958* during this period.
6 Hans Kelsen, 'Sovereignty and International Law' (1960) 48(4) *Georgetown Law Journal* 627, 627.

DOI: 10.4324/9781003515852-3

possibly problematic but, because of its continued use, impossible to discard.[7] To identify the definitions and uses of sovereignty relevant to this inquiry, the chapter firstly introduces the concept and the problems it poses. Secondly the chapter surveys the philosophical and historical development and function of the concept from its European roots to its function in colonisation. Thirdly the chapter places these definitions in an Australian context by providing background to the evolving nature of the status of Australia as a sovereign nation. Within this Australian context the chapter then refines the nature of sovereignty asserted by the Australian state's representatives by examining contemporary challenges to sovereignty.

Luigi Condorelli and Antonio Cassese identify the contemporary challenges to state sovereignty as internal strife, international human rights and globalisation.[8] The chapter examines the first two of these challenges in an Australian context, identifying the internal challenge as the assertion of Indigenous sovereignty and not the rebel fighters that Condorelli and Cassese envisioned.[9] These two areas, Indigenous sovereignty and human rights, are examined because of what they reveal of the nature of the sovereignty asserted by migration lawmakers. The third challenge, the categorisation of globalisation as a threat to state sovereignty that 'tests the limits of a state centric world community', will be more thoroughly examined in the next chapter.[10]

II The Problem of Defining Sovereignty

Sovereignty denotes the idea of supreme power, and is often applied to a state's power over a territory and its people.[11] It can be understood as inter-

7 Hans Kelsen, 'Sovereignty and International Law' (1960) 48(4) *Georgetown Law Journal* 627, 627. See also James Crawford, *The Creation of States in International Law* (Oxford University Press, 2006) 32–3 ('*Creation*'); WJ Stankiewicz, 'In Defense of Sovereignty: A Critique and an Interpretation', in WJ Stankiewicz (ed), *In Defense of Sovereignty* (Oxford University Press, 1969) 1, 3–38; Daniel Philpott, 'Sovereignty: An Introduction and Brief History' (1995) 48(2) *Journal of International Affairs* 353, 354–5; Joseph A Camilleri and Jim Falk, *The End of Sovereignty? The Politics of a Shrinking and Fragmenting World* (Edward Elgar, 1992) 31.

8 Luigi Condorelli and Antonio Cassese, 'Is Leviathan Still Holding Sway Over International Dealings?', in Antonio Cassese (ed), *Realizing Utopia: The Future of International Law* (Oxford University Press, 2012) 14, 22. Hilary Charlesworth also characterised globalisation as a challenge to state sovereignty: Hilary Charlesworth, 'Dangerous Liaisons: Globalisation and Australian Public Law' (1998) 20 *Adelaide Law Review* 57.

9 Condorelli and Cassese (n 8) 22–4.

10 Antonio Cassese, 'Gathering Up the Main Threads', in Antonio Cassese (ed), *Realizing Utopia: The Future of International Law* (Oxford University Press, 2012) 653.

11 Kelsen (n 6) 627; Philpott (n 7) 353, 357; Antonio Cassese, *International Law* (Oxford University Press, 2nd ed, 2005) 49 ('*International*'); Stephen Hall, *Principles of International Law* (Lexis Nexis, 6th ed, 2019) 3–4; *Netherlands v US* (1928) 2 RIAA 829, 838 ('*Islands of Palmas Case*'); Gillian Triggs, *International Law: Contemporary Principles and Practices*

nal and external, and this is mirrored in domestic and international law and politics.[12]

Internal sovereignty has been defined as a right to hold supreme authority and command obedience,[13] not just superior force, within a state.[14] It is a legitimate authority within the state,[15] with legitimacy that can be sourced from 'law, tradition, consent or divine command'.[16] It is not dependent on democratic legitimacy.[17] It is described as 'a fundamental authority relation within states between rulers and ruled which is usually defined by a state's constitution'.[18]

External sovereignty can be defined negatively as the absence of a superior authority over a defined territory and its people.[19] It is marked by the independence of the state from other authorities.[20] From the perspective of international law the sovereignty of a state, both internal and external, is 'limited only by the requirements of international law'.[21] Eminent international legal scholar James Crawford defines legal sovereignty as 'the totality of powers a state may have under international law'.[22] Judgments in international courts and tribunals have identified the rights and mutual obligations of sovereign states. As early as 1928 the arbitrator Max Huber noted in the *Islands of Palmas Case* that, along with the 'exclusive competence' of the state within its territorial boundaries, there was also an obligation to protect the 'right to integrity and inviolability' of other states.[23] The definition of sovereignty in international law was also discussed in the *Lotus Case*.[24] The principle

(Lexis Nexis Butterworth, 2nd ed, 2011) 271; *Mabo v Queensland [No 2]* (1992) 175 CLR 1, 82, 36 (Brennan J) ('*Mabo*'); Robert Jackson, 'Sovereignty in World Politics: A Glance at the Conceptual and Historical Landscape', in Neil Walker (ed), *Relocating Sovereignty* (Dartmouth Publishing Company, 2006) 3, 5.

12 Oppenheim, *International Law: A Treatise*, ed H Lauterpact (David Mckay Company, 8th ed, 1955) 37.

13 Philpott (n 7) 355. Note that Crawford disputes that sovereignty is a right, preferring the term 'attribute', because to be a state under international law is to be sovereign. See Crawford, *Creation* (n 7) 33.

14 FH Hinsley, *Sovereignty* (Cambridge University Press, 2nd ed, 1986) 25.

15 Philpott (n 7).

16 Philpott (n 7) 54.

17 James Crawford, 'Chance, Order, Change: The Course of International Law' (2013) 365 *Recueil des Cours* 9, 70, 89 ('Chance').

18 Jackson (n 11).

19 Hall (n 11) 3–4; Hinsley (n 14) 215.

20 Jackson (n 11). James Crawford discusses the development of this internal/external definition, citing Henry Wheaton, *Elements* (3rd ed, 1846) pt I, ch II, 6 in Crawford, *Creation* (n 7) 8–9.

21 Hall (n 11) 4; see also Hinsley (n 14).

22 Crawford, *Creation* (n 7) 33. See also Hall (n 11); Kelsen (n 6).

23 *Islands of Palmas Case* (n 11) 838.

24 PCIJ, *SS Lotus Case* (France v Turkey), PCIJ Rep, (1927) Series A No 10, 18–19.

derived from this case, that a state is free to act unless the action has been prohibited by a rule to which the state has become bound on the basis of consent, has been used to further define state authority, but its relevance and interpretation in an increasingly interdependent world and a context of more developed international law have been questioned.[25]

A strand of this modern international law is human rights law, which since the middle of the 20th century could be seen to have blurred the distinction between internal and external sovereignty.[26] The increasing globalised movement of people also tests this distinction between internal and external sovereignty.[27]

The attributes of sovereignty identified in these definitions raise theoretical and practical issues. Two are relevant to the discussion of the internal challenge of Indigenous sovereignty. The first of these is the divisibility of sovereignty, that is whether sovereign power can be shared internally. The second is the issue of the source of the legitimacy of Australia's claim to sovereignty. Relevant to the discussion of the external challenge of human rights law is the issue of the relationship of international law and state sovereignty. If the essence of sovereignty is supreme authority over a territory and its people,[28] how can state sovereignty be limited? Oppenheim described this as the 'problem of sovereignty' in the 20th century.[29] Addressing this paradox, Jacques Maritain suggested the concept of sovereignty itself was problematic and should be discarded.[30] Hans Kelsen pointed to politics, not law, for a resolution.[31] He argued that, if sovereignty is the supreme authority of a legal order, then the question of whether that supremacy lies in international law or domestic law lies beyond the realm of legal arguments.[32] Oppenheim's solution was that a state's sovereignty is conditioned by 'a partial surrender of their sovereignty' in order to maintain peace and operate international

25 An Hertogen, 'Letting Lotus Bloom' (2015) 26 *European Journal of International Law* 901; Anne Peters, 'Does Kosovo Lie in the Lotus-Land of Freedom' (2011) 24 *Leiden Journal of International Law* 95; Crawford, 'Chance' (n 17) 73–4.

26 Antonio Cassese, *International Law in a Divided World* (Oxford University Press, 1986) ('*Divided*').

27 For a discussion of the practical and humanitarian dilemmas produced by concepts of sovereignty at the domestic and international law interface see Chantal Thomas, 'What Does the Emerging International Law of Migration Mean for Sovereignty' (2013) 4 *Melbourne Journal of International Law* 392, 393–9; Eve Lester, *Making Migration Law: The Foreigner, Sovereignty, and the Case of Australia* (Cambridge University Press, 2018). See especially 8–158.

28 Cassese, *International* (n 11) 49; Hinsley (n 14) 215.

29 Oppenheim (n 12) 122–3.

30 Jacques Maritain, 'The Concept of Sovereignty', in WJ Stankiewicz (ed), *In Defense of Sovereignty* (Oxford University Press, 1969) 41, 51. James Crawford expresses a similar sentiment but accepts the need to retain the term in Crawford, *Creation* (n 7) 32.

31 Kelsen (n 6) 638.

32 Kelsen (n 6) 638.

legal institutions.[33] How Australia addresses this problem of the interface of state sovereignty with international law in the area of human rights law, particularly in the treatment of migrants and asylum seekers, is discussed in Section VI.

III The Philosophy and Function of Sovereignty

The following brief account of sovereignty's philosophical development and historical function provides a conceptual framework and background to understand sovereignty and assess its function in Australian migration legislative processes in 2000–20.[34] For clarity this section examines these aspects, the philosophical development and historical function, separately, but scholars such as Martii Koskenniemi, Harald Bauder, Antony Anghie and Eve Lester argue that across the history of sovereignty the function was constitutive of the concept.[35] As Koskenniemi writes, 'sovereignty did not arise as a philosophical invention but out of Europe's exhaustion from religious conflict'.[36] The attraction was not to a 'transcendental idea' but a practical way to harness the power of a secular ruler to ensure the security and welfare of the population.[37]

A Philosophical Development

The particular interest of this inquiry is how the relationship of sovereignty and law was theorised. The modern philosophical development of sovereignty as both a legal and political concept is most often traced to European philosophers such as Jean Bodin and Thomas Hobbes. Jean Bodin introduced the concept in 1577, from the French 'souverain' meaning an 'authority which had no authority above itself'.[38] Bodin defined sovereignty as an 'absolute' and 'perpetual' power,[39] subject only to God and the law of nature and not human-made law.[40] For Bodin, 'the bare word of a prince should be

33 Oppenheim (n 12) 123.
34 Camilleri and Falk (n 7) 17 suggest that sovereignty must be understood in the context of specific times and places.
35 Martii Koskenniemi, 'What Use of Sovereignty Today?' (2011) 1 *Asian Journal of International Law* 61, 65 ('What Use'); Harald Bauder, 'State of Exemption: Migration Policy and the Enactment of Sovereignty' (2021) 9(5) *Territory, Politics, Governance* 675; Antony Anghie, *Imperialism, Sovereignty and the Making of International Law* (Cambridge University Press, 2004) 13–114; Lester (n 27) 94–108.
36 Koskenniemi, 'What Use' (n 35) 65.
37 Koskenniemi, 'What Use' (n 35) 65.
38 Oppenheim (n 12) 120; Maritain (n 30) 49.
39 Jean Bodin, *Six Books of the Commonwealth*, tr and abridged MJ Tooley (Basil Blackwell, 1955) 25–30.
40 Oppenheim (n 12) 121.

as sacred as a divine pronouncement'.[41] A century later Hobbes theorised an omnipotent 'Mortall God',[42] using unlimited sovereign power for the protection and good of those who had traded their personal sovereignty, which in their natural state would lead to war, for the protection and security of the sovereign. He describes this sovereign as a 'Common Power' for 'Common Benefit' completely concentrated in a single sovereign who by 'Power and Strength' forces community harmony and defence against external enemies.[43] For Hobbes it was the duty of this sovereign to make and execute 'good Lawes'.[44] This sovereign was the lawmaker. For both Bodin and Hobbes the concept of sovereignty was the indivisible power of the sovereign.[45] In a reaction to Hobbes' concept of the omnipotent indivisible sovereign as the shield against anarchy, English philosopher and influential proponent of liberalism John Locke asserted, 'Where law ends tyranny begins'.[46] Locke proposed instead a constitutional partnership, grounded in natural law.[47] Locke traced the power of the sovereign 'to the positive grant and commission delegated to them by the governed'.[48] Rousseau criticised this constitutional approach as a 'dismembering of the social body'.[49] He agreed with Hobbes that sovereignty was indivisible but disputed its source.[50] In his theory of the social contract the source of sovereignty was 'the will of the [whole] body of the people . . . and constitutes law'.[51] For all these philosophers the source of law is the sovereign but this power was sourced variously in God, a singular 'Common Power', a constitution or the people.

In the early 20th century, responding to what he saw as the inadequacy of the liberal constitutionalism of the 18th and 19th centuries,[52] of which Locke was an early proponent,[53] and its conceptualisation of sovereignty as

41 Bodin (n 39) 30.
42 Thomas Hobbes, *Leviathan*, tr Karl Schulmann and GAJ Rogers (Bloomsbury, 2006) 136.
43 Thomas Hobbes, *Leviathan*, tr Karl Schulmann and GAJ Rogers (Bloomsbury, 2006) 36.
44 Thomas Hobbes, *Leviathan*, tr Karl Schulmann and GAJ Rogers (Bloomsbury, 2006) 175.
45 Oppenheim (n 12) 121.
46 John Locke, 'Of Civil Government', in John Locke, *Two Treaties of Government and a Letter of Toleration*, ed Ian Shapiro (Yale University Press, 2003) 189.
47 John Locke's understanding of natural law is captured in 'The state of nature has a law of nature to govern it, which obliges every one: and reason, which is that law, teaches all mankind, who will but consult it, that being all equal and independent, no one ought to harm another in his life, health, liberty, or possessions'. John Locke, 'Of Civil Government', in John Locke, *Two Treaties of Government and a Letter of Toleration*, ed Ian Shapiro (Yale University Press, 2003) 102.
48 John Locke, 'Of Civil Government', in John Locke, *Two Treaties of Government and a Letter of Toleration*, ed Ian Shapiro (Yale University Press, 2003) 167; Camilleri and Falk (n 7) 20–1.
49 Jean-Jacques Rousseau, *The Social Contract*, tr Maurice Cranston (Penguin Books, 1968) 71.
50 Camilleri and Falk (n 7) 20–1.
51 Rousseau (n 49) 70, 59–62.
52 For a discussion of the development of the constitutional state see Hinsley (n 14) 156–7.
53 For a discussion of the development of the constitutional state see Hinsley (n 14) 156–7.

a set of legal norms,[54] Carl Schmitt theorised sovereignty as 'he who decides on the exception', that is to say, when legal norms do not apply.[55] Schmitt claimed conceptual continuity with both Bodin and Hobbes. He linked his theory to Bodin's concept of sovereignty as indivisible, and not bound by law or obligation.[56] He related his ideas to Hobbes' positioning of authority, not God or nature, as the key element of sovereignty.[57] He theorised that, in the application of sovereignty beyond an abstract theory, legal liberalism was false in imagining that legal norms cover all situations.[58] Schmitt placed the sovereign necessarily outside the legal order, deciding in a situation of conflict what constitutes 'the public interest or interest of the state, public safety and order' and whether the constitution should be suspended.[59] For Schmitt this suspension is distinguished from anarchy and chaos, instead being a different kind of order.[60] This sovereignty is 'a space beyond law, a space where law recedes leaving the legally unconstrained [sovereign] state to act'.[61] In the late 20th century Giorgio Agamben positioned law and sovereignty differently. He theorised sovereignty on the edge, not outside of law,[62] and that edge marks inclusion and exclusion.[63] He dismissed both Schmitt's categorisation of sovereignty as a purely political concept and Kelsen's concept that sovereignty is at the apex of a juridical order.[64] Agamben replaces Schmitt's definition of the pairing of friend/enemy[65] of the state as the expression of sovereign power with the categorial pairing of inclusion and exclusion.[66] For

54 Carl Schmitt, *Political Theology: Four Chapters on the Concept of Sovereignty*, tr George Schwab (Massachusetts Institute of Technology, 1985) 13–14.
55 Carl Schmitt, *Political Theology: Four Chapters on the Concept of Sovereignty*, tr George Schwab (Massachusetts Institute of Technology, 1985) 5.
56 Carl Schmitt, *Political Theology: Four Chapters on the Concept of Sovereignty*, tr George Schwab (Massachusetts Institute of Technology, 1985) 8.
57 David Dyzenhaus notes that Schmitt liked to quote Hobbes that 'authority not truth makes law': David Dyzenhaus, *The Constitution of Law: Legality in a Time of Emergency* (Cambridge University Press, 2006) 12.
58 John P McCormick, 'Schmittian Positions on Law and Politics – CLS and Derrida' (2000) 21 *Cardozo Law Review* 1693, 1695; Dyzenhaus (n 57) 4.
59 Schmitt, *Political Theology* (n 54) 6–7.
60 Schmitt, *Political Theology* (n 54) 12.
61 Dyzenhaus (n 57) 39.
62 Giorgio Agamben, *Homo Sacer*, tr Daniel Heller-Roazen (Stanford University Press, 1998) 28–9.
63 Giorgio Agamben, *Homo Sacer*, tr Daniel Heller-Roazen (Stanford University Press, 1998) 181.
64 Giorgio Agamben, *Homo Sacer*, tr Daniel Heller-Roazen (Stanford University Press, 1998) 28–9. See also Kelsen's discussion of sovereignty in national and international law in Kelsen (n 6).
65 Carl Schmitt, *The Concept of the Political*, tr G Schwabb (University of Chicago Press, 2007) 26–7. Note Schmitt is careful to remove from this concept of enemy any moral or aesthetic judgment. He defines the enemy as a stranger with whom it is possible to be in conflict if there is a threat to one's way of life.
66 Agamben (n 62) 8.

Agamben the work of sovereign power is to create the space where 'The law applies in no longer applying'.[67] The excluded are not unaffected by the law, but placed in a position of being 'abandoned', 'exposed' and 'threatened'.[68]

B The Historical Function of Sovereignty

All of these conceptual developments, from Bodin's sovereignty as the voice of God,[69] to Hobbes' sovereignty as omnipotent protector[70] to Agamben's sovereignty marking exclusion at the edge of law,[71] occurred within a historical political and legal context.[72] Two strands of that history illustrate the functions sovereignty has played: sovereignty as a cure for war and sovereignty as a tool for imperial expansion and colonisation.

Sovereignty functioning as a cure for war, as Koskenniemi argues, is a theme running through its history.[73] This history, developed in parallel with the concept of the state,[74] can be traced to Ancient Rome,[75] but the Peace of Westphalia at the end of the Thirty Years' War in 1648 is most often viewed as the beginning of the modern history of sovereignty.[76] Through the Westphalian treaties, the supremacy of the political authority of the state within its territorial borders was enshrined as subject to no other authority.[77] 'Absolute, perfect and full sovereignty' was ascribed to internally and externally independent monarchs.[78] The treaties made under the Peace of Westphalia allowed for resolution of interstate conflict. The dominant European powers secured their sovereign power in further collective action in 1815 with the

67 Agamben (n 62) 28.
68 Agamben (n 62) 28.
69 Bodin (n 39) 30.
70 Hobbes (n 42) 136.
71 Agamben (n 62) 181.
72 For example, Carl Schmitt is seen as providing theoretical underpinnings and a language for Nazis in Germany in 1939 in Ville Suuronen, 'Carl Schmitt as a Theorist of the Nazi Revolution: "The Difficult Task of Rethinking and Recultivating Traditional Concepts"' (2021) 20(2) *Contemporary Political Theory* 341.
73 Koskenniemi, 'What Use' (n 35).
74 Hinsley (n 14) 24 sees the development of the state as essential to the concept of sovereignty. Crawford, *Creation* (n 7) states that in international law the legal consequences of state sovereignty and statehood are synonymous.
75 Hinsley (n 14) 43.
76 Note that the significance of Westphalia is disputed. Andreas Osiander suggests that the Peace of Westphalia was only a milestone in a process that had already begun and not 'a revolutionary new phenomenon'. Andreas Osiander, 'Sovereignty, International Relations and the Westphalian Myth' (2001) 55(2) *Spring International Organization* 251, 287. See also Crawford, *Creation* (n 7) 10; Ignacio de la Rasilla del Moral, 'Sovereignty through the Inter-Disciplinary Kaleidoscope' (2015) 84 *Nordic Journal of International Law* 130.
77 Triggs (n 12) 10.
78 Oppenheim (n 12) 121 notes that not all monarchs were ascribed absolute sovereignty. Those who were dependent on another monarch for defence or other state functions were attributed 'relative sovereignty'.

Final Act of the Congress of Vienna, which aimed to secure states against revolutionary forces within and without.[79] This demonstrates the growing understanding among sovereign states that it was in their own interest to respect the sovereignty of other states.

This function of sovereignty as a cure for war continued into the 20th century. The response of the victors in both the First World War and the Second World War was to establish international collaborations to prevent future war, forming the League of Nations in 1919 and the United Nations in 1945.[80] The focus of both these international institutions, just as with the Peace of Westphalia, was the prevention of war.

Those nations eligible to become members of the League of Nations and later the United Nations were generally sovereign states recognised by the victors after the respective world wars. These international institutions recognised the sovereignty of the member states. Article 2 of the UN Charter notes that the United Nations is 'based on the principle of sovereign equality'.[81] At paragraph 7 the charter commits to a respect for, and non-intervention in, 'matters which are essentially within the domestic jurisdiction of any state'.[82] Being a United Nations member state is a recognition of the individual state's sovereignty and the equality of that sovereignty with that of other nations.[83]

Parallel to sovereignty functioning in this way as a cure for war, however imperfect, the concept of sovereignty was instrumental in creating the circumstances to secure wealth and land through imperial expansion.[84] This second historical function of sovereignty was as a tool for this imperialist expansion and colonisation.[85] As Europe emerged from the conflicts of the 17th century

79 Hall (n 11) 5.

80 Hall (n 11) 6–7; Oppenheim (n 12) 381, 392, 400–48.

81 *Charter of the United Nations* art 2(1). For a discussion of sovereign equality and current issues see B Rutledge, 'Toward a Functional Approach to Sovereign Equality' (2012) 53 *Virginia Journal of International Law* 181, 185–91; Cassese, *Divided* (n 26) 31–2; Michail Risvas, 'Non-discrimination in International Law and Sovereign Equality of States: An Historical Perspective' (2017) 39 *Houston Journal of International Law* 79; Brad R Roth, 'Coming to Terms with Ruthlessness: Sovereign Equality, Global Pluralism, and the Limits of International Criminal Justice' (2010) 8 *Santa Clara Journal of International Law* 231.

82 *Charter of the United Nations* art 2(7).

83 Cassese, *International* (n 11); Ann Kent, 'Influences on National Participation in International Institutions: Liberal v Neoliberal States', in Hilary Charlesworth, Madelaine Chaim, Devika Hovell and George Williams (eds), *The Fluid State* (Federation Press, 2005) 251, 252–4.

84 See, e.g., Martii Koskenniemi, 'Sovereignty, Property and Empire: Early Modern English Contexts' (2017) 18(2) *Theoretical Inquiries in Law* 355 ('Sovereignty, Property'); Lester (n 27) 11, 81–111. See also Andrew Fitzmaurice, *Sovereignty, Property and Empire, 1500–2000* (Cambridge University Press, 2014) especially chs 2–4.

85 See, e.g., Martii Koskenniemi, 'Sovereignty, Property and Empire: Early Modern English Contexts' (2017) 18(2) *Theoretical Inquiries in Law* 355 ('Sovereignty, Property'); Lester (n 27) 11, 81–111. See also Andrew Fitzmaurice, *Sovereignty, Property and Empire, 1500–2000* (Cambridge University Press, 2014) especially chs 2–4.

the dominant European powers co-opted the concept of sovereignty as they looked to secure their power and wealth beyond Europe, as Koskenniemi's analysis of the English experience demonstrates.[86] He concludes that the British empire of free trade was created both by sovereignty and property.[87] In the public sphere sovereignty created the boundaries within which the private sphere of property could thrive. In turn property created the wealth to support and defend the assertion of sovereignty.[88] Lester's research also illustrates this relationship between the concept of sovereignty and the production of wealth. Lester shows that, concurrently with European expansion, a common law doctrine of absolute sovereignty was developed that gave colonisers the unfettered right to exclude or impose conditions on the entry of aliens and that this was used to access cheap labour essential to build new enterprises.[89]

Antony Anghie also argues that the concept of sovereignty was developed, and not merely applied, to justify this imperial endeavour.[90] Anghie argues that the elements of sovereignty were shaped through the encounter of the European sovereign state with the colonised. Anghie traces sovereignty not to Bodin or Hobbes but to the 16th century Spanish theologian and jurist Francisco de Vitoria.[91] Vitoria defined the colonised (in his case the Indigenous peoples of the Americas) against 'universal natural law' and European (in his case Spanish) cultural and religious norms.[92] Using these standards, he concluded that Indigenous Americans possessed universal reason but were uncivilised.[93] Anghie explains how this ethnocentric analysis resulted in Indigenous Americans being judged as lacking the sovereignty recognised between sovereign European states.[94] It also resulted, Anghie argues, in justifying unconstrained war against any resistance from Indigenous Americans, because, possessing reason, they could be judged as transgressing universal natural law.[95]

Ethnocentric concepts of civilisation were also used to deny the sovereignty of Australia's Indigenous peoples.[96] In Australia the doctrine of terra

86 Koskenniemi, 'Sovereignty, Property' (n 84).
87 Koskenniemi, 'Sovereignty, Property' (n 84) 388–9.
88 Koskenniemi, 'Sovereignty, Property' (n 84) 388–9.
89 Lester (n 27) 11, 81–111.
90 Anghie (n 35) 13–31.
91 Anghie (n 35) 13–31.
92 Anghie (n 35) 13–31.
93 Anghie (n 35) 13–31.
94 Anghie (n 35) 13–31.
95 Anghie (n 35) 13–31.
96 Irene Watson, 'Re-Centring Indigenous Knowledge and Places in a Terra Nullius Space' (2014) 10(5) *AlternNative* 508; Allan Ardill, 'Sociobiology, Racism and Australian Colonisation' (2009) 18 *Griffith Law Review* 82.

nullius (land belonging to no one) was used to justify colonisation. Brennan J in *Mabo v Queensland* provides this description:

> As among themselves, the European nations parcelled out the territories newly discovered to the sovereigns of the respective discoverers, provided the discovery was confirmed by occupation and provided the indigenous inhabitants were not organised in a society that was united permanently for political action. To these territories the European colonial nations applied the doctrines relating to acquisition of territory that was terra nullius. They recognised sovereignty of the respective European nations over the territory of 'backward peoples' and, by State practice, permitted the acquisition of sovereignty of such territory by occupation rather than by conquest.[97]

For a sovereign nation such as England, which claimed that its law was 'grounded upon the law of God and extends itself to the original law of nature and the universal law of nations',[98] taking ownership of territory with local inhabitants for the sake of economic enterprise was viewed by some as an uneasy fit. For example, in the early 18th century the prominent English jurist William Blackstone, while supporting 'sending colonies [of settlers] to find out new habitations', and the 'right of migration when the mother country was overcharged with inhabitants' cautioned that such activity be 'kept strictly within the limits of the law of nature'.[99] Blackstone questioned:

> Seising on countries already peopled, and driving out or massacring the innocent and defenceless natives, merely because they differed from their invaders in language, in religion, in customs, in government, or in colour;

97 *Mabo* (n 11) 32. For a discussion of the development of the concept of terra nullius, the legitimacy of original title and the history of these concepts from colonial to postcolonial international law see Sookyeon Huh, 'Title to Territory in the Post-Colonial Era: Original Title and Terra Nullius in the ICJ Judgments on Cases Concerning Ligitan/Sipadan (2002) and Pedra Branca (2008)' (2015) 26(3) *European Journal of International Law* 709. Barbara Hocking traces the correction of the legal interpretation of Australia as terra nullius from *Milirrpum v Nabalco and the Commonwealth* 2 (1971) 17 FLR 141 to *Cooper v Stuart* (1889) 14 App Cas 286 to *Mabo*: Barbara Hocking, 'Aboriginal Law Does Now Run in Australia: Reflections on the *Mabo* Case from *Cooper v Stuart* through *Milirrpum* to *Mabo*' (1993) 15 *Sydney Law Review* 187. See also Garth Nettheim, 'The Consent of the Natives: Mabo and Indigenous Political Rights' (1993) 15 *Sydney Law Review* 223; Darryl Cronin, *Trapped by History: The Indigenous – State Relationship in Australia* (Rowman & Littlefield, 2021) 51–64; Watson (n 96).

98 Koskenniemi 'Sovereignty, Property' (n 84) 360, quoting *Calvin v Smith* (1608) 77 ER 377 (KB) (Lord Chancellor Ellesmore).

99 William Blackstone, *Commentaries on the Laws of England* (1765) bk2 ch 1 <https://avalon.law.yale.edu/18th_century/blackstone_bk2ch1.asp>.

> how far such a conduct was consonant to nature, to reason, or to christianity, deserved well to be considered by those, who have rendered their names immortal by thus civilizing mankind.[100]

Such uncomfortable inconsistencies required that this economic expansion be rationalised within a legal, philosophical and moral framework. This was provided by an expansion of the meaning of terra nullius justified in part by the application of teachings such as those of influential Swiss jurist Emer Vattel to the use of land.[101] Vattel taught that it was the duty of the sovereign to ensure that the territory controlled was cultivated as much as possible.[102] He judged that living by hunting was idle and a misuse of land and that those who lived in this way did not inhabit the land.[103] This Eurocentric view of land use justified the broadening of the concept of terra nullius from the literal meaning of 'belonging to no-one'.[104] It was used by the European colonisers to justify claiming legal original title to any land subjectively judged by the coloniser as inadequately utilised or civilised.[105] The term was applied where 'indigenous inhabitants were not organized in a society that was united permanently for political action', that is, was not in a form in which the European notion of sovereignty was recognised.[106] This justified the acquisition of property: taking territory, goods and even the bodies of local and neighbouring inhabitants as slaves.[107] Resistance by indigenous inhabitants was not to be tolerated. The policy of the colonising power was, 'whilst

100 William Blackstone, *Commentaries on the Laws of England* (1765) bk2 ch 1 <https://avalon.law.yale.edu/18th_century/blackstone_bk2ch1.asp>.

101 Emer de Vattel, *The Law of Nations*, ed Béla Kapossy and Richard Whatmore (Liberty Fund, 2008) 128–30. The book was first published in 1758. For discussion of the justifications of the treatment of those deemed uncivilised by the European standard see Wayne Glausser, 'Three Approaches to Locke and the Slave Trade' (1990) 51(2) *Journal of the History of Ideas* 199, 215. See Irene Watson (n 96) for a discussion of the continuing effects of terra nullius. See also Rowan Nicholson's analysis of this expanded concept of terra nullius in Rowan Nicholson, 'Was the Colonisation of Australia an Invasion of Sovereign Territory?' (2019) 20 *Melbourne Journal of International Law* 1, 10–14.

102 Vattel (n 101) 128.

103 Vattel (n 101) 130.

104 Bruce Moore (ed), *Australian Pocket Oxford Dictionary* (Oxford University Press, 6th ed, 2007) 1110.

105 Sookyeon Huh, 'Title to Territory in the Post-Colonial Era: Original Title and Terra Nullius in the ICJ Judgments on Cases Concerning Ligitan/Sipadan (2002) and Pedra Branca (2008)' (2015) 26(3) *European Journal of International Law* 709, 716.

106 *Mabo* (n 11) 32, citing Mark Frank Lindley, *The Acquisition and Government of Backward Territory in International Law* (Longmans, Green and Co, 1926) chh 3, 4.

107 For a discussion of this history and politics in Australia see, e.g., Tracey Banivanua-Mar, *Violence and Colonial Dialogue: The Australian-Pacific Indentured Labor Trade* (University of Hawai'i Press, 2007); Emma Christopher, 'The Saviour and the Revolutionary: Afro-Caribbean Responses in a Queensland/New Guinea Kidnapping Case' (2018) 40(2) *Slavery & Abolition* 321.

the aboriginal inhabitants were not to be ill-treated, settlement was not to be impeded by any claim which those inhabitants might seek to exert over the land'.[108] The legal framework of the expanded notion of terra nullius allowed the colonisers to judge these claims as invalid.

These two strands of history, sovereignty as a cure for war and sovereignty as a tool for imperialism, show sovereignty functioning both to tame and to unleash the power of those recognised as sovereign states. Concepts of sovereignty protected the internal sovereignty of sovereign states from the aggression of other states and justified sovereign states' imperial territorial conquests and colonisation of those judged 'backward',[109] and not inhabitants of their land.[110] They were excluded from the benefits of this sovereignty.

IV Sovereignty in an Australian Context

Before examining two of the possible challenges to Australian state sovereignty, the indigenous challenge and the international human rights challenge, this section provides context concerning two issues, namely the source of the legitimacy of the sovereignty of the Australian state and the locus of that supreme power within the state.

The source of legitimacy is argued in 'traditional legal theory'[111] to have been an Imperial Act of Parliament of the UK. At Federation the legitimacy of the Australian Constitution, the foundation of Australian law, derived from the enactment of the *Commonwealth of Australia Constitution Act 1900* (UK).[112] High Court Justice Owen Dixon[113] described the Crown as 'the visible sign of national power'.[114] The new federation was a federated group of self-governing colonies of the British Empire.[115] Sovereignty, supreme power, across the British Empire of which Australia was a part was the sovereignty of the Imperial Parliament which had the power to change the common law.[116] The gradual concessions of power made by this Imperial Parliament to the colonies of Australia and then to the federation were the acts of sovereign

108 *Mabo* (n 11) (Dawson J) 142. For a list of archival material and other original sources documenting settler violence in Australia see Lyndall Ryan et al., 'Colonial Frontier Massacres in Australia 1788–1930', University of Newcastle (Website, 2019). <https://c21ch.newcastle.edu.au/colonialmassacres/>.
109 *Mabo* (n 11).
110 Vattel (n 101) 130.
111 *Kirmani v Captain Cook Cruises Pty Ltd [No 1]* (1985) 159 CLR 351, 442 (Deane J).
112 *Commonwealth of Australia Constitution Act 1900* (UK).
113 At the time a Justice of the High Court, later the Chief Justice and recipient of a knighthood.
114 Owen Dixon, 'The Law and the Constitution' (1935) 35 *Law Quarterly Review* 590, 614.
115 Owen Dixon, 'The Law and the Constitution' (1935) 35 *Law Quarterly Review* 592–3.
116 Owen Dixon, 'The Law and the Constitution' (1935) 35 *Law Quarterly Review* 592.

power of that British Parliament.[117] The date when the United Kingdom formally lost the last of its legal power over Australia was 1986.[118] In March of that year the British Parliament and the Australian Parliament passed acts that terminated the power of the British Parliament to legislate for Australia and ended the capacity for appeals from state supreme courts to be heard by the Privy Council in Britain.[119] The Australian legislation declared that this was recognition of Australia as a 'sovereign, independent and federal nation'[120] and the validity of that legislation was grounded in the Constitution s 51(38),[121] which itself continued unchanged under both the UK and Australian Acts.[122] Geoff Lindell argues that this unbroken 'chain of legislative authority' provides the legal legitimacy for the Australian Constitution as it sets the boundaries of the legislative processes and the share of power across institutions of government in the state.[123] As Justice Kirby has put it, the Australian Constitution remains attached 'like a legal umbilical cord' to the legislation of the Imperial Parliament.[124]

An alternative account argues from this same history that the legitimacy of Australian sovereignty ultimately resides in the will of the Australian people. This account notes that the preamble of the *Commonwealth of Australia Constitution Act 1900* (UK) begins: 'whereas the people . . . have agreed' and the Constitution includes s 128 allowing the people to vote on any change to the basis of their law. Murphy J's statement in 1976 that 'The original authority for our Constitution was the United Kingdom Parliament, but the existing authority is its continuing acceptance by the Australian people'[125]

117 *Colonial Laws Validity Act 1865* (UK); *Statute of Westminster 1931* (UK) adopted by Australia in *Statute of Westminster Adoption Act 1942* (Cth); *Australia Act 1986* (UK) reflected in *Australia Act 1986* (Cth).

118 Note Edelman J states that by 1948 Australia was a country where the sovereign 'had a separate identity in relation to Australia': *Checuti v Commonwealth* (2021) 95 ALJR 704, 707. See Alison Pert, 'The Development of Australia's International Legal Personality' (2017) 34 *Australian Yearbook of International Law* 149. She surveys the arguable dates for Australia's independence up to 1986. See also Anne Twomey, 'International Law and the Executive', in Brian R Opeskin and Donald R Rothwell (eds), *International Law and Australian Federalism* (Melbourne University Press, 1997) 69, 69–76.

119 *Australia Act 1986* (UK) s 11.

120 *Australia Act 1986* (Cth) long title.

121 This section allows the Australian Parliament to legislate with respect to 'the exercise within the Commonwealth, at the request or with the concurrence of the Parliaments of all the States directly concerned, of any power which can at the establishment of this Constitution be exercised only by the Parliament of the United Kingdom or by the Federal Council of Australasia'.

122 *Australia Act 1986* (UK) s 5; *Australia Act 1986* (Cth) s 5.

123 GJ Lindell, 'Why Is Australia's Constitution Binding? The Reasons in 1900 and Now, and the Effect of Independence' (1986) 16 *Federal Law Review* 29, 37.

124 Michael D Kirby, 'Deakin: Popular Sovereignty and the True Foundation of the Australian Constitution' (1996) 3 *Deakin Law Review* 129, 138.

125 *Bistricic v Rokov* (1976) 135 CLR 552, 566.

was not explicitly endorsed by other High Court Justices at that time but within a decade Deane J doubted whether

> traditional legal theory can properly be regarded as providing an adequate explanation of the process which culminated in the acquisition by Australia of full 'independence and Sovereignty'. Plainly, there is something to be said for the view that any explanation of the legal nature of that process is incomplete if it fails to acknowledge and examine the relevance and importance, under both international law and internal law, of that social compact, of those international agreements, of the 'established constitutional position' to which the Statute of Westminster expressly refers and of international recognition of Australia as an independent and sovereign State whose only de jure government is that which is locally based.[126]

By 1996 McHugh J stated clearly that

> the political and legal sovereignty of Australia now resides in the people of Australia. But the only authority that the people have given to the parliaments of the nation is to enact laws in accordance with the terms of the Constitution.[127]

The first part of McHugh J's statement addresses the issue of the source of legitimacy of Australia's contemporary claim to sovereignty. The second part addresses the issue of the locus of this sovereignty: it resides in the people through their representation in the Parliament and through their power to change the Constitution. The Australian Constitution shares the administration of this sovereign authority across the institutions of the judiciary, the Parliament and the executive government. The limits of the power of each of these institutions is the subject of constitutional interpretation by the judiciary.[128] Two of the proposed challenges to the legitimacy and extent of the power of this Australian state sovereignty are discussed shortly.

V Indigenous Challenge to Sovereignty

The first challenge to sovereignty discussed here is an internal challenge. Condorelli and Cassese give the example of groups of rebels and insurgents,

126 *Kirmani v Captain Cook Cruises Pty Ltd [No 1]* (1985) 159 CLR 351, 442.

127 *McGinty v Western Australia* (1996) 70 ALJR 200, 239 (McHugh J).

128 Note that when Sir Anthony Mason was Chief Justice of the High Court he argued that because the judiciary had inherited from the British model an 'an ingrained belief . . . in the supremacy of parliament' the Court conducted its interpretive role in a legalistic and apolitical manner. See Anthony Mason, 'The Role of a Constitutional Court in a Federation – A Comparison of the Australian and the United States Experience' (1986) 16 *Federal Law Review* 1, 4.

motivated by ethnic or other tensions, who instigate civil wars in countries emerging from a colonial past.[129] While Australia has not seen a tangible and disruptive internal challenge on this scale,[130] this chapter argues that the assertion of Indigenous sovereignty is in some respects comparable to an internal rebellion. Asserting Indigenous sovereignty is an internal rebellion against the concept of state sovereignty which was developed and imported from Europe at colonisation, which operates within the Australian state and which is supported by international law and institutions.[131] The assertion of Indigenous sovereignty is a philosophical challenge to the dominant concept of sovereignty, a political challenge to the distribution of sovereign power and a legal challenge to the legitimacy of the state's claim to sovereignty.[132]

To examine the philosophical challenge of Indigenous sovereignty, Agamben's philosophy of sovereignty provides a helpful framework. Agamben posits that sovereignty has its existence and definition in its capacity to comprehensively exclude.[133] He gives the example of the bandit, stripped of rights, fleeing capture 'but caught in the sovereign ban [categorically paired with the good citizen] . . . no life is more "political" than his.'[134] This concept is poignantly enacted in the concentration camp. Agamben also gives the example of the concentration camp inmate, who at the 'extreme limit of pain' exists in a space where the distinction between 'fact and law . . . nature and politics' is indistinct.[135] The inmate embodies the power of the sovereign. 'Nothing "natural" or "common" is left in him'.[136] As Agamben puts it: 'Where there is a People [the embodied sovereignty] there will be bare life [the people excluded from political existence]'.[137] On this definition sovereignty is not just

129 Condorelli and Cassese (n 8) 22–4.
130 Challenges to the colonists were a feature of Australia's pre-Federation past as Indigenous populations attempted unsuccessfully to resist the colonists. See, e.g., Henry Reynolds, *The Other Side of the Frontier* (Penguin Books Australia, 1982) 61–127; Henry Reynolds, *Frontier* (Allen and Unwin Australia, 1987) 3–57. Note Aileen Moreton-Robinson argues that Australia since the moment of colonisation has been engaged in a 'race war' in Aileen Moreton-Robinson, 'Imagining the Good Indigenous Citizen: Race War and the Pathology of Patriarchal White Sovereignty' (2009) 15(2) *Cultural Studies Review* 61.
131 Watson (n 96); Megan Davis and Marcia Langton (eds), *It's Our Country: Indigenous Arguments For Meaningful Constitutional Recognition and Reform* (Melbourne University Press, 2016) 87, 93. See also Shireen Morris and Noel Pearson, 'Indigenous Constitutional Recognition: Paths to Failure and Possible Paths to Success' (2017) 91 *Australian Law Journal* 350, 351.
132 For discussions of Indigenous sovereignty see Watson (n 96); Gerry Simpson, 'Mabo, International Law, Terra Nullius and the Stories of Settlement: An Unresolved Jurisprudence' (1993) 19 *Melbourne University Law Review* 195; Sarah Maddison, 'Recognise What? The Limitations of Settler Colonial Constitutional Reform' (2017) 52(1) *Australian Journal of Political Science* 3.
133 Agamben (n 62) 8.
134 Agamben (n 62) 183.
135 Agamben (n 62) 185.
136 Agamben (n 62) 185.
137 Agamben (n 62) 185.

the power of exclusion: it is the power of life and death invested in the state. To illustrate this idea Agamben uses the story of a young woman held in an apparent vegetative state by the law which will not allow her to die.[138] She embodies the law in her flesh: a 'legal being as much as a biological being', dependent on the law for life or death.[139]

It is not difficult to ground this commentary in the colonised experience of Indigenous peoples whose territories are classified as terra nullius (belonging to no one), and who themselves are labelled 'backward'.[140] Indigenous people were once excluded from political existence, condemned by Australian state sovereignty to 'bare life', and this resulted in well-documented gross disadvantage.[141] Even government initiatives such as Closing the Gap[142] can be viewed as expressing Agamben's model of sovereignty. Closing the Gap purports to help Indigenous people 'catch up' to the non-Indigenous standard.[143] Such an apparently benevolent initiative as Closing the Gap reveals the ongoing exclusion of Indigenous people, captured by the non-Indigenous standard by which the government now attempts to judge Indigenous people.[144] Just as in Agamben's analysis, under the coloniser's sovereignty Indigenous people embody the law and the demarcation between what is and is not included.

However, unlike Agamben's metaphoric images (the bandit, the prison camp inmate or the young woman in a vegetative state stripped of political agency), Indigenous people have asserted their political existence embodied within a different sovereignty, which they assert coexists alongside the dominant colonising sovereignty.[145] This assertion challenges the philosophical legitimacy of the state model. While Indigenous people are positioned like Agamben's camp inmate within the dominant model of European state sovereignty, they have a different place in their own Indigenous conception of sovereignty. This positioning is eloquently expressed in the Uluru Statement from the Heart (Uluru Statement).[146] This is a statement of the Indigenous National Constitutional Convention which met over four days in May 2017.

138 Agamben (n 62) 186.
139 Agamben (n 62) 186.
140 *Mabo* (n 11).
141 See the series of reports by the Productivity Commission, 'Overcoming Indigenous Disadvantage' (Web Page) <www.pc.gov.au/research/ongoing/overcoming-indigenous-disadvantage>.
142 Closing the Gap is an Australian government initiative. For more information see Department of Prime Minister and Cabinet, *Closing the Gap* (Report, 2019).
143 Closing the Gap is an Australian government initiative. For more information see Department of Prime Minister and Cabinet, *Closing the Gap* (Report, 2019).
144 Heather McCrae et al., *Indigenous Legal Issues: Commentary & Materials* (Thomson Reuters (Professional) Australia, 4th ed, 2009) 55. See also Angie's (n 35) analysis of Vittoria's rationalisation of treatment of Indians.
145 Watson (n 96).
146 Referendum Council, *Final Report of the Referendum Council* (Report, 2017) <www.referendumcouncil.org.au/sites/default/files/report_attachments/Referendum_Council_Final_Rep ort.pdf>.

Convened by the Referendum Council,[147] it was the defining statement of sovereignty from 250 Indigenous Australians gathered after an extensive national consultation process. The Uluru Statement describes Australian Indigenous sovereignty in this way:

> This sovereignty is a spiritual notion: the ancestral tie between the land, or 'mother nature', and the Aboriginal and Torres Strait Islander peoples who were born there from, remain attached thereto, and must one day return thither to be united with our ancestors. This link is the basis of the ownership of the soil, or better, of sovereignty. It has never been ceded or extinguished and co-exists with the sovereignty of the Crown. How could it be otherwise? That peoples possessed a land for sixty millennia and this sacred link disappears from world history in merely the last two hundred years?
>
> With substantive constitutional change and structural reform, we believe this ancient sovereignty can shine through as a fuller expression of Australia's nationhood.[148]

The philosophical challenge of Indigenous sovereignty expressed in the Uluru Statement is to conceptualise sovereignty as a spiritual, historical and continuing connection to the physical environment, the territory, that can co-exist and cannot be excluded by the dominant model. The concept of the co-existence of authorities to include or exclude cannot be part of a concept of sovereignty that is based on the existence of an absolute and final authority. By proposing coexistence, Indigenous sovereignty rejects a model of sovereignty that is an imposition of a legal framework that is defined by its capacity to exclude Indigenous sovereignty.

The political challenge that comes with the assertion of Indigenous sovereignty is the proposal for 'a redistribution of public power'.[149] In 2016 in his foreword to a collection of essays by Indigenous academics and leaders, Fred Chaney expressed the political nature of this challenge:

> First nations come to the table as stakeholders, not supplicants. They can determine what they wish to negotiate. They do not have to be limited by the legal complexities of native title law. As the Yorta Yorta proclaimed

147 The Referendum Council was jointly appointed by the prime minister and the leader of the opposition to advise on how to recognise Indigenous peoples in the *Constitution*. Referendum Council, 'The Council' (Web Page, 2 January 2019) <www.referendumcouncil.org.au/council.html>.

148 Referendum Council (n 146) i.

149 Megan Davis, 'Ships That Pass in the Night', in Megan Davis and Marcia Langton (eds), *It's Our Country: Indigenous Arguments For Meaningful Constitutional Recognition and Reform* (Melbourne University Press, 2016) 86, 87. See also Morris and Pearson (n 131).

> after the High Court denied their native title claim: we are here, and you have to deal with us. Assertion of first nation state[150] is a political action rather than a necessarily circumscribed legal claim.[151]

The Uluru Statement called for a share of power for Indigenous people. The statement included proposals for 'substantive constitutional change and structural reform'. These were a constitutionally founded 'First Nations Voice' to Parliament and a treaty-making process which required a political response.[152] In 2000 Prime Minister John Howard had dismissed a treaty with Indigenous people as divisive:

> Now a treaty will divide this country. Countries don't make treaties with themselves, they make treaties with other nations and the very notion of a treaty in this context conjures up the idea that we are two separate nations. Now I thought the whole idea of reconciliation was to prevent that occurring.[153]

In 2017 the government's response to the Uluru Statement was silent on treaty making and focussed only on the proposal for a 'First Nations Voice to Parliament'. This proposal was for a constitutionally enshrined Indigenous body. This was rejected as neither 'desirable or capable of winning acceptance at referendum'.[154] The government criticised the proposal for a constitu-

150 Note I interpret the term state as equivalent to sovereignty, consistent with Crawford, *Creation* (n 7) 33.

151 Fred Chaney, 'Foreword', in Megan Davis and Marcia Langton (eds), *It's Our Country: Indigenous Arguments For Meaningful Constitutional Recognition and Reform* (Melbourne University Press, 2016) v, vii. Note Fred Chaney was a member of the Australian Parliament from 1974 to 1993 and held several ministries including Aboriginal Affairs from 1978 to 1980: David Hough, 'Chaney, Frederick Michael (1941–)', *The Biographical Dictionary of the Australian Senate* (Web Page, 2022) https://biography.senate.gov.au/chaney-frederick-michael/; see also *Yorta Yorta Aboriginal Community v Victoria* (2002) 214 CLR 422.

152 Referendum Council (n 146). Constitutional change requires a vote by the electorate. See *Australian Constitution* s 128. Note in June 1998 a five-step treaty-making proposal was put to Prime Minister Bob Hawke. He accepted it and committed his government to respond positively but by 1990 he had been unable to make progress: Bob Hawke, 'Speech at Barunga Sports and Cultural Festival, Northern Territory', *PM Transcripts* (Speech, 12 June 1988); Bob Hawke, 'News Conference, Sheraton Hotel, Brisbane', *PM Transcripts* (9 March 1990) <https://pmtranscripts.pmc.gov.au/release/transcript-7947>.

153 Tim Lester, 'Interview with Tim Lester, 7.30 Report', *PM Transcripts* (Interview, 29 May 2000) <https://pmtranscripts.pmc.gov.au/release/transcript-22789>.

154 Malcolm Turnbull, 'Response to Referendum Council's Report on Constitutional Recognition', *PM Transcripts* (26 October 2017) <https://pmtranscripts.pmc.gov.au/release/transcript-41263>. This proved prescient. When this proposal was finally put to the Australian people by a new government in a 2023 referendum it was defeated.

tional voice as creating a 'new national representative assembly open only to some Australians'[155] and that this would undermine 'the universal principles of unity, equality and "one person one vote"'.[156] The claim to the universality of these principles can be seen as an ethnocentric assertion of the imported European model of sovereignty as the supreme power and demonstrates what constitutional law academic Megan Davis describes as the 'tin ear' of successive governments when confronted with this challenge.[157] This response from the government, like that in 2000, claims that recognition of Indigenous sovereignty is a threat to national unity. Such an objection is a political position and does not rely on any constitutional legal issues that the voice proposal raises. As discussed previously the Australian model of sovereignty operating is already a model of shared 'internal authority and rights'.[158] Under the Constitution power is shared between the federal government and the states and within the federal government between the executive, the parliament and the courts.[159] On this basis it was possible within the framework of public law to redistribute power, that is to share sovereignty. What can be concluded from the 2017 government's response is that, while assertions of Indigenous sovereignty might have moral and ethical weight,[160] its proponents have lacked

155 Malcolm Turnbull, 'Response to Referendum Council's Report on Constitutional Recognition', *PM Transcripts* (26 October 2017) <https://pmtranscripts.pmc.gov.au/release/transcript-41263>. This proved prescient. When this proposal was finally put to the Australian people by a new government in a 2023 referendum it was defeated.

156 Malcolm Turnbull, 'Response to Referendum Council's Report on Constitutional Recognition', *PM Transcripts* (26 October 2017) <https://pmtranscripts.pmc.gov.au/release/transcript-41263>. This proved prescient. When this proposal was finally put to the Australian people by a new government in a 2023 referendum it was defeated.

157 Davis (n 149) 86.

158 Sean Brennan, Brenda Gunn and George Williams, '"Sovereignty" and Its Relevance to Treaty Making Between Indigenous people and Australian Governments' (2004) 26 *Sydney Law Review* 308, 350.

159 Sean Brennan, Brenda Gunn and George Williams, '"Sovereignty" and Its Relevance to Treaty Making Between Indigenous people and Australian Governments' (2004) 26 *Sydney Law Review* 320.

160 See, e.g., Bob Hawke's 1988 commitment to a treaty: 'At the end of this process when these things are done my fervent wish that I expressed, as you'll recall last year, my fervent wish is that at the end of that process a position will have been reached in which the non-Aboriginal people of Australia will recognise the injustices of the past, will recognise the obligations that we have to create an Australia in which your culture and traditions will not only be able to survive but to flourish, in which you the Aboriginal people will have the opportunity of living in dignity, living in an environment in which you will have the opportunity for self-management, in which your law and tribal customs will be able to apply to the maximum possible extent, that these things will be done, that you will have that sort of Australia in which to live and that you on your part will accept then that Australia has accepted and will continue to discharge its commitment'. Hawke, 'Transcript of News Conference' (n 152.)

the necessary political power to achieve a redistribution of public power, that is a share of sovereignty.

The legal challenge of the assertion of Indigenous sovereignty is more fundamental and not one that can be addressed by the municipal courts whose authority is based on the Constitution.[161] The legal challenge concerns the issue of identifying the legal basis in British and international law on which the British colonised Australia and declared British sovereignty and which has culminated, as outlined previously, in the Australian state having internal and external sovereignty. At the time of British entry to Australia, international law and British common law recognised conquest, cession and occupation of land judged to be terra nullius as three ways for a European nation to acquire sovereignty over territory.[162] Occupation, through a finding of terra nullius, allowed the law of the British colonisers to automatically apply.[163] Australian state sovereignty and with it the common law remain despite the finding in *Mabo v Queensland [No 2]* that 'terra nullius' was misapplied to Australia.[164] However in *Mabo v Queensland [No 2]* the High Court held back from a positive finding on what legal basis Australia was colonised.[165] Davis describes the implications of this 'unfinished business':

> Sovereignty was not passed from the Aboriginal people through any significant legal act. The British did not ask permission to settle. Aboriginal people did not consent, and no one ceded. Neither the English nor Australian courts have yet declared in what legally sanctioned way English sovereignty, and with it the common law, was imposed.[166]

The assertion of Indigenous sovereignty, such as that made in the Uluru Statement, is positioned as one sovereign people speaking to another: not a citizen or group of citizens appealing to a government through a municipal court.[167] This is a positioning that the *United Nations Declaration on the Rights of Indigenous Peoples* (UNDRIP) only partially addresses.[168] It gives a right to

161 *Mabo* (n 11).
162 *Mabo* (n 11) 32 (Brennan J).
163 *Mabo* (n 11) 36.
164 Davis (n 149) 93.
165 Simpson (n 134) 197.
166 Davis (n 149) 93. See also Rowan Nicholson's conclusions that the Australian colonisation was an 'invasion of sovereign territory' under international law in Nicholson (n 101) 35.
167 See Warren Mundine's history of these appeals and his argument that the requirement is for a 'nation to nation' encounter, which requires a treaty, in Warren Mundine, 'Unfinished Business', in Megan Davis and Marcia Langton (eds), *It's Our Country: Indigenous Arguments For Meaningful Constitutional Recognition and Reform* (Melbourne University Press, 2016) 128, 134–7.
168 *United Nations Declaration on the Rights of Indigenous Peoples*, opened for signature 13 September 2007 (entered into force 13 September 2007) (UNDRIP).

Indigenous peoples to 'autonomy or self-government',[169] but fails to grant the equal standing of a nation by declaring:

> Nothing in this Declaration may be interpreted as implying for any State, people, group or person any right to engage in any activity or to perform any act contrary to the Charter of the United Nations or construed as authorizing or encouraging any action which would dismember or impair, totally or in part, the territorial integrity or political unity of sovereign and independent States.[170]

Davis sees the Australian Parliament as responsible for the resolution of this matter.[171] Under the Australian Constitution the Parliament could return to the people as the source of the authority to change the Australian Constitution and seek a referendum.[172] At the time of Davis' writing the federal Parliament had not taken up her challenge.[173]

What can be concluded about the nature and function of state sovereignty in Australia from the response to the philosophical, political and legal challenge of Indigenous sovereignty? Firstly, state sovereignty is based on the acquisition of territory made without a declared legal basis that answers the assertion of Indigenous sovereignty and the finding in *Mabo v Queensland [No 2]* regarding the misapplication of terra nullius. Secondly the state's response demonstrates an ethnocentric European model of sovereignty that is defined by the exclusion of other models of sovereignty. Thirdly this ethnocentric model is sustained by superior political power that allows the state to ignore the ambiguity of its legitimacy and to resist responding to assertions of Indigenous sovereignty from within, such as the Uluru Statement and from without, such as the approximations of sovereignty described as a right in UNDRIP. Fourthly there seems to be no legal impediment in Australian public law to the state sharing 'rights and authority' with Indigenous people. Together these conclusions suggest that when Indigenous people ask of the state, 'What legitimises your entry?'[174] the answer might echo Jacques Derrida and Nicolas Onuf. Derrida argues that the inherent violence at the

169 *United Nations Declaration on the Rights of Indigenous Peoples*, opened for signature 13 September 2007 (entered into force 13 September 2007) arts 3–5.
170 *United Nations Declaration on the Rights of Indigenous Peoples*, opened for signature 13 September 2007 (entered into force 13 September 2007) art 46.
171 Davis (n 149) 93.
172 *Constitution* s 128.
173 A 2023 Referendum was conducted by a newly elected Labor Government and failed. Racism was named as at least one of the causes. See Mike Berry, 'The Voice Referendum' (Summer 2024) (92) *The Journal of Australian Political Economy* 240–8.
174 Irene Watson, 'Aboriginal Laws and the Sovereignty of Terra Nullius' (2002) 1(2) *borderlands ejournal* 15.

source of the establishment of sovereignty is delegitimising: 'There is no law without enforceability, and no applicability or enforceability of the law without force'.[175] Nicholas Onuf criticises Derrida's analysis and calls for a focus only on the types of violence that 'institute, effectuate, validate and perpetuate dominance'.[176] The tentative conclusion is that the enactment of state sovereignty in Australia has, conceptually, the violent origins that Derrida sees as delegitimising and the continued comprehensive dominance that Onuf says is more relevant. The state's response to the assertion of Indigenous sovereignty shows a state sovereignty legitimised by the superior power of numbers which allows it to ignore the unfinished business of the past and the effect of this on the present. The model of sovereignty that is revealed is one that is static, refusing to notice that, like the Yorta Yorta people, Indigenous sovereignty is here. The state's model of sovereignty is unable to accommodate this other reality.[177]

VI International Law: A Challenge to Sovereignty?

The second challenge to sovereignty proposed here is an external challenge. It is a challenge to the limits on internal sovereign power posed by the growing body of international law, particularly in the areas of human rights, refugee rights and immigration control. This challenge is recognised by the government. In 2019 Scott Morrison, Coalition Prime Minister of Australia 2018–22, expressed a concern about a 'new variant of globalism that seeks to elevate global institutions above the authority of nation states to direct national policies'.[178] On coming to office, he characterised internal sovereignty as 'a right to run our own show'.[179] However, if this is a right it is no longer unfettered.[180] The post-World War II focus on human rights and the transnational movement of people marks a key moment in the history of sovereignty and the relationship between internal and external sovereignty.

175 Jacques Derrida, 'Force of Law: The "Mystical Foundation of Authority"' (1990) 11(5–6) *Cardozo Law Review* 920, 925–6.
176 Nicholas Onuf, 'Old Mistakes: Bourdieu, Derrida and the "Force of Law"' (2010) 4(3) *International Political Sociology* 315, 318.
177 See Chaney (n 151). Yorta Yorta are the people of the Yorta Yorta nation which exists on land which is also known as the Central Murray Goulburn region. Yorta Yorta Nation Aboriginal Corporation <https://yynac.com.au>.
178 Scott Morrison, 'In Our Interest' (Speech, Lowey Lecture, 3 October 2019).
179 Scott Morrison, 'The Beliefs That Guide Us', *Prime Minister Media Centre* (Speech, Asia Briefing Live, 1 November 2018) <www.pm.gov.au/media>.
180 Crawford, *Creation* (n 7) 33, citing *Heller v US*, 776 F 2d 92, 96–7 (3rd Cir 1985). See also the discussion of domestic and international law in Australia in IA Shearer, 'The Relationship between International Law and Domestic Law', in Brian R Opeskin and Donald Rothwell (eds), *International Law and Australian Federalism* (Melbourne University Press, 1997) 34.

Whether this is an example of a new globalism placing global institutions above state authority, and in this way being a challenge to Australian state sovereignty, is doubtful.

Human rights have not always been a focus of international law. Like the concept of state sovereignty, international law began as a reflection of European ideas and is grounded in positivist principles of law which emerged in the late 18th century.[181] Under this positivist approach international law focussed on treaties and customary norms. International law has historically had a primary focus on relationships between states and on providing mechanisms other than armed conflict for solving disputes over territory or at least attempting to 'humanize the violence of war'.[182] The rights and obligations of states was the focus of international law, that is external sovereignty, but this broadened at the end of World War II.[183] The Charter of the United Nations as well as many other international treaties reflected the dual concerns of the international community: the historic concern for peace and a newer concern for human rights.[184] Article 1(3) of the UN Charter called for the establishment of a framework for protecting 'human rights and . . . fundamental freedoms for all without distinction as to race, sex, language, or religion'. Important in this framework was the Universal Declaration of

181 Triggs (n 11) 12–13.

182 David Bates, 'Constitutional Violence' (2007) 34(1) *Journal of Law and Society* 14, 19.

183 See Donald R Rothwell et al., *International Law: Cases and Materials with Australian Perspectives* (Cambridge University Press, 3rd ed, 2018) 454. They note the earliest beginnings after World War I.

184 *International Convention on the Elimination of All Forms of Racial Discrimination*, opened for signature 21 December 1965, 660 UNTS 195 (entered into force 4 January 1969); *International Covenant on Civil and Political Rights*, opened for signature 16 December 1965, 999 UNTS 171 (entered into force 3 March 1976); *Optional Protocol to the International Covenant on Civil and Political Rights*, opened for signature16 December 1966, 999 UNTS 171 (entered into force 23 March 1976); *Second Optional Protocol to the International Covenant on Civil and Political Rights*, opened for signature 15 December 1989 (entered into force15 December 1989); *International Covenant on Economic Social and Cultural Rights*, opened for signature 16 December 1966, 993 UNTS 3 (entered into force 3 January 1976); *Convention on the Elimination of All Forms of Discrimination against Women* opened for signature 18 December 1979, 1249 UNTS 13 (entered into force 3 September 1981); *Convention against Torture and Other Cruel, Inhuman or Degrading Treatment or Punishment*, opened for signature 10 December 1984, 1465 UNTS 85 (entered into force 26 June 1987); *Convention on the Rights of the Child*, opened for signature 20 November 1989, 1577 UNTS 3 (entered into force 2 September 1990); *International Convention on the Protection of the Rights of All Migrant Workers and Members of Their Families*, opened for signature 18 December 1990 (entered into force 18 December 1990); *International Convention for the Protection of All Persons from Enforced Disappearance*, opened for signature 20 December 2006 (entered into force 23 December 2010); *Convention on the Rights of Persons with Disabilities*, opened for signature 24 January 2007 (entered into force 3 May 2008); *Convention relating to the Status of Refugees*, opened for signature 28 July 1951, 189 UNTS 150 (entered into force 22 April 1954); UNDRIP arts 3–5 (n 168).

Human Rights, the International Covenant on Civil and Political Rights (ICCPR) and the International Covenant on Economic, Social and Cultural Rights. (ICESCR). This framework of rights ascribes rights to individuals and obligations to states.

The United Nations' broadened focus encompassing human rights signalled a distinction between the Westphalian sovereignty of unfettered freedom of states within their territory, and what Cassese terms the post-World War II 'Charter sovereignty', which has tempered the internal sovereignty of states through international agreements.[185] Individuals are now positioned in international law to 'claim respect for their human rights' and states can be challenged for breaches of the human rights of their citizens or foreigners.

The question of whether this development of international human rights law, including the UN Convention Relating to the Status of Refugees 1951 (Refugee Convention) and the Protocol Relating to the Status of Refugees 1967 (Refugee Protocol), challenges sovereignty can be approached in three ways. The first approach concerns the definition of sovereignty adopted by the state. International human rights law threatens an outdated Westphalian definition of internal sovereignty as an indivisible, unfettered, supreme power that a state can wield over its inhabitants.[186] It does not threaten a definition of sovereignty that is the supreme power of the state over a territory and its people 'limited only by the requirements of international law'.[187]

Another approach examines the agency of the state at the interface of internal and external sovereignty. This returns the discussion back to the problem of the competing sovereignty of domestic and international law. Oppenheim's solution was that the sovereignty of states is conditioned by 'a partial surrender of their sovereignty' in order to maintain peace and operate international legal institutions,[188] and since World War II this has included human rights law. At the core of this solution is the agency of the state. It is the state that surrenders. International law cannot be seen as an external challenge to sovereignty because it was not imposed against the sovereign will of the state. For example, Brian Opeskin addresses this question in the context of migration law and human rights.[189] He concludes that international legal norms do constrain states, but this constraint has been voluntarily adopted.[190] Condorelli

185 Cassese, *Divided* (n 26) 13–14.

186 Condorelli and Cassese (n 8) 19; Stephen D Krasner, *Sovereignty: Organized Hypocrisy* (Princeton University Press, 1999) 123.

187 Hall (n 11) 4.

188 Oppenheim (n 12) 123.

189 Brian Opeskin, 'Managing International Migration in Australia: Human Rights and the "Last Redoubt of Unfettered National Sovereignty"' (2012) 46(3) *International Migration Review* 551, 578.

190 Brian Opeskin, 'Managing International Migration in Australia: Human Rights and the "Last Redoubt of Unfettered National Sovereignty"' (2012) 46(3) *International Migration Review* 551, 578. Koskenniemi makes a similar point: Koskenniemi, 'What Use' (n 35) 62.

and Cassese make a similar point. While they recognise that constraints on states' sovereignty are a consequence of the growth of international agencies, they point out that it is not a case of 'expropriation [of sovereignty] but rather that of assignment, transfer, or delegation'.[191] The states are willing participants and it is only through states that any enforcement of international law occurs: 'international law has no arms or legs of its own'.[192] Further emphasising this state sovereignty as the power of international law, Condorelli and Cassese note that even the Security Council only operates to give permission to willing states to act to resist threats to peace.[193] The measure of the effectiveness of international law is necessarily a measure of the sovereignty, the political power, of the participating states.

The third approach to understanding whether international human rights law, including the Refugee Convention, challenges sovereignty is to examine Australia's record of ratification and compliance with its commitments. Australia's record of signing international treaties is illustrative. Australia delayed for many years, for nine and fourteen respectively, before ratifying the ICCPR and the ICESCR.[194] Australia, along with Canada, New Zealand and the United States, has not ratified the International Labour Organization's 1975 *Convention Concerning Migrations in Abusive Conditions and the Promotion of Equality of Opportunity and Treatment of Migrant Workers* nor the *International Convention on the Protection of the Rights of All Migrant Workers and Members of their Families*.[195] This is despite Australia's high reliance on skilled migrant labour. Such reluctance might be surprising considering that Australia was a member of the group of military victors who led the establishment of the United Nations.[196] Australia exercises state sovereignty in its choice of which treaties to endorse and the extent to which these are incorporated into domestic law. In Australia's circumstances Opeskin's analysis is supported: constraints from international law are the 'natural consequence of the [free] exercise of state power at an earlier time'.[197] One of those natural consequences flows from Australia's status as a founding member of the United Nations. While the UN Charter commits to respect non-intervention in 'matters which are essentially within the domestic jurisdiction of any state'[198] the Preamble of the UN Charter also affirms

191 Condorelli and Cassese (n 8) 15–16.
192 Condorelli and Cassese (n 8) 16.
193 Condorelli and Cassese (n 8) 18.
194 Annemarie Devereux suggests this delay was because of conflict concerning respective roles of the states and the Commonwealth in the area of human rights: Annemarie Devereux, 'Australia's Journey to Ratification of the ICESCR and ICCPR' (2019) 36(1) *Australian Year Book of International Law Online* 163.
195 Opeskin (n 188) 559.
196 Dag Hammarskjold Library, 'Founding Member States', *United Nations* (Web Page, 10 August 2022) <https://research.un.org/en/unmembers/founders>.
197 Opeskin (n 188) 578.
198 *Charter of the United Nations* art 2(7).

belief in the 'fundamental human rights' of humans and the equality of men and women.[199]

Since Australia ratified the ICCPR in 1991 individuals have taken their cases to the UN Human Rights Committee when their domestic options for relief have been exhausted. Cases have concerned, for example, the rights of homosexual people to privacy,[200] their rights to government recognition of their relationships for pension purposes,[201] and rights of liberty from arbitrary detention,[202] including how such detention impacts on the rights of the child under the ICCPR.[203] Australia's response to the case of *D&E v Australia*[204] is instructive. The committee's decision and commentary in *D&E v Australia* concerned the administrative immigration detention of an asylum-seeking Iranian couple who arrived by boat to Australia. The committee found that Australia had breached article 9 paragraph 1 of the ICCPR and should give D&E a remedy and compensation. The committee also reminded Australia of the basis on which it demanded compliance with this judgment:

> by becoming a party to the Optional Protocol, the State party has recognized the competence of the Committee to determine whether there has been a violation of the Covenant or not and that, pursuant to article 2 of the Covenant, that State party has undertaken to ensure all individuals within its territory or subject to its jurisdiction the rights recognized in the Covenant and to provide an effective and enforceable remedy in case a violation has been established.[205]

Despite Australia's ratification of the ICCPR and the logic of the committee's reasoning that its only power was that given to it by Australia, Australia has

199 It is beyond the scope of this book to fully discuss how the definition and protection of these human rights coexist with a commitment to non-intervention in state affairs. For a discussion on one aspect of this issue see, e.g., Thomas (n 27) 393 who notes the incompatibility of the concept of international human rights with an international legal system based on sovereign nation states. Another aspect of this issue is the development of the principle of the responsibility to protect, which emerged in international law in 2001. See Rothwell et al (n 182) 717–27. Ramesh Thakur notes the importance of the responsibility rather than the authority of sovereignty in this principle in Ramesh Thakur, *The United Nations, Peace and Security* (Cambridge University Press, 2007) 255. Hilary Charlesworth criticises the lack of female lived experience in the development of this principle in Hilary Charlesworth, 'Feminist Reflections on the Responsibility to Protect' (2010) 2(3) *Global Responsibility to Protect* 232.

200 Human Rights Committee Communication No 488/1992 (*Toonen v Australia*).

201 Human Rights Committee Communication No 941/2000 (*Young v Australia*).

202 Human Rights Committee Communication No 560/1993 (*A v Australia*); Human Rights Committee Communication No. 1050/2002 (*D & E v Australia*).

203 Human Rights Committee Communication No 1069/2002 (*Bakhtiyari v Australia*).

204 *D and E v Australia*, Merits, Communication No 1050/2002, UN Doc CCPR/C/87/D/1050/2002 (2006) 14 IHRR 14, IHRL 1587 (UNHRC 2006) (11 July 2006).

205 Human Rights Committee Communication No 1050/2002 (*D & E v Australia*) 9–10.

failed to adequately address the committee's concerns about its mandatory detention policy under the *Migration Act 1958* (Cth), which is also the circumstance of other cases before the committee.[206] The policy of mandatory detention, except for a small cohort, continues to the time of writing.[207]

Australia's position as a sovereign state means that the committee might persuade, instruct or even embarrass Australia into compliance with Australia's commitments but this falls short of impinging on state sovereignty.[208] It cannot be concluded that international human rights law impinges on the enactment of Australian sovereignty.

Another practical way that human rights law might be characterised in Australia as a challenge to sovereignty is in its influence on domestic statutory interpretation. Australian state sovereignty is the constitutional shared authority of the executive, the Parliament and the judiciary. The executive or Parliament might perceive a challenge if there is a possibility that international human rights law could materially influence statutory interpretation by the judiciary.[209] For example Kirby J in *Malika Holdings Pty Ltd v Stretton*[210] proposed that the Universal Declaration of Human Rights and the International Covenant on Civil and Political Rights could aid in defining a 'fundamental' right in Australian law.[211] Again, in the case of immigration detainee Al-Kateb, *Al-Kateb v Godwin*[212] Kirby J (in dissent) promoted the importance of the context of international law:

> The Australian Constitution was understood and applied in 1945 in a completely different international context from that prevailing today. . . . Whatever may have been possible in the world of 1945, the complete

206 Opeskin (n 188) 570–3.

207 See discussion in Chapter 6 regarding *NZYQ v Minister for Immigration, Citizenship and Multicultural Affairs* (2023) HCA 37 [2] and *ASF17 v Commonwealth of Australia* (2024) HCA 19; 98 ALJR 782.

208 For further analysis on the gap between Australia's commitment to international human rights instruments and domestic practice see Madeline Gleeson, 'Monitoring Places of Immigration Detention in Australia under OPCAT' (2019) 25 *Australian Journal of Human Rights* 150; Ben Saul, 'Dark Justice: Australia's Indefinite Detention of Refugees on Security Grounds under International Human Rights Law' (2012) 13(2) *Melbourne Journal of International Law* 685; Matthew T Stubbs, 'Arbitrary Detention in Australia: Detention of Unlawful Non-citizens under the Migration Act 1958 (Cth)' (2006) 25 *Australian Year Book of International Law* 273.

209 Note that this is perhaps only a theoretical concern. See Michael Head's view that the court has moved away from what he terms a traditional principle of making judgments where possible that are not inconsistent with international law in Michael Head, 'High Court Sanctions Indefinite Detention of Asylum Seekers' (2004) 8 *University of Western Sydney Law Review* 153, 163.

210 *Malika Holdings Pty Ltd v Stretton* (2001) 204 CLR 290, 328.

211 *Malika Holdings Pty Ltd v Stretton* (2001) 204 CLR 290, 328.

212 (2004) 219 CLR 562.

> isolation of constitutional law from the dynamic impact of international law is neither possible nor desirable today. That is why national courts, and especially national constitutional courts such as this, have a duty, so far as possible, to interpret their constitutional texts in a way that is generally harmonious with the basic principles of international law, including as that law states human rights and fundamental freedoms.[213]

The removal of direct references to the Refugee Convention from the *Migration Act 1958* (Cth) in 2014 might suggest the government's concern that the High Court is a possible channel for this challenge from international law.[214] Kirby J's judgment quoted previously demonstrates the pathway for this challenge through the High Court.

From this analysis it seems that only a Westphalian view of internal sovereignty could support the idea that international human rights law, including the application of those rights to the unwanted migrant, is a challenge to Australian state sovereignty. Australia chooses what commitments it makes and with what judgments of international bodies it will comply. However international human rights law might challenge Australia politically by exposing the gap between the status Australia has as a sovereign member of the United Nations and a signatory to human rights instruments, and how it wields domestic sovereign power.

VII Conclusion

There is no single definition of sovereignty. Its core meaning denotes supreme power. This concept of the supreme power of the state over a territory and its people is applied internally as the supreme authority within the state, and externally to mark the independence of the state from any external authority. This modern concept of sovereignty as an attribute of the state arose in Europe in the 16th century. The nature of this power, its source of legitimacy and its relationship to law have been variously characterised as the voice of God speaking law through the monarch, a constitutional monarch guided by parliaments, a decision-maker external to the law or a power defined by those it excludes. The historical function of this concept has been as a cure for war and a justification for European economic and cultural imperialism and colonial expansion.

The British colonisation of Australia, justified by the application of terra nullius, brought the common law of the British and the sovereignty of the

213 (2004) 219 CLR 634.

214 This removal was affected by the codification of Australia's interpretation of its protection obligations. *Migration and Maritime Powers Legislation Amendment (Resolving the Asylum Legacy Caseload) Act 2014* (Cth).

British monarch to Australia. The legal and political sovereignty of the Australian state and the status of the Australian Constitution is sourced to both the legislation of the Imperial Parliament and to the will of the Australian people. Under the Constitution sovereignty remains symbolised by the British monarch, as the monarch of Australia, and is administered by the institutions of Parliament, the executive and the judiciary.

The assertion of Indigenous sovereignty challenges this conception of an exclusive sovereignty. The philosophical challenge of this assertion is that it resists definition within the dominant model. Indigenous sovereignty is a refusal to be placed at the edge of or excluded from the dominant European model of sovereignty, and asserts its presence. The political challenge is a challenge to the distribution of power and the ongoing reality of Indigenous people. The response from governments up to 2022 to reject or ignore this challenge relied on the political power of superior numbers and an assertion of a need for unity that is based on the dominant European model of sovereignty, not on legal justifications. That reliance was demonstrated in the successful opposition to the Voice referendum led by the leader from the previous government. The legal challenge of Indigenous sovereignty is a challenge to the legitimacy of the legal basis of Australian sovereignty. Australian state sovereignty is revealed as static and enabled by superior political power, allowing the state to refuse to acknowledge or respond to this challenge.

An argument that international human rights law and its application to the unwanted migrant is an external challenge to the Australian state's internal sovereignty is difficult to sustain. Only a concept of sovereignty that existed before the establishment of the United Nations, what some term Westphalian sovereignty, could be understood as impinged on by international human rights law. The Australian state has chosen when to engage with international legal institutions and Australia remains in control of its level of compliance when human rights decisions are made against it. One such choice is Parliament's attempt to limit the influence of international human rights law on statutory interpretation of the *Migration Act 1958* (Cth) by removing references to the Refugee Convention. Australian state sovereignty is revealed as resistant to the challenge posed by international human rights law. It is vulnerable only to embarrassment.

A third challenge to sovereignty posed by Condorelli and Cassese as well as by Brown and Dauvergne is globalisation.[215] This chapter has argued that the purported challenges of Indigenous sovereignty and international human rights law have done little to impinge on Australian state sovereignty. The next chapter examines some of the phenomena of globalisation and in what way they might challenge the sovereignty of the state as the supreme authority over a territory and its people.

215 Condorelli and Cassese (n 8); Dauvergne (n 1); Brown (n 1).

Chapter 3

Globalisation as a Threat to Sovereignty in the 21st Century

I Introduction

The previous chapter surveyed the concept and function of state sovereignty and concluded that sovereignty has functioned historically to tame the power of states to wage war and simultaneously to unleash the power of states on non-European territory and peoples through colonisation. The chapter also examined two purported challenges to state sovereignty. Luigi Condorelli and Antonio Cassese suggest that three 'extra-legal trends' restrain the traditional sovereign prerogatives of states.[1] They identify these as the spread of international human rights, internal rebellion and globalisation.[2] The previous chapter examined the first challenge and concluded that international human rights law can only be understood as a threat to a Westphalian definition of sovereignty of absolute internal control and that the Australian state remains in control of its commitment to, and compliance with, international law. On the second challenge it concluded that, while the assertion of Australian Indigenous people's sovereignty is a rebellion against the exclusivity of state sovereignty and a challenge to its legitimacy, the Australian government has the political power to ignore this challenge. The purpose of this chapter is to examine the third 'extra-legal trend': globalisation and how it might be understood as a threat to sovereignty.

To begin this examination the chapter firstly introduces the concept of globalisation and four approaches to theorising and researching this phenomenon: an historical approach, a transnational approach, a microglobalisation approach and the globalisation of a value. It then examines how these approaches might be applied to contemporary events and how they might

1 Luigi Condorelli and Antonio Cassese, 'Is Leviathan Still Holding Sway Over International Dealings?', in Antonio Cassese (ed), *Realizing Utopia: The Future of International Law* (Oxford University Press, 2012) 14, 23.
2 Luigi Condorelli and Antonio Cassese, 'Is Leviathan Still Holding Sway Over International Dealings?', in Antonio Cassese (ed), *Realizing Utopia: The Future of International Law* (Oxford University Press, 2012) 14, 23.

DOI: 10.4324/9781003515852-4

be relevant to the Australian context in which amendments to the *Migration Act 1958* (Cth) were made. These approaches overlap and represent globalisation from various vantage points. None provide a comprehensive framework. The definitional debate continues about what globalisation comprises and how it can be fruitfully analysed. This discussion encompasses a historical approach which traces globalisation to the global empires of past imperialists and challenges the idea that the globalisation of the 21st century is unique; a transnational approach which understands globalisation as capitalist globalisation that is driven by a transnational capitalist class; and a micro-globalisation analysis which demonstrates how harnessing new technologies challenges the traditional idea of territorial boundaries.[3] The historical approach is examined because of the importance to this analysis of whether contemporary globalisation is qualitatively different from past comparable instances and this examination will be further developed across other chapters particularly in an Australian immigration context. The transnational and micro-globalisation approaches have been chosen because the economic aspects of globalisation and the enabling new technologies are facilitators of cultural and other forms of globalisation including migration.[4] This section will conclude with an examination of the philosophical underpinnings of globalisation in the period 2009–20.

Secondly, the chapter draws on the theories of Catherine Dauvergne and Wendy Brown concerning the interface of globalisation and sovereignty to examine the extent to which globalisation is a threat to a sovereignty and how these theories apply in an Australian context.[5] The chapter will examine the impact of globalisation on state sovereignty and how states respond. In an era that has encompassed the COVID-19 pandemic, US president Donald Trump and Britain's exit from the European Union (Brexit), accelerating climate change and deepening social and economic inequality, the possibility of withdrawal from globalisation behind stronger state borders and the benefits and disadvantages of such a withdrawal are pressing issues.

3 Leslie Sklair, 'A Transnational Framework for Theory and Research in the Study of Globalization', in Ino Rossi (ed), *Frontiers of Globalisation Research: Theoretical and Methodological Approaches* (Springer Science and Business Media, 2007) 93, 100.

4 Catherine Dauvergne, *Making People Illegal: What Globalization Means for Migration Law* (Cambridge University Press, 2008) 30 ('*Making People Illegal*').

5 Wendy Brown, *Walled States, Waning Sovereignty* (Zone Books, 2010) ('*Walled States*'); Wendy Brown, *Undoing the Demos: Neo Liberalism's Stealth Revolution* (Zone Books, 2015) 9–10 ('*Undoing the Demos*'); Catherine Dauvergne, 'Sovereignty, Migration, and the Rule of Law in Global Times' (2004) 67(4) *Modern Law Review* 588 ('Sovereignty, Migration'); Dauvergne, *Making People Illegal* (n 4).

II Four Ways of Defining Globalisation

Situating the 'nebulous phenomena' that compose globalisation in a coherent framework is a complex task and possibly not achievable.[6] There is, however, general agreement among theorists in both legal and sociological disciplines that a core characteristic of globalisation is dramatically increased interaction and interdependence across the globe.[7] This can be seen in areas such as economic, financial, commercial, security, cultural and information exchange.[8] Stella Ladi also makes a case that policy research institutions have been agents for policy globalisation, which she argues is shaped by ideas, not just shared economic goals.[9] It is enabled by technological change that is so swift that analyses can be outdated before they are published.[10] It is also enabled by the increased mobility of the world population.[11]

How to best theorise and research globalisation is debated.[12] Four overlapping approaches are discussed shortly: a historical approach that understands globalisation as the waxing and waning of hegemony between states; a transnational approach that situates globalisation as internal and external to the state, reducing the significance of territorial sovereignty; a micro-globalisation approach which focuses on the impact of technology to defy previous time and spatial limitations; and an approach which examines the underlying values of the contemporary phenomena that compose globalisation. These approaches are selected for their explanatory power to understand the ways in which globalisation can challenge state sovereignty.

6 Janet Abu-Lughod, 'In Search of a Paradigm', in Ino Rossi (ed), *Frontiers of Globalisation Research: Theoretical and Methodological Approaches* (Springer Science and Business Media, 2007) 397, 353.
7 See, e.g., Abu-Lughod (n 6) 354; Condorelli and Cassese (n 1) 14; Hilary Charlesworth, 'Dangerous Liaisons: Globalisation and Australian Public Law' (1998) 20 *Adelaide Law Review* 57; Kim Rubenstein, 'Globalization and Citizenship and Nationality', in Catherine Dauvergne (ed), *Jurisprudence for an Interconnected Globe* (Ashgate Publishing, 2003) 159, 165–8. See also Kenichi Ohmae, *The End of the Nation* (Free Press, 1995) especially 27, 40 describing a new 'melting pot' of a borderless economy.
8 Condorelli and Cassese (n 1) 23.
9 Stella Ladi, *Globalisation, Policy Transfer and Policy Research Institutes* (Edward Elgar Publishing, 2005) 2.
10 See, e.g., Karin Knorr Cetina, 'Microglobalization', in Ino Rossi (ed), *Frontiers of Globalisation Research: Theoretical and Methodological Approaches* (Springer Science and Business Media, 2007) 65. At the time of writing the technology on which she bases her terrorism case study has been overtaken by live streaming.
11 Graeme Hugo, 'Globalization and Changes in Australian International Migration' (2006) 23(2) *Journal of Population Research* 107. See especially the summary of drivers of increased mobility at 109–10.
12 Ino Rossi, 'Preface', in Ino Rossi (ed), *Frontiers of Globalisation Research Theoretical and Methodological Approaches* (Springer Science and Business Media, LLC, 2007) v.

A An Historical Approach

Historical research helps to answer the question of whether globalisation is a qualitatively new phenomenon or is a continuation of historical trends or a replication of historical processes.[13] Historians identify several waves of globalisation beginning in the 15th century or even earlier with the 'march of the Mongols'.[14] Raymond Grew suggests that a study of these historical instances shows that globalisation should be viewed 'not as an external force imposed from outside but rather as a reciprocal process in which local, regional, and national changes interact with global changes, all of them reconstituted in continuing mutation'.[15] Grew argues that a historical approach can help to counter the idea that globalisation is irresistible and of an inevitable end to which the world is heading. An historical approach allows a view of how a 'process comes about, creates resistance, and dissolves'.[16]

Applying an historical perspective, contemporary globalisation could be viewed as a version of imperialism powered by a technological revolution.[17] Is the current form of globalisation just American imperialism replacing European imperialism and now being threatened by Chinese imperialism? Within Rossi's description of 'the continuing usage by the global North, (previously termed the West) of cosmopolitan ideologies at the service of its nationalistic interests' can be seen elements of imperialism.[18] Rossi's description invites a conclusion that globalisation is the vehicle for this new imperialism by powerful states.[19] Cha's comparison of the United States' role in globalisa-

13 Raymond Grew, 'Finding Frontiers in Historical Research on Globalization', in Ino Rossi (ed), *Frontiers of Globalisation Research: Theoretical and Methodological Approaches* (Springer Science and Business Media, 2007) 271, 271–2.

14 Raymond Grew, 'Finding Frontiers in Historical Research on Globalization', in Ino Rossi (ed), *Frontiers of Globalisation Research: Theoretical and Methodological Approaches* (Springer Science and Business Media, 2007) 277–8.

15 Raymond Grew, 'Finding Frontiers in Historical Research on Globalization', in Ino Rossi (ed), *Frontiers of Globalisation Research: Theoretical and Methodological Approaches* (Springer Science and Business Media, 2007) 278. For an example see Jeffrey G Williamson, *Globalization and the Poor Periphery Before 1950* (MIT Press, 2006). He identifies the shift in poor countries from providing primary produce to a focus on providing manufactured products from cheap labour as a factor in promoting engagement in world markets.

16 Grew (n 13) 272. See as an example of this approach historian Adam M McKeon, *Melancholy Order: Asian Migration and the Globalization* of Borders (Columbia University Press, 2008).

17 Abu-Lughod (n 6) 354.

18 Ino Rossi, 'From Cosmopolitanism to a Global Perspective: Paradigmatic Discontinuity (Beck, Ritzer, Postmodernism, and Albrow) Versus Continuity (Alexander and Collins) and Emergent Conceptualizations (Contributors to This Volume)', in Ino Rossi (ed), *Frontiers of Globalisation Research: Theoretical and Methodological Approaches* (Springer Science and Business Media, 2007) 397, 435.

19 Ino Rossi, 'From Cosmopolitanism to a Global Perspective: Paradigmatic Discontinuity (Beck, Ritzer, Postmodernism, and Albrow) Versus Continuity (Alexander and Collins) and

tion with Britain's role in the 19th century also supports the interpretation of globalisation as a new imperialism.[20]

Such an analysis might help to explain the events of 2016: the rise of Trump to the US presidency and the referendum in which British voters opted to withdraw from the European Union (Brexit), which were accompanied by threats of protectionist policies.[21] This has been characterised as a popular 'backlash [in Grew's model 'resistance'] against the forces and values underpinning the processes of globalisation'.[22] For future historians there will be empirical evidence about whether the current kind of globalisation will dissolve in the face of resistance just as past instances of phenomena that could be labelled globalisation have dissolved, or whether this era of globalisation is qualitatively different from past instances and independent of state resistance. Taesuh Cha draws comparisons with what has been termed the first globalisation during the Pax Britannica which ended after World War I.[23] He asks 'whether globalization was a passing fancy artificially produced by the US liberal project in the unipolar moment, not a fundamental spatiotemporal transformation of human existence caused by economic and technological shifts'.[24] He answers this question with 'wait and see', suggesting that an historical and empirical approach will reveal the answer.[25]

B A Transnational Approach

Sklair argues that globalisation cannot be understood as a new type of imperialism and colonisation.[26] He argues that an approach which analyses globalisation in the old paradigm of a more powerful state diminishing the

Emergent Conceptualizations (Contributors to This Volume)', in Ino Rossi (ed), *Frontiers of Globalisation Research: Theoretical and Methodological Approaches* (Springer Science and Business Media, 2007) 397, 435.

20 Taesuh Cha, 'Is Anybody Still a Globalist? Rereading the Trajectory of US Grand Strategy and the End of the Transnational Moment' (2020) 17(1) *Globalizations* 60, 71.

21 Joseph E Stiglitz, 'Rethinking Globalization in the Trump Era: US-China Relations' (2018) 13(2) *Frontiers of Economics in China* 133, 134.

22 Valentina Kostadinova, 'Brexit Is Unlikely to Provide Answers to Governance Problems under Globalisation' (2017) 37(1) *Economic Affairs* 135, 135.

23 Cha (n 20). Pax Britannica refers to the period after the end of the Napoleonic Wars in 1815 which left Britain as a dominant world military and industrial power without rival. As Matzke notes, the dominant military power of the British navy was promoted as a force for peace, deterring challengers: Rebecca Berens Matzke, *Deterrence through Strength: British Naval Power and Foreign Policy under Pax Britannica* (University of Nebraska Press, 2011) 1–10.

24 Rebecca Berens Matzke, *Deterrence through Strength: British Naval Power and Foreign Policy under Pax Britannica* (University of Nebraska Press, 2011) 61.

25 Rebecca Berens Matzke, *Deterrence through Strength: British Naval Power and Foreign Policy under Pax Britannica* (University of Nebraska Press, 2011) 71.

26 Sklair (n 3) 94.

sovereignty of another less powerful state is inadequate for analysing aspects of globalisation that are beyond the state or interstate interaction.[27] Sassen seems to support this.[28] She describes how 'global processes, supported by new technologies, materialise in and push the transformation of national institutional arrangements and economies'.[29] Sklair goes further, describing states as active participants, not just objects of global forces.[30] This matches the previous chapter's analysis of Australia's active role in supporting and resisting international law.

Sklair proposes that a transnational theoretical framework is the most useful for analysis. His transnational framework analyses the 'changing role of state actors and agencies in sustaining the hegemony of capitalist globalisation'.[31] Sklair argues that contemporary globalisation can best be understood as capitalist globalisation. He analyses globalisation in terms of 'transnational practices that cross state boundaries but do not originate with state institutions, agencies or actors' but can involve them.[32] His concept of globalisation is beyond interstate interaction.[33] He introduces a concept of economic, political and cultural–ideological power that is independent of, but interreacting with, states. Sklair identifies the economic element of his model as the transnational corporation, the political element as a transnational capital class and the cultural–ideological element as consumerism.[34]

Sklair's transnational capitalist class has four elements: controllers of transnational corporations, state and interstate bureaucrats and politicians, technocrats and merchants and the media. He argues that this capitalist class has global rather than national interests but at the same time is key to the intertwining of globalisation into the national and local and that it plays an active role in workplaces through economic, political and cultural influence. To maintain control of workers, members of the class promote the threat of foreign competition to both workers and consumerism.[35] Their message is both work harder for less or you will lose your job and spend more of what you earn to be happy.[36] The wealth of this class is derived from markets that may not coincide with national borders. Its shareholders are not

27 Sklair (n 3) 94.
28 Saskia Sassen, *Losing Control? Sovereignty in an Age of Globalization* (Columbia University Press, 1995) xii.
29 Saskia Sassen, *Losing Control? Sovereignty in an Age of Globalization* (Columbia University Press, 1995) xii.
30 Sklair (n 3). Also see the discussion of the government's involvement in the international student industry in Chapter 5.
31 Sklair (n 3) 95.
32 Sklair (n 3) 97.
33 Sklair (n 3) 97.
34 Sklair (n 3) 100.
35 Sklair (n 3) 99–100.
36 Sklair (n 3) 99.

nationally limited.[37] Neither are their corporate and personal investments confined to the national. Members of this class brand themselves with similar consumer lifestyles and they promote themselves as 'citizens of the world': even their nationality is changed to suit their corporate interests, as exemplified by Rupert Murdoch, an Australian media magnate who has adopted US citizenship.[38]

Saskia Sassen proposes a more complex model that names the effect of these phenomena. Rather than Sklair's transnational corporate class, Sassen proposes 'predatory "formations," a mix of elites and systemic capacities with finance a key enabler', that push toward acute concentration of wealth and power.[39] She describes a complex interaction, where governments are the enablers, resulting in the normalisation of extremes of poverty and inequality.[40] As part of her account of current phenomena she describes the reciprocal trends of 'the rise of displaced populations in the Global South and the rising rates of incarceration in the Global North'.[41] Her concern is for those expelled, those who are not counted in the economic logic that dominates.[42]

C *Micro-globalisation*

While the transnational approach focusses on the visible political, economic and ideological face of globalisation, micro-globalisation addresses a more elusive element: how a globally dispersed group of people, lacking the military, social, economic or political power of dominant states, can organise and implement global terror attacks.

The elements of micro-globalism are the microstructure, which is powered by increasingly sophisticated information technology. This microstructure defies spatial boundaries, giving it global reach. Karin Knorr Cetina explains how: 'Global systems based on microstructural principles do not exhibit institutional complexity but rather the asymmetries, unpredictability, and playfulness of complex (and dispersed) interaction patterns, a complexity that . . . is always intertwined with chaos'.[43]

37 Sklair (n 3) 99.
38 Sklair (n 3) 99.
39 Saskia Sassen, *Expulsions: Brutality and Complexity in the Global Economy* (Harvard University Press, 2014) 13.
40 Saskia Sassen, *Expulsions: Brutality and Complexity in the Global Economy* (Harvard University Press, 2014) 29.
41 Saskia Sassen, *Expulsions: Brutality and Complexity in the Global Economy* (Harvard University Press, 2014) 29.
42 Saskia Sassen, *Expulsions: Brutality and Complexity in the Global Economy* (Harvard University Press, 2014) 37.
43 Knorr Cetina (n 10) 66.

Chaos is hard to control by imposing state boundaries and by traditional structures. Micro-globalisation is characterised by 'response-presence-based social forms' bound together by information technologies, not spatially tied, and constantly creating and recreating time-based (not spatial) structures to achieve their outcomes.[44] It is the opposite of orderliness or predictability. Knorr Cetina notes how microstructures utilise rather than control technologies from outside their micro-organisation. Their model is not to acquire but to utilise. The microstructure contrasts with the dominant organisational models of government and business, which are characterised by 'interiorized systems of control and expertise' that at worst can be inward focussed and unresponsive bureaucracies.[45] Traditional structures require order, not chaos.

Knorr Cetina uses the concept 'scopic media' to describe the way in which terrorist microstructures utilise technologies both to promote a terrorist event to a global audience and simulataneously to record and interpret events to build a sense of integration for globally dispersed individuals.[46] Through this scopic media a single event can be interpreted and reinterpreted to both individual participants and global audiences. In this way the terrorism microstructure, not weighed down by a hierarchy, constantly transforms and has impact beyond the places where it performs terrorist events and out of proportion to its lack of traditional economic and social power and complex hierarchy and bureaucracy.[47]

Knorr Cetina described the model of micro-globalisation soon after the attack by Al-Qaeda on the twin towers in New York in September 2001, known as 9/11, and President George W Bush's prosecution of what he termed a 'War on Terror'. The technologies that amplified this event beyond its spatial reality were 'TV channels, the Web, videotapes and audiotapes, and their producers'.[48] Knorr Cetina notes that these lacked the 'synchronicity, continuity, and temporal immediacy that locked together participants and activities in the global [financial] market' which she also uses as an example of micro-globalisation.[49]

However, since the publication of her analysis, technology has developed to provide this synchronicity, continuity and temporal immediacy. Through live streaming a global audience can virtually participate in the terrorist event, defeating temporal and spatial limitations. For example, the perpetrator of

44 Knorr Cetina (n 10) 66.
45 Knorr Cetina (n 10) 79.
46 Knorr Cetina (n 10) 82.
47 Knorr Cetina (n 10) 79.
48 Knorr Cetina (n 10) 82.
49 Knorr Cetina (n 10) 82.

the New Zealand Christchurch massacre of 2019 used this technology.[50] In the money market the

> technical systems gather up a lifeworld,[51] while simultaneously projecting it . . . project layers of context and horizons that are out of reach in ordinary lifeworlds; they deliver not only transnational situations, but a global world spanning all major time zones.[52]

Terrorism now has the same capacity.

D The Globalisation of a Value

The three theoretical approaches discussed previously provide an analytical framework for globalisation but to understand the challenge of globalisation it is also necessary to examine the philosophical and legal values that are being globalised. It is these philosophies and legal values that underpin the transnational structures that Sassen and Sklair describe and which, through the processes of micro-globalisation, others such as terrorists react against. They are enabled by the technology that supports economic, social and political action unlimited by sovereign borders.

This philosophical basis has been described as neoliberalism, a philosophy developed as a reaction to both welfare state polices and a confidence in market forces.[53] Martin Krygier highlights the drift of neoliberalism from liberalism's traditional strengths. He contrasts liberalism, 'a powerful tradition of political thought with a strenuous political morality which also had an economic component', with neoliberalism, which is focussed on and inspired by the economic, a shrunken, diminished liberalism.[54] Framing globalisation as 'neo-liberal globalisation', Paul O'Connell emphasises the importance of understanding this neoliberal philosophical basis of contemporary globalisation and bemoans the 'failure (of researchers) to interrogate the concept (of globalisation)' and the consequent acceptance of globalisation as an

50 Yasmin Ibrahim, 'Livestreaming the "Wretched of the Earth": The Christchurch Massacre and the "Death-Bound Subject"' (2020) 20(5) *Ethnicities* 803.

51 Defined as 'the sum of immediate experiences, activities, and contacts that make up the world of an individual, or of a corporate, life' in 'Life-world', *Oxford English Dictionary* (online, 4 July 2022).

52 Knorr Cetina (n 10) 71.

53 Martin Krygier, 'Transformations of the Rule of Law: Legal, Liberal and Neo', in Ben Golder and Daniel McLoughlin (eds), *The Politics of Legality in a Neoliberal Age* (Routledge, 2018) 19, 27–31. It should be noted that neoliberalism suffers from similar definitional challenges as globalisation and can be theorised through many disciplines. See Ben Golder and Daniel McLoughlin, 'Introduction', in Ben Golder and Daniel McLoughlin (eds), *The Politics of Legality in a Neoliberal Age* (Routledge, 2018) 1, 1–7.

54 Krygier (n 53).

'apolitical and natural given'.[55] A strand of the critique of neoliberalism and its values most relevant to the examination of Australian migration law centres around the relationship between neoliberalism and the spread of international human rights.

The central question for some is whether neoliberalism is an agent of the spread of human rights or a malign accomplice.[56] What Sassen describes as a concerning and growing worldwide problem for the excluded,[57] others describe as the globalisation of a neoliberal logic that has the positive impact of spreading international human rights as an international value. For example Kellner suggests that, as well as the globalisation of a 'neoliberal global corporate economy', globalisation has meant the promotion of values such as human rights and democracy.[58] This is despite the process of state-level interpretation that, Kellner suggests, renders some human rights commitments meaningless, for example China's ratification of the International Covenant on Civil and Political Rights.[59] However Kellner argues that were states to neglect this global project vulnerable groups could suffer.

By contrast O'Connell argues that the structures and values of the 'global political economy' are causes of human rights violations.[60] He argues, along with Wendy Brown,[61] that promotion of the market by globalised neoliberalism undermines democracy.[62] O'Connell suggests this must be countered by 'domestic legal and global structures' that provide democratic controls and an assurance that the market works to benefit the majority and ensures the protection of human rights.[63]

Samuel Moyn's solution is not an enforcement of international human rights, despite their worthiness. He sees a debate about human rights and neoliberalism as a distraction from the central issue of inequality, an issue which international human rights does not set out to address.[64] He describes international human rights as at most providing a 'minimum floor of human protection' but doing nothing about the threat to the value of equality from

55 Paul O'Connell, 'On Reconciling Irreconcilables: Neo-Liberal Globalisation and Human Rights' (2007) 7 *Human Rights Law Review* 483, 485.
56 Samuel Moyn, 'A Powerless Companion: Human Rights in the Age of Neoliberalism' (2014) 77 *Law and Contemporary Problems* 147, 148.
57 Sassen (n 39).
58 Douglas Kellner, 'Donald Trump, Globalization, and Modernity' (2018) 11 *Fudan Journal of Humanities and Social Sciences* 265, 271.
59 JA Rabkin, *Law without Nations? Why Constitutional Government Requires Sovereign States* (Princeton University Press, 2007) 251.
60 O'Connell (n 55) 488.
61 Wendy Brown, *Undoing the Demos* (n 5) 9–10.
62 O'Connell (n 55) 509.
63 O'Connell (n 55) 509.
64 Moyn (n 56) 151.

neoliberalism.[65] This is not a merely theoretical debate, the World Economic Forum Global Risk Reports from 2019 to 2021 warn of growing inequality within and between nation-states.[66]

The tensions which are apparent in this debate can be seen worked out in the amendments to the *Migration Act 1958* (Cth) of 2000–20. The rise of the multinational company challenges the state's authority over the economy. The philosophy of neoliberalism places governments as free market facilitators, but also as competitors in that market against other nations, as the Australian example of competing in the international student market, discussed in Chapter 5, demonstrates.

III Globalisation as a Challenge to Sovereignty?

This section examines ways that states respond to globalisation and its purported threats to sovereignty in two areas: economic globalisation and the increased movement of people. This examination will draw on philosopher Wendy Brown's theorising of the relationship between globalisation and sovereignty.

Brown argues that globalisation simultaneously produces tensions between 'national interests and the global market', 'global networks and local nationalisms', 'virtual power and physical power' and the 'security of the subject and the movements of capital'.[67] She characterises the building of physical walls across the globe as a response to this tension: a 'hypersovereignty' in response to waning sovereignty.[68] Brown notes that this hypersovereignty exemplified in wall building is not a defence against other sovereign states, the traditional challenger of a state's sovereignty.[69] Instead the walls exclude non-state actors, the unwanted including the 'poor people, workers, or asylum seekers'.[70] Brown defines the sovereignty that is waning as the theoretical Westphalian sovereignty of the indivisible and supreme power, that sits above human-made law, the absolute sovereign of Hobbes, Bodin and Schmitt.[71] While this absolute sovereignty might never have been fully realised in any national state, Brown postulates that this concept of sovereignty remains a 'potent fiction' underpinning the hypersovereignty of wall building.[72] Yet paradoxically this

65 Moyn (n 56) 151.

66 World Economic Forum, *The Global Risks Report 2019* (Report, 15 January 2019) 6, 24; World Economic Forum, *The Global Risks Report 2020* (Report, 15 January 2020) 6; World Economic Forum, *The Global Risks Report 2021* (Report, 19 January 2021) 7.

67 Brown, *Walled States* (n 5) 19–20.

68 Brown, *Walled States* (n 5) 76–9.

69 See the discussion in the previous chapter on the function of sovereignty as a cure for war.

70 Brown, *Walled States* (n 5) 32.

71 Brown, *Walled States* (n 5) 34. Also see the previous chapter's discussion of the theories of sovereignty of Jean Bodin, Thomas Hobbes and Carl Schmitt.

72 Brown, *Walled States* (n 5).

hypersovereignty of wall building is ineffective against the actual challenges of globalisation, which she identifies as neoliberalism. Brown argues that the neoliberal logic of globalisation places the market as sovereign, replacing the political sovereign and substituting the liberal values of 'universal inclusion, equality, liberty and the rule of law' with the values of the market.[73] Brown sees the walls as symbols of the erosion of sovereignty, not its assertion.

A *The Challenge of Economic Globalisation*[74]

Economic globalisation is argued to have brought new economic benefits and vulnerabilities.[75] One argument is that economic globalisation is not a challenge to sovereignty because economic globalisation is the result of states using their sovereign power for their own benefit. Nobel prizewinning economist Joseph Stiglitz, writing in 2017, extolled the benefits of globalisation, crediting it with moving hundreds of millions of people across the globe out of poverty.[76] He counselled China against the 'foolish New Protectionism' that then US president Donald Trump promoted and which Stiglitz presciently predicted would deliver a lower standard of living for Americans and a drop in the value of the US dollar.[77] Stiglitz promoted globalisation to China as a pathway to improved standards of living for China and across the globe.[78] He urged China to continue its pathway to increased engagement through what he describes as a strategy of 'enlightened self-interest'.[79] The logic of this argument is not that nations give up power to economic globalisation but that they act in the interest of accumulating wealth to embrace it.[80] Just as in the discussion of international human rights law in the previous chapter, in Stiglitz' argument, states are agents, not passive victims of economic globalisation.

Kostadinova echoes this argument that states are agents who participate in economic globalisation as enlightened self-interest.[81] In a discussion of the European Union, Kostadinova argues that increased connectedness is a

73 Brown, *Walled States* (n 5) 34.
74 I use the term 'economic globalisation' because the economy is the focus of much of the discourse regarding globalisation. It incorporates other aspects of globalisation such as social, cultural and political and is facilitated by the technology that is described as micro-globalisation of the finance market. See Knorr Cetina's analysis at Knorr Cetina (n 10) 70–9.
75 See the discussion of attempts to measure the impact, not merely the output, of globalisation in Niklas Potrafke, 'The Evidence on Globalisation' (2015) 38(3) *The World Economy* 509; Axel Dreher, Noel Gaston and Pim Martens, *Measuring Globalisation: Gauging Its Consequences* (Springer Science+Business Media, 2007).
76 Stiglitz (n 21) 133.
77 Stiglitz (n 21) 141.
78 Stiglitz (n 21) 146.
79 Stiglitz (n 21) 144.
80 Stiglitz (n 21) 144.
81 Kostadinova (n 22).

pragmatic and responsive way for states to achieve their outcomes.[82] She suggests that the 'surge in complex dependencies' that globalisation brings has frustrated the capacity of states to attain the outcomes they want.[83] This has driven states to heightened levels of cooperation as they strive to achieve their goals.[84] Sovereign states cooperate by giving up some of their sovereign discretion for their own and others' welfare but throughout this cooperation states retain what Alvarez calls 'exit and voice': the capacity to withdraw and the capacity to shape and direct the multistate engagement.[85] Global agreements concerning trade are part of this process. The existential threat of climate change can also be understood as a global challenge exemplifying interdependency and the need for cooperation. Following Stiglitz' logic of self-interest this cooperative behaviour can be understood as an expression of the state's sovereignty which at its core has the same authority as the Westphalian model but is adapted to more complex global realities. Economic globalisation can be understood as states using their sovereign power to act with enlightened self-interest.

However, such an argument flattens out the economic inequality between states and perhaps overemphasises some states' power to act unilaterally. The choice for a state not to participate in economic globalisation might be merely theoretical for all but the most powerful. For those states economic globalisation could be seen as a challenge to sovereignty. Axel Dreher, Noel Gaston and Pim Martens demonstrate the mechanisms that drive this inequality in their economic analysis of globalisation.[86] They found that globalisation changes 'the underlying structure of economies causing a shift of workers and other factors of production across industries and countries'.[87] One aspect of this change is the trend toward privatisation. The World Economic Forum reported that for the last forty years there have been large transfers of capital ownership from public to private control: 'public wealth is now negative or close to zero in rich countries'.[88] The transnational corporations who now wield this economic power are not, as Sklair argues, attached to a national identity or loyalty or – critical to this discussion – controlled by an individual state.[89] It is only through cooperation with other states, in agreeing for example on taxation levels, that states can address these non-state actors.[90]

82 Kostadinova (n 22) 138.
83 Kostadinova (n 22) 138.
84 Kostadinova (n 22) 138.
85 Jose E Alvarez, 'State Sovereignty Is Not Withering Away: A Few Lessons For the Future', in Antonio Cassese (ed), *Realizing Utopia: The Future of International Law* (Oxford University Press, 2012) 26, 37.
86 Dreher et al (n 75).
87 Dreher et al (n 75) 177.
88 World Economic Forum, *The Global Risks Report 2019* (n 66) 10.
89 Sklair (n 3) 100.
90 For example, through mechanisms such as the General Agreement on Tariffs and Trade 1947.

The effect of this restructuring of the world economy is the creation of winners and losers at the level of individuals, groups and states. These losers are the victims of a paradox created by economic globalisation. To compensate the losers would be difficult in practice and would risk global adverse systemic economic market disincentives.[91] Dreher et al. found that the result of these processes is that 'globalisation increases economic growth but also inequality'.[92] In this way the cooperation to achieve a state's goals that Kostadinova describes can increase the vulnerability of already economically weak states. As argued previously, the neoliberal philosophy underpinning contemporary globalisation can mean a less powerful state must trade domestic social[93] and political values[94] for short-term economic gain or even survival.[95]

This is not to suggest that economically powerful states are not vulnerable to the challenge of economic globalisation's impact on their sovereign control of economies, just that they do not suffer its loss so acutely. Condorelli and Cassese argue that the vulnerabilities produced by economic globalisation impact the internal sovereignty of all states.[96] They argue that this vulnerability is a product of connection and interchange in areas from finance to information and culture and means that 'no state can escape dramatic events that occur in other parts of the world'.[97] Such vulnerabilities challenge the capacity of the state to control its territory and to deliver the public goods of territorial and economic security and a secure public and private business environment. The processes of micro-globalisation, enabled by increasingly sophisticated technology, challenge the capacity of government lawmakers and regulators.[98] The Global Financial Crisis of 2008 is an example of such vulnerability: banks, financial institutions and governments are globally intertwined.[99] Just as seen in the COVID-19 pandemic, in a connected world

91 Dreher et al. (n 75).

92 Dreher et al. (n 75).

93 For a discussion of the impact of globalisation on social welfare provision see Sulemana Adams Achanso, 'The Impact of Globalisation on the Provision of Social Welfare' (2014) 32 *Journal of Law, Policy and Globalization* 15.

94 See discussion of the impact of globalisation on democracy in O'Connell (n 55); Brown, *Undoing the Demos* (n 61). See also the conclusions of the 'Workshop on the Impact of Globalisation on the Full Enjoyment of Economic, Social and Cultural Rights and the Right to Development – Agreed Conclusions' (2002) 3 *Asia-Pacific Journal on Human Rights and the Law* 232, 233.

95 For a further discussion of the economically weak state and globalisation see Isaac OC Igwe, 'Recognising the Various Trends of Globalisation: Inequality in International Economic Relations' (2019) 5 *Athens Journal of Law* 1.

96 Condorelli and Cassese (n 1) 23.

97 Condorelli and Cassese (n 1) 23.

98 Knorr Cetina (n 10) 65–82.

99 Sharon Horgan, 'The Impact of Globalisation and the Global Financial Crisis' (2014) 17 *International Trade and Business Law Review* 43, 63.

'an outbreak anywhere is a risk everywhere'.[100] Condorelli and Cassese conclude that in this highly connected world 'not even the superpower is able always to act unilaterally any longer'.[101] They predict 'a slow [but not immediate] dwindling of the immense power of the states' over the decades.[102] Kenichi Ohmae argues that states are almost fatally constrained. It is the nature of globalisation that the more a state seeks to control its economy the more likely it is to lose the benefits of the globalised market.[103]

This is not a certain future. Grew warned against the rhetoric of globalisation that suggests inevitability.[104] World events since 2016 show signs of withdrawal from international engagement. Despite the argued overall economic benefit of globalisation, it could be seen that its challenge to the potent fiction of a state's historical absolute sovereignty, indivisible, above the law and supremely powerful, has not been uniformly responded to by increased cooperation between states.[105] In 2019 Cha suggested that the 'transnational moment, which seemed to open a new time-space beyond the Westphalian paradigm during the past decades, has imploded under its own contradictions'.[106] The 2019 *Global Risks Report* notes 'the world's move into a new phase of strongly state centred politics', a worldwide trend of states 'taking back control'.[107] The 2021 report sees this trend accelerating.[108] Contrary to Condorelli and Cassese's assessment in 2012 that even superpowers cannot act unilaterally because of globalisation's interdependencies, the US, as a Trump-led superpower, and Britain through Brexit, attempted just that.

Two inextricably linked features of globalisation can be seen in these examples as drivers of this attempt by the UK and the US to withdraw. These are firstly the loss of political agency in the globalisation process and secondly the failure to equally share the wealth that globalisation has brought.[109]

Addressing a loss of political agency, Koskenniemi asks, 'What use for sovereignty today?' and gives the answer that 'it stands as an obscure representative of an ideal against disillusionment with global power and expert rule' and an angry reaction to transnational private interests and the dominance of politics by economic and technical discourses underpinned by

100 World Economic Forum, *The Global Risks Report 2021* (n 64) 73.
101 Condorelli and Cassese (n 1) 23.
102 Condorelli and Cassese (n 1) 24.
103 Ohmae (n 7) 11–12.
104 Grew (n 13) 278.
105 Brown, *Walled States* (n 5) 34.
106 Cha (n 20) 60.
107 World Economic Forum, *The Global Risks Report 2019* (n 66) 6.
108 World Economic Forum, *The Global Risks Report 2021* (n 66).
109 See, e.g., Kostadinvova (n 22) and Pencheva and Maronitis who note the systemic inequalities within the state as possible causes of the populist demand or at least acceptance of retreat. Denny Pencheva and Kostas Maronitis, 'Fetishizing Sovereignty in the Remain and Leave Campaigns' (2018) 19(5) *European Politics and Society* 526, 537.

values that those who promote sovereignty had no role in choosing or prioritising.[110] Sovereignty, he says, gives people the opportunity for agency: to be 'the master of one's own life'.[111] Dyzenhaus too notes states' anxiety about the increasing loss of power as international and transnational bodies make decisions that impact on them.[112] Brown however argues that the challenge derives from the neoliberal philosophy that underpins globalisation. She sees the Western liberal democracies 'hollowed out from within' because they have taken on the globalised neoliberal values with the result that the concept of democracy, which she defines as 'political self-rule by the people', is diminished.[113]

Addressing inequality, the economic analysis of globalisation, outlined previously, concludes that globalisation increases both growth and inequality.[114] The benefits of economic globalisation come at an unequally borne economic cost and this inequality is not exclusively between states.[115] By 2019 globalisation had brought a diminishing of global inequality but within countries inequality continues to rise.[116] The impact of COVID-19 worsened this. The pandemic's 'livelihood crisis' caused inequality between both groups and countries.[117]

The events of 2016 to 2020 in the UK and the US are illustrative of these two impacts of globalisation: a concern with a loss of political agency and economic inequality within the state. In the UK the decision by voters in a referendum to withdraw from the European Union suggests firstly that the people believed their political agency was diminished. The European Union might once have been thought to 'satisfy democratic demands in the nations subject to its superintending control' by providing 'indirect forms of accountability' and a 'sufficiently democratic atmosphere'.[118] However, Brexit suggests that the British people were not satisfied. Kostadinova argues that what Britain lost in the heightened cooperation of the European Union

110 Martti Koskenniemi, 'What Use for Sovereignty Today?' (2011) 1 *Asian Journal of International Law* 61, 61.
111 Martti Koskenniemi, 'What Use for Sovereignty Today?' (2011) 1 *Asian Journal of International Law* 70.
112 David Dyzenhaus, 'Constitutionalism in an Old Key: Legality and Constituent Power' (2012) 1(2) *Cambridge University Press* 229, 231–2.
113 Brown, *Undoing the Demos* (n 61) 20. See similar arguments in Kostadinova (n 22) 135; Margaret S Archer, 'Social Integration, System Integration, and Global Governance', in Ino Rossi (ed), *Frontiers of Globalisation Research: Theoretical and Methodological Approaches* (Springer Science and Business Media, 2007) 221.
114 Dreher et al. (n 75).
115 World Economic Forum, *The Global Risks Report 2019* (n 66) 2, 16; Dreher et al. (n 75); Achanso (n 93).
116 World Economic Forum, *The Global Risks Report 2019* (n 66) 2, 16.
117 World Economic Forum, *The Global Risks Report 2021* (n 66) 7.
118 Rabkin (n 59) 255.

is the form of accountability that governments in Western democracies are held to. Accurately or not, the Brexiteers blamed the European Union supranational governance for their dissatisfaction.[119] Secondly, as Kostadinova's research also identified, inequality was a driver of the vote to leave the European Union. She demonstrates the link between the British vote to leave the European Union and inequality among the British population. She found that those who voted for Britain to leave the European Union were socially and economically less well off. In addition, those regions of Britain most impacted by Chinese imports were also more likely to vote to leave.[120] Kostadinova also shows evidence for a popular belief among the leave voters that British decision-makers would protect British interests.[121] The extent to which Britain will gain or lose from Brexit might be hard to measure, as entangled as it will be with the impact of the COVID-19 pandemic and other world events.[122]

Similar issues were leveraged for political advantage in the US. Donald Trump blamed an ill-defined global elite for the loss of jobs and economic hardship of some Americans. Trump harnessed the term globalisation to 'denote an economy run by global elites that had given workers a rotten deal'.[123] Kellner notes the irony of global capitalist Trump winning the presidency on such a platform only to implement policies that benefited these corporations including his own personal international interests.[124] Trump's speech at a midterm campaign rally demonstrated the electoral strategy of asserting sovereignty by blaming others. Following one of his threats to withdraw from NATO if other nations did not meet their funding commitments, he said: 'Now they respect us. They respect our country again. They didn't respect our country. They didn't respect our country'.[125]

Can it be concluded from these examples that economic globalisation challenged the state sovereignty of the UK and US? In 2016 in both these states, globalisation was named and blamed in political rhetoric as a threat to sovereignty.[126] It is undeniable that global economic trends impacted on the jobs and livelihoods of their citizens. It can be argued that the governments'

119 Kostadinova (n 22) 136.
120 Kostadinova (n 22) 136.
121 Kostadinova (n 22) 136.
122 See for example Michaela Benson, Nando Sigona and Elena Zambelli, 'The UK's "Safe and Legal" Humanitarian Routes: From Colonial Ties to Privatising Protection' (April/June 2024) 95(2) *The Political Quarterly* 263.
123 Kellner (n 58) 221.
124 Kellner (n 58) 281–2.
125 Donald Trump, 'Trump Confirms He Threatened to Withdraw from NATO', *Atlantic Council* (Blog Post, 21 August 2018) <www.atlanticcouncil.org/blogs/natosource/trump-confirms-he-threatened-to-withdraw-from-nato>.
126 In their detailed analysis of the Brexit campaign rhetoric, Pencheva and Maronitis (n 109) argue that sovereignty was re-imagined and promoted as a personal possession of each UK citizen and that it was threatened by the outsider.

failure to protect the livelihoods of some of their citizens is an example of Brown's argument that liberal democracy is 'hollowed out from within' by the neoliberal logic of globalisation.[127] It is less clear that this is a challenge to the sovereignty of these wealthy and powerful states for two reasons. Firstly, both the US and the UK have played major historical roles in creating and benefiting from the globalised economy.[128] It is their sovereign actions of the past that they now confront. Secondly as sovereign states they remain architects of their own global engagement and the social distribution of wealth within the state. The UK made the decision to deepen its engagement with Europe and successive governments did not judge it in the interest of their sovereign state to withdraw, despite concerns about rising inequality. It also made the decision concerning its distribution of the benefits of globalisation. In the post-Cold War period the US emerged as a lone global economic and political superpower. The US fostered the economic, political and ideological globalisation from which President Trump purported to withdraw and which has delivered the wealth that the US has failed to share equitably among its population.

The impact of this trend toward a less cooperative global engagement, of which the UK and the US are examples, will be assessed by future analysts. The World Economic Forum warns of dire consequences of any withdrawal from globalisation.[129] The 2019 *Global Risks Report* warned that the effort states put into 'taking back control' is at the cost of developing the cooperation necessary to deal with future global crises.[130] This prediction was manifested in the COVID-19 pandemic. The World Health Organization lacked the authority to investigate and sanction.[131] Member states of the G7 were constrained by political considerations.[132] Individual states competed for medical equipment and supplies, hampering efforts to build the necessary global coordinated response.[133] One key finding was the unequal impact of the pandemic on the poor: inequality, already a concern, was exacerbated.[134] The report in 2021 notes that the livelihoods of 'youth, unskilled workers, working parents – especially mothers – and already-disadvantaged minorities have been especially hard hit'.[135] A similar analysis was made of the climate crisis. Environment-related risks have accounted for three of the five likely risks and four of the most impactful in the *Global Risks Report 2019*.[136]

127 Brown, *Undoing the Demos* (n 61) 20.
128 See, e.g., Cha's discussion of Britain in Cha (n 20) and Stiglitz on the US in Stiglitz (n 21).
129 World Economic Forum, *The Global Risks Report 2019* (n 66) 9.
130 World Economic Forum, *The Global Risks Report 2019* (n 66).
131 World Economic Forum, *The Global Risks Report 2021* (n 66) 73.
132 World Economic Forum, *The Global Risks Report 2019* (n 66) 73.
133 World Economic Forum, *The Global Risks Report 2019* (n 66) 73–5.
134 World Economic Forum, *The Global Risks Report 2019* (n 66) 17.
135 World Economic Forum, *The Global Risks Report 2019* (n 66) 17.
136 World Economic Forum, *The Global Risks Report 2019* (n 66) 15.

In 2021 climate action failure is rated the most impactful and second most likely long-term risk.[137] It seems that, despite the efforts of leaders such as Trump to withdraw, such action might risk catastrophic disease and environmental destruction.[138]

While this account of risks is compelling it must be noted that this analysis of the consequences of the withdrawal from global engagement is the perception sponsored by the World Economic Forum, which is a nonprofit organisation of '1,000 leading companies' whose mission is to 'shape a better world'.[139] These companies fit into Sklair's category of the transnational global company and the global class.[140] They are the businesses benefiting from the freeing up of global markets. A nonprofit using its combined economic power to shape a better world may seem benign. What is not considered in this analysis is what is lost in global engagement and who is defining the goal of the better world. Such is Koskenniemi's concern that a judgment made by a global elite about what a better world would be has no input from any but the elite in that world.[141] The local is disenfranchised.

However, if taking back control means that states neglect the indisputable global risks of climate change and pandemics, the reassertion of a form of state sovereignty that more closely matches a Westphalian model could be a pyrrhic victory. In this predicament there is an opportunity for states to express sovereignty in a more sophisticated and complex way that might better meet the global challenges and reassert values that are more than the shrunken version of liberalism that diminishes the individual and local community and values only the economic.[142]

B *Globalisation and International Migration*[143]

To examine whether the 21st-century movement of people is a phenomenon of globalisation and a threat to sovereignty, this section will firstly provide background and context to this international migration before considering how it could be characterised as a threat to sovereignty.

137 World Economic Forum, *The Global Risks Report 2021* (n 66) 9.

138 Condorelli and Cassese (n 1) 23.

139 World Economic Forum, 'Our Partners' (Web Page, 2022) <www.weforum.org/about/our-members-and-partners>.

140 Sklair (n 3) 100.

141 Koskenniemi (n 110) 69.

142 Krygier (n 53); Brown, *Undoing the Demos*(n 61) 17–45. See also O'Connell (n 55) 509; Moyn (n 56) 151.

143 Consistent with United Nations definitions, an international migrant is defined as a long-term international migrant if they change their usual residence for at least one year and short-term if the change is between three months and one year. United Nations Department of Economic and Social Affairs Population Division Migration Section, *Toolkit on International Migration* (Toolkit, June 2012) <www.un.org/en/development/desa/population/migration/publications/others/docs/toolkit_DESA_June% 202012.pdf>.

Whether or not the current movement of people across the globe is unprecedented compared to the past or is just an accelerating wave is yet to be finally assessed both in number and impact.[144] What is known is that the wave is growing. Over the two decades from 2000, the number of international migrants has increased by 108 million to 281 million people.[145] Of these, 12% are recognised as refugees and 34 million are displaced persons, a doubling from 2000.[146] The COVID-19 pandemic and the disruption to international travel was predicted to marginally reduce the growth of this wave by 2 million.[147]

What is also known is that some of the phenomena of globalisation are drivers of this migration. In a complex interaction the globalised labour market[148] combines with increasing inequality, globalised media and social networks, that inform people about opportunities, and improved and more accessible transport, to drive people to migrate to achieve better economic outcomes.[149] What is argued is that the doubling of displaced people and the increase in refugees is driven by the failure of states and the international community to address the drivers of these trends: the effects of greed, climate change, poverty, violence, war, human rights abuses, persecution, a failure of state governance or a combination of these factors.[150] In this way the increase in international migration can be seen as a phenomenon, or a result, of globalisation.

In 1999 David Held, Anthony McGrew, David Goldblatt and Jonathan Perraton concluded that one feature of the current migration was the imperfect ability of states to keep out 'illegal migrants'.[151] An important driver of this issue and an attempt at a global response was addressed in the 2016 UN New York Declaration for Refugees and Migrants.[152] The declaration aimed to solve the 'growing global phenomenon of large movements of refugees

144 David Held et al., *Global Transformations: Politics, Economics and Culture* (Polity Press, 1999) 312. See also detailed discussion at 281–326. Note as well the claim to unprecedented movement of people in *New York Declaration for Refugees and Migrants*, UN Doc A/RES/71/1 (3 October 2016).

145 United Nations Department of Economic and Social Affairs, Population Division, *International Migration 2020 Highlights*, ST/ESA/SER.A/452 (January 2020) 1.

146 United Nations Department of Economic and Social Affairs, Population Division, *International Migration 2020 Highlights*, ST/ESA/SER.A/452 (January 2020) 1.

147 United Nations Department of Economic and Social Affairs, Population Division, *International Migration 2020 Highlights*, ST/ESA/SER.A/452 (January 2020) 1.

148 United Nations Department of Economic and Social Affairs, Population Division, *International Migration 2020 Highlights*, ST/ESA/SER.A/452 (January 2020) 303.

149 Hugo (n 11) 109. See also Archer (n 113) 239–2.

150 Hugo (n 11).

151 Held et al. (n 143) 321.

152 *New York Declaration for Refugees and Migrants*, UN Doc A/RES/71/1 (3 October 2016).

and migrants' in 'unprecedented' numbers.[153] By 2018 two Global Compacts were developed. These were the Global Compact on Refugees (GPR) and the Global Compact for Safe, Orderly and Regular Migration (GCM). Jane McAdam believed they signal 'new moral and political undertakings by the world's governments . . . at least on paper'.[154] The GPR affirmed the already agreed upon refugee regime. The GCM was an unprecedented attempt to agree on state cooperation on migration within the framework of existing human rights law and other principles of international law.[155] Neither compact is legally binding.[156] Despite this, both the US and Australia declined to endorse the GCM on the grounds that it would compromise their sovereignty.[157]

How then is this issue a challenge to state sovereignty? Dauvergne theorises that as globalisation compromises sovereign state control of other areas of policy, such as the economic challenges described in the previous section on economic globalisation, migration appears as a site where sovereign control can be demonstrated.[158] Dauvergne characterises migration law as the 'new last bastion of sovereignty' in a globalising world.[159] Dauvergne's analysis is helpful in explaining this response in the context of globalisation. It complements Brown's analysis of wall building as a signifier of waning sovereign power. Brown noted that one of the paradoxes of sovereignty is that it can only exist in relation to another.[160] Sovereignty can only stand for independence and control if there is another from whom to be independent. Brown observes that in a globalising world the relational other of sovereignty is no longer the other state. The wall building indicates that the relational other is the unwanted migrant. Dauvergne theorises that migration law is positioned in a similar way. Applying Dauvergne's theory, it is the migrant and migration law that is the site where sovereignty is expressed. Dauvergne argues that migration law creates a category of people who are labelled

153 *New York Declaration for Refugees and Migrants*, UN Doc A/RES/71/1 (3 October 2016).
154 Jane McAdam, 'The Global Compacts on Refugees and Migration: A New Era for International Protection?' (2018) 30(4) *International Journal of Refugee Law* 571, 571.
155 Jane McAdam, 'The Global Compacts on Refugees and Migration: A New Era for International Protection?' (2018) 30(4) *International Journal of Refugee Law* 573.
156 United Nations, 'World Leaders Adopt First-Ever Global Compact on Migration, Outlining Framework to Protect Millions of Migrants, Support Countries Accommodating Them' (Meetings Coverage, DEV/3375, 10 December 2018).
157 United States Mission to the United Nations, 'National Statement of the United States of America on the Adoption of the Global Compact for Safe, Orderly, and Regular Migration' (Media Release, 7 December 2018). Amy Remeikis and Ben Doherty, 'Dutton Says Australia Won't "Surrender our Sovereignty" by Signing UN Migration Deal', *The Guardian* (online, 25 July 2018) <www.theguardian.com/australia-news/2018/jul/25/dutton-says-australia-wont-surrender-our-sovereignty-by-signing-un-migration-deal>.
158 Dauvergne, *Making People Illegal* (n 4).
159 Dauvergne, 'Sovereignty, Migration' (n 5); Dauvergne, *Making People Illegal* (n 4) 169.
160 Brown, *Walled States* (n 5) 65.

illegal so that even when they have breached the territorial border the state maintains its control of their membership and their identity.[161] For Brown and Dauvergne these acts of exclusion, walls and migration laws to exclude the unwanted migrant are signifiers of the state's loss of the Westphalian sovereign control they once held or imagined.

IV Conclusion

Cassese describes globalisation as 'testing the limits of a state-centric world society'[162] and creating interdependency and vulnerability that constrain unilateral action.[163] This chapter has acknowledged the complexity of globalisation and explored globalisation as a historical, transnational and micro-globalisation set of phenomena and has applied these approaches to recent historical developments in the UK and the USA. The chapter has identified neoliberalism as the underpinning philosophy of the current period of globalisation. The chapter notes that neoliberal globalisation promotes economic competition and success and positions the state as the market facilitator rather than the absolute authority at a more granular level. The chapter also notes that this globalised philosophy has been argued to result in increasing inequality. The chapter has demonstrated the explanatory power of these approaches for globalisation and the events of the 21st century. The chapter tested in what way these phenomena of globalisation threaten sovereignty in the area of economic globalisation and the increased movement of people.

Firstly focussing on economic globalisation, broadly defined, it was found that globalisation has a positive economic impact globally but the failure to equally share the gains has increased inequality. This is a driver, together with the perception of a loss of political agency, of a trend of withdrawal from international cooperation and engagement. It was noted that, while some aspects of globalisation challenge the concept of sovereign control of territory, the sovereign decisions of powerful states, such as the UK and the USA, have contributed to the globalisation from which they have benefited in the past and from which they at times this decade have sought to withdraw. However, less economically powerful states do not have the same agency. The chapter notes the tension between a move by states to take back control,

161 Dauvergne, *Making People Illegal* (n 4) 169. See also Alastair Davidson's discussion of the failure of Australia to take a global approach to its liberal democratic identity, instead making immigration decisions based on narrow national interest in Alastair Davidson, 'The Politics of Exclusion in an Era of Globalisation', in Laksiri Jayasuriya, David Walker and Jan Gothard (eds), *Legacies of White Australia: Race, Culture and Nation* (University of Western Australia Press, 2003) 129, 133–4.

162 Antonio Cassese, 'Gathering Up the Main Threads', in Antonio Cassese (ed), *Realizing Utopia: The Future of International Law* (Oxford University Press, 2012) 653.

163 Condorelli and Cassese (n 1) 23.

a complex global economy and the global importance of strong international systems of collaboration to address global changes such as climate change and the risks of pandemics. On one hand a return to an historic Westphalian definition of sovereignty might be a pyrrhic victory for individual states and for the globe. The pandemic which began in 2019 and the continuing climate crisis provide examples of global interdependence. However, on the other hand such a withdrawal could be understood as reasserting national values and for the West a reassertion of liberal values.

Secondly the chapter defined how the globalised movement of people can be understood as a globalisation phenomenon linked to economic globalisation and to the inequities and opportunities it creates. The chapter examined how the theories of Brown and Dauvergne explain the link between globalisation, sovereignty and migration. They theorise that the exclusion of the unwanted migrant through, for Brown, wall building and, for Dauvergne, migration lawmaking is states' response to a loss of a Westphalian version of internal sovereignty in other areas of policy.

How Australian lawmakers from 2000 to 2020 have responded to these concerns at the nexus of globalisation, sovereignty and migration law in Australia is taken up in later chapters. The next chapter sets out a historical benchmark against which to assess the influence of globalisation and the nature of sovereignty in later chapters.

Chapter 4

Migration Law and Sovereignty in Australia

1901, 1958, 1978

I Introduction

As discussed in the previous chapter, Wendy Brown and Catherine Dauvergne argue that the focus of the expression of the state's sovereignty on exclusion signals a loss of control over other areas of state authority and that this loss is the result of the pressures of globalisation.[1] Brown's neat juxtaposition of 'hypersovereignty' and 'waning sovereignty', the one a compensation for the other, encapsulates this argument.[2] Both Brown and Dauvergne theorise that the exclusion of the unwanted migrant paradoxically signifies the waning of state sovereignty that is accelerating a shift from the absolute control of a territory and its people that, at least theoretically, defined Westphalian sovereignty.[3]

Referencing the historical approaches of Grew and Cha, discussed in the previous chapter,[4] the purpose of this chapter is to provide a historical benchmark against which to answer, in later chapters, to what extent the Australian migration law of the 21st century can be seen as Australia expressing hypersovereignty as a response to new challenges of globalisation. To establish this historical benchmark the chapter examines the legislative processes, issues, objectives and techniques as expressed through the debates and legislation, used to achieve and then continue the White Australia policy and one instance of policy making that replaced it. The first two instances

1 See Chapter 3.

2 Wendy Brown, *Walled States, Waning Sovereignty* (Zone Books, 2010) 67, 107.

3 Wendy Brown, *Walled States, Waning Sovereignty* (Zone Books, 2010) 67, 107; Catherine Dauvergne, 'Sovereignty, Migration and the Rule of Law in Global Times' (2004) 67(4) *Modern Law Review* 588. For a discussion of Westphalian sovereignty see Chapter 3 Section III.

4 Raymond Grew, 'Finding Frontiers in Historical Research on Globalization', in Ino Rossi (ed), *Frontiers of Globalisation Research: Theoretical and Methodological Approaches* (Springer Science and Business Media, 2007) 271, 271–2, 278; Taesuh Cha, 'Is Anybody Still a Globalist? Rereading the Trajectory of US Grand Strategy and the End of the Transnational Moment' (2019) 17(1) *Globalizations* 60, 71. See discussion of this historical approach in Chapter 3 Section II A.

DOI: 10.4324/9781003515852-5

are examined from a period when the White Australia policy was still official government policy.[5] The first instance is the debate which led to the passing of the *Immigration Restriction Act 1901* (Cth) and the *Pacific Island Labourers Act 1901* (Cth). The second instance is the passing of the *Migration Act 1958* (Cth). The third instance is a policy statement made in 1978 that replaced racial discrimination as a rationale for immigration restriction.

The chapter argues that these instances of lawmaking give some support to a view that Brown's hypersovereignty might not be a new phenomenon for Australia as it responds to the interdependencies and vulnerabilities of globalisation. Rather, from federation in 1901, migration legislation to exclude has been a significant site for expressing both sovereign power and its vulnerability.

II Immigration Restriction Act 1901 and Pacific Island Labourers Act 1901

This section examines Australia's response to the vulnerabilities and interdependencies in 1901 when Australia was a newly formed federation of colonies of the British Empire at a time when Britain still had the global hegemony later enjoyed by the USA and now challenged by China.[6] This examination of the migration legislative processes of 1901 demonstrates both the high priority that the first Parliament placed on migration control and the legislative techniques that were adopted in response to the external vulnerabilities and interdependencies of the new Federation.[7]

A *Key Issues in the First Parliament*

The priority given to migration control was evident from the earliest debates following the Australian governor-general's first speech in May 1901.[8] The

5 See Gwenda Tavan, who notes especially the political efficacy of reviving the racism that is latent in the Australian community up to 2001: Gwenda Tavan, *The Long, Slow Death of White Australia* (Scribe Publications, 2005) especially ch 11. George Williams notes that discredited 19th-century concepts of race remain 'embedded in Australia's constitutional DNA': George Williams, 'Removing Racism from Australia's Constitutional DNA' (2012) 37(3) *Alternative Law Journal* 151. See also Stefano Gulmanelli, 'John Howard and the "Anglospherist" Reshaping of Australia' (2014) 49(4) *Australian Journal of Political Science* 581.

6 Joseph E Stiglitz, 'Rethinking Globalization in the Trump Era: US-China Relations' (2018) 13(2) *Frontiers of Economics in China* 133.

7 See discussion of Australia's slowly evolving internal sovereignty in Chapter 2 Section IV.

8 Commonwealth, *Parliamentary Debates*, Senate, 10 May 1901 (His Excellency Governor) 28. Note this was an occasion when the members of the House of Representatives were invited to enter the senate chamber. The first governor-general was the Right Honourable John Adrian Louis Hope, 7th Earl of Hopetoun www.gg.gov.au/about-governor-general/former-governors-general.

parliamentarians were concerned with two related issues, one practical and one ideological. The first concern was whether Australia would adopt a free trade policy.[9] The second was how Australia would adopt a racially discriminatory migration policy.[10] The Parliament felt little need to debate the merits of this migration policy. Before Federation the colonies had already separately adopted racially discriminatory legislation and had agreed that this was a priority for Federation.[11]

The two issues of trade and migration policy were closely connected and debated. The debate on trade issues discussed the economic vulnerability and dependency of the new nation. Alexander Paterson, Member for Capricornia, Queensland, noted:

> that the United States have become an enormously rich country, and that their people are able to invest money in other countries. Americans own an immense amount of property in England and have sunk a great deal of money in commercial ventures there; and to-day the finest commercial buildings in Sydney and Melbourne are buildings which have been put up with American money.[12]

There was a recognition of world markets and the vulnerabilities that trade can bring. Sir Langdon Bonython, Member for Barker, South Australia, argued that there was logic in being a proponent of free trade when, and only when, a nation is the 'master of the markets of the world'.[13] In tension with the desire for economic prosperity through trade was the aspect of trade policy that concerned labour. Members of that first Parliament debated the balance that should be struck between economic outcomes and achieving an immigration policy that excluded people on the basis of colour, what the parliamentarians called a 'white Australia'.[14]

An argument put against wholesale restriction of non-white migrants was the economic advantage that would be given to other nations if Australia

9 See for example the first speech in reply to the governor-general made by Senator Norman Kirkwood Ewing, senator for Western Australia 1901–1903: Commonwealth, *Parliamentary Debates*, Senate, 21 May 1901 (Norman Ewing) 69–7.

10 See for example the first speech in reply to the governor-general made by Senator Norman Kirkwood Ewing, senator for Western Australia 1901–1903: Commonwealth, *Parliamentary Debates*, Senate, 21 May 1901 (Norman Ewing) 69–7.

11 Myra Willard, *History of the White Australia Policy to 1920* (Melbourne University Press, 1923) 17–119.

12 Commonwealth, *Parliamentary Debates*, House of Representatives, 5 June 1901, 696 (Alexander Paterson).

13 Commonwealth, *Parliamentary Debates*, House of Representatives, 5 June 1901, 691 (Langdon Bonython).

14 Commonwealth, *Parliamentary Debates*, House of Representatives, 5 June 1901, 691 (Langdon Bonython) 688.

did not take advantage of cheap Pacific Islander and Asian labour, but at the same time adopted a free trade policy:[15]

> I am in favour of a white Australia, and no one could advocate that more strongly than I but I would like to ask gentlemen who have been talking so much about free-trade in the past, what free-trade means. Does it not mean free trade in goods, and, if so, would it not mean free-trade in labour. Would they restrict kanakas from entering the country, and not allow Asiatics to come in, while at the same time they would allow the free importation of goods made by those races elsewhere? Free-traders would stop our manufacturers from using this cheap labour, but, at the same time, they do not wish to stop the produce of that cheap labour from entering the country.[16]

The counterargument was concerned with competition for employment. For example, James Manifold, Member for Corangamite, Victoria argued that Pacific Islander labour took employment from 'our own', presumably white people.[17] He noted that white labourers could perform the work but might be reluctant to do these jobs.[18] Despite this debate on the details of a free trade policy and the possibility of an economic detriment if a free trade policy was combined with a prohibition on non-white labour, Alexander Paterson, Member for Capricornia, Queensland, articulated the majority view:

> Even if it could be proved that we cannot carry on the industry without a certain loss of cultivation, I say it is still better, a thousand times, to

15 Note the term kanaka is avoided in this book except when quoted. In 21st-century Australia it is understood as an offensive term for South Sea Islanders. Imelda Miller, 'Sugar Slaves', *Queensland Historical Atlas* (Web Page, 22 October 2010) <www.qhatlas.com.au/content/sugar-slaves>.

16 Commonwealth, *Parliamentary Debates*, House of Representatives, 5 June 1901, 692 (James Manifold). Note the term Asiatic is now considered an offensive term for Asian as it is associated with the polices of colonialism. 'Asiatic', *Merriam Webster Dictionary* (online, 1 September 2022) <www.merriam-webster.com/dictionary/Asiatic>. Note also that in this chapter I use the concept and terminology of race reluctantly, but for convenience. Modern discourse disputes the biological basis of the idea of distinct races, with many arguing that race is merely a social construction; see Robin O Andreasen, 'Race: Biological Reality or Social Construct?' (2000) 67(S3) *Philosophy of Science* 653. In spite of this, the concept of race remains part of Australian law. It is in the *Constitution* and in legislation such as the *Racial Discrimination Act 1975* (Cth).

17 Commonwealth, *Parliamentary Debates*, House of Representatives, 5 June 1901, 693 (James Manifold). See also Commonwealth, *Parliamentary Debates*, House of Representatives, 5 June 1901, 698 (Alexander Patterson).

18 Commonwealth, *Parliamentary Debates*, House of Representatives, 5 June 1901, 703 (James Manifold).

> dispense with black labour, and to convert these dark plantations into smiling fields cultivated by free and white labour.[19]

The importance of a white Australia was declared and contributions to the debate reinforced the commitment to this goal. Bonython noted with approval that the governor-general's speech at the opening of the first session included mention of 'Bills for the firm restriction of the immigration of Asiatics, and for the diminution and gradual abolition of the introduction of labour from the South Sea Islands'.[20] Bonython said: 'I take that statement to be a declaration in favour of a white Australia, and a white Australia will have my hearty support'.[21] He demonstrated this support by noting that South Australia had refused a financially beneficial offer for the Northern Territory that would have allowed 'alien races . . . [to enter and that would] be injurious to the whole of Australia'.[22] The superiority and vulnerability of white people was encapsulated by Thomas Kennedy, member for Moira, Queensland. He argued that education could not close the gap of inferiority of others to white people while at the same time, despite their proposed superiority, he characterised white people as vulnerable to degradation:

> There is no challenging the fact that wherever we have Asiatics in numbers amidst a white people, diffuse whatever educational influences we may amongst them, we can never educate them up to the level of the white. Do what we will, the Asiatics will always demoralize and degrade a certain portion of our own population, and when we cannot force people resident amongst us up to our own standard of living, I say that we should rigorously exclude them.[23]

19 Commonwealth, *Parliamentary Debates*, House of Representatives, 5 June 1901, 695 (Alexander Patterson). For a brief overview of the politics of this era see Marija Taflaga, 'A Short Political History of Australia', in Peter J Chen et al (eds), *Australian Politics and Policy* (Sydney University Press, 2019) 18, 20–4.

20 Commonwealth, *Parliamentary Debates*, House of Representatives, 5 June 1901, 688 (Langdon Bonython).

21 Commonwealth, *Parliamentary Debates*, House of Representatives, 5 June 1901, 688 (Langdon Bonython).

22 Commonwealth, *Parliamentary Debates*, House of Representatives, 5 June 1901, 688 (Langdon Bonython) 689.

23 Commonwealth, *Parliamentary Debates*, House of Representatives, 5 June 1901, 703 (Thomas Kennedy). See Alanna Kamp's textual analysis of the debates which provides numerical evidence on which she bases a conclusion that Whiteness was integral to definitions of belonging and exclusion in the parliamentary debates on the *Immigration Restriction Act 1901* in Alanna Kamp, 'Formative Geographies of Belonging in White Australia: Constructing the National Self and Other in Parliamentary Debate, 1901' (2010) 48(4) *Geographical Research* 411, 413, 424. For a history of the White Australia policy see Tavan (n 5); HI London, *Non-White Immigration and the 'White Australia' Policy* (Sydney University Press, 1970).

B Acts To Create a White Australia

In December 1901, the governor-general gave royal assent to two bills to enact a white Australia, the *Immigration Restriction Act 1901* and the *Pacific Island Labourers Act 1901*. The passing of these two acts by the first Parliament translated into positive law the high priority placed on controlling the composition of the citizenship of the new nation.[24]

The exclusion of non-Europeans was the central concern of the *Immigration Restriction Act 1901*: a person was deemed a prohibited immigrant and not allowed to enter Australia if they failed a dictation test in a European language of the administering official's choice.[25] The *Immigration Restriction Act 1901* also included other grounds of exclusion. Immigration into the Commonwealth was prohibited for 'any person who has within three years been convicted of an offence, not being a mere political offence, and has been sentenced to imprisonment for one year or longer therefor, and has not received a pardon'.[26]

Combining the concerns of the character test and the capacity to discriminate on the basis of race, the act also provided for grounds for deportation of immigrants already in Australia. Excluded from the pool of immigrants who could be subject to the test were a 'British subject either natural-born or naturalized under a law of the United Kingdom or of the Commonwealth or of a State'.[27] Other immigrants were subject to this test:

> [A person] who is convicted of any crime of violence against the person, shall be liable, upon the expiration of any term of imprisonment imposed on him therefor, to be required to write out at dictation and sign in the presence of an officer a passage of fifty words in length in an European language directed by the officer, and if he fails to do so shall be deemed to be a prohibited immigrant and shall be deported from the Commonwealth pursuant to any order of the Minister.[28]

The priority of race over criminal history is clear. Through this provision the impact of committing a violent crime on the immigration status of the perpetrator was negated if the perpetrator was literate in the European language of the test. The criteria for the choice of European language were not specified. This was left to the discretion of the 'officer' administering the test who was under the direction of the immigration minister.[29] This provision gave

24 See generally Willard (n 11).
25 *Immigration Restriction Act 1901* s 3(a).
26 *Immigration Restriction Act 1901* s 3(e).
27 *Immigration Restriction Act 1901* s 8.
28 *Immigration Restriction Act 1901* s 8.
29 *Immigration Restriction Act 1901* s 8.

the officers the capacity to manipulate the education test to achieve a desired outcome, namely to exclude anyone the officer wished, or was directed, to exclude.[30] The Parliament was charged with monitoring the implementation of the education test and it required the immigration minister to report annually to Parliament.[31] Information about the criminal history of those allowed to remain residents was not reported. The immigration minister was required only to report on the numbers and national origin of prohibited immigrants and of those passing and failing the education test.[32] This demonstrated that race and the broad discretion to deport were more important criteria in the legislation than a criminal conviction. The objective of the other piece of legislation, the *Pacific Island Labourers Act 1901*, was to ban Pacific Islander labourers from Australia after 1906.[33] This act legislated a staggered exit from 1901 and banned new licences to employ Pacific Islanders from 1904.[34] Under the act any Pacific Islander or anyone who appeared to a public servant to be a Pacific Islander, and could not show that they were currently employed, was liable to arrest and deportation.[35] The act also stated that anyone 'alleged to be a Pacific Island labourer shall be deemed to be a Pacific Island labourer until the contrary is shown'.[36] This reversal of the onus of proof of those targeted for deportation allowed for discrimination by appearance including skin colour and ignored long-term residence or birth in an Australian state or other ethnicity. This demonstrates how the high value placed on whiteness and the low tolerance for any possibility that a non-white person could avoid deportation was built into the positive law.

The lack of opposition to the priority of exclusion on racial grounds meant that the main issue in the debate on banning Pacific Islanders was economic, echoing the concerns expressed in response to the governor-general's speech. Objections to the bill concerned the impact on the Queensland sugar industry such as that from Richard Edwards, Member for Oxley, Queensland.[37] Even those who warned of 'disaster to many thousands of our [white

30 *Immigration Restriction Act 1901* ss 3(a), 3(e), 8.

31 *Immigration Restriction Act 1901* s 17.

32 *Pacific Island Labourers Act 1901*: 'An Act to provide for the Regulation, Restriction, and Prohibition of the Introduction of Labourers from the Pacific Islands and for other purposes'.

33 For a history of Queensland's indentured Pacific Islander labour scheme see Tracey Banivanua-Mar, *Violence and Colonial Dialogue: The Australian-Pacific Indentured Labor Trade* (University of Hawai'i Press, 2007) especially ch 4 which highlights the agency of the labourers in contrast to the racialised myths of their indocility and ch 5 which describes the treatment of indentured labourers as resembling a legally sanctioned system of slavery, with high levels of violence, morbidity and mortality.

34 *Pacific Island Labourers Act 1901* s 7; ss 3–6.

35 *Pacific Island Labourers Act 1901* s 8(1).

36 *Pacific Island Labourers Act 1901* s 10.

37 Commonwealth, *Parliamentary Debates*, House of Representatives, 30 May 1901, 533 (Richard Edwards).

Australian] people' if the act was passed and the impact on the sugar business came about pledged themselves as supporters of a racially discriminatory migration policy.[38]

C *Interdependency, Vulnerability and Sovereign Power: 'That Right Exists'*[39]

The parliamentary debate leading up to the passing of the *Immigration Restriction Act 1901* and the *Pacific Island Labourers Act 1901* demonstrates that creating a white Australia was viewed as critical to the new nation.[40] The problem the Parliament faced was firstly whether the parliament had the right to discriminate on the basis of colour and secondly how to deliver on this policy priority in the context of the new Federation's economic, defence and diplomatic dependencies and vulnerabilities.

In the debate on the *Immigration Restriction Act 1901* the issues were not whether to discriminate based on race but how to do it without creating a problem for the new nation. Firstly the Parliament had to establish that it had the right to exclude unwelcome migrants. In his second reading of his speech Edmund Barton, Prime and External Affairs Minister 1901–3, stated the right of the British Empire, of which Australia was at that time a part, to exclude 'such persons from their territory as seem to them undesirable'.[41] He then proposed that relying on a 'mere right' to discriminate would 'lead to trouble', unspecified at that point, and that the right needed to be reinforced in 'our own internal law' to 'satisfy conditions laid down by the Empire in its dealing with other powers'.[42] In this he demonstrated a careful attempt to balance the emerging sense of the power of the new national government with dependency on the British Empire.[43] That ambiguity was commented

38 Commonwealth, *Parliamentary Debates*, House of Representatives, 30 May 1901, 533 (Richard Edwards).

39 Commonwealth, *Parliamentary Debates*, House of Representatives, 7 August 1901, 3500 (Edmund Barton).

40 Commonwealth, *Parliamentary Debates*, Senate, 15 November 1901, 7332 (James Stewart).

41 Commonwealth, *Parliamentary Debates*, House of Representatives, 7 August 1901, 3500 (Edmund Barton). Note by 1905 this power was codified in Britian with the passing of the *Aliens Act 1905* (UK), the first migration legislation passed by the British parliament.

42 Commonwealth, *Parliamentary Debates*, House of Representatives, 7 August 1901, 3500 (Edmund Barton). Note by 1905 this power was codified in Britian with the passing of the *Aliens Act 1905* (UK), the first migration legislation passed by the British parliament.

43 See the discussion of the use of the term sovereignty to describe the power of the Australian government in 1906 in the comments of the Parliament's contemporary A Berriedale Keith. One of his conclusions is that, despite the dependency on the sovereignty of the Imperial Parliament, the Australian Parliament had authority to legislate. A Berriedale Keith, 'The Legal Interpretation of the Constitution of the Commonwealth' (1910) 11 *Journal of the Society of Comparative Legislation* 220, 228–31. See also Commonwealth, *Parliamentary Debates*, Senate, 6 December 1901, 8366 (Henry Dobson).

upon in 1910 by A Berriedale Keith who, while noting that it was the Imperial Parliament that had sovereign authority, believed that sovereignty was a useful way to describe the authority of the Commonwealth. The Commonwealth's power was not merely delegated power from the Imperial Parliament but sovereign authority to the extent authorised by the Constitution, which could be called internal sovereignty.[44]

Secondly the Parliament had to agree on the optimal legislative mechanism to deliver a white Australia. This debate also reveals an attempt to balance the achievement of a white Australia with external dependencies and vulnerabilities. The key dependency was on the British Empire. The Parliament wrestled with how to introduce racially discriminatory legislation while still fulfilling what was seen as Australia's duty: 'to conserve the interests of the British Empire'.[45] The key vulnerability was a perceived threat from Japan.[46]

This was the challenge facing the Parliament:

> We all desire to attain the same object [a white Australia], and we are equally unanimous and desirous of attaining it in a way which will cause the least embarrassment to the mother country, and at the same time give the least offence to friendly powers.[47]

'Friendly powers' referred to Japan.[48] 'It is a delicate matter to legislate for the exclusion of the subjects of a power that is an ally of Great Britain'.[49] The 'embarrassment to the mother country' was the problem of implementing a racially discriminatory policy while belonging to an Empire which included non-white people. It was argued,

> It was once our boast that if the negro set his foot on our shores, from that moment he was free. We are, no doubt, under peculiar exigencies and under special local circumstances, reversing that great principle of British freedom and British refuge.[50]

44 Keith (n 43) 231.

45 Commonwealth, *Parliamentary Debates*, House of Representatives, 5 June 1901, 692 (Langdon Bonython).

46 See discussion of the British Empire's relationship with Japan in Cees Heere, *Empire Ascendant: The British World, Race and the Rise of Japan, 1894–1914* (Oxford University Press, 2019) 8–45.

47 Commonwealth, *Parliamentary Debates*, House of Representatives, 20 September 1901, 5076 (Allan McLean).

48 Heere (n 46).

49 Heere (n 46) 5075.

50 Commonwealth, *Parliamentary Debates*, House of Representatives, 6 September 1901, 4627 (William McMillan).

Barton likened the two sides of the debate over the mechanism as 'two fires'.[51] On one side it was argued that the decision about the mechanism in the test, a mechanism which was to deliver a policy of the highest priority for the new nation, concerned 'the policy of the Empire', not Australia.[52] Henry Dobson, senator for Tasmania 1901–10, argued that to think of it as Australian policy was acting as an 'Australian Jingo',[53] that is an extreme nationalist. He noted that the education test had the support of the imperial government made explicit at the 1897 Imperial Conference.[54] The test was modelled on Natal's *Immigration Restriction Act 1897* which had been used successfully to exclude Indian immigrants without explicitly mentioning race.[55] It in turn was modelled on American immigration legislation.[56] Dobson urged parliamentarians not to 'dictate a policy to the Empire' and to remember that 'our self-government and free institutions were a gift from the motherland'.[57] He argued that 'Australia [should] fall into line with their views when they are carrying out a policy on behalf of the Empire'.[58]

Apart from gratitude and loyalty to the empire, the Parliament was also reminded of Australia's reliance on Britain for defence:

> We should not close our eyes to the fact that our immunity from attack has been due to the fact that the British Empire has been behind us, and that any country contemplating an invasion of our territory would have to reckon with the British navy before they could get at us.[59]

Barton's other 'fire', opposing this view, was the argument for a straightforward declaration in a 'manly fashion' of the races the Parliament intended to exclude and arguing against the 'miserable subterfuge of the education test'.[60]

51 Commonwealth, *Parliamentary Debates*, House of Representatives, 7 August 1901, 3500 (Edmund Barton).
52 Commonwealth, *Parliamentary Debates*, Senate, 6 December 1901, 8366 (Henry Dobson).
53 Commonwealth, *Parliamentary Debates*, Senate, 6 December 1901, 8366 (Henry Dobson).
54 AT Yarwood, *Asian Migration to Australia: The Background to Exclusion* (Melbourne University Press, 1964) 1–13.
55 Jeremy Marten, 'A Transnational History of Immigration Restriction: Natal and New South Wales, 1896–97' (2006) 34 *Journal of Imperial and Commonwealth History* 323, 324.
56 Jeremy Marten, 'A Transnational History of Immigration Restriction: Natal and New South Wales, 1896–97' (2006) 34 *Journal of Imperial and Commonwealth History* 323, 324.
57 Commonwealth, *Parliamentary Debates*, Senate, 6 December 1901, 8366 (Henry Dobson).
58 Commonwealth, *Parliamentary Debates*, Senate, 6 December 1901, 8366 (Henry Dobson) 8366–7.
59 Commonwealth, *Parliamentary Debates*, House of Representatives, 20 September 1901, 5075 (Allan McLean).
60 Commonwealth, *Parliamentary Debates*, Senate, 15 November 1901, 7332 (James Stewart) 7332. Jupp, writing one hundred years later, labels the legislative solution strange and 'hypocritical' and a denial of the racial discrimination that the act allowed, but explains it only in terms of Australia's dependency on Britain. James Jupp, *From White Australia to Woomera: The Story of Australian Immigration* (Cambridge University Press, 2002) 8–9.

James Stewart, senator for Queensland 1901–17, reminded the Parliament of the political argument for decisive exclusion. He noted the wide support in the recent election, the 'resounding cry [that]went up from one end of the continent to the other that the coloured races must go'.[61] Stewart also argued the inferiority and social incompatibility of non-whites but also the danger to white people of allowing 'other races' into Australia.[62] He echoed the concerns of Thomas Kennedy, Member for Moira, Victoria 1901–6,[63] characterising any non-white immigrant as a threat. To Stewart it was a 'matter of life and death to the people of Australia'.[64] He characterised achievement of a white Australia as a hard-fought victory. White Australia represented patriotism, freedom and survival:

> I cannot forget the desperate nature of the struggles which my forefathers in Great Britain underwent. I cannot forget that many of them went to prison, that many were transported, that some even went to the gallows so that we might enjoy the measure of liberty we possess, and might be in a better position than they were in. I should be a traitor to my country, to my race, and to those of our ancestors who have conferred benefits upon us, if I were a party to anything which would allow these Asiatics to come here and destroy at one fell swoop all the efforts of centuries.[65]

For Stewart the debate over the education test also revealed a class struggle:

> In my opinion, the better educated these people [non-white people] are the more undesirable citizens of Australia they most undoubtedly will be. It is in the interests of the capitalistic class that these people should be permitted to enter, but against the interests of the working classes. As the large majority of the people of Australia are workers, they would be foolish if they permitted Asiatic subjects of the King of England, or of the Mikado of Japan, or of the Emperor or Empress of China to enter.[66]

In the end, despite admitting that it was 'a sidewind' and that 'we are not saying all we mean in this Bill – that we mean a great deal more than we say'[67] and 'we do not intend to apply the test all round; we only intend to apply it

61 Jupp (n 60).
62 Jupp (n 60).
63 Commonwealth, *Parliamentary Debates*, House of Representatives, 5 June 1901, 703 (Thomas Kennedy).
64 Commonwealth, *Parliamentary Debates*, Senate, 15 November 1901, 7332 (James Stewart).
65 Commonwealth, *Parliamentary Debates*, Senate, 15 November 1901, 7332 (James Stewart).
66 Commonwealth, *Parliamentary Debates*, Senate, 5 December 1901, 8309 (James Stewart).
67 Commonwealth, *Parliamentary Debates*, House of Representatives, 20 September 1901, 5075 (Allan McLean).

where it is necessary',[68] the education test was adopted as the only option that would effectively exclude the undesirable immigrants who had been characterised as such a threat in the debate, without dangerously offending the empire or provoking foreign nations.

D Legislative Techniques Foreshadowing the Future: Executive Discretion To Avoid Saying All We Mean[69]

It is significant that the Parliament accepted that the vulnerabilities and dependencies of the new nation were such that it believed 'one of the most important matters with regard to the future of Australia that can engage the attention of this House'[70] should be achieved through legislation that was deliberately ambiguous and relied on the discretion of the immigration minister and how effectively he could convey the unlegislated intentions to his officers.[71]

The ambiguous nature of the *Immigration Restriction Act 1901*, that through it 'we mean a great deal more than we say',[72] meant that administering the act in compliance with the strong support expressed in the parliamentary debate for exclusion on racial grounds was left to the discretion of the immigration minister. Legislating ministerial discretion avoided explicitly stating in legislation that 'everyone of a certain nationality or colour shall be restricted, while other persons are not' and this avoided 'trouble and objection'.[73] It also allowed the immigration minister to make exceptions for 'desirable civilized immigrants'.[74] Without legislation the officers administering the education test had the responsibility and discretion to identify who should be asked to sit the test, to choose the European language,[75] later broadened to a 'prescribed language', and to identify people, even those currently living in Australia for

68 Commonwealth, *Parliamentary Debates*, House of Representatives, 20 September 1901, 5075 (Allan McLean).
69 Commonwealth, *Parliamentary Debates*, House of Representatives, 20 September 1901, 5075 (Allan McLean).
70 Commonwealth, *Parliamentary Debates*, House of Representatives, 7 August 1901, 3497 (Edmund Barton).
71 Jupp (n 60) 8–9 labels the legislative solution 'hypocritical' and a denial of the racial discrimination that the act allowed, but explains it only in terms of Australia's dependency on Britain.
72 Commonwealth, *Parliamentary Debates*, House of Representatives, 20 September 1901, 5075 (Allan McLean).
73 Commonwealth, *Parliamentary Debates*, House of Representatives, 7 August 1901, 3500 (Edmund Barton).
74 Commonwealth, *Parliamentary Debates*, House of Representatives, 7 August 1901, 3500 (Edmund Barton).
75 'It is for the officer and not the immigrant to select the European language for the purpose of applying the test under s 3(a) of the *Immigration Restriction Act 1901*': *Gee, Kow Chee, Seet & Quin v Martin* (1905) 3 CLR 649, 649.

less than twelve months, to perform the test.[76] By 1905 this discretion was extended to 'any member of the police force of a State'.[77]

Ministerial discretion was also an issue of debate concerning Pacific Islander labourers although on a much smaller scale. The blatantly racist language in this act was not judged to risk offence to other nations or embarrassing the empire. This was likely because the exclusion was aimed at those not considered people from one of the 'civilized powers', which to Barton included non-white Japan but not Pacific Islands.[78] The destination of the deportee under the *Pacific Island Labourers Act 1901* was left to the immigration minister's discretion despite it being of concern to at least one member of the Parliament that the legislation would ensure humane treatment.[79] Alfred Conroy, Member for Werriwa, Victoria, 1901–6, for example argued that the same care should be given to the deportees as the Parliament would expect for 'our own men'. He said:

> The Parliament that is dead to all considerations of right and wrong is not fit to legislate for the people of Australia, and if we do injustice in a case of this kind Nemesis will surely pursue us. A nation has to pay for its wrong-doing in just the same way as has the individual.[80]

Despite this concern the parliamentary majority agreed to the government's request to trust 'common sense' and the 'justice and humanity which has always characterised the British people'.[81]

These acts were soon tested in the High Court in 1906 in the case of *Robtelmes v Brenan*,[82] which appealed a ruling under the *Pacific Island Labourers Act 1901*, and confirmed in 1907 in the case of *Ah Yin v Christie*,[83] which appealed a ruling under the *Immigration Restriction Act 1901*. The judgments characterised the immigration power as essential to the expression of sovereignty.[84] In *Robtelmes v Brenan* Chief Justice Griffiths described as 'settled law of the British empire' that it 'was an essential prerogative of a sovereign

76 *Immigration Restriction Act 1901* ss 3(a), 5(2).
77 *Immigration Restriction Amendment Act 1905* s 3.
78 Commonwealth, *Parliamentary Debates*, House of Representatives, 7 August 1901, 3500 (Edmund Barton).
79 Commonwealth, *Parliamentary Debates*, House of Representatives, 12 December 1901, 8633 (Alfred Conroy).
80 Commonwealth, *Parliamentary Debates*, House of Representatives, 12 December 1901, 8633 (Alfred Conroy).
81 Commonwealth, *Parliamentary Debates*, House of Representatives, 12 December 1901, 8635 (Francis McLean); Commonwealth, *Parliamentary Debates*, House of Representatives, 7 August 1901, 3500 (Edmund Barton).
82 (1906) 4 CLR 395.
83 (1907) 4 CLR 1428.
84 *Robtelmes v Brenan* (1906) 4 CLR 395, 401–3 *Ah Yin v Christie* (1907) 4 CLR 1428, 1431.

State to determine who shall be allowed to come within its dominions, share in its privileges, take part in its government, or even share in the products of its soil'.[85] In *Ah Yin v Christie* he stated: 'The Commonwealth has under the Constitution power to exclude any person, whether an alien or not.'[86]

The parliamentary debates on these two acts reveal the purpose to which this assertion of sovereignty through migration law was put: an unquestioning belief in white superiority, its vulnerability to degradation and the priority of its protection even at an economic cost. The legislative techniques to which the Parliament agreed to achieve a white Australia were chosen to avoid 'trouble'.[87] This trouble stemmed from the vulnerabilities and interdependencies which could have led to diplomatic, trade and defence concerns if explicit, racially discriminatory legislation had been passed. The ambiguity of the legislation and the consequent need to legislate a high level of ministerial discretion to achieve the intention of the Parliament was the result. The nation's first migration law delivered the highest priority policy for the new nation through legislation that avoided stating its objective and was instead legislated broad ministerial discretion, trusting the immigration minister's judgement to deliver.

III Migration Act 1958

This section examines how the policy objective of a white Australia, still followed by the government in 1958, was to be delivered under the new migration legislation. The 1958 parliamentary debate, detailed shortly, demonstrates that, despite Australia's involvement in two world wars and the postwar arrival of 170,000 displaced persons from Europe,[88] the policy objective and legislative techniques match the *Immigration Restriction Act 1901* and can be argued to have further loosened the accountability and increased the discretion of the immigration minister.[89]

The new *Migration Act* did not change the policy of achieving a white Australia. The issue of achieving a racially discriminatory migration policy without damaging the diplomatic relationships of postwar Australia echoed

85 *Robtelmes v Brenan* (1906) 4 CLR 395, 401–3.

86 *Ah Yin v Christie* (1907) 4 CLR 1428, 1431. See also the previous discussion on the use of the term sovereignty at this time in Australia's constitutional history. Keith (n 43).

87 Commonwealth, *Parliamentary Debates*, House of Representatives, 7 August 1901, 3500 (Edmund Barton).

88 Jayne Persian, '"Chifley Liked Them Blond": Dp Immigrants for Australia' (2015) 12(2) *History Australia* 80.

89 For a discussion of this postwar migration see Gwenda Tavan, 'Leadership: Arthur Calwell and the Post-War Immigration Program' (2012) 58(2) *Australian Journal of Politics and History* 203; Matthew Jordan, 'The Reappraisal of the White Australia Policy against the Background of a Changing Asia, 1945–67' (2006) 52(1) *Australian Journal of Politics and History* 224.

the same concerns of 1901. In the second reading speech that introduced the legislation as a bill to be debated in the Parliament, Alexander Downer, Minister for Immigration (1958–63) in the Menzies Coalition Government, characterised the bill as a technical document concerning implementation and not policy change.[90] However, he did announce one significant change.[91] Welcomed in the debate in both the House of Representatives and later the Senate was the abolition of the dictation test.[92] Downer praised the test as 'ingenious' but criticised it as 'heavy handed . . . out of keeping with the ideas of the second half of the 20th century . . . [and] the cause of much resentment outside Australia'.[93] By this time it seems the diplomatic trouble that Barton had hoped to avoid in 1901 was materialising. However, Downer did not criticise the test's purpose and its achievement: to prevent entry or to deport within five years of entry 'both Europeans and Asians'.[94]

The new legislation replaced this test with an entry permit system which Downer described as a 'neat simple expedient'.[95] The improvement which the entry test delivered did not change the racially discriminatory policy or declare it in legislation. Downer stated that it was to save the unwelcome immigrant from being 'humiliated and bedazzled' by the dictation test.[96] Downer described the process which would replace the dictation test. He explained that the immigration officer would identify a person who according to the 'policy or instructions approved by the Minister' was ineligible to enter Australia.[97] The officer would then 'quietly' inform them.[98] The selection of those ineligible to enter remained on racial grounds. The outcome, refusal of entry and the threat of arrest and deportation, remained the same.[99]

90 Commonwealth, *Parliamentary Debates*, House of Representatives, 1 May 1958, 1396 (Alexander Downer).

91 Commonwealth, *Parliamentary Debates*, House of Representatives, 1 May 1958, 1396 (Alexander Downer) 1396–7.

92 The test had been introduced (as discussed in Section II B) by the *Immigration Restriction Act 1901* s 3(a).

93 Commonwealth, *Parliamentary Debates*, House of Representatives, 1 May 1958, 1396 (Alexander Downer).

94 Commonwealth, *Parliamentary Debates*, House of Representatives, 1 May 1958, 1396 (Alexander Downer).

95 Commonwealth, *Parliamentary Debates*, House of Representatives, 1 May 1958, 1396 (Alexander Downer). *Migration Act 1958* (Cth) s 6 (as made).

96 Commonwealth, *Parliamentary Debates*, House of Representatives, 1 May 1958, 1397 (Alexander Downer).

97 Commonwealth, *Parliamentary Debates*, House of Representatives, 1 May 1958, 1397 (Alexander Downer).

98 Commonwealth, *Parliamentary Debates*, House of Representatives, 1 May 1958, 1397 (Alexander Downer).

99 Commonwealth, *Parliamentary Debates*, House of Representatives, 1 May 1958, 1397 (Alexander Downer).

The strongly held ideas about the importance of discrimination by race continued from 1901 and were made clear in debate, as the following illustrates. Hon Henry Bruce, Member for Leichardt, Queensland, lamented that the death rate in World War I had robbed Australia of the chance to build a population from purely British stock.[100] This purely British population is what Sir William McMillan, Member for Wentworth, New South Wales, had hoped for in 1901.[101] However Bruce noted that building a population was similar to 'breeding thoroughbred horses' and as such an injection of new blood from Northern, not Southern, Italians, Germans and 'Nordic blood' would be promising.[102] Downer made it clear, however, that under no circumstances would a 'small colony of Japanese migrants' be given an opportunity to develop.[103]

What also remained from the *Immigration Restriction Act 1901* in the new legislation was the reliance on the discretion of the immigration minister for the delivery of this parliamentary intention: to 'build up a fine balanced population'.[104] The reason for the high level of discretion had also not changed since 1901: it was diplomatically unacceptable to overtly discriminate based on skin colour. Just as in 1901, in 1958 ministerial discretion was used to deliver a policy that might cause the 'trouble' that Barton in 1901 was keen to avoid. To justify the discretion given by the bill to the minister, Senator John McCallum, Liberal senator for NSW, 1950–62, said:

> in matters relating to the admission to this country of people from abroad we cannot clearly lay down in an act the whole of our policy. To do so would be very unwise and might cause considerable trouble with certain foreign countries. As everybody knows, we have a limited immigration policy in the sense that we limit the people who can come here.[105]

100 Commonwealth, *Parliamentary Debates*, House of Representatives, 16 September 1958, 1256 (Henry Bruce).
101 Commonwealth, *Parliamentary Debates*, House of Representatives, 6 September 1901, 4625–6 (William McMillan).
102 Commonwealth, *Parliamentary Debates*, House of Representatives, 16 September 1958, 1255 (Henry Bruce).
103 Commonwealth, *Parliamentary Debates*, House of Representatives. 29 March 1960. 701 (Alexander Downer). Downer's view was possibly influenced by his experience as a prisoner of war in World War II. See IR Hancock, 'Downer, Sir Alexander Russell (Alick) (1910–1981)'. *Australian Dictionary of Biography*, National Centre of Biography, Australian National University.
104 Commonwealth, *Parliamentary Debates*, House of Representatives, 16 September 1958, 1253 (Charles Anderson).
105 Commonwealth, *Parliamentary Debates*, Senate, 30 September 1958, 698 (John McCallum).

The bill maintained the ministerial discretion but introduced what Downer described as 'important checks on . . . [the minister's] authority in order to ensure a further degree of justice for the individual'.[106] One curb on the discretion was that the immigration minister's decisions could be reviewed by an independent commissioner with legal training and experience.[107] The commissioner would purportedly guard against the abuse of the deportation power against an innocent person who has 'displeased the minister of the day'.[108] A person could only be deported within five years of entry and on the recommendation of this commissioner who reviewed ministerial decisions to deport, but only if the deportee requested.[109] Limits were also placed on officers' discretion. For example, the bill proposed that anyone arrested as a suspected prohibited immigrant should be brought before a 'prescribed authority' within forty-eight hours and that a search warrant would be necessary to search premises or vehicles for prohibited immigrants or deportees.[110] The bill also introduced a measure to detain deportees in a detention centre and no longer a jail. Downer noted that 'very often the deportee has a blameless record: his only offence is a statutory one'.[111] Those in custody were also to be provided with legal assistance.[112]

Despite the claims that the ministerial discretion in the new legislation was being limited, the weakness of the measures to curb ministerial and officer discretion was argued in the debate even by members of the immigration minister's own party as the upcoming discussion illustrates. While not objecting to the policy on racial discrimination, there was concern that the discretion could be used in other ways.[113] For example, Reginald Wright, Liberal senator for Tasmania, 1950–78, expressed a view that the reform did not limit discretion but instead enshrined the immigration minister's opinion in legislation.[114] He complained that what the proposed commissioner had to investigate was whether the 'proposed deportee's conduct is such as appears

106 Commonwealth, *Parliamentary Debates*, House of Representatives, 1 May 1958, 1397 (Alexander Downer).
107 *Migration Act 1958* (Cth) as made ss 14 (3)–(8), 67.
108 Commonwealth, *Parliamentary Debates*, House of Representatives, 1 May 1958, 1397 (Alexander Downer). *Migration Act 1958* (Cth) as made s 7(4).
109 Commonwealth, *Parliamentary Debates*, House of Representatives, 1 May 1958, 1397 (Alexander Downer).
110 *Migration Act 1958* (Cth) as made ss 38(2), 37(3)–(4).
111 Commonwealth, *Parliamentary Debates*, House of Representatives, 1 May 1958, 1397 (Alexander Downer).
112 *Migration Act 1958* (Cth) as made s 40.
113 Commonwealth, *Parliamentary Debates*, Senate, 30 September 1958, 719 (Reginald Wright); Commonwealth, *Parliamentary Debates*, House of Representatives, 17 September 1958, 1307–8 (Gordon Bryant).
114 Commonwealth, *Parliamentary Debates*, Senate, 30 September 1958, 719 (Reginald Wright).

to the immigration minister to make the immigrant a person who should not be allowed to remain in Australia'.[115] He asked rhetorically: 'What criterion is that upon which anybody in this country, so long as it is to be ruled by law and not by men, should act?'[116] He noted with concern that this allowed the immigration minister to deport a 'British subject who has not been convicted of a crime'.[117] He suggested that before the immigration minister made the decision the officers should 'submit the cases to law'.[118] He also urged, in the name of the 'spirit of the rule of law', that the kinds of misconduct that would lead to deportation should be specified in the act and that detention should be subject to bail applications and conditions and should not be indefinite.[119] Opposition member Gordon Bryant, Member for Wills, Victoria, 1955–80, questioned the purported necessity for a power of deportation, especially of a permanent resident whose only offence was a connection with a militant trade union.[120] He expressed dissatisfaction with the 'general attitude to defining the rights of the potential deportee'[121] and suggested that enshrining a right to deport based on the immigration minister's subjective assessment of a person's political activity was a worse evil than any possible unwelcome political agitation.[122]

None of these concerns about how the legislated discretion given to the immigration minister weakened the rule of law were translated into the new *Migration Act 1958*. Just as in 1901, the Parliament agreed to an act that failed to unambiguously specify the Parliament's intention to control the racial composition of the population. Just as in 1901 the Parliament thought it necessary to give wide discretion to the immigration minister to translate the undocumented policy into practice, because to be specific was diplomatically dangerous.[123] What did change from 1901 was that in the 1958 act, ministerial accountability mechanisms appear to have been loosened.

115 Commonwealth, *Parliamentary Debates*, Senate, 30 September 1958, 719 (Reginald Wright).
116 Commonwealth, *Parliamentary Debates*, Senate, 30 September 1958, 719 (Reginald Wright).
117 Commonwealth, *Parliamentary Debates*, Senate, 30 September 1958, 719 (Reginald Wright).
118 Commonwealth, *Parliamentary Debates*, Senate, 30 September 1958, 719 (Reginald Wright).
119 Commonwealth, *Parliamentary Debates*, Senate, 30 September 1958, 719 (Reginald Wright).
120 Commonwealth, *Parliamentary Debates*, House of Representatives, 17 September 1958, 1307–8 (Gordon Bryant).
121 Commonwealth, *Parliamentary Debates*, House of Representatives, 17 September 1958, 1307–8 (Gordon Bryant) 1307.
122 Commonwealth, *Parliamentary Debates*, House of Representatives, 17 September 1958, 1307–8 (Gordon Bryant) 1308.
123 Commonwealth, *Parliamentary Debates*, Senate, 30 September 1958, 698 (John McCallum).

McCallum noted in debate that, with such a 'considerable degree of discretion to the Minister', the Parliament would need to be 'vigilant to see that the act is administered according to the principles of British justice'.[124] However, without specific mention in the second reading speech, the requirement to report annually to the Parliament on the operation of the new entry permit system, as previously required for the dictation test by the *Immigration Restriction Act* s 17, was dropped, leaving scrutiny to parliamentary questioning. The immigration minister was to be trusted, despite misgivings and possible past abuses,[125] to act with a 'general sense of equity and justice'.[126]

The extent to which the Parliament had relied on ministerial discretion to deliver its nation-defining policy over its first seven decades was illustrated in 1973 when a newly elected government had a new policy 'to remove all forms of racial discrimination'.[127] Al Grassby, Minister for Immigration 1972–4 in the Whitlam Labor government, celebrated this new policy. He said: 'It will also at long last enable us to ratify the International Convention on the Elimination of all forms of Racial Discrimination'.[128] To implement this policy the only change necessary to the *Migration Act 1958* was to remove the restriction on Indigenous people travelling overseas.[129] Nowhere visible in the *Immigration Restriction Act 1901* or the *Migration Act 1958* was the White Australia policy, which was so central to the intent of the Parliament for its first decades. It had been entrusted only to the discretion of the immigration minister.

These two instances of parliamentary debates and legislative processes in 1901 and 1958 are significant in four ways. Firstly, they illustrate the enduring high priority given to exclusion on racial grounds, even over economic gain, which was justified as a right by Barton and confirmed by the High Court as an expression of sovereign power.[130] Secondly, they illustrate the

124 Commonwealth, *Parliamentary Debates*, Senate, 30 September 1958, 698 (John McCallum) 699.

125 Commonwealth, *Parliamentary Debates*, Senate, 30 September 1958, 699 (John McCallum).

126 Commonwealth, *Parliamentary Debates*, Senate, 30 September 1958, 699 (John McCallum).

127 Commonwealth, *Parliamentary Debates*, House of Representatives, 28 February 1973, 53 (Al Grassby).

128 Commonwealth, *Parliamentary Debates*, House of Representatives, 28 February 1973, 53 (Al Grassby).

129 *Migration Amendment Act 1973* ss 3–6. For a discussion on the decades of political change which led to a dismantling of the White Australia policy see Gwenda Tavan, 'The Limits of Discretion: The Role of the Liberal Party in the Dismantling of the White Australia Policy' (2005) 51(3) *Australian Journal of Politics and History* 418.

130 Commonwealth, *Parliamentary Debates*, House of Representatives, 7 August 1901, 3500 (Edmund Barton); *Robtelmes v Brenan* (1906) 4 CLR 395; *Ah Yin v Christie* (1907) 4 CLR 1428 (n 84). See also Tavan, *The Long, Slow Death* (n 5).

external danger and vulnerability, expressed by one speaker as a life and death struggle,[131] that the Parliament believed this racially discriminatory policy defended against and which itself might cause.[132] Thirdly, they illustrate that the Parliament's solution to this dilemma was to legislate broad ministerial discretion to deliver a policy they did not dare to plainly state. Fourthly, they illustrate that through migration legislative processes the Parliament moved away from the principles of British common law.[133] This is demonstrated in comments such as in the 1901 debate when McMillan excused the racial discriminatory policy which 'reversed that great principle of British freedom and British refuge' as necessary because of the new Commonwealth's local circumstances.[134] Later in the 1958 debate MacCallum and Wright recognised that the principles of British justice were now taken out of the Parliament's hands and left up to the minister's discretion.[135] Together these four aspects of the legislative process show what the Parliament was willing to trade to achieve a white population: economic gain, parliamentary power and inherited legal principles.

IV 1978: Replacing Racial Discrimination With Sovereignty as a Rationale for Migration Law

The purported end of the White Australia policy[136] did not signal the end of a restrictive migration policy.[137] The issue for lawmakers was to find a new rationale to justify these restrictions. In the 1901 and 1958 parliamentary debates, racial discrimination was openly espoused as the rationale for the legislation as detailed previously. Once the White Australia policy was declared officially over, a new rationale for restriction emerged and

131 Commonwealth, *Parliamentary Debates*, Senate, 15 November 1901, 7332 (James Stewart).

132 See sections II and III.

133 These principles are discussed in chapters 7 and 8.

134 Commonwealth, *Parliamentary Debates*, House of Representatives, 6 September 1901, 4627 (William McMillan).

135 Commonwealth, *Parliamentary Debates*, Senate, 30 September 1958, 719 (Reginald Wright); Commonwealth, *Parliamentary Debates*, Senate, 30 September 1958, 699 (John McCallum).

136 Commonwealth, *Parliamentary Debates*, House of Representatives, 28 February 1973, 53 (Al Grassby). Kim Beazley, Leader of the Labor Opposition, recounted in a condolence speech on the death of Al Grassby that Al Grassby was questioned in the Philippines about the White Australia policy in 1973 and that he had responded: 'It is dead – give me a shovel and I will bury it'. Commonwealth, *Parliamentary Debates*, House of Representatives, 10 May 2005, 9 (Kim Beazley).

137 Tavan, *The Long, Slow Death* (n 5) 235–9. Tavan argues that even though in 1973 Grassby declared the White Australia policy was dead and buried, racism remained a factor in the electorate and in migration policy.

sovereignty was overtly asserted to justify what was presented as a new policy framework for migration, as discussed shortly.

In June 1978, Michael Mackellar, Minister for Immigration and Ethnic Affairs (1975–9) in the Fraser Coalition government, declared to the Parliament that the 'issue of Indo-Chinese refugees has brought all Australians face to face with the reality that no longer are we insulated and isolated from immigration questions of immense significance'.[138] To address this challenge the immigration minister set out nine principles for immigration policy. His stated purpose was that both Australians and other countries would understand Australia's 'goals, obligations and constraints'.[139] He claimed the principles were based on 'the interests of Australia and its people, compassion and international responsibility'.[140] The first principle echoed Chief Justice Griffith's words in *Robtelmes* in 1906,[141] but unlike that judgment McKellar ascribed this power not to the sovereign state or even the Parliament, but to the 'Australian Government alone'.[142] Mackellar stated that it was 'fundamental to national sovereignty that the Australian Government alone should determine who will be admitted to Australia'.[143] The other eight principles covered issues such as the importance of the migrant being beneficial to the Australian community, non-discrimination on the basis 'race, colour, nationality, descent, national or ethnic origin or sex' (religion was not listed), the avoidance of threats to social cohesion and only allowing families, not 'community groups', to apply.

Families were defined only as 'husband, wife and minor unmarried children'. There was also an expectation that migrants 'should integrate into Australian society'.[144]

What was the threat to sovereignty to which the immigration minister was responding by asserting this as his first principle of migration policy? Two changes had occurred which impacted on the government's capacity to exert its authority over the territory to exclude migrants. The first, and the one around which the immigration minister framed his speech, was the arrival

138 Commonwealth, *Parliamentary Debates*, House of Representatives, 7 June 1978, 3153 (Michael Mackellar).
139 Commonwealth, *Parliamentary Debates*, House of Representatives, 7 June 1978, 3153 (Michael Mackellar) 3154.
140 Commonwealth, *Parliamentary Debates*, House of Representatives, 7 June 1978, 3153 (Michael Mackellar) 3155.
141 *Robtelmes v Brenan* (1906) 4 CLR 395, 403.
142 Commonwealth, *Parliamentary Debates*, House of Representatives, 7 June 1978, 3155 (Michael Mackellar) 3155.
143 Commonwealth, *Parliamentary Debates*, House of Representatives, 7 June 1978, 3155 (Michael Mackellar) 3154.
144 Commonwealth, *Parliamentary Debates*, House of Representatives, 7 June 1978, 3155 (Michael Mackellar) 3155.

of Indo-Chinese refugees to Australia.[145] By the time Mackellar launched his nine principles the number of Vietnamese 'boat people' had reached approximately 1,700.[146] To attempt to stop these unauthorised boat arrivals, a refugee intake of Indo-Chinese refugees was initiated as well as other measures to prevent boats from leaving their overseas ports.[147]

While the phenomena of 'boat people' began to be and remains a political concern, the biggest numerical challenge to asserting sovereignty through migration policy did not come from 'boat people'. At the same time as McKellar's launch of the new migration principles there were an estimated 57,000 prohibited immigrants in Australia and, in a change from the past when most people travelled by boat, '98 per cent of arrivals are by air'.[148] Air travel and increased temporary migration had created administrative demands on the immigration administration to identify and deny entry to potential prohibited immigrants.[149] Yet the focus of the announcement was the people arriving on boats.

This final historical instance highlights three elements. The first was the challenge to the continuing tight control of migration at a time when distance and geography were no longer the barrier they had been in the past. The second was that, even though since 1973 the White Australia policy had been officially abandoned, community sentiment was divided.[150] Mackellar noted that 'Few issues have attracted so wide a spectrum of sentiment [on migration policy], from the extreme of the virtual open door to the absolute of the door nailed firmly shut'.[151] The third was the need to justify exclusion, when racial discrimination was no longer available. In the immigration minister's speech an assertion of sovereignty, as power located in 'the Australian Government alone',[152] replaced racial discrimination as the first principle of migration policy. A power replaced a policy.

Nine immigration ministers followed McKellar across the last decades of the 20th century serving in both Coalition and Labor governments before the Howard Coalition government came to office in 1996. Only one mentioned

145 See detailed account in N Viviani, *The Long Journey* (Melbourne University Press, 1984). See also Tavan, *The Long, Slow Death* (n 5) 214; Katharine Betts, 'Boatpeople and Public Opinion in Australia' (2001) 9(4) *People and Place* 34.

146 Betts (n 145) 34–6.

147 Betts (n 145) 34–6.

148 Commonwealth, *Parliamentary Debates*, House of Representatives, 10 May 1979, 2095 (Raymond Groom).

149 Commonwealth, *Parliamentary Debates*, House of Representatives, 10 May 1979, 2095 (Raymond Groom).

150 Tavan, *The Long, Slow Death* (n 5) 215–18; Betts (n 145) 40–1.

151 Commonwealth, *Parliamentary Debates*, House of Representatives, 7 June 1978, 3153 (Michael Mackellar).

152 Commonwealth, *Parliamentary Debates*, House of Representatives, 7 June 1978, 3153 (Michael Mackellar).

this first principle of migration policy. On two occasions in early 1986 Chris Hurford, Minister for Immigration and Ethnic Affairs 1984–7 in the Hawke Labor government, repeated McKellar's first principle. Hurford noted that it was 'fundamental to national sovereignty that the Australian Government alone should decide who will be admitted to Australia'.[153] This language of sovereignty in relation to migration was not taken up by prime ministers, including John Howard, until 2001.

V Conclusion

The nexus of migration law, sovereignty and globalisation might be understood, at least in part, by a reference to history. This chapter set a historical benchmark of issues, objectives and legislative techniques against which, in later chapters, to test the application of the concept of hypersovereignty to migration lawmaking between 2000 and 2020. In the first Parliament of the newly formed Australian Federation one of the most important issues was the implementation of a racially discriminatory migration policy to keep out all but white immigrants, preferably British, and to remove Pacific Island labourers from Australia. The removal of Pacific Island labourers was straightforwardly legislated as the *Pacific Island Labourers Act 1901*. It set out the policy of removal of this group and the Parliament empowered the immigration minister to deport anyone suspected of being a Pacific Island labourer to any destination the immigration minister saw fit. Keeping out all but white migrants was much more problematic. The policy needed to be implemented without offending the British Empire of which the new nation was a part and on which it was dependent, and without offending powerful neighbours such as Japan against whom the new nation was vulnerable. The strategy agreed upon implemented the policy through the *Immigration Restriction Act 1901* which legislated wide discretion to the immigration minister to use an education test, later known as the dictation test, to exclude those judged by the immigration minister to be undesirable. Almost sixty years later the passing of the *Migration Act 1958* (Cth) did not change this racially discriminatory policy nor the wide discretion of the immigration minister. The only change was the replacement of the dictation test with a permit system on the basis that this would be more acceptable internationally. By 1973 when the newly elected government announced it wished to rid legislation of any racial discrimination, the only change necessary to the *Migration Act 1958* (Cth) concerned the previous ban on Indigenous people travelling overseas. The policy of discrimination, believed so crucial to the nation, had been delivered

153 Commonwealth, *Parliamentary Debates*, House of Representatives, 20 February 1986, 952 (Chris Hurford); Commonwealth, *Parliamentary Debates*, House of Representatives, 10 April 1986, 1969 (Chris Hurford).

through ministerial discretion to avoid censure, damage to trade and possible aggression from Japan. By 1978 the White Australia policy was officially abandoned. The justification for exclusion was no longer overtly racial discrimination. The first principle of migration policy was now sovereignty located in the Australian government, the executive, alone.

These first two instances of migration legislative processes demonstrate the overt policy goal of racial discrimination and how it was achieved by a Parliament that was acutely aware of Australia's dependencies and vulnerability. The third instance, a declaration of policy to the Parliament, demonstrates that the concept of sovereignty replaced racial discrimination as a central rationale for exclusion. In what ways these instances compare with the objectives, issues and techniques used in migration lawmaking in 2000–20 is taken up over the following chapters.

Part Two

How Sovereignty Is Used To Justify Exclusion

Chapter 5

The Clash of Neoliberalism and Sovereignty

I Introduction

The previous chapter demonstrated that exclusion of the unwanted migrant has been a key feature of migration law in Australia. It was justified for more than half of the twentieth century by a policy of racial discrimination and, because of external vulnerabilities and dependencies, it was achieved by legislation which avoided enunciating the policy. Alongside this central theme the parliamentary debates also showed the tension between these exclusionary objectives and the importance of migration law and policy to economic development. This tension was demonstrated from the earliest debate in 1901 over Pacific Islander labour.[1] This chapter explores this tension by examining amendments made to the *Migration Act 1958* (Cth) between 2000 and 2020 where the economic benefit of globalisation and the assertion of sovereignty collided. The purpose of this chapter is to test the nature of sovereignty in this globalised era by examining how the Parliament attempted to resolve this tension.

Before beginning this discussion one further aspect of migration law and policy should be noted as context. From around 2000 there was a shift to an economic focus in migration policy, as is demonstrated by the dramatic increase in skilled migration as a proportion of the migrant intake.[2] However, unlike the amendments made in this period aimed to exclude,[3] this shift to an economic focus did not require legislative amendment. The broad

1 See Chapter 4 Section II. See also Gwenda Tavan, *The Long, Slow Death of White Australia* (Scribe Publications, 2005); Katrina Stats, 'Characteristically Generous? Australian Responses to Refugees Prior to 1951' (2014) 60(2) *Australian Journal of Politics and History* 177, 184.

2 Andrew Markus, James Jupp and Peter McDonald, *Australia's Immigration Revolution* (Allen & Unwin, 2009) 11–13; Harriet Spinks, 'Australia's Migration Program' (Parliamentary Library Background Note, Parliament of Australia, 29 October 2016); Department of Home Affairs, 'Migration Program Planning Levels' (Web Page, 16 August 2022) <https://immi.homeaffairs.gov.au/what-we-do/migration-program-planning-levels>.

3 See Chapter 6.

DOI: 10.4324/9781003515852-7

discretionary power of the immigration minister allows quite impactful policy changes to be made without legislative change.[4]

Using the example of the four amendments to the international student visa legislation,[5] the student amendments, the chapter explores how the parliamentary debates and legislative processes expressed the neoliberal value of globalisation and at the same time defended a Westphalian concept of sovereign authority against the challenge of globalisation through migration control and the right to exclude. The chapter argues that while the emphasis in the debate on amendments to the student visa legislation was on the student as a customer of a highly lucrative product, the Parliament's rationale for the migration measures is not justified by economics alone. In these parliamentary debates on migration and the resulting legislation the limit of the Parliament's adoption of the neoliberal logic of globalisation is reached. At this limit an expression of state sovereignty as the power to exclude, little changed since Federation, is prioritised over the opportunity for economic gain.

The chapter makes this argument by firstly setting out two alternate hypotheses, one concerning the continuity of Westphalian notions of absolute sovereignty expressed through exclusion and the other the logic of neoliberalism that drives current globalisation trends. These hypotheses are tested for their explanatory power in discerning the underpinning objectives and values of these legislative processes.

Secondly the chapter examines the policy context in which these student amendments to the *Migration Act 1958* (Cth) were enacted. The chapter does this through an examination of how the prime ministers and immigration ministers over the period 2000–20 used the specific language of globalisation and how they represented globalisation both within and outside the Parliament. Thirdly the chapter applies the two hypotheses to the student amendments as an example of amendments with an economic objective where the values of neoliberalism and Westphalian sovereignty competed in the Parliament's deliberations.

The chapter draws from parliamentary debate, ministerial speeches and comment and judicial comment, using them as the primary sources for analysis. The focus of this analysis is on the words of the lawmakers and the law

4 For examples of this see Sudrishti Reich, 'Great Expectations and the Twilight Zone: The Human Consequences of the Linking of Australia's International Student and Skilled Migration Programs and the Dismantling of that Scheme', in Marianne Dickie, Dorota Gozdecka and Sudrishti Reich (eds), *Unintended Consequences: The Impact of Migration Law and Policy* (ANU Press, 2016) 31; Sanmati Verma, 'Pathways to Illegality, or What became of the International Students', in Marianne Dickie, Dorota Gozdecka and Sudrishti Reich (eds), *Unintended Consequences: The Impact of Migration Law and Policy* (ANU Press, 2016) 9.

5 *Migration Legislation Amendment (Overseas Students) Act 2000* (Cth); *Education Services for Overseas Students Legislation Amendment (2006 Measures No 2) Act 2006* (Cth); *Education Services for Overseas Students Legislation Amendment Act 2007* (Cth); *Migration Legislation Amendment (Student Visas) Act 2012* (Cth).

itself. They reveal the values, interests and priorities that are the ingredients of the legislative process.[6] The rationale for this choice is that in the decisions of those who sit in Parliament and decide on the content of legislation and in the judiciary's interpretation of that legislation lies the sovereign power of the state as enshrined in the Australian Constitution.[7]

II Two Hypotheses: Neoliberalism v Westphalian Sovereignty

The examination of the student migration amendments will test two hypotheses. They are central to this book's analysis of the nature of sovereignty expressed in Australian migration law. They contribute to discerning the extent to which the legislative process can be understood as a defence of waning sovereignty in a globalising world, the hypersovereignty that Wendy Brown discusses, and the use of migration law as the 'new last bastion of sovereignty' in a globalising world that Catherine Dauvergne identifies.[8]

The first hypothesis proposes that Australian migration law since Federation has been central to the way Australia has expressed national sovereignty and the vulnerabilities and interdependencies of globalisation had little impact on migration legislative processes in 2000–20. This is because Australia has focussed its assertion of sovereign power through migration law since Federation in 1901.[9] This hypothesis sees the current period of globalisation as part of a cycle of historical processes of responding to external forces, such as the waves of European, British and US imperialism and the rise of China.[10] The hypothesis suggests that the aspects of globalisation to which migration lawmakers have responded since 2000 is comparable to the external forces that have impacted on Australia's migration policy choices and legislative techniques since Federation.

6 See also Chapters 7 and 8.

7 See Chapter 2 Section IV.

8 Wendy Brown, *Walled States, Waning Sovereignty* (Zone Books, 2010) 67, 107 ('*Walled States*'); Catherine Dauvergne, 'Sovereignty, Migration and the Rule of Law in Global Times' (2004) 67(4) *Modern Law Review* 588, 588. See discussion of these theories in Chapter 2 Section III.

9 See Chapter 4.

10 Raymond Grew, 'Finding Frontiers in Historical Research on Globalization', in Ino Rossi (ed), *Frontiers of Globalisation Research: Theoretical and Methodological Approaches* (Springer Science and Business Media, 2007) 271, 271–8; Taesuh Cha, 'Is Anybody Still a Globalist? Rereading the Trajectory of US Grand Strategy and the End of the Transnational Moment' (2019) 17(1) *Globalizations* 60, 71; Ino Rossi, 'From Cosmopolitanism to a Global Perspective: Paradigmatic Discontinuity (Beck, Ritzer, Postmodernism, and Albrow) Versus Continuity (Alexander and Collins) and Emergent Conceptualizations (Contributors to This Volume)', in Ino Rossi (ed), *Frontiers of Globalisation Research: Theoretical and Methodological Approaches* (Springer Science and Business Media, 2007) 397, 435. See discussion of this historical approach in Chapter 2 Section II A.

This hypothesis also identifies a continuum of legislative techniques in migration law since the enacting of the *Immigration Restriction Act 1901*, which was discussed in the previous chapter. A government speaker in that first Parliament expressed this technique as: 'we are not saying all we mean in this Bill – that we mean a great deal more than we say'.[11] This hypothesis suggests that, just as in 1901, the Parliament making the 2000–20 amendments avoided explicitly enacting 'what we mean', as it is politically and diplomatically sensitive, and relies on a high level of ministerial discretion to select and exclude. The hypothesis of a continuum suggests that, rather than a new phenomenon of 'hypersovereignty' as a response to waning sovereignty in a globalised world, Australia's migration legislative processes have always been the arena where governments expressed sovereignty and broad ministerial discretion has been the technique used to enact policy since 1901, removing the underlying policy values from legislative expression, judicial comment or public scrutiny.

The second hypothesis, in conflict with the first, is that these student visa amendments, instead, signal a break in the continuum, a qualitatively different response. This hypothesis proposes that the legislative processes represent an embrace of a globalised neoliberal logic that values the success of the corporation, and the individual is valued exclusively as an economic entity to be measured by skill and productivity.[12] Drawing on Krygier's work, this hypothesis suggests that the traditional function of the rule of law, to protect the individual from arbitrary power, has been largely abandoned in these amendments.[13] Rather the law is used to protect free enterprise to maximise its profit, a neoliberal rule-of-law function.[14] This hypothesis suggests that this neoliberal logic diminishes the importance of state sovereignty in favour of the sovereignty of capital and triggers a hypersovereignty response that manifests as a reassertion of sovereign power in an area where the state can exercise Westphalian sovereignty by controlling territorial borders through migration law.[15]

11 Commonwealth, *Parliamentary Debates*, House of Representatives, 20 September 1901, 5075 (Allan McLean). See the context of this quotation in Chapter 1 Section II C – D.

12 Saskia Sassen, *Expulsions: Brutality and Complexity in the Global Economy* (Harvard University Press, 2014) 213–16; Wendy Brown, *Undoing the Demos: Neo Liberalism's Stealth Revolution* (Zone Books, 2015) 9–10.

13 Martin Krygier, 'Transformations of the Rule of Law Legal, Liberal, and Neo-', in Ben Golder and Daniel McLoughlin (eds), *The Politics of Legality in a Neoliberal Age* (Routledge, 2018) 19, 20–1.

14 Martin Krygier, 'Transformations of the Rule of Law Legal, Liberal, and Neo-', in Ben Golder and Daniel McLoughlin (eds), *The Politics of Legality in a Neoliberal Age* (Routledge, 2018) 19, 20–1.

15 See discussion of these theories in Chapter 3 Section III.

III Globalisation and the Parliament

Over the two decades 2000–2020 the Parliament developed its understanding of globalisation as both an opportunity and a threat. Economic globalisation remained the focus over the decades even while the threat of a 'dissolution of boundaries between nations'[16] to a Westphalian concept of sovereign control became more apparent. Terrorism and security threats were seen as key globalisation threats but, as is seen shortly, they were not a focus of the discussion of globalisation and were kept separate from economic goals until the COVID-19 pandemic stuck Australia in 2020.

In order to understand the broad policy framework in which economic amendments were made during this period, this section draws primarily on prime ministerial statements and comment. This is for two reasons. Firstly, the making of prime ministerial statements and comments on an issue suggests that the issue is one of critical national importance. Secondly, the way the leader of the government represents an issue, such as globalisation, indicates the broad policy framework in which legislation is proposed to the Parliament, in this case the economic amendments to the *Migration Act 1958* (Cth).

This examination begins just before the period 2000–21, with Paul Keating, Labor prime minister (1991–6), the first prime minister to name the cluster of phenomena as globalisation in Parliament,[17] and with opposition and government spokespersons, Anthony Albanese, Labor Member for Grayndler, and Marise Payne, Liberal senator for NSW. While neither of the latter speakers were yet in leadership positions in their political parties they are referenced for two reasons. Firstly, they made the only speeches in Parliament solely on the issue of globalisation. Secondly, their speeches summarise the risks of economic globalisation that were given little attention in the speeches and comments of more prominent speakers. Following this introduction, the chapter traces the contexts and representations of globalisation by prime ministers and their immigration ministers as they voiced the policy framework for responding to these phenomena.

A Globalisation as an Economic Opportunity

By 2000 the Parliament was aware of the phenomenon of economic globalisation and characterised it as an opportunity for wealth but also a threat

16 John Howard, 'Radio Interview Keith Conlon 5AN', *PM Transcripts* (Radio interview, 5 July 1996) <pmtranscripts.pmc.gov.au>.

17 Paul Keating, 'World Conference of the International Council for Small Business, Sydney' *PM Transcripts* (Speech, 21 June 1995) <pmtranscripts.pmc.gov.au>. Note that the first mention of the term globalisation in the Parliament was in 1987 when Senator Vigor reported unanimous support by the Committee on Legal and Constitutional Affairs for national securities laws to support Australian business in a new globalised business environment. Commonwealth, *Parliamentary Debates*, Senate, 29 April 1987, 2017 (David Vigor).

to nations' economic sovereignty.[18] Speakers from both sides of the Parliament had specifically addressed the issue of globalisation in Parliament a year before. Both sides of Parliament emphasised the economic opportunity of globalisation and proposed international cooperation between states to mitigate any threat to sovereignty.

While opposition speaker Albanese acknowledged that globalisation 'could bring enormous benefit', he highlighted two areas of debate: the impact of globalisation on the state, when almost half of the largest economies were corporations, not states, and the effect of globalisation on working people.[19] He warned of two concerns: firstly, the protection of working people and secondly, the protection of developing nations. His proposed solutions relied on cooperation between states. His first solution was for internationally agreed regulation linking trade to workers' rights. His second was a tax on international financial transactions that would be used to support developing nations.[20] Neither proposal was progressed in debate.

The government's position emphasised the economic opportunity of globalisation and expressed confidence that the threats could be ameliorated.[21] Payne defined globalisation as a beneficial significant increase in trade. She acknowledged the twin concerns regarding working conditions and state sovereignty.[22] Payne, like Albanese, proposed international cooperation to control globalisation.[23] Payne noted that globalisation had many benefits for those countries who chose to constructively engage through international bodies. Payne argued that nations remained in control, not losing sovereignty, because national agreement to join international mechanisms, such as the World Trade Organization, was necessary to 'ratify any form of positive globalisation'.[24] Corporate interests could be tamed, she claimed, by nations uniting to harmonise regulations through international and bilateral cooperation.

18 Commonwealth, *Parliamentary Debates*, House of Representatives, 30 August 1999, 9383 (Anthony Albanese).

19 Commonwealth, *Parliamentary Debates*, House of Representatives, 30 August 1999, 9383 (Anthony Albanese). See also previous discussion of the proposed irrelevance of national boundaries in Chapter 2 Section II B on Leslie Sklair's theory of globalisation and Saskia Sassen's consistent theory. Leslie Sklair, 'A Transnational Framework for Theory and Research in the Study of Globalization', in Ino Rossi (ed), *Frontiers of Globalisation Research: Theoretical and Methodological Approaches* (Springer Science and Business Media, 2007) 93, 100; Saskia Sassen, *Losing Control? Sovereignty in an Age of Globalization* (Columbia University Press, 1995) xii.

20 Commonwealth, *Parliamentary Debates*, House of Representatives, 30 August 1999, 9383 (Anthony Albanese).

21 Commonwealth, *Parliamentary Debates*, Senate, 1 November 2000, 18816 (Marise Payne).

22 Commonwealth, *Parliamentary Debates*, Senate, 1 November 2000, 18816 (Marise Payne).

23 Commonwealth, *Parliamentary Debates*, Senate, 1 November 2000, 18816 (Marise Payne).

24 Commonwealth, *Parliamentary Debates*, Senate, 1 November 2000, 18816 (Marise Payne).

This would be effective, she argued, because simplicity of regulation was what 'businesses prefer' and because disparity could create loopholes for abuse.[25] Those same international mechanisms, she argued, could remedy parliamentarians' concerns about workers' rights and state sovereignty. In particular these mechanisms could limit the possibility that international corporations, which Payne seemed to personify as 'globalisation', might benefit from globalisation, and not states themselves.[26]

Both speakers seemed to be aware that the entities jostling for economic dominance were no longer all states. While Albanese raised the issue of the power of multinational corporations that rival states,[27] Payne did not raise this issue directly. However, her personification of globalisation as an entity able to receive a benefit reveals her awareness that the globalisation of which she spoke was actually the growth of corporations, not tied to national identity, that rivalled the economic dominance of states, as Albanese had noted.[28] Despite this recognition of new powerful non-state actors, neither Payne nor Albanese proposed a way to engage these multinationals in international cooperation. Their solution was for states to unite against a common threat through jointly agreed upon mechanisms such as taxation and regulation.[29] Their solution seems to have underestimated the power of multinationals that Sklair discusses,[30] and the individual national economic competitiveness between states that, as outlined shortly, was promoted by prime ministers from 2000 to 2020.

While Payne and Albanese proposed international cooperation as the solution, an analysis of statements from the six prime ministers across the period 2000 to 2020 shows a less consistent approach. Four of these prime ministers, along with their predecessor Paul Keating, emphasised both competition and international cooperation with other states as strategies to manage the opportunities and threats of economic globalisation. Keating suggested that to capitalise on globalisation's economic benefits there needs to be 'both competition and cooperation between states'.[31] Kevin Rudd, Labor prime minister 2007–10, urged that to embrace the challenges of globalisation Australia

25 Commonwealth, *Parliamentary Debates*, Senate, 1 November 2000, 18816 (Marise Payne).
26 Commonwealth, *Parliamentary Debates*, Senate, 1 November 2000, 18816 (Marise Payne) 18815.
27 Commonwealth, *Parliamentary Debates*, House of Representatives, 30 August 1999, 9383 (Anthony Albanese) 9383.
28 Commonwealth, *Parliamentary Debates*, House of Representatives, 30 August 1999, 9383 (Anthony Albanese) 9383.
29 Commonwealth, *Parliamentary Debates*, Senate, 1 November 2000, 18815 (Marise Payne); Commonwealth, *Parliamentary Debates*, House of Representatives, 30 August 1999, 9383 (Anthony Albanese).
30 Sklair (n 19).
31 Paul Keating, 'United Nations Social Summit Copenhagen', *PM Transcripts* (Speech, 12 March 1995) <pmtranscripts.pmc.gov.au>.

needed to 'work in partnership with others to reform our institutions of global governance'.[32] Julia Gillard, Labor prime minister 2010–3, saw globalisation as presenting an array of 'transnational challenges' that needed to be 'collectively managed . . . on a regional level' but she did not directly address the power of the multinational corporation rivalling that of nations.[33] Malcolm Turnbull, Coalition prime minister 2015–8, made comments that, like Keating's, seem to embrace competing approaches, promoting both aggressive competition and cooperation. For example, Turnbull deflected a question by a journalist about whether he shared the German chancellor's concerns about US president Trump's protectionist approach that characterised globalisation as a 'matter of winners and losers rather than working toward cooperation between nations'.[34] However, Turnbull had already stated months before that Australia needed 'to compete aggressively for global export markets' and that 'we cannot retreat into the bleak dead-end of protectionism'.[35] At the same time as promoting aggressive competition he urged at an international forum 'that in age of globalisation . . . now it is more important than ever that we work together'.[36]

Some of these prime ministers also specifically raised the issue of the impact of the rise of multinational corporations. For example, Keating noted that 'more than one third of world trade is now conducted by firms trading within their own structures across national boundaries'.[37] Tony Abbott, Coalition prime minister, 2013–5, expressed concern that businesses could 'take advantage of different countries' tax regimes . . . generating profits to chase tax opportunities rather than market ones'.[38] His solution was for the G20 to tackle this.

John Howard, Coalition prime minister (1996–2007) and the longest serving of the period, was the only prime minister of the five not to propose cooperation between states as part of a strategy to address the threats of economic globalisation. Howard saw globalisation as the 'most potent economic force in the world

32 Kevin Rudd, 'Hard Heads, Soft Hearts: A Future Reform Agenda for the New Australian Government, Progressive Governance Conference, London', *PM Transcripts* (Speech, 4 April 2008) <pmtranscripts.pmc.gov.au>.
33 Julia Gillard, 'Address to the Parliament of New Zealand', *PM Transcripts* (Speech, 16 February 2011) <pmtranscripts.pmc.gov.au>.
34 Malcolm Turnbull, 'Doorstop, Hamburg, Germany', *PM Transcripts* (7 July 2017) <pmtranscripts.pmc.gov.au>.
35 Malcolm Turnbull, 'Press Statement at the Indian Ocean Rim Association Leaders' Summit Jakarta, Indonesia', *PM Transcripts* (7 March 2017) <pmtranscripts.pmc.gov.au>.
36 Malcolm Turnbull, 'Press Statement at the Indian Ocean Rim Association Leaders' Summit Jakarta, Indonesia', *PM Transcripts* (7 March 2017) <pmtranscripts.pmc.gov.au>.
37 Keating, 'World Conference' (n 17).
38 Tony Abbott, 'Address to the World Economic Forum, Davos, Switzerland', *PM Transcripts* (Speech, 23 January 2014) <pmtranscripts.pmc.gov.au>.

today'[39] and stated that 'globalisation, technological change and the communications revolution'[40] were the 'driving forces of change and opportunity'.[41]

In Howard's earliest mention of globalisation, in a report to Parliament on his APEC meeting,[42] he said his government 'would take account of what other governments were doing', but that his government believed that the liberalisation of trade that was economic globalisation would benefit the economy.[43] He characterised the government's role in pursuing this liberalisation of trade as explaining the benefits to the electorate, not protecting it from an adverse impact.[44] His earliest comments outside the Parliament show him doing this. In radio interviews and speeches at this time he lamented that globalisation had brought an increased 'dissolution of boundaries between nations'.[45] He noted that 'we can't reverse the globalisation of the economy. We can't tell companies who are answerable to their shareholders that they've got to invest here and there'.[46] His solution was not international cooperation but to 'try and work with them [the corporations] and we've also got to remind them of their social obligations'.[47] Howard's solution seemed to be to rely on the good nature of the multinationals and on government-to-business dealmaking with the multinational companies, which he recognised as new powerful economic players. He welcomed the business community's involvement in APEC as 'insurance that APEC would focus on business's needs'.[48] Howard's comments about globalisation continued across his time in office to emphasise the importance of competition, of individual nations taking

39 Commonwealth, *Parliamentary Debates*, House of Representatives, 11 December 1996, 7514 (John Howard).
40 Commonwealth, *Parliamentary Debates*, House of Representatives, 27 February 1997, 1578 (John Howard).
41 Commonwealth, *Parliamentary Debates*, House of Representatives, 27 February 1997, 1578 (John Howard).
42 APEC is the Asia-Pacific Economic Cooperation forum, which describes itself as 'a regional economic forum established in 1989 to leverage the growing interdependence of the Asia-Pacific. APEC's 21 members aim to create greater prosperity for the people of the region by promoting balanced, inclusive, sustainable, innovative and secure growth and by accelerating regional economic integration'. APEC, 'What Is Asia-Pacific Economic Cooperation?' (Web Page, September 2021) <www.apec.org/about-us/about-apec>.
43 Commonwealth, *Parliamentary Debates*, House of Representatives, 11 December 1996, 7514 (John Howard).
44 Commonwealth, *Parliamentary Debates*, House of Representatives, 11 December 1996, 7514 (John Howard). However see the discussion of globalisation and inequality in Chapter 3 Sections II B, D and III A.
45 Howard, 'Radio Interview Keith Conlon' (n 16).
46 John Howard, 'Radio Interview with John Stanley 2UE', *PM Transcripts* (Radio interview, 13 May 1997) <pmtranscripts.pmc.gov.au>.
47 John Howard, 'Radio Interview with John Stanley 2UE', *PM Transcripts* (Radio interview, 13 May 1997) <pmtranscripts.pmc.gov.au>.
48 Commonwealth, *Parliamentary Debates*, House of Representatives, 11 December 1996, 7514 (John Howard).

advantage of globalisation and selling its benefits.[49] Australia's role in building international cooperation or as an international leader protecting developing nations, as Albanese had suggested, is largely missing.

Howard, more explicitly than other prime ministers of the period, characterised globalisation as irreversible and the state as powerless against multinational corporations.[50] As Raymond Grew suggests, an acceptance that globalisation is inevitable overlooks the agency of states.[51] In this way Howard's characterisation is a failure to recognise, or perhaps a failure to acknowledge, the agency of governments who embraced the economic gains that globalisation promised.[52] What can be seen is a prioritising of economic gain and an embrace of the market over the Westphalian views of sovereignty that he later expressed in the context of migration.[53]

B A Security Threat

After the 2001 terrorist attack known as 9/11, terrorism and security issues were also characterised as a threat from globalisation. Howard lamented that beyond the economic benefits of globalisation was the threat of terrorism: 'One of the curses of globalisation is that it means that borders are inevitably more porous, communications are more rapid and the capacity of terrorists' was enhanced.[54] By 2007 Howard said that 'globalisation means a range and number of events affecting our security and prosperity will continue to grow'.[55] His response to this security threat, apparent in the introduction of a range of national security measures, is beyond the scope of this book. Howard's successor Rudd, while necessarily addressing the Global Financial Crisis of 2008, did not retreat from economic globalisation.[56] At the same time Rudd also saw globalisation as a security issue to be addressed, suggesting a continuation of Howard's strategy (although not attributed to him) of partnership within Australia between industry, state governments and the community.[57]

49 John Howard, 'Address to the Business Luncheon, Diwan-I-Am Room, New Delhi', *PM Transcripts* (Speech, 6 March 2006) <pmtranscripts.pmc.gov.au>.
50 Howard, 'Radio Interview Keith Conlon' (n 16); Howard, 'Radio Interview with John Stanley' (n 46).
51 Grew (n 10) 278; See also Chapter 3 Section II A.
52 A reading of Ino Rossi suggests that Australia, with other ideologically if not geographically Global North nations, has driven globalisation as an economic imperialism and gained from it. See Rossi (n 10) 435.
53 Discussed in Chapter 5.
54 John Howard, 'Address at the Asia Society Luncheon, Peninsula Hotel, Manila', *PM Transcripts* (Speech, 15 July 2003) <pmtranscripts.pmc.gov.au>.
55 John Howard, 'Address to the Millennium Forum Four Seasons Hotel, Sydney', *PM Transcripts* (Speech, 20 August 2007) <pmtranscripts.pmc.gov.au>.
56 Rudd, 'Hard Heads' (n 32).
57 Kevin Rudd, 'The First National Security Statement to the Parliament', *PM Transcripts* (Speech, 4 December 2008) <pmtranscripts.pmc.gov.au>.

C *Globalisation After COVID-19: The Threat to Sovereignty of 'Hyper-globalisation'*[58]

It is notable that, faced with the opportunity and threats identified in globalisation, understood as economic globalisation, the protection of state sovereignty was not identified as a central issue by five of the period's prime ministers. This absence is most pronounced in Prime Minister Howard's statement, quoted previously, that the government had no power to direct multinational companies where to invest and had to rely on their sense of duty to the community.[59] The economic opportunity was the priority. In summary, before the COVID-19 pandemic economic competitiveness, rather than cooperation, was emphasised as the solution to any economic threat from globalisation. The security threat was identified by Howard as 'porous borders', which was not contradicted by his successors. These twin understandings had implications for migration law.

The exception to this failure to represent globalisation as a threat to sovereignty is the response to the COVID-19 pandemic. Before the COVID-19 pandemic impacted Australia Scott Morrison, Coalition prime minister (2018–22) and the sixth and last prime minister of the period, mentioned globalisation only as economic globalisation, in line with his predecessors. He listed globalisation as a 'headwind' along with 'trade tensions, geo-political instability, digital disruption and climate change'.[60] He claimed that his government had already ensured that Australia had reduced income inequality 'in the context of globalisation'.[61] He stated: 'Challenges are not new, even existential ones. Their existence is no cause for crisis settings'.[62] However, after the pandemic globalisation was represented as an existential threat and by 2022 Morrison characterised 'hyper-globalisation' as a threat to 'sovereign national interest'.[63]

In an address to parliament in 2020 when the pandemic had entered Australia, its rapid spread enabled by globalisation phenomena,[64] Morri-

58 Scott Morrison, 'A Modern Manufacturing Strategy for Australia, National Press Club', *ACT* (Speech, 1 October 2020). Note Morrison also used the term 'hyper-globalisation' in Scott Morrison, 'Transcript Address and Q&A, State of the World Virtual Address World Economic Forum: The Davos Agenda', *PM Transcripts* (Speech, 21 January 2022) <pmtranscripts.pmc.gov.au>.

59 Howard, 'Radio Interview with John Stanley' (n 46).

60 Scott Morrison, 'Business Council of Australia Annual Dinner, Sydney', *PM Transcripts* (Speech, 21 November 2019) <pmtranscripts.pmc.gov.au>.

61 Scott Morrison, 'Business Council of Australia Annual Dinner, Sydney', *PM Transcripts* (Speech, 21 November 2019) <pmtranscripts.pmc.gov.au>.

62 Scott Morrison, 'Business Council of Australia Annual Dinner, Sydney', *PM Transcripts* (Speech, 21 November 2019) <pmtranscripts.pmc.gov.au>.

63 Morrison, 'A Modern Manufacturing' (n 58).

64 One of these phenomena is increased population mobility. For a summary of the drivers of mobility see Graeme Hugo, 'Globalization and Changes in Australian International Migration' (2006) 23(2) *Journal of Population Research* 107, 109–10.

son focussed his address on the risk to national sovereignty and protecting national sovereignty in 'a fight we will win'.[65] That fight was not only against a virus but against 'foreign interests' that might prey on vulnerable Australian businesses.[66] Morrison defined sovereignty as 'our capacity and freedom to live our lives as we choose in a free, open and democratic society', 'having a vibrant market economy that underpins our standard of living that gives all Australians the opportunity to fulfil their potential, to have a go and to get a go', the 'quality of life we afford Australians, with world class health, education, disability, aged care, and a social safety net that guarantees the essentials that Australians rely on' and 'what we believe as Australians, what we value, and hold most dear, our principles, our way of doing things'.[67]

Morrison's speech to Parliament had two important omissions. Firstly, he did not mention international cooperation, a key strategy according to the World Economic Forum and missing in the response in Parliament to the COVID-19 pandemic, for addressing global crises.[68] While his definition of the sovereignty he was protecting alludes to beliefs, values, principles and strategies, these are not defined except by the actions the speech announced. His focus was the competitive position of Australia, not cooperation against a global challenge. His language was that of war: 'we are up to the fight. We will pay the price'.[69]

Secondly he failed to mention those in the Australian community who might not be embraced by the social 'social safety net that guarantees the essentials that Australians rely on'.[70] His strategies were to defend Australian assets and businesses through scrutiny of foreign investment and economic support.[71] The only mention of temporary visa holders was a reference to the agricultural workers brought from the Pacific Islands to work in rural Australia. These workers were now to be allowed to work in Australia for up to one extra year. There are parallels of this policy with the debate on the phasing out of Pacific Islander labour in 1901.[72] Just as in 1901, workers were allowed to stay temporarily for the sake of an industry.

65 Commonwealth, *Parliamentary Debates*, House of Representatives, 8 April 2020, 2909 (Scott Morrison).
66 Commonwealth, *Parliamentary Debates*, House of Representatives, 8 April 2020, 2909 (Scott Morrison) 2912.
67 Commonwealth, *Parliamentary Debates*, House of Representatives, 8 April 2020, 2909 (Scott Morrison) 2909.
68 World Economic Forum, *The Global Risks Report 2021* (Report, 19 January 2021) 72–81.
69 Commonwealth, *Parliamentary Debates*, House of Representatives, 8 April 2020, 2912 (Scott Morrison).
70 Commonwealth, *Parliamentary Debates*, House of Representatives, 8 April 2020, 2912 (Scott Morrison) 2909.
71 Commonwealth, *Parliamentary Debates*, House of Representatives, 8 April 2020, 2912 (Scott Morrison) 2911.
72 See Chapter 4 on the *Pacific Island Labourers Act 1901*.

Morrison also failed to mention the 706,242 international students enrolled in Australia at that time as full fee-paying consumers of the fourth largest export industry.[73] This absence was noted by opposition speakers, but they framed their criticism as a lack of support for the industry and its workers or the poor treatment of the student customer.[74] Only the opposition spokesperson for education and one other noted the impact on international student welfare and urged the government to provide welfare support.[75]

It is significant that Morrison moved quickly to support agriculture, which ranks relatively low among export industries and imports low-skilled manual labour,[76] but did nothing to support the fourth largest export industry whose consumers at that time were told to 'go home'.[77] An economic rationale is not credible.[78]

Outside the Parliament in further responses to the pandemic Morrison continued to use the language of sovereignty, heightening the gravity of his concerns. He stated the need to secure 'sovereign capability in areas of national interest' against the 'hyper-globalisation' that had left the Australian economy vulnerable.[79] In a final shift Morrison took an historical approach to globalisation that aligned with Taesuh Cha and Grew.[80] In the same way as Cha, who compares the global hegemony of the US with the imperial dominance of Britain in a previous age,[81] Morrison emphasised a view of globalisation through a historical lens. He focussed on shifts in power and dominant value systems, not, as previously, economic opportunity. In a 2022

73 Australian Trade and Investment Commission, 'Summaries and News' (Web Page) <www.austrade.gov.au/australian/education/education-data/current-data/summaries-and-news>. For a discussion of the negative impact of the Australian Government's refusal to extend adequate COVID-19 support measures to international students see Oanh (Olena) Thi Kim Nguyen and Varsha Devi Balakrishnan, 'International Students in Australia – During and After COVID-19' (2020) 39(7) *Higher Education Research & Development* 1372; J Gibson and A Moran, 'As Coronavirus Spreads, "It's Time to Go Home" Scott Morrison Tells Visitors and International Students', *ABC News* (online, 4 April 2020) <www.abc.net.au/news/2020-04-03/coronavirus-pm-tells-international-students-time-to-go-to-home/12119568>.

74 Commonwealth, *Parliamentary Debates*, Senate, 14 May 2020, 3507 (Giles); Commonwealth, *Parliamentary Debates*, Senate, 10 June 2020, 3666 (Hill); Commonwealth, *Parliamentary Debates*, Senate, 10 June 2020, 3773 (Coker).

75 Commonwealth, *Parliamentary Debates*, House of Representatives, 8 April 2020, 2948 (Tanya Plibersek); Commonwealth, *Parliamentary Debates*, House of Representatives 10 June 2020, 3805 (Milton Dick).

76 Department for Foreign Affairs and Trade, 'Trade and Investment at a Glance' (Web Page, 2020) <www.dfat.gov.au/publications/trade-and-investment/trade-and-investment-glance-2020>.

77 Gibson and Moran (n 73).

78 The economic and other objectives of the international student visa will be taken up in Section IV.

79 Morrison, 'A Modern Manufacturing' (n 58).

80 See Chapter 3 Section II A.

81 Cha (n 10) 71. See also Chapter 2 Section II A.

speech he positioned globalisation as a product of the global hegemony of Western liberal democracies.[82] He characterised the contemporary globalisation of the world economy (which since the pandemic he had termed 'hyper-globalisation'), as a product of the 'great power at the centre of our global systems' which he did not name but, from the juxtaposition of this with his mention of Western liberal democracies,[83] it can be inferred that he meant the United States, acting as the great power or supported by other liberal democracies. Obliquely referencing Russia and China, he warned that the 'nature of the great power at the centre of our global systems matters decisively – together with their animating ideas and ideals' and that this is under threat.[84] He stated bluntly: 'global economics is downstream from global politics'.[85] His statement is significant to this discussion of globalisation because, unlike Howard who expressed the view that globalisation was inevitable,[86] Morrison identified a state or states as having agency in globalisation, aligning with Grew's and Cha's approaches.[87] Certain states created the globalised economy and benefit from it. The challenge Morrison identified to sovereignty is not from globalisation but to globalisation under a change in global power balances.

D *Globalisation and the Movement of People*

Within the broad policy framework established by their prime ministers, which addressed globalisation as economic globalisation, as discussed previously, immigration ministers also embraced the economic opportunity of economic globalisation. As early as 1995 Prime Minister Keating had recognised that one of the phenomena of globalisation was the increased movement of people. Stating that 'the movement of people and information rather than goods is the fastest growing segment of world trade',[88] he conceptualised these migrants in the language of the market as an economic product.[89] Immigration ministers since 2000, the beginning of the period being examined, did the same. They positioned Australia as a competitor for skills in a

82 Scott Morrison, 'Virtual Address, AFR Business Summit' (Speech, 8 March 2022).
83 Scott Morrison, 'Virtual Address, AFR Business Summit' (Speech, 8 March 2022).
84 Scott Morrison, 'Virtual Address, AFR Business Summit' (Speech, 8 March 2022).
85 Scott Morrison, 'Virtual Address, AFR Business Summit' (Speech, 8 March 2022).
86 See Howard, 'Radio Interview with John Stanley' (n 46).
87 See Chapter 3 Section II A. Also for a discussion of how the contemporary legal and political field can be understood in terms of imperialism see James Tully, 'On Law, Democracy and Imperialism', in Emilios Christodoulidis and Stephen Tierney (eds), *Public Law and Politics* (Ashgate, 2008) 69. See also Gavin Anderson's response to Tully in Gavin W Anderson, 'Imperialism and Constitutionalism', in Emilios Christodoulidis and Stephen Tierney (eds), *Public Law and Politics* (Ashgate, 2008) 129.
88 Keating, 'World Conference' (n 17) 2.
89 See Sassen (n 12) and Brown (n 12) on the conceptualisation of people in market terms.

global market.[90] Demonstrating the government's optimism, Philip Ruddock, the Minister for Immigration and Multicultural Affairs (1996–2003) in the Howard Coalition government, declared that globalisation signalled a different world.[91] He positioned his skilled migration program in the international market for mobile young skilled workers with good English skills.[92] The dramatic rebalancing of the composition of the migration program over the two decades following demonstrates the significance of this response: people with skills were the new commodity of trade in the new world. In 1999/2000 the ratio of family to skilled migration was .96, 32,000 to 33,350. The number and difference grew. By 2009/10 it was .56, 60,354 to 107,686.[93] Planned for 2019/20 was 47,732 to 108,682, a ratio of .44 to 1.[94] This is a refocussing over the two decades from reuniting family members and welcoming new citizens to achieving economic outcomes. Migrants were now seen as economic units, not future citizens.

Migrants as an economic opportunity remained a priority but by 2018 David Coleman, Minister for Immigration, Citizenship and Multicultural Affairs (2018–9) in the Morrison Coalition government, also linked his migration decision-making about this economic opportunity to a sovereign right to make choices. Upon his appointment Coleman characterised his migration responsibilities in two ways. Firstly, he declared Australia's sovereignty: 'It is our immigration programme, and it must reflect our choices'.[95] Within a year he built on this theme of control. In 2019 he summarised his immigration policy as 'sovereign, focussed and fair'.[96]

Secondly, he declared that this sovereign power would be used exclusively for economic benefit: 'I can tell you today that the choices I make

90 For a discussion of the primacy of skills over nationality as a migration selection criteria in this market see Marion Panizzon, 'Migration and Trade: Prospects for Bilateralism in the Face of Skill-Selective Mobility Laws' (2011) 12 *Melbourne Journal of International Law* 95.

91 Philip Ruddock, 'Australian Immigration: Grasping the New Reality' (Speech, Nation Skilling: Migration Labour and the Law Symposium, 23 November 2000).

92 Philip Ruddock, 'Australian Immigration: Grasping the New Reality' (Speech, Nation Skilling: Migration Labour and the Law Symposium, 23 November 2000). The issue of the English language and testing for proficiency has been prominent since 1901. See Chapter 4 Section II and Chapter 7 Sections II and V. See also Laurie Berg, '"Mate Speak English, You're in Australia Now": English Language Requirements in Skilled Migration' (2011) 36(2) *Alternative Law Journal* 110; Dominic Npoanlari Dagbanja, 'The Invisible Border Wall in Australia' (2019) 23(2) *UCLA Journal of International and Foreign Affairs* 221. Note too that in 2018 the Australian government reported more than three hundred languages were spoken in Australia. This does not count Indigenous languages. See Treasury and Department of Home Affairs, *Shaping a Nation* (Report, 16 April 2018).

93 Spinks (n 2).

94 Department of Home Affairs (n 2).

95 David Coleman, 'Address to the Sydney Institute' (Speech, Sydney Institute, 13 August 2019).

96 David Coleman, 'Address to the Sydney Institute' (Speech, Sydney Institute, 13 August 2019).

about our immigration programme will have a sharp focus on the economic benefits to Australia'.[97] To achieve this economic benefit he stated that migrants were most beneficial to the economy if they were: highly skilled, employer-sponsored, young so that they have many years ahead in the workforce, able to speak English and placed in regional areas. In summary these would be migrants who could be immediately economically productive in areas of high need. He announced that 'skilled migration is the lynchpin of our approach, accounting for close to 70% of the intake'.[98]

However, despite Coleman's bold statements characterising migrants as economic units and justifying policy choices as a sovereign right, the examination of the following legislative processes shows that economic benefit was balanced against other concerns. This reflects the way the Parliament understood the aspect of globalisation that had increased the movement of people as a security threat as well as an economic threat and opportunity. The economic goals of migration were tempered in a portfolio where the senior minister, Peter Dutton, Minister for Home Affairs (2017–21) in the Turnbull and Morrison Coalition governments, had declared the priority was security. The portfolio's purpose was to ensure 'a nationally consistent approach to terrorism, cyber security, organised and transnational crime, while securing the integrity of Australia's migration programmes and protecting our borders by managing the movement of people and goods'.[99] Dutton's statement declares the priority: the prevention of the migration program being misused, intentionally or negligently, for any purpose other than intended and to protect the border, that is the physical entry point to Australian territory. These priorities of maintaining control of the migration program and of safety and security were translated into the mission for the new department: 'work together with the trust of our partners and community to keep Australia safe and secure and support a cohesive and united Australia open for global engagement'.[100] Coleman's comments made it clear that 'open' meant only open for business.

This tension between priorities in migration policy is not new. As detailed in the previous chapter, parliamentary debate on migration has consistently featured an economic theme in competition for priority with other concerns. In 1901 and 1958 the concern was about race, expressed explicitly in parliamentary debate.[101] Later this concern was expressed in coded terms such as social cohesion.[102] Dutton's statement suggests the balancing concern in

97 David Coleman, 'Address to the Sydney Institute' (Speech, Sydney Institute, 13 August 2019).

98 David Coleman, 'Address to the Sydney Institute' (Speech, Sydney Institute, 13 August 2019).

99 Peter Dutton, 'A New Era of National Security' (Media Release, Department of Home Affairs, 20 December 2017).

100 Department of Home Affairs, *Annual Report 2018/19* (Report, 2019).

101 See, e.g., Commonwealth, *Parliamentary Debates*, House of Representatives, 5 June 1901, 688 (Langdon Bonython).

102 See, e.g., Commonwealth, Parliamentary Debates, House of Representatives, 7 June 1978, 3155 (Michael Mackellar). After the official ending of the White Australia policy and a

these recent two decades (2000–20) has been safety and security as well as social cohesion.[103] How these competing priorities, economic opportunity and migration control, the same competing issues that concerned the first Parliament,[104] played out in the making of the amendments to the international student visa is examined shortly.

IV 'Overseas Students'[105]: Importing Customers

The international student industry which the student visa legislation enables is used as an example of the tension between economic gain offered by globalisation and migration control because of its unique combination of factors. International students have become a multibillion-dollar industry eclipsing traditional exports[106] and the development of this export industry has been largely concentrated in the 21st century.[107] In addition, it is an export industry that relies on immigration not, primarily, to secure skilled workers, although this has been significant,[108] but to import consumers of a legislatively narrowly defined product. The impact of COVID-19 pandemic border closures on the education sector illustrates this dependence on importing consumers.[109] The final reason to use this visa as an example is because, unlike migration to attract labour which has been an aspect of migration since 1901, importing students for economic benefit was new.

By 2000 Australia's relationship to overseas students had shifted from a diplomatic interest to an economic interest.[110] The aim of the Colombo Plan

change in government the Minister for Immigration announced a set of policy principles. Social cohesion was one of these principles. The term continued to be used to represent a reason to control migration.

103 Dutton (n 99).

104 See discussion in Chapter 4 Section II A.

105 Commonwealth, *Parliamentary Debates*, House of Representatives, 30 August 2000, 19613 (David Kemp).

106 David Coleman, 'Address to the Migration Institute of Australia National Conference, Sydney' (Speech, 19 October 2018). See also Eric Meadows, 'From Aid to Industry: A History of International Education in Australia', in Dorothy Davis and Bruce Mackintosh (eds), *Making a Difference: Australian International Education* (University of New South Wales Press, 2011) 50.

107 Spinks (n 2); Department of Home Affairs (n 2).

108 See, e.g., the analysis in Joanna Howe, Sara Charlesworth and Deborah Brennan, 'Migration Pathways for Frontline Care Workers in Australia and New Zealand: Front Doors, Side Doors, Back Doors and Trapdoors' (2019) 42(1) *UNSW Law Journal* 211.

109 Victoria University estimates the Australian university sector could lose up to $19 billion dollars due to the impact of COVID-19. Victoria University, 'University Sector Faces Losing Up to $19 Billion Due to COVID-19' (Web Page, 17 April 2020) <www.vu.edu.au/mitchell-institute/tertiary-education/university-sector-faces-losing-up-to-19-billion-due-to-covid-19>. See discussion of Scott Morrison's COVID-19 response in Section III C.

110 Markus, Jupp and McDonald (n 2).

of 1950 was 'to have the wide-reaching – if ambiguous – goal of neutralising anti-Western sentiment directed towards Australia'.[111] The Colombo Plan, which included bringing Asian students to study in Australia, was conceived as 'an instrument of Australian foreign policy in the fight against communism'.[112] One impact of the Colombo Plan was skills enhancement for the origin countries of students.[113] In contrast, by 2000, overseas students had become part of a significant export industry in which Australia was competing for students on a global scale. International students were the consumers in an important new export industry market.[114]

In a speech in 2000 made just three days after the introduction of a package of amendments designed to reform the overseas student sector, Ruddock signalled his enthusiasm for international students. He made a link between international students and assisting the skill shortages in Australia's labour market of aging workers.[115] Ruddock boasted that '50% of all skilled applicants [for skilled migrant visas] had Australian qualifications'.[116] He stated that it was in the national interest to compete vigorously in the new global marketplace for mobile, young, skilled migrants with good English language skills.

As well as in Australia characterising overseas students as consumers of an export product accelerated in Canada, the United Kingdom and the United States.[117]

111 Daniel Oakman, *Facing Asia: A History of the Colombo Plan* (ANU E-Press, 2010) 60.
112 Daniel Oakman, *Facing Asia: A History of the Colombo Plan* (ANU E-Press, 2010) 2.
113 Markus, Jupp and McDonald (n 2).
114 This chapter's focus is the parliamentary debate, the legislation and judicial comment. Beyond the scope of this analysis is the human cost to the countries of origin. See Markus, Jupp and McDonald (n 2) 13. Also beyond its scope is the human cost to students of the policy shifts that the immigration minister's broad discretionary power enables without legislative amendment. These human costs are well detailed by researchers such as Joanna Howe and others. See Joanna Howe, Andrew Stewart and Rosemary Owens, 'Temporary Migrant Labour and Unpaid Work in Australia' (2018) 40 *Sydney Law Review* 183; Marianne Dickie, Dorota Gozdecka and Sudrishti Reich (eds), *Unintended Consequences: The Impact of Migration Law and Policy* (ANU Press, 2016); Alexander Reilly, 'The Ethics of Seasonal Labour Migration' (2011) 20(1) *Griffith Law Review* 127; Yao-Tai Li and Katherine Whitworth, 'When the State Becomes Part of the Exploitation: Migrants' Agency within the Institutional Constraints in Australia' (2016) 54(6) *International Migration* 138.
115 Philip Ruddock, 'Australian Immigration: Grasping the New Reality' (Speech, Nation Skilling: Migration Labour and the Law Symposium, Sydney, 23 November 2000).
116 Philip Ruddock, 'Australian Immigration: Grasping the New Reality' (Speech, Nation Skilling: Migration Labour and the Law Symposium, Sydney, 23 November 2000).
117 Sandra Schinnerl and Antje Ellermann, 'The Education-Immigration Nexus: Situating Canadian Higher Education as Institutions of Immigrant Recruitment' (2003) 24(3) *Journal of International Migration and Integration* 5599, 5601; Anita Gopal, 'Visa and Immigration Trends: A Comparative Examination of International Student Mobility in Canada, Australia, the United Kingdom, and the United States' (2016) 4(3) *Strategic Enrolment Management Quarterly* 130.

In 2018 Coleman, immigration minister, highlighted the economic value to Australia of the international student market:

> In 2017, Education Services generated $30 billion in export revenue for Australia. It is our third largest export industry. To put that into perspective, we generated four times as much revenue from education as we did from beef, at $7 billion, and five times as much as we did from wheat, at $6 billion.
>
> International students in Australia generate substantial economic benefits through tuition fees, accommodation and living expenses and expenditure on goods and services. Visits by family and friends of international students also contribute to our tourism, hospitality and retail sectors, both in metropolitan and regional Australia.[118]

The immigration minister's contribution to this growing education export industry is to administer and reform the legal basis for entry of noncitizens to support Australia's competitive position. The levers at a minister's disposal to create this legal basis are legislation, regulations and in 2000 a recently strengthened capacity for the minister to circumvent the deportation law by using the character test to deport even long-term residents.[119] The themes and strategies of the legislative process for amending this consumer visa are examined shortly.

A *Migration Legislation Amendment (Overseas Students) Act 2000*

The *Migration Legislation Amendment (Overseas Students) Act 2000* was the first of the amendments made to the *Migration Act 1958* concerning students since 1998 and was led in Parliament by David Kemp, Minister for Schools, Vocational Education and Training (1996–2001) in the Howard Coalition government. The expectation raised by Ruddock's enthusiasm in his speech in 2000 was that this amendment would be designed to promote

118 David Coleman, 'Address to the Sydney Institute' (Speech, Sydney Institute, 13 August 2019).

119 *Migration Act 1958* (Cth) ss 499, 501. See also discussion in Chapter 8 Section V; Michelle Foster, 'An "Alien" by the Barest of Threads: The Legality of the Deportation of Long Term Residents from Australia' (2009) 33 *Melbourne University Law Review* 483, 484–5; Samuel C Duckett White, 'God-Like Powers: The Character Test and Unfettered Ministerial Discretion' (2020) 41 *Adelaide Law Review* 1; Rights Advocacy Project, *Playing God: The Immigration Minister's Unrestrained Power* (Report, Liberty Victoria, 2017). Also see cases concerning long-term residents' deportation under the character test: *Minister for Immigration and Multicultural and Indigenous Affairs v Nystrom* (2006) 228 CLR 566, 572; *Falzon v Minister for Immigration and Border Protection* (2018) HCA 2, [1]; *Caric v Minister for Immigration and Border Protection* (2017) FCA 1391, [19], [21].

Australia as a destination for study.[120] It was, but as the upcoming discussion demonstrates, students were welcome only under strict conditions which created a status of illegality for those who did not comply.

The Migration Legislation Amendment (Overseas Students) Bill 2000 (Overseas Student Migration Amendment 2000) legislation was introduced as part of a set of measures to improve the regulation of the education and training export industry.[121] These measures were set out in the Education Services for Overseas Students (or ESOS) Bill and other consequential ESOS Bills.[122] The second reading speech for the ESOS Bill that introduced this package of measures and the debate and commentary from across the Parliament emphasised the economic importance of the 'education and training export industry' as a rapidly growing $3.7 billion industry comparable in importance to Australia's traditional exports of wool and wheat.[123] The very rapid growth of the industry was noted and used as a rationale for reforming regulation to protect students' prepaid course fees in cases of provider insolvency and to rid the industry of 'unscrupulous providers'.[124]

The Overseas Student Migration Amendment 2000 was part of this education industry package. That package had three stated objectives: firstly, to ensure that overseas students are treated with equity and fairness; secondly to provide a positive basis for promoting Australia's international reputation as a provider of reliable, high-quality education and training; and thirdly to strengthen the integrity of the student visa program.[125]

The emphasis in the legislation was on the third objective of strengthening integrity. So concerned was the government to admit only those they considered genuine students that the migration amendment contained three enhanced compliance measures that carried the threat of visa cancellation, migration detention and criminal sanctions and only one measure directly concerned with economic outcomes. The objective of equity and fairness received negligible discussion or elaboration in debate.

120 Phillip Ruddock, 'Australian Immigration: Grasping the New Reality' (Speech, Nation Skilling: Migration Labour and the Law Symposium Sydney, 23 November 2000).

121 Commonwealth, *Parliamentary Debates*, House of Representatives, 30 August 2000, 19609 (David Kemp).

122 Education Services for Overseas Students Bill 2000; Education Services for Overseas Students (Consequential and Transitional) Bill 2000; Education Services for Overseas Students (Registration Charges) Amendment Bill 2000; Education Services for Overseas Students (Assurance Fund Contributions) Bill 2000.

123 Commonwealth, *Parliamentary Debates*, House of Representatives, 30 August 2000, 19609 (David Kemp).

124 Commonwealth, *Parliamentary Debates*, House of Representatives, 30 August 2000, 19609 (David Kemp). See Mary Crock and Laura Berg's discussion of this legislation as a response to past providers' collapse in Mary Crock and Laura Berg, *Immigration, Refugees and Forced Migration* (Federation Press, 2011) 315.

125 Explanatory Memorandum, Migration Legislation Amendment (Overseas Students) Bill 2000 (Cth) 2.

The first compliance measure in the Overseas Student Migration Amendment 2000 complemented the introduction in the ESOS Bill of a measure requiring the education provider to send notices of visa breaches.[126] The legislation allowed automatic cancellation of a student's visa if the student failed to attend a meeting and explain the breach to an officer within twenty-eight days of the notice being sent.[127] Attendance and explanation did not guarantee that the student would avoid visa cancellation, just that the automatic cancellation process, under the new amendment, was halted.[128] It was still available to the immigration minister to cancel the visa under other provisions in the *Migration Act 1958* such as s 116. It was also possible for the immigration minister to revoke a cancellation if an application was made in a time frame that was effectively less than a week for those in immigration detention as a consequence of the cancellation.[129] In addition the legislation explicitly ruled out of consideration an explanation from the student that the notice was not received: 'The Minister must not revoke the cancellation on the ground that the non-citizen was unaware of the notice or the effect of section 137J'.[130] Any misunderstanding by the student was put beyond the immigration minister's discretion. The immigration minister and his department were shielded from the burden of a duty to examine an individual student's set of unfortunate circumstances that could have led to not receiving or overlooking an item of mail. The Federal Court was also excluded from judicially reviewing this automatic cancellation process as demonstrated in the judgment in *Kumar v Minister for Immigration and Citizenship*.[131] In that case the court found that automatic cancellation was not an administrative decision and therefore the court had no jurisdiction.[132]

Despite the changes that reduced the immigration minister's responsibilities and reduced the avenues of appeal for international students, the immigration minister's long-established broad discretion was preserved.[133] Section 137N(1) allowed the immigration minister, on the basis of 'public interest', to take the initiative to revoke a cancellation, but s 137N(4) ensured they had a duty to act. Public interest was not defined in the legislation.

The Parliament did not debate the detail or implications of this first compliance measure. It was explained as necessary streamlining to lighten the

126 Education Services for Overseas Students Bill 2000 s 20; Commonwealth, *Parliamentary Debates*, House of Representatives 30 August 2000, 19610 (David Kemp).

127 Explanatory Memorandum, Migration Legislation Amendment (Overseas Students) Bill 2000 (Cth) 7. The Bill inserted sections 137J–137P.

128 Explanatory Memorandum, Migration Legislation Amendment (Overseas Students) Bill 2000 (Cth) 7. The Bill inserted sections 137J–137P [9] 7.

129 *Migration Legislation Amendment (Overseas Students) Act 2000* (Cth) s 137K(3).

130 *Migration Legislation Amendment (Overseas Students) Act 2000* (Cth) s 137L (2).

131 (2008) 221 FLR 361, 365 [26].

132 (2008) 221 FLR 361, 365 [26]. See also *Sahi v Minister for Immigration and Citizenship* (2012) 271 (FLR) 54, 63–4.

133 See Chapter 4.

administrative burden on government. Minister Kemp said his department 'receives hundreds of non-compliance notices from education providers each month. Effective management of these notices is an enormous task and must be streamlined'.[134] The burden of this process was shifted to the individual overseas student to comply or risk severe consequences. The cancellation of a student's visa resulted in the student becoming an illegal noncitizen, that is a noncitizen without a visa, and would oblige an immigration department 'officer' to place them in immigration detention.[135]

The second compliance measure increased the investigative power of these officers to ensure that education providers were monitoring student compliance as required.[136] The amendment gave officers power to 'require the production of, or to search for and inspect, and in some cases seize, relevant records of overseas students held by education providers'.[137] The maintenance of these records by providers, records which included current student addresses and attendance data, was now legislated. Education providers became legally obliged to report any deviation from compliance with visa conditions. So determined was the government to closely control student behaviour that criminal sanctions applied to offences such as failing to comply with a notice or giving false or misleading information or a document.[138] Penalties ranged from six to twelve months' imprisonment.[139] The legislation obliged education providers to provide documents or information even if it incriminated themselves or others.[140]

The third compliance measure was made in response to a Federal Court ruling that overturned a visa cancellation.[141] In the case of *Nong v Minister for Immigration and Multicultural Affairs* (6 November 2000) the immigration minister had argued that subsection (b) of condition 8202 'should be applied in a progressive fashion' rather than at the completion of a term or

134 Commonwealth, *Parliamentary Debates*, House of Representatives, 30 August 2000, 19613 (David Kemp).

135 *Migration Act 1958* (Cth) s 189.

136 Migration Legislation Amendment (Overseas Students) Bill 2000, Schedule 2 – Monitoring compliance with student visa conditions.

137 Explanatory Memorandum, Migration Legislation Amendment (Overseas Students) Bill 2000 (Cth) 2.

138 Migration Legislation Amendment (Overseas Students) Bill 2000 (Cth) ss 268BH, 268BI.

139 Migration Legislation Amendment (Overseas Students) Bill 2000 (Cth) ss 268BH, 268BI.

140 Migration Legislation Amendment (Overseas Students) Bill 2000 (Cth) ss 268BH, 268BI s 268BK.

141 Supplementary Explanatory Memorandum, Migration Legislation Amendment (Overseas Students) Bill 2000 (Cth) 1: 'The amendments are a direct Government response to the decision of the Federal Court in the recent case of *Nong v Minister for Immigration and Multicultural Affairs* (6 November 2000). In that decision, the Court set aside a decision of the Migration Review Tribunal to cancel a student visa on the basis that it had erred in the construction it gave to paragraph (b) of condition 8202'.

semester.[142] The court did not accept this.[143] The new measure 'established a general power in ss 116(1) of the *Migration Act 1958* for the Immigration Minister to cancel student visas where the holder is no longer a genuine or continuing student'.[144] This new power added ss 116(3): 'If the Minister may cancel a visa under subsection (1), the Minister must do so if there exist prescribed circumstances in which a visa must be cancelled'.[145] This closed a loophole in the legislation which had made it more in the student's interest to ignore a s 20 notice sent under the *ESOS Act* by a provider and be assessed by the Immigration Minister under s 116, than to comply.

The rationale for these measures was to provide a 'significant deterrent to overseas students considering breaching visa conditions'.[146] These visa conditions could include attendance of at least 80% per term and seeking the immigration minister's permission before changing courses.[147] The rationale was also to shift the cost of the growing administrative burden of the compliance regime from the government department responsible. This burden was now to be borne by education providers and students.[148] A notice of pending cancellation was to be sent directly to the student and a cancellation followed if the student failed to adequately respond.[149] In this way education providers were legally obliged and vulnerable to criminal sanctions if they failed to administer the legislated scrutiny of student visa holders' compliance.

The fourth measure was the only one not focussed on compliance. This measure increased the immigration minister's discretion to control who would be allowed to access other visa opportunities. This was not discussed in debate and simply explained by Kemp as a measure to 'increase flexibility'.[150] However, the context of this measure indicates that the government granted itself the flexibility to increase at a more granular level its control over which students would be allowed to remain in Australia and solve skill shortages,

142 *Nong v Minister for Immigration and Multicultural Affairs* (Federal Court, 6 November 2000) [46].
143 *Nong v Minister for Immigration and Multicultural Affairs* (Federal Court, 6 November 2000) [44].
144 *Nong v Minister for Immigration and Multicultural Affairs* (Federal Court, 6 November 2000) [44].
145 Supplementary Explanatory Memorandum, Migration Legislation Amendment (Overseas Students) Bill 2000 (Cth) 1.
146 Commonwealth, *Parliamentary Debates*, House of Representatives, 30 August 2000, 19613 (David Kemp).
147 *Migration Regulations 1994* (Cth) sch 8 reg 8202(3)(b), reg 8203.
148 Commonwealth, *Parliamentary Debates*, House of Representatives, 30 August 2000, 19613 (David Kemp).
149 Commonwealth, *Parliamentary Debates*, House of Representatives, 30 August 2000, 19613 (David Kemp).
150 Commonwealth, *Parliamentary Debates*, House of Representatives, 30 August 2000, 19613 (David Kemp).

that is, which students the immigration minister judged would be of most economic value or in other ways more desirable. The measure gave the immigration minister discretion to waive what was then the prohibition on students applying for other visas, apart from protection or bridging visas.[151] The new measure made it possible, for example, for students to apply for skilled migrant visas that could eventually lead to permanent residence.[152]

The focus in the debate was on compliance. The apparent tension between the economic and migration control objectives in this package of bills, on one hand to build a major export industry and on the other to closely and punitively control the presence and behaviour of students, was given little attention during the debate. The justification for a strengthened compliance regime was explained in several ways. A primary one was economic. Opposition speakers criticised the government's past performance on student visa compliance and claimed that the tightening of visa management was essential for the success of the industry. Speakers claimed that Australia's reputation as a study destination, and by implication its competitiveness in this market, was suffering overseas because of continued visa rorting.[153] In his second reading speech Minister Kemp had addressed this issue. He stated that there was a need to strengthen public confidence in the student visa program. He positioned the amendment as building on the 'successful measures' that had led to the numbers of cancellations of student visas growing significantly since 1998. One speaker summarised the objective of the package of bills was to strike the right balance that 'attracts bona fide overseas students without threatening the integrity of the Australian immigration program'.[154] The method to achieve this was to impose a range of visa conditions, the threat of visa cancellation and criminal sanctions for education providers.

While these economic justifications make a logical link between the objectives of attracting overseas students and reputational issues that tight control over student visa system would address, two other reasons were also presented in the debate by the government. The first was political. Kemp's reference to public confidence can be understood as both the domestic and international public. Margaret May, Liberal Member for McPherson, Queensland, was more forthright. She characterised students who breach visa conditions as 'deceptive fraudsters' whom the Australian community would expect to be deprived of a visa.[155]

151 Explanatory Memorandum, Migration Legislation Amendment (Overseas Students) Bill 2000 (Cth) 36.

152 Bob Birrell and Bronwen Perry, 'Immigration Policy Change and the International Student Industry' (2009) 17(2) *People and Place* 64, 65.

153 Commonwealth, *Parliamentary Debates*, House of Representatives, 9 November 2000, 22594 (Frank Mossfield).

154 Commonwealth, *Parliamentary Debates*, House of Representatives, 9 November 2000, 22568 (Ian Macfarlane).

155 Commonwealth, *Parliamentary Debates*, House of Representatives, 9 November 2000, 22575 (Margaret May).

The second reason proffered in debate for supporting the tight control of student compliance is not logically linked to a concrete benefit to the economy or to political success. It squarely addresses the tension between the economic and sovereignty themes historically central to Australia's migration law.[156] A government member said:

> the integrity of our immigration system is a cornerstone of Australia's society and, while we are keen to facilitate the expansion of the education industry, we as a government will not compromise our stand on ensuring that Australia's immigration standards are maintained.[157]

The burgeoning $3.7 billion industry was not to be given priority over a threat to 'the integrity of the Australian immigration program'.[158] While it would seem logical to control entry to ensure the appropriate students were admitted, this alludes to control for a different purposc.

The *ESOS Act* and *Overseas Students Amendment 2000* established a 'hybrid' status of international students in legislation: lucrative customer and potential illegal noncitizen. This hybrid status was itself justified on economic grounds.[159] The Parliament justified the tight control as the need to filter out the non-genuine student for the sake of market confidence. The obligations owed to students derive from their market value. However, when the student, through a breach of conditions, ceases to be a consumer they become an illegal noncitizen, liable to be deprived of liberty in immigration detention even while appealing the change in their status.[160]

B *Education Services for Overseas Students Legislation Amendment (2006 Measures No 2) Act 2006*

The further three amendments made to the overseas student visa legislation did not change the objective of the migration measures in this legislative package. Amendments in 2006 and 2007 completed the government's program of reform.

156 See Chapter 4 Section II.

157 Commonwealth, *Parliamentary Debates*, House of Representatives, 9 November 2000, 22568 (Ian Macfarlane).

158 Commonwealth, *Parliamentary Debates*, House of Representatives, 9 November 2000, 22568 (Ian Macfarlane).

159 Commonwealth, *Parliamentary Debates*, House of Representatives, 13 September 2006, 11 (Craig Emerson); Commonwealth, *Parliamentary Debates*, House of Representatives, 13 September 2006, 118 (Brendan O'Connor).

160 Segrave, Forbes-Mewett and Keel note that overseas students occupy a 'hybrid' status. They suggest they are both economically attractive temporary migrants but also noncitizens whose presence in Australia is highly controlled. Marie Segrave, Helen Forbes-Mewett and Chloe Keel, 'Migration Review Tribunal Decisions in Student Visa Cancellation Appeals: Sympathy, Hardship and Exceptional Circumstances' (2017) 29 *Current Issues in Criminal Justice* 1. See also Crock and Berg (n 123) 299–318.

By 2006 the *Education Services for Overseas Students Legislation Amendment (2006 Measures No 2) Act 2006* made one change to the *Migration Act 1958*. The amendment changed a note to s 137J(1), removing attendance and satisfactory performance, issues central to the functioning of the student visa automatic cancellation, as the criteria for an automatic breach. In the place of these criteria would be criteria 'prescribed by regulation'.[161] This removed debate about this key definition.[162] This was in response to education sector's concern that the 'full weight' of the migration law was being brought to bear too early in the compliance monitoring process.[163] The amendment was unopposed and the change to the *Migration Act 1958* largely ignored in the debate.

The international student was the international consumer and amendments were understood as contributing to market competitiveness. The parliamentary debate reveals the extent to which student migrants were seen exclusively as consumers and the amendments to the *Migration Act 1958* justified by purely economic arguments. For example, the purpose of 'extending consumer protection' was to safeguard the education product's reputation.[164] Australia 'needed to be branded as a quality destination'.[165] Martin Ferguson, Labor Shadow Minister for Primary Industries, Resources, Forestry and Tourism 2005–6, distinguished between Australian and overseas students. He justified consumer protection for overseas students because they provided 'enormous financial benefit'.[166] The economic benefit of overseas students was a solution to skills shortages that would also boost tourism.[167] While acknowledging that overseas students also 'contributed to the social and cultural makeup of the society',[168] the link even for this was made in terms of economic outcomes.[169] The central issue was to remain competitive in the market.[170]

161 Education Services for Overseas Students Legislation Amendment (2006 Measures No. 2) Bill 2006 (Cth) s 7.
162 Commonwealth, *Parliamentary Debates*, House of Representatives, 13 September 2006, 105 (Michael Hatton).
163 Commonwealth, *Parliamentary Debates*, House of Representatives, 13 September 2006, 53 (Kirsten Livermore).
164 Commonwealth, *Parliamentary Debates*, House of Representatives, 13 September 2006, 53 (Kirsten Livermore) 56; Commonwealth, *Parliamentary Debates*, House of Representatives, 13 September 2006, 60 (Martin Ferguson) 60.
165 Commonwealth, *Parliamentary Debates*, House of Representatives, 13 September 2006, 60 (Kirsten Livermore).
166 Commonwealth, *Parliamentary Debates*, House of Representatives 13 September 2006, 60 (Martin Ferguson).
167 Commonwealth, *Parliamentary Debates*, House of Representatives 13 September 2006, 60 (Martin Ferguson) 106, 108.
168 Commonwealth, *Parliamentary Debates*, House of Representatives 13 September 2006, 60 (Martin Ferguson) 108.
169 Commonwealth, *Parliamentary Debates*, House of Representatives, 13 September 2006, 11 (Craig Emerson); Commonwealth, *Parliamentary Debates*, House of Representatives, 13 September 2006, 118 (Brendan O'Connor).
170 Commonwealth, *Parliamentary Debates*, House of Representatives, 13 September 2006, 121 (Bronwyn Bishop).

The only substantive issue relating to the migration implications of the bill was the need to exclude unsuitable students. Ferguson voiced this concern. He agreed that, unless the measures in the debate were put in place, unsuitable students might find a 'back door' way to citizenship.[171] This high level of concern was not balanced by a discussion of whether the consequences for some students not complying with all visa conditions was commensurate with their breach.

C *Education Services for Overseas Students Legislation Amendment Act 2007*

A year later in 2007 the government further amended the act. The government recognised that the legislative concept of conditions of compliance did not necessarily match how education was delivered. The solution was to give providers more discretion to use their 'educational judgement . . . as to when they elect to report a student for breaches of visa conditions'.[172] In addition, departmental officers would no longer 'look behind the educational judgement of the provider'.[173] The amendment also strengthened what was called 'consumer support mechanisms of the provider', referring to independent dispute resolution.

The migration law aspect of this amendment aimed to 'ensure that the provider is responsible for educational issues. The role of the Department of Immigration and Citizenship will be to finalise the student's visa status'.[174] That meant that the department would take the advice of the provider concerning a breach of conditions, the trigger for visa cancellation. The role of immigration law was to provide 'necessary visa and immigration services that enhance and secure this education services trade which is so important to Australia'.[175] Migration legislation was the market enabler. The education provider could now decide whether a student should automatically lose their visa. In essence the power to cancel a visa was privatised to the education provider.

Another issue in relation to the control of the visa program arose at the intersection of a number of competing factors: the desired student of the

171 Commonwealth, *Parliamentary Debates*, House of Representatives, 13 September 2006, 106 (Martin Ferguson). For a discussion of the limit of the idea that the only option for students was to stay in Australia or return home see George Tan and Graeme Hugo, 'The Transnational Migration Strategies of Chinese and Indian Students in Australia' (2017) 23 *Population Space Place* 1.

172 Commonwealth, *Parliamentary Debates*, House of Representatives, 22 March 2007, 2 (Andrew Robb).

173 Commonwealth, *Parliamentary Debates*, House of Representatives, 22 March 2007, 2 (Andrew Robb).

174 Commonwealth, *Parliamentary Debates*, House of Representatives, 22 March 2007, 2 (Andrew Robb) 3.

175 Commonwealth, *Parliamentary Debates*, House of Representatives, 29 March 2007, 72 (Brendan O'Connor).

policy objective, the selection of students for enrolment by providers, the valuable, increasingly necessary additional income these enrolments brought to education providers and the motivation of students. Ferguson pointed to research that indicated that 'a large minority' of students, mostly from East Asia, were not attracted so much by the education opportunity as the chance for permanent residence in Australia.[176] Ferguson noted that the government spokesperson boasted of student numbers from Canada, North America and Europe, but these were a tiny minority.[177] His comments foreshadowed the next amendment to the visa program. The picture of skilled, mobile, young people with good English skills, which in 2000 Immigration Minister Ruddock saw as a lucrative source of funds and a cure for the skills gap, did not match the more complex reality of the students and providers this international market was attracting.[178]

By 2009 the research was showing a different picture. Birrell and Perry demonstrated that the market was not working as the previous government had hoped. The policy settings were such that the minimal qualification of even a one-year vocational education and training (VET) course in Certificate III Hospitality in Australia could be a pathway to permanent residence. The numbers are revealing. From 2005 to 2008 higher education enrolments increased by 20.7% while VET enrolments increased by 183%. Students from India accounted for almost half of this increase.[179] A significant minority of the international student cohort to whom the immigration department was granting student visas wanted to live in Australia and had undertaken the minimum qualification for that purpose.[180]

Policy adjustments in 2010, made by a new Labor government in response to rising Australian unemployment, greatly limited the chance for these TAFE

176 Commonwealth, *Parliamentary Debates*, House of Representatives, 29 March 2007, 59 (Martin Ferguson).

177 Commonwealth, *Parliamentary Debates*, House of Representatives, 29 March 2007, 59 (Martin Ferguson).

178 Note Castles predicted that enforcing border control would become increasingly difficult. One reason is a weakness in states' approach of discounting human agency, seeing migration as something that can be turned on and off 'like a tap' through border control. Legal positivism blinds states, he suggests, to the character of migration as a collective process, driven by families and communities. These families and communities now have better information about the world and easier and cheaper access to transport. See Stephen Castles, 'Migration and Community Formation under Conditions of Globalisation' (2006) 36(4) *International Migration Review* 1143, 1144. Note that even in an island state such as Australia these forces are at play. See, e.g., Rosie Roberts, '"His Visa Is Made of Rubber": Tactics, Risk and Temporary Moorings under Conditions of Multistage Migration to Australia' (2021) 22(3) *Social & Cultural Geography* 319.

179 Birrell and Perry (n 151) 66.

180 Birrell and Perry (n 151) 64; Department of Immigration and Citizenship, 'Strategic Review of the Student Visa Program 2011: Regulation Impact Statement', 2 <www.aph.gov.au/Parliamentary_Business/Bills_Legislation/Bills_Search_Results/Result?bId=r4779>.

graduates to gain the further residential visa which the previous policy would have made a likelihood. Moreover, the low-level Australian qualifications they had earned were unlikely to be valuable to them in their home country.[181] The subsequent human cost of this policy change both to the students and to their families in their home countries is well documented.[182] The dramatic impacts were implemented with minimal parliamentary scrutiny or debate through policy changes within the immigration minister's discretion.

D *Migration Legislation Amendment (Student Visas) Act 2012*

The last amendment, up to the time of writing, made to the student visa legislation was the *Migration Legislation Amendment (Student Visas) Act 2012*. This amendment abolished the automatic cancellation of student visas because it was ineffective and inefficient.[183] This was effected by an amendment to the *Education for Overseas Students Act 2000* and a second note at the end of *Migration Act 1958* ss 137J(1). This note simply stated: 'Note 2: Under subsection 20(4A) of that Act, a registered provider must not send a notice on or after the day that subsection commences.' The power to automatically cancel a student visa remains in the *Migration Act 1958* and could be reactivated by a change in the *Education for Overseas Students Act 2000*.

The visa cancellation power was placed back into the hands of the immigration minister under the discretionary power in the *Migration Act 1958*. The amendment was a response to the 'adverse commentary from the Federal Court, with the majority of automatic cancellations made between May 2001 and December 2009 having been overturned, affecting some 19,000 cases'.[184] The Knight Review of the student visa system had reported that 'the courts are not impressed'.[185] The legislation formed part of the new Labor government's response.

The act aimed to 'provide for a fairer, merits based cancellation process and allow integrity and compliance resources to be more targeted to areas of high risk'.[186] This risk-based approach removed 'blanket cancellation rules'

181 Birrell and Perry (n 151) 64; Department of Immigration and Citizenship, 'Strategic Review of the Student Visa Program 2011: Regulation Impact Statement', 2 <www.aph.gov.au/Parliamentary_Business/Bills_Legislation/Bills_Search_Results/Result?bId=r4779>.

182 For example Reich (n 4).

183 Commonwealth, *Parliamentary Debates*, House of Representatives, 22 March 2012, 3952–54 (Chris Bowen).

184 Commonwealth, *Parliamentary Debates*, House of Representatives, 22 March 2012, 3952–54 (Chris Bowen) 3953.

185 Commonwealth, *Strategic Review of the Student Visa Program 2011* (Report, 30 June 2011) (Knight Review) 95.

186 Commonwealth, *Parliamentary Debates*, House of Representatives, 9 March 2012, 3952 (Chris Bowen).

and replaced them with the use of the immigration minister's discretionary power in *Migration Act 1958* s 116 to prioritise 'according to risk [of a breach of visa conditions]'.[187] The immigration minister said the new law would allow him to focus on breaches that were 'wilful or intentional and egregious'.[188]

The amendment rebalanced the power over visa cancellation. The 'extraordinary powers' that were previously given to education providers over students were now shifted to the immigration minister and his delegates who use their discretion to target cancelation.[189] Bowen noted that these cancellation powers had sometimes been used 'carelessly or even maliciously'.[190] The new act now transferred these powers of cancellation to departmental officers who, he implied, would not behave in this way.

While the immigration minister justified the risk-prioritising approach as enabling a focus of the department's resources on a breach of the visa conditions, another element of risk was raised by an opposition member. Approving a risk assessment approach to migration compliance of student visas, he noted:

> We know that our main markets for foreign students – India and China – are treated as high-risk countries, and that makes it harder for students to obtain visas, particularly Indians. The rejection rates are around 60 per cent. Streamlined arrangements are welcome in this regard, and that is why we are not going to oppose the intent of this bill or the passage of it. Streamlining these things is a good thing, and focusing on the risks, rather than the administration, is a superior model of the government's choosing.[191]

Here the immigration minister's discretion is seen as an opportunity to respond to the market demand by overcoming the constraint of the high-risk rating on Indian and Chinese students without the need to legislate specifically.

187 Commonwealth, *Parliamentary Debates*, House of Representatives, 9 May 2012, 4377 (Scott Morrison).

188 Commonwealth, *Parliamentary Debates*, House of Representatives, 10 May 2012, 4519 (Chris Bowen). Note that education providers are responsible for recruiting students who are low risk. If after recruitment and grant of a visa a student's visa is cancelled, or they become unlawful by overstaying their visa or they apply for an onshore protection visa they are counted against the education provider as a risk to the integrity of the visa program. Department of Home Affairs, *Simplified Student Visa Framework (SSFF) Appraisal* (May 2018) 7.

189 Commonwealth, *Parliamentary Debates*, House of Representatives, 22 March 2012, 3952 (Chris Bowen).

190 Commonwealth, *Parliamentary Debates*, House of Representatives, 22 March 2012, 3952 (Chris Bowen).

191 Commonwealth, *Parliamentary Debates*, House of Representatives, 10 May 2012, 4518 (Alex Hawke).

However, the broadening of the immigration minister's discretion did not go unchallenged. Commenting on the increased discretion, Don Randall, Shadow Parliamentary Secretary for Local Government 2010–3 said:

> it is not clear what mechanism or circumstance will trigger an investigation or prove severe enough to prompt visa cancellation. These questions are hanging out there now. They have not been addressed, I understand, in any of the explanatory memoranda which accompany this bill. I hope that we have not opened the door for the use of ad hoc discretionary powers by the minister, which, as I said, could be fraught with danger.[192]

The opposition supported this amendment, with the shadow minister summarising its position as: 'The coalition is committed to the integrity of our immigration program. We believe strongly in our immigration program. We want to see it succeed and to see it welcomed, appreciated and supported in the Australian community'.[193] This statement promotes the migration system as an end in itself and can be understood in a similar way to the comments in earlier debates that went beyond the language of the market used in debates on the student visa.[194]

E *Judicial Comment Since 2012*

Since 2012 there have been no further legislative amendments to the student visa provisions. The immigration minister's broad discretion to cancel a visa under the general cancellation power of *Migration Act 1958* s 116 remains. The High Court, however, has enforced some limits.

In *Wei v Minister for Immigration and Border Protection* the High Court found jurisdictional error in the decision to cancel Mr Wei's student visa.[195] Mr Wei was enrolled at Macquarie University, but his enrolment was not entered into a database available for the government department to monitor compliance. He did not receive letters sent to him and did not receive an email sent to him because his email address was misspelt by the university. In this case what Gaegler J and Keane J termed 'an imperative duty' had not been carried out by a staff member at Macquarie University.[196] This

192 Commonwealth, *Parliamentary Debates*, House of Representatives, 10 May 2012, 4501 (Don Randall).
193 Commonwealth, *Parliamentary Debates*, House of Representatives, 9 May 2012, 4379 (Scott Morrison).
194 See Commonwealth, *Parliamentary Debates*, House of Representatives, 9 November 2000, 22568 (Ian Macfarlane).
195 *Wei v Minister for Immigration and Border Protection* (2015) 257 CLR 22, 34–5.
196 *Wei v Minister for Immigration and Border Protection* (2015) 257 CLR 22, 34–5.

failure 'tainted' the fact-finding that was a necessary part of the delegate's decision-making.[197] Mr Wei won his appeal.

The 2012 amendment removed the prohibition on the immigration minister taking into account the fact that a student did not receive a notice of a breach of visa conditions and a subsequent cancellation of a visa. However, despite this, student visas were still in danger of being cancelled without the student receiving written notification, as *Wei* demonstrates. The 'carelessness or maliciousness'[198] that it was expected would be overcome if the visa cancellation process was managed by the immigration minister's department was apparently not completely eradicated.

As the facts of the case were explained to the High Court in *Wei*, Keane J inquired, 'If someone had spoken to the University, would it not have been able to say that the plaintiff was enrolled?' Counsel for Mr Wei replied: 'We assume it would have said that if it had been asked that question'. However, the delegate did not ask. The representative continued, 'Compliance with the scheme was of such importance that non-compliance by the education provider prevented the delegate from reaching his state of satisfaction on what the law required to be before him'. No explanation was given on why the simple question had not been asked.

It is beyond the scope of this book to assess to what extent Mr Wei's case is representative of the quality of compliance monitoring in place since the 2012 amendment. Mr Wei's case does, however, illustrate the multilayered processes in place to exclude and the reliance on sanctions in the compliance measures to control education providers as well as students. The hybrid status of the student as lucrative customer and potential illegal noncitizen is clearly on display.[199] Also on display is the technique of legislating ministerial discretion to solve the difficulties of controlling students' behaviour at a granular level.

V Sovereignty versus Globalised Neoliberalism

The parliamentary debates, ministerial statements and judicial comment on the student visa amendments encapsulate the tension between on one hand the Parliament's adoption of a neoliberal logic in order to benefit from economic globalisation and on the other hand the importance the Parliament places on migration control. This tension illustrates the incompatibility between the adoption of a neoliberal market approach to overseas students and the maintenance of migration law as an expression of an Australian sovereignty akin

197 *Wei v Minister for Immigration and Border Protection* (2015) 257 CLR 22, 34–5.

198 Commonwealth, *Parliamentary Debates*, House of Representatives, 10 May 2012, 4506 (Ewen Jones).

199 Segrave et al. (n 159).

to the Westphalian sovereignty that was understood in 1901 but, as Brown argues, is an anachronism in this post-Westphalian world.[200] The debate demonstrates the point where a neoliberal logic of the market is in conflict with a foundational policy of expressing sovereignty through migration law which attempts to tightly control the composition of the Australian population.

Up until the amendment in 2012, the direction of the development of this aspect of migration law was for the law to free the market to operate. Migration legislation was used to support the operation of the market and to minimise interference in this process including from the judiciary. By adding ss 137J–137P to the *Migration Act 1958* (Cth) in 2000 judicial review was eliminated. The amendment did this by introducing automatic cancellation of a student visa if certain conditions were not met. This automatic cancellation was not a decision of the immigration minister and therefore it could not be judicially reviewed. The power to trigger this automatic cancellation of student visas was increasingly transferred to education providers, in essence allowing these market actors to select and reject their consumers. In this way the function of the migration law over the period 2000–12 increasingly became that of a market facilitator.

By 2012 research showed the flaws in this approach. The migration amendments that increasingly empowered market actors did not deliver on the policy objectives the government had desired. Instead, the market showed that for a significant minority an important aspect of the product being offered was permanent residency and citizenship, not education. Providers delivered this pathway to citizenship through VET courses for skills that Australia did not need. The government's attempts to maintain tight control of the Australian international student market, coordinating policy and legislation across several government agencies while at the same time devolving compliance monitoring to the market, was shown to be flawed. Its attempt to construct an automatic cancellation process that was immune from judicial oversight also failed, as the Knight Review noted.

The automatic cancellation policy showed the extreme of this policy of control and was justified by a market logic that targeted only bona fide consumers of the education product. The legislation placed international students at risk of incarceration if they breached any of the prescriptive requirements of the visa. A risk-based approach replaced automatic cancellation. This legislation retained the consequences for a breach of conditions, incarceration and deportation, but allowed the immigration minister to target those to be excluded. It was justified as efficiency but, as Hawke's comment implies,[201]

200 Brown, *Walled States* (n 8) 52–3.

201 See contribution to debate made by Alex Hawke, Liberal Member for Mitchell (2007–current), such as Commonwealth, *Parliamentary Debates*, House of Representatives, 10 May 2012, 4518 (Alex Hawke).

it also meant that the immigration minister could more selectively choose from groups labelled as high risk such as Indian and Chinese students. This echoes the legislative technique of giving the immigration minister discretion to avoid making plain an unpalatable policy, or an inconsistency such as favouring the wealthy or those placed in a high-risk group,[202] echoing the debates of 1901 and 1958.[203]

Control of migration in the student visa debates was not explicitly expressed as asserting or protecting sovereignty. This is in sharp contrast to the debates on asylum seekers or other visa applicants considered undesirable, discussed in the next chapter. However, while the debate emphasised the economic objectives and used the neoliberal language of the market, a link to sovereignty can be inferred from assertions such as the suggestion by a member of the Coalition government that migration law is the 'cornerstone of Australia's society',[204] and Opposition spokesperson Scott Morrison's statement that 'We believe strongly in our immigration program. We want to see it succeed and to see it welcomed, appreciated, and supported in the Australian community'.[205] These are statements of belief and values, not economic facts derived from analysis of the market. The control of students entering and remaining in Australia was not completely justified by the links speakers made to the competitiveness of the education product in the market.

In parliamentary debate from 2000 to 2012 the migration system was accorded a value in itself, rivalling economic opportunity. Even with this critical export industry, in a competitive global environment, excluding those who failed to comply with visa conditions defined at a granular level and motivating compliance with the threat of detention and deportation were accepted as priorities. Also accepted, when the Knight Review highlighted the problems found with the student visa system, was a legislative technique that left it to the immigration minister's discretion to exclude. That broad ministerial power available under the act remains.

VI Conclusion

This chapter has argued that in the amendments to the *Migration Act 1958* (Cth) made between 2000 and 2020 with an objective of economic gain, as exemplified by the student visa legislation, the Parliament wrestled with two competing philosophies: neoliberalism and a version of Westphalian

202 Commonwealth, *Parliamentary Debates*, House of Representatives, 7 August 1901, 3500 (Edmund Barton).

203 See Chapter 4.

204 Commonwealth, *Parliamentary Debates*, House of Representatives, 9 November 2000, 22568 (Ian Macfarlane).

205 Commonwealth, *Parliamentary Debates*, House of Representatives, 9 May 2012, 4379 (Scott Morrison).

sovereignty that is expressed through migration control. The chapter found that prime ministers and immigration ministers viewed globalisation as largely an economic opportunity. Their statements on migration policy demonstrated that they saw migration as a tool to maximise economic gain that could be used without legislative amendment, through ministerial policy-making discretion. The government's changed priority, over the period, from migration for family reunion to a focus on economic outcomes is an indicator of how this understanding of globalisation shaped the migration program.

Using the example of the amendments to the international student visa legislation, the chapter has explored how the competing philosophies were expressed in parliamentary debate and ministerial comment. The philosophy of neoliberalism can be seen in legislative processes that positioned the law as a market facilitator and the student as a customer of a highly lucrative product. However, the Parliament's rationale for the migration measures was not justified by economics alone. Prime Minister Morrison's neglect of international students in his first response to the COVID-19 pandemic, which he framed as protecting sovereignty, was at odds with a neoliberal market philosophy. His development of that response positioned protecting the current global political power balance that facilitated globalisation as a part of protecting sovereignty. The chapter concludes that, even given the reality of a major export industry, a Westphalian sovereignty that emphasises authority over territory and people, through border control, was prioritised.

While not conclusive, there are parallels between these student visa debates prioritising the exclusion of the undesirable student visa holder over economic outcomes and the 1901 debates that placed a white Australia as a priority over economic gain.[206] As Alexander Patterson, Member for Capricornia, Queensland, said in Parliament in 1901, articulating the majority view:

> Even if it could be proved that we cannot carry on the industry without a certain loss of cultivation, I say it is still better, a thousand times, to dispense with black labour, and to convert these dark plantations into smiling fields cultivated by free and white labour.[207]

What is certain is that the policy priority of identifying and excluding the unwanted migrant through migration law and the use of ministerial discretion to achieve this has remained constant.

206 See Chapter 4 Section II.

207 Commonwealth, *Parliamentary Debates*, House of Representatives, 5 June 1901, 695 (Alexander Patterson). For a brief overview of the politics of this era see Marija Taflaga, 'A Short Political History of Australia', in Peter J Chen et al (eds), *Australian Politics and Policy* (Sydney University Press, 2019) 18, 20–4.

Chapter 6

Sovereignty To Justify 'Keeping Out' and 'Kicking Out'

I Introduction

The previous chapter examined how the two competing philosophies of neoliberalism and a conception of Westphalian sovereignty of absolute control over territory and people competed in the making of amendments to student visa legislation, which facilitated a major export industry. Even with that major economic objective, the importance of ensuring exclusion of all those not considered the ideal consumer of that export product remained an important focus of the amendments. The purpose of this chapter is to examine the function of a Westphalian concept of sovereignty in the making of the amendments to the *Migration Act 1958* (Cth) in the same period, 2000–20, which had the stated objective of exclusion. These amendments aimed to exclude the unwanted noncitizen[1] by preventing their entry onto Australian territory or by expelling those already present.

By examining these amendments, the chapter aims to uncover the nature and function of the sovereignty that successive governments have asserted as their justification. The chapter tests the extent to which these amendments can be characterised as hypersovereignty, a turn to migration law as a way of expressing Westphalian sovereignty of absolute control in response to the loss of control and the interdependence, and vulnerability to events and decisions beyond a state's individual control, that globalisation brings.[2]

The chapter begins by examining the policy context in which these 'exclusion' amendments to the *Migration Act 1958* (Cth) were enacted. The chapter does this through an examination of how, in respect of migration law, the prime ministers over the period 2000–20 used the specific language of sovereignty when addressing the increased movement of people, a phenomenon of globalisation. This focus is because prime ministerial statements and

1 The noncitizen is defined in *Migration Act 1958* (Cth) s 5 as 'a person who is not a citizen'. The *Australian Citizenship Act 2007* (Cth) defines an Australian citizen in s 4 and in detail in pt 2 div 1 and 2.

2 See discussion in Chapter 3 Section III.

DOI: 10.4324/9781003515852-8

comments signal that an issue is one of critical national importance. The policy context in which immigration ministers proposed and argued for the amendments to exclude can be understood by examining the representations of the policy problem, using the language of sovereignty, by their prime ministers. The sources for this analysis are parliamentary debates and also some limited commentary made outside the Parliament or formal speeches, such as in radio interviews, in order to fully demonstrate the policy context.[3]

Secondly the chapter examines the function and nature of sovereignty used in the justification for the amendments made in this period in two categories: firstly, those with the stated aim of preventing a person from entering Australian territory, and secondly those with the stated aim of removing a person from Australian territory. The analysis demonstrates that the pairing of sovereignty with a physical territorial border in the rhetoric of government initiatives such as 'Operation Sovereign Borders' hides the functions for which sovereignty is deployed. The chief of these functions is the justification of absolute executive government control over migration decisions to exclude.[4]

Thirdly the chapter draws from both theory and history to further inquire into the nature of the sovereignty used to justify the exclusion amendments. The chapter compares the legislative process with the philosophies of

3 Aspects of this context were highly politicised. Some of these aspects are well documented. See, e.g., David Marr and Marian Wilkinson, *Dark Victory* (Allen and Unwin, 2003); Peter Mares, *Borderline: Australia's Response to Refugees and Asylum Seekers in the Wake of the Tampa* (UNSW Press, 2nd ed, 2002); James Jupp, *An Immigrant Nation Seeks Cohesion: Australia from 1788* (Cambridge University Press, 2018) especially ch 18; Gwenda Tavan, *The Long, Slow Death of White Australia* (Scribe Publications, 2005) 229–33; Alex Reilly, 'Explainer: The Medevac Repeal and What It Means for Asylum Seekers on Manus Island and Nauru', *The Conversation* (online, 4 December 2019) <https://theconversation.com/explainer-the-medevac-repeal-and-what-it-means-for-asylum-seekers-on-manus-island-and-nauru-128118>; Kate Walton, '"Dark Day": Australia Repeals Medical Evacuation for Refugees', *Aljazeera* (online, 19 December 2019) <www.aljazeera.com/news/2019/12/4/dark-day-australia-repeals-medical-evacuation-for-refugees>; Australian Human Rights Commission, *Lives on Hold: Refugees and Asylum Seekers in the 'Legacy Caseload'* (Report, 2019); John Flannery and Maria Hawthorne, 'Asylum Seeker Death Was Preventable', *Australian Medicine* (online, 13 August 2018) 8.

4 Executive control can be validly sourced from executive power under legislation and also in limited circumstances from the *Constitution* s 61 executive power. *Constitution* s 61 states: 'The executive power of the Commonwealth is vested in the Queen and is exercisable by the Governor-General as the Queen's representative, and extends to the execution and maintenance of this Constitution, and of the laws of the Commonwealth'. The majority decision in the *MV Tampa Case* held, in summary, that the government had executive power to prevent entry and that this was not extinguished by statute 'absent of clear words or inescapable implications' that this was the Parliament's intention. *Ruddock v Vadarlis* [2001] FCA 1329, [185] ('*MV Tampa Case*').

sovereignty proposed by Carl Schmitt,[5] Giorgio Agamben,[6] Wendy Brown[7] and Catherine Dauvergne[8] and with historical benchmarks from Australia's migration law and policy of the 20th century.[9]

II The Australian Migration Policy Context: Linking Sovereignty and Exclusion

The policy position proclaimed and politicised in 2001 by John Howard, Coalition prime minister 1996–2007, which explicitly linked the concept of sovereignty to excluding unwanted asylum seekers, established the broad policy rationale for the amendments to exclude which successive prime ministers followed and elaborated.[10] Howard took the 1978 policy principle quietly pronounced to replace the White Australia policy, and hardly mentioned of Minister Michael Mackellar, Minister for Immigration and Ethnic Affairs (1975–9) in the Fraser Coalition government,[11] to a rallying cry for twenty first century migration.

Howard, arguing for the Border Protection Bill 2001, declared to the Parliament:

> The protection of our sovereignty, including Australia's sovereign right to determine who shall enter Australia, is a matter for the Australian government and this parliament.
>
> It is essential to the maintenance of Australian sovereignty, including our sovereign right to determine who will enter and reside in Australia.[12]

5 Carl Schmitt, *The Concept of the Political*, tr G Schwabb (University of Chicago Press, 2007); Carl Schmitt, *Political Theology: Four Chapters on the Concept of Sovereignty*, tr George Schwab (Massachusetts Institute of Technology, 1985).

6 Giorgio Agamben, *Homo Sacer: Sovereign Power and Bare Life*, tr Daniel Heller-Roazen (Stanford University Press, 1998).

7 Wendy Brown, *Walled States, Waning Sovereignty* (Zone Books, 2010) 19–20 ('*Walled States*').

8 Catherine Dauvergne, 'Sovereignty, Migration, and the Rule of Law in Global Times' (2004) 67(4) *Modern Law Review* 588.

9 See Chapter 4.

10 Note that, writing at the end of the Howard prime ministership in 2008, Jane McAdam and Kate Purcell comment on the significance of the Howard influence on exclusion of the unwanted migrant through his rhetoric and lawmaking. They argue that these measures were a breach of good faith under international law in Jane McAdam and Kate Purcell, 'Refugee Protection in the Howard Years: Obstructing the Right to Seek Asylum' (2008) 27 *Australian Year Book of International Law* 87, 111–13.

11 Commonwealth, *Parliamentary Debates*, House of Representatives, 7 June 1978, 3153–5 (Michael Mackellar).

12 Commonwealth, *Parliamentary Debates*, House of Representatives, 29 August 2001, 30569 (John Howard). The purpose of this discussion is not to debate the accuracy of this statement. It is however interesting to note that a major international law text stated both that

In 2018 Scott Morrison, Coalition prime minister 2018–22, characterised sovereignty as the 'right to run our own show',[13] and as keeping Australians safe.[14] Elaborating on the theme of safety, he linked sovereignty to 'making sure our kids are safe from predators and . . . kicking those people out of this country who would be predators against them'.[15]

The making of prime ministerial statements and comments such as these suggests the issue is one of critical national importance. The policy context in which immigration ministers proposed and argued for the amendments to exclude can be understood by examining the representations of the policy problem, using the language of sovereignty, by their prime ministers.[16] In 2001 Howard's statement, quoted previously,[17] echoed the declaration of a characteristic of a sovereign state made in a High Court judgment in 1906, which found the newly formed Australian Parliament had the power to pass legislation to exclude.[18] Howard used it as a justification for the government's

---

'Emigration is in fact entirely a matter of internal legislation of the different states', supporting Howard's assertion, and that 'The Law of nations does not, as yet, grant a right of emigration to every individual, although it is frequently maintained that it is a "natural" right of every individual to emigrate from his own State'. It goes on to state: 'It is a moral right which could fittingly find a place in any international recognition of the Rights of man'. L Oppenheim, *International Law: A Treatise,* ed H Lauterpacht (David Mckay Company, 8th ed, 1955) 647–8. For a history of the right to leave one's country see Jane McAdam, 'An Intellectual History of Freedom of Movement in International Law: The Right to Leave as a Personal Liberty', in Mary Crock and Tom D Campbell (eds), *Refugees and Rights* (Taylor & Francis Group, 2015) 3. Note McAdam contrasts the origin of the right, which is now embedded in human rights law as an enabler of other rights, with the restriction of this right in practice. She sees the individual right and state rights as not yet reconciled.

13 Scott Morrison, 'The Beliefs That Guide Us: Key Note Address to Asia Briefing', *Prime Minister Media Centre* (Speech, Asia Society Australia, 1 November 2018) <pm.gov.au/media>.

14 Scott Morrison, 'Until the Bell Rings', *Prime Minister Media Centre* (Speech, Menzies Research Centre, 6 September 2018) <pm.gov.au/media>.

15 Scott Morrison, 'Until the Bell Rings', *Prime Minister Media Centre* (Speech, Menzies Research Centre, 6 September 2018) <pm.gov.au/media>.

16 These amendments were also made in a social and broader political and geopolitical context referenced in the previous chapters. However most relevant to the context in which the migration amendments to exclude were made was the context of international migration law and norms. For a discussion of these in relation to Australia in particular see Jane McAdam and Fiona Chong, *Refugees: Why Seeking Asylum Is Legal, and Australia's Policies Are Not* (UNSW Press, 2014) especially 9–36, 170–80. For a broader discussion see James C Hathaway, *The Rights of Refugees under International Law* (Cambridge University Press, 2005). For a critique of international refugee law and practice see Patricia Tuitt, *False Images: Law's Construction of the Refugee* (Pluto Press, 1996); Michelle Foster, *International Refugee Law and Socio-Economic Rights: Refuge from Deprivation* (Cambridge University Press, 2007).

17 Commonwealth, *Parliamentary Debates*, House of Representatives, 20 August 2001, 30569 (John Howard).

18 See the discussion of Australia's developing constitutional sovereignty and international sovereign status in Chapter 2 Section III; and Chapter 4, citing *Robtelmes v Brenan* (1906) 4 CLR 395, 401 reiterated in *Ah Yin v Christie* (1907) 4 CLR 1428, 1431.

actions in the *MV Tampa* incident and as a rationale for a suite of amendments to the *Migration Act 1958* (Cth). This was a new use of the language of sovereignty by a prime minister.[19] Pairing the attempted maritime entry of asylum seekers with sovereignty raised asylum seekers to an existential threat to the absolute authority of the Australian state over its territory.

This use of sovereignty contrasts with the same prime minister's position on economic globalisation and the threat to economic sovereignty posed by multinational companies.[20] On that issue he suggested that the government had no power to direct investment and that Australia must rely on asking these companies to respect their social obligations.[21] He accepted that this was largely unchallengeable. The political motivation at that time for pairing sovereignty and asylum seekers has been extensively discussed and is beyond the scope of this thesis.[22] What matters for present purposes is that the different responses to asylum seekers and to multinational companies provides support for characterising the migration amendments as an exercise of hyper-sovereignty, the performance of exclusion as a demonstration of sovereign power that simultaneously signals the waning capacity to wield Westphalian sovereignty, and a turning towards migration law where absolute control still seems possible. The investigation of the legislative processes of these amendments from 2000 to 2020 elucidates the nature and function of the sovereignty being asserted.

19 Before the 2001 *MV Tampa* incident in which Prime Minister John Howard refused to allow a Norwegian tanker to dock at Christmas Island to enable a group of asylum seekers rescued at sea to disembark on Australian soil, he linked sovereignty to a migration matter only once in his then four years in office. When asked by a journalist whether the denial of an entry visa to an Uzbek boxer to attend the 2000 Sydney Olympics was an issue of sovereignty, Howard agreed it was. John Howard, 'Interview with Prime Minister John Howard (Murray Olds and Julie Flynn, 2UE Radio)', *PM Transcripts* (Radio interview, 9 September 2000) <pmtranscripts.pmc.gov.au>. See also the discussion in Chapter 4 Section IV. Note also that a search of comments of all prime ministers post-World War II shows that no prime minister before Howard made this overt pairing of sovereignty and migration.

20 John Howard, 'Radio Interview with John Stanley 2UE', *PM Transcripts* (Radio interview, 13 May 1997) <pmtranscripts.pmc.gov.au>.

21 John Howard, 'Radio Interview with John Stanley 2UE', *PM Transcripts* (Radio interview, 13 May 1997) <pmtranscripts.pmc.gov.au>.

22 See, e.g., references listed in n 3. See also William Maley on politicisation in 2001 in William Maley, 'Asylum-Seekers in Australia's International Relations' (2003) 57(1) *Australian Journal of International Affairs* 187, 192. See Savitri Taylor's critique of the post-9/11 anti-terrorism legislative amendments and their potential impact on asylum seekers. She called for 'the principle of proportionality [to] be applied in all areas of national security activity. In the present context, this means insisting on a case-by-case demonstration that the cost of procedural restrictions on the individual asylum-seeker is not disproportionate to the seriousness and likelihood of the danger to Australia of permitting that particular individual in those particular circumstances access to the usual procedural safeguards'. Savitri Taylor, 'Guarding the Enemy from Oppression: Asylum-Seeker Rights Post-September 11' (2002) 26 *Melbourne University Law Review* 396, 405–8.

In his speech to Parliament quoted previously,[23] and in other speeches and comments, Howard elaborated on how the attempted arrival of asylum seekers threatened Australia's sovereignty. The threats he identified, which are detailed shortly, are indicators of the function of sovereignty in this migration lawmaking. What was meant by sovereignty is revealed in what it was used to protect and exclude.

The first threat Howard identified is what he described as 'the rising flood of unauthorised arrivals'.[24] This referred to an increase of asylum seekers attempting to reach Australia by boat.[25] The economic or social impact was not argued. The global drivers of unauthorised asylum seeking were seldom considered in the debate. This contrasts with the approach to globalisation where the opportunities were identified and embraced and the threat to economic sovereignty of multinational companies was not represented as a threat to sovereignty but rather as a driver for international cooperation,[26] or of a need to call on the social conscience of the companies.[27] International students were characterised as consumers, and overseas skilled workers were seen as a solution to Australia's skills shortage.[28] These economic considerations were generally missing when asylum seekers were addressed. Asylum seekers were homogenised as the unauthorised, and the opportunities they might present – for example to boost the skilled workforce or to consume – went unexamined and unimagined.

The second threat to sovereignty that Howard identified was the Australian court system. Howard argued, 'It is in the national interest that the courts of Australia do not have the right to overturn something that rightly belongs to the determination of the Australian people'.[29] In this way sovereignty was represented as the will of the Australian people and was protected by shielding the use of this power from the scrutiny of the court.[30]

23 Commonwealth, *Parliamentary Debates*, House of Representatives, 29 August 2001, 30569 (John Howard).
24 Commonwealth, *Parliamentary Debates*, House of Representatives, 29 August 2001, 30569 (John Howard).
25 This referred to a sudden increase from 17 boats with 200 people in 1998 to 86, 51 and 43 boats with a total of 12,176 people from 1999 to 2001: Parliamentary Library, 'Boat Arrivals in Australia Since 1976: Statistical Appendix' (Research Paper, 23 July 2013) Appendix A <www.aph.gov.au/about_parliament/parliamentary_departments/parliamentary_library/pubs/bn/2012-2013/boatarrivals>.
26 See Chapter 5 Section III A.
27 See Chapter 5 Section III A.
28 Phillip Ruddock, 'Australian Immigration: Grasping the New Reality' (Speech, Nation Skilling: Migration Labour and the Law Symposium Sydney, 23 November 2000).
29 Commonwealth, *Parliamentary Debates*, House of Representatives, 29 August 2001, 30570 (John Howard).
30 Note Justice of the High Court Stephen Gaegler highlights the historical legacy of the executive using legislation to overcome judicial declarations of the law in Stephen Gaegler, 'A Tale

The third threat presented by Howard was a threat to a right. He claimed 'a right to control borders' and asserted that 'they [the asylum seekers] don't have any legal right to be in Australia'.[31] The now infamous decision to represent the government's refusal to allow the asylum seekers on the *MV Tampa* to come to Australia as the assertion of a sovereign nation's well-established right in international law to control its territorial borders has been well analysed over the last twenty years. The interpretation and application of this legal right remains contested.[32] What cannot be contested is that there was some doubt about the validity of the Howard government's actions. In the parliamentary debate in support of the Border Protection Bill 2001 Howard said, 'While the government believes that there is appropriate legal authority at present, for more abundant caution this legislation will ensure that there is no doubt about the government's ability to order such vessels to leave our territorial waters.'[33] The threat he was combating was the possibility of the illegality of his actions. Sovereignty functioned to legitimise government action against asylum seekers, which at the time was legally ambiguous.

The fourth threat is one the prime minister seemed reluctant to discuss. This was the threat that Australia's own domestic laws might thwart the government's actions and objectives. During a radio interview the prime minister claimed that the asylum seekers onboard the *MV Tampa* did not have claims as 'meritorious' as those of asylum seekers who came to Australia from overseas refugee camps after assessment by the UNHCR.[34] At the same time as making this assertion he admitted he had little information about the asylum seekers on board the *MV Tampa*, and he referred to 'legal reasons' that meant it was not a good idea for Australia to inquire further about them:

Interviewer: Do we know anything about the people on board the *MV Tampa*?

Prime Minister: We only have very sketchy information. I would imagine we'll be accumulating a bit more information, but we have to be rather careful about the extent to which we engage them about their histories and backgrounds for certain potential legal reasons.

---

of Two Ships: The MV Tampa and the SS Afghan' (2019) 40(3) *Adelaide Law Review* 615; see especially 625–6.

31 John Howard, 'Interview with Prime Minister John Howard (Neil Mitchell, Radio 3AW)', *PM Transcripts* (Radio interview, 31 August 2001) <pmtranscripts.pmc.gov.au>.

32 See, e.g., Penelope Mathews, 'Australian Refugee Protection in the Wake of the Tampa' (2002) 96(3) *American Journal of International Law* 661, 665–76. Chantal Marie-Jeanne Bostock, 'The International Legal Obligations Owed to the Asylum Seekers on the MV Tampa' (2002) 14(2–3) *International Journal of Refugee Law* 279, 294–7. See also further discussion in Section III A,1.

33 Commonwealth, *Parliamentary Debates*, House of Representatives, 29 August 2001, 30570 (John Howard).

34 Howard, 'Interview with Prime Minister John Howard' (n 31). See Chapter 1 for discussion of *MV Tampa*.

Interviewer: The . . . what, gives them some rights somehow?
Prime Minister: Well I just don't . . .
Interviewer: You're not allowed to talk to them?
Prime Minister: No it's not a question of allowed. It's not a question of being allowed to talk to them, but we have to take those sort of things into account.[35]

It can be inferred from the prime minister's obfuscation in this interview that he feared that if allowed to set foot on Australian territory the asylum seekers might establish a claim for protection under the *Migration Act 1958* (Cth) at that time.[36] His defence of sovereignty was against the operation of Australian law. An assertion of sovereignty allowed the prime minister to avoid the possibility that the international obligation to which the Australian sovereign nation had committed, in ratifying the *Refugee Convention* and transforming it into provisions of the *Migration Act 1958*(Cth), would force him to accept the *MV Tampa* asylum seekers and assess their claims on shore.[37]

The last overlapping threat against which sovereignty was asserted was a consequence of Australia's obligations under international law.[38] The assertion of sovereignty to repel asylum seekers raised the problem of what to do with those attempting to enter. The government at that time immediately established an offshore processing facility where asylum seekers could be detained while being processed by Australian officials.[39] The prime minister used sovereignty as both a rationale for the need for offshore processing and to try to absolve Australia of the international implications of this policy. He explained that the people on the *MV Tampa* would have to 'be taken somewhere and processed and [have] their refugee status determined and that country can't be Australia'. This was, he said, because he needed to 'draw a line' on 'uncontrollable illegal migration' and to control how Australia's

35 Howard, 'Interview with Prime Minister John Howard' (n 31). See Chapter 1 for discussion of *MV Tampa*.
36 *Migration Act 1958* (Cth), as amended taking into account amendments up to Act No 85 of 2001.
37 See Hathaway (n 16) 171–4 on the rights of refugees who are merely physically present, whether legally or illegally on a Refugee Convention contracting state's territory and his footnote on the case of *Minister for Immigration and Multicultural Affairs v Khawar* [2002] HCA 14. Hathaway disputes the judgment of McHugh and Gummow JJ for raising the issue that the convention did not define what 'within a state' meant. Hathaway suggests this omission by the convention drafters implies the meaning is self-evident.
38 See discussion in Chapter 2, Section VII.
39 Mary Crock et al. note that Papua New Guinea accepted $1 million from Australia for the right to use their sovereign territory and the UNHCR refused to assist Australia with processing, in Mary Crock, Ben Saul and Azadeh Dastyari, *Future Seekers II* (Federation Press, 2006) 125. This attempt to outsource international obligations and the cost is discussed by Tania Penovic and Azadeh Dastyari, who document the history of offshore detention and the issues of cost, humanitarian concerns and breaches of international obligations in Tania Penovic and Azadeh Dastyari, 'Boatloads of Incongruity: The Evolution of Australia's Offshore Processing Regime' (2007) 13(1) *Australian Journal of Human Rights* 33.

'warm hearted' approach to refugees was dispensed.[40] The *MV Tampa* incident was an opportunity to 'demonstrate a point'.[41] He used the concept of national sovereignty to justify indefinite detention even for those assessed as refugees, which he acknowledged was immigration detention with no certain end date:[42]

> The Government is not prepared to set limits on the time allowed for resettlement as this may have the effect of entitling a person to enter Australia and unjustifiably undermine our territorial sovereignty and would encourage people not to cooperate with efforts to process and resettle them.[43]

He also used the concept of sovereignty to absolve Australia of responsibility for the consequences of this policy, including placing children in detention: 'Accommodation at an OPC [offshore processing centre] is not detention under Australian law . . . host countries are sovereign nations.'[44] By purchasing the sovereignty of another nation, through funding offshore processing arrangements, Australia could avoid the international obligations arising from Australia's ratification of the ICCPR in November 1980 and the *Convention on the Rights of the Child* in December 1990.[45]

What was threatened was the executive's exclusive control over migration decisions. The representation of these five threats as threats to sovereignty indicates that the nature of the sovereignty that Howard asserted was the sovereign will of the executive to be asserted against asylum seekers, the courts, Australian legislation, international law and international opprobrium. The function of sovereignty as a justification was to exclude impediments to executive power based on the democratic will of the Australian

40 Howard, 'Interview with Prime Minister John Howard' (n 31). See Maley (n 22) especially 190 and from 192 for a refutation of the assertion that there was, at least logistically, 'uncontrollable illegal migration'.

41 Howard, 'Interview with Prime Minister John Howard' (n 31).

42 John Howard, 'Offshore Processing', *PM Transcripts* (Media Release, Department of Prime Minister and Cabinet, 21 June 2006) <pmtranscripts.pmc.gov.au>.

43 John Howard, 'Offshore Processing', *PM Transcripts* (Media Release, Department of Prime Minister and Cabinet, 21 June 2006) <pmtranscripts.pmc.gov.au>.

44 John Howard, 'Offshore Processing', *PM Transcripts* (Media Release, Department of Prime Minister and Cabinet, 21 June 2006) <pmtranscripts.pmc.gov.au>.

45 *International Covenant on Civil and Political Rights*, opened for signature 16 December 1965, 2200A (XXI) UNTS (entered into force 3 March 1976); *Optional Protocol to the International Covenant on Civil and Political Rights*, opened for signature 16 December 1966, 2200A (XXI) UNTS, (entered into force 23 March 1976); *Second Optional Protocol to the International Covenant on Civil and Political Rights*, opened for signature 15 December 1989, TTS 44/128 (entered into force 15 December 1989); *Convention on the Rights of the Child*, opened for signature, 20 November 1989 (entered into force 2 September 1990).

electorate. Howard stated, 'The protection of our sovereignty, including Australia's sovereign right to determine who shall enter Australia, is a matter for the Australian government and this parliament'.[46]

Under the next four prime ministers, the migration law which had been justified as an important expression of sovereignty continued. Howard's immediate successors, Labor Prime Ministers Kevin Rudd and Julia Gillard, made no use of the language of sovereignty for the exclusion of noncitizens, but under their governments, except for a brief suspension of offshore processing from 2008 to 2010, the law remained unchanged.[47]

However Tony Abbott, Coalition prime minister 2013–5, characterised boats of asylum seekers attempting to reach Australia as a 'very serious affront to our national sovereignty'.[48] Under his leadership Scott Morrison, Minister for Immigration 2013–4, established a military-led cross-portfolio initiative, the authority for which was within Morrison's discretion, which included towing back asylum seeker boats to Indonesia and the destruction of those boats. It was conducted within the legislated discretion already available to the minister.[49] This initiative was named Operation Sovereign Borders, which continued the characterisation of asylum seekers arriving on Australian territory as a threat to sovereignty and heightened this threat with military language that implied these asylum seekers were the enemy. They become an issue of border security, not international obligation.[50] Malcolm Turnbull, Coalition prime minister 2015–8, made little use of the language of sovereignty but did on one occasion characterise the border protection policy

46 Commonwealth, *Parliamentary Debates*, House of Representatives, 29 August 2001, 30569 (John Howard).

47 Refugee Council of Australia, 'Australia's Offshore Processing Regime: The Facts' (Web Page, 20 May 2020) <www.refugeecouncil.org.au/offshore-processing-facts/3>.

48 Tony Abbott, 'Leigh Sales, 7.30, ABC Television', *PM Transcripts* (Interview, 13 November 2013) <pmtranscripts.pmc.gov.au>.

49 Work Health and Safety (Operation Sovereign Borders) Declaration 2013. This was the only legislation needed. It made changes to the *Work Health and Safety Act 2011* (Cth) to allow public servants to work in what was described as a 'hazardous, uncertain and high-tempo operational environment, having to board vessels, and control and potentially transfer uncooperative persons'.

50 For a background on the Operation Sovereign Borders policy and its interaction with obligations under international law see Joyce Chia, Jane McAdam and Kate Purcell, 'Asylum in Australia: "Operation Sovereign Borders" and International Law' (2014) 32 *Australian Year Book of International Law* 33; Azadeh Dastyari and Asher Hirsch, 'The Ring of Steel: Extraterritorial Migration Controls in Indonesia and Libya and the Complicity of Australia and Italy' (2019) 19 *Human Rights Law Review* 435. See Patrick Emerton and Maria O'Sullivan's discussion of the characterisation of asylum seekers as a border security issue in Patrick Emerton and Maria O'Sullivan, 'Rethinking Asylum Seeker Detention at Sea: The Power to Detain Asylum Seekers at Sea Under the *Maritime Powers Act 2013* (Cth)' (2020) 38(2) *UNSW Law Journal* 695, 695–6.

as 'protecting our national sovereignty'.[51] This policy, he noted, included offshore detention and not allowing people who had sought asylum by boat to ever settle in Australia.[52]

Morrison, the last prime minister of the period, in office 2018–22, continued and strengthened the defences against the same threats that Howard had identified: uninvited asylum seekers arriving on boats, the scrutiny of the judiciary, contemporary Australian law and the implications of international law that might impede the assertion of Westphalian sovereignty. On taking office Morrison asserted that Operation Sovereign Borders, which he had led as immigration minister, was one of 'Australia's greatest national security policy successes'.[53] This success was based, he suggested, on lifelong bans from settling in Australia, regional processing and disrupting people smuggling including by physically turning back asylum seeker vessels.[54] Unlike all previous prime ministers of the period, except Howard, Morrison made regular use of the language of sovereignty in the context of migration.

Morrison also broadened the function of sovereignty to justify excluding the unwanted migrant, by characterising the unwanted migrant as a threat to community safety. Referencing Howard's 2001 election speech[55] Morrison said:

> But there's one great principle that John Howard, I think, put it best in Sydney many years ago: 'Our sovereignty in keeping Australians safe is critical,' and that means – we decide. We decide, as he said, who comes to the country.[56]

This is a misrepresentation. Firstly, although Howard asserted 'we will decide who comes to this country and the circumstances in which they come', he added, 'we'll do that within the framework of the decency for which Australians have always been renowned'.[57] Secondly, Howard's speech was made during the 2001 election campaign which followed soon after the *MV Tampa* incident and the terrorist incident of 9/11. Even in that climate of heightened awareness of terrorist threats, Howard did not characterise asylum seekers as a threat from which Australian people need to be protected. Rather he

51 Malcolm Turnbull, 'Press Gallery, Commonwealth Parliamentary Offices, Sydney', *PM Transcripts* (9 October 2015) <pmtranscripts.pmc.gov.au>.

52 Malcolm Turnbull, 'Press Gallery, Commonwealth Parliamentary Offices, Sydney', *PM Transcripts* (9 October 2015) <pmtranscripts.pmc.gov.au>.

53 Morrison, 'Until the Bell Rings' (n 14).

54 Morrison, 'Until the Bell Rings' (n 14).

55 John Howard, 'Address at the Federal Liberal Party Campaign Launch, Sydney', *PM Transcripts* (Speech, 28 October 2001) <https://pmtranscripts.pmc.gov.au/release/transcript-12389>.

56 Morrison, 'Until the Bell Rings' (n 14).

57 Howard, 'Address at the Federal Liberal Party' (n 55).

characterised his position on sovereignty as resisting demands of people who 'quite literally present themselves at Australia's borders and demand entry no matter what the background or no matter what the circumstances are',[58] or as excluding people not morally worthy of being in Australia.[59] His position is echoed more by Prime Minister Abbott's assertion that asylum seeker boats were a 'serious affront' to sovereignty.[60]

It is Morrison, not Howard, who linked with sovereignty the concept of keeping individual Australians safe. As well as conceptualising sovereignty as a right of a nation, the 'right to run our own show',[61] Morrison linked sovereignty to 'making sure our kids are safe from predators and . . . kicking those people out of this country who would be predators against them'.[62] Removing the unwanted citizen was now personal, expressed as the duty of a parent to a child. He praised Peter Dutton, his Minister for Home Affairs 2017–21, responsible for a portfolio including migration, for achieving this.[63] This broadening of the concept of sovereignty brought the exclusion of people already in Australia, which included asylum seekers but encompassed any noncitizen, within the justification of sovereignty. A suggestion that asylum seekers might be a threat to the population was not itself new. The concern over the inferiority and immorality of the migrant had been expressed before.[64] As recently as 2015 Abbott had warned of the migrant who might be the 'threat in our midst'.[65] What was new in this era was the representation of these personal threats as a threat to national sovereignty.

Morrison elaborated his broadened concept of sovereignty in his first speech to Parliament about the closure of the border in response to the COVID-19 pandemic.[66] Protection of sovereignty was the motif of this speech.[67] In it he characterised an idealised Australian way of life being

58 John Howard, 'Address at the Launch of "A Stronger Tasmania Policy"', *PM Transcripts* (Speech, 2 November 2001) <pmtranscripts.pmc.gov.au>.

59 John Howard, 'Interview with Phillip Clarke, Radio 2GB', *PM Transcripts* (Interview, 8 October 2001) <https://pmtranscripts.pmc.gov.au/release/transcript-12107>; Senate, *Senate Select Committee on the Scrafton Evidence* (Report, December 2004) ch 2 <www.aph.gov.au/Parliamentary_Business/Committees/Senate/Former_Committees/scrafton/report/c02>.

60 Abbott (n 48).

61 Scott Morrison, 'Beliefs That Guide Us' (n 13).

62 Morrison, 'Until the Bell Rings' (n 14).

63 Morrison, 'Until the Bell Rings' (n 14).

64 See Chapter 4 Section II A.

65 Tony Abbott, 'Joint Press Conference, Transcript, Department of Prime Minister and Cabinet', *PM Transcripts* (26 May 2015) <https://pmtranscripts.pmc.gov.au/release/transcript-24499>.

66 Commonwealth, *Parliamentary Debates*, House of Representatives, 8 April 2020, 2909 (Scott Morrison). See Chapter 5 Section III C.

67 Commonwealth, *Parliamentary Debates*, House of Representatives, 8 April 2020, 2909 (Scott Morrison).

protected by sovereignty from the dangerous outsider.[68] This rhetoric echoes his US and UK contemporaries, Donald Trump (US president 2017–21) and Boris Johnson (the former Brexit campaigner and UK prime minister 2019–present), who linked the concept of sovereignty to personal well-being and characterised the uninvited immigrant as a threat to this well-being.[69] Along with those contemporaries Morrison used the concept of sovereignty to position the executive as the protector of individuals' welfare.

In summary, Howard's interpretation of sovereignty as a Westphalian sovereignty of absolute unfettered control, when applied to unwanted asylum seekers, established the broad policy rationale for the amendments to exclude which are examined shortly. The succeeding four prime ministers made less use of the language of sovereignty but continued and strengthened the policy direction originally justified as an assertion of sovereignty. In 2018 as the newly appointed prime minister, Morrison built on this problematising of the entry of asylum seekers as a threat to national sovereignty. He broadened the function of sovereignty to justify 'kicking out', not just preventing entry.[70] He broadened the nature of sovereignty from an assertion of a right to decide who should enter territory. Sovereignty was now about the protection of Australia's vulnerable individuals and a vulnerable way of life. He broadened the threat to sovereignty to include those noncitizens who failed the character test in the *Migration Act 1958* (Cth) s 501 (implied by his use of 'predators'[71]) and not just asylum seekers. The rationale of sovereignty now more explicitly justified all exclusion under the *Migration Act 1958* (Cth) as a right to decide and as an act of protecting the vulnerable.

Concurrent with this, prime ministers gave little attention to the phenomena of globalisation that were driving this unwanted and rapidly growing movement of people.[72] This is the policy context for the amendments to

68 See discussion of this in Chapter 5 Section III C. Commonwealth, *Parliamentary Debates*, House of Representatives, 8 April 2020, 2909–12 (Scott Morrison).

69 See, e.g., Denny Pencheva and Kostas Maronitis, 'Fetishizing Sovereignty in the Remain and Leave Campaigns' (2018) 19(5) *European Politics and Society* 526, 537; Valentina Kostadinova, 'Brexit Is Unlikely to Provide Answers to Governance Problems Under Globalisation' (2017) 37(1) *Economic Affairs* 135; Joseph E Stiglitz, 'Rethinking Globalization in the Trump Era: US-China Relations' (2018) 13(2) *Frontiers of Economics in China* 133, 135, 139.

70 Morrison, 'Until the Bell Rings' (n 14).

71 Morrison, 'Until the Bell Rings' (n 14).

72 See discussion over the rapidly growing movement of people in the period in, for example, Graeme Hugo, 'Globalization and Changes in Australian International Migration' (2006) 23(2) *Journal of Population Research* 107, especially the summary of drivers of increased mobility at 109–10. See also Saskia Sassen, *Expulsions: Brutality and Complexity in the Global Economy* (Harvard University Press, 2014) 13; United Nations, 'World Leaders Adopt First-Ever Global Compact on Migration, Outlining Framework to Protect Millions of Migrants, Support Countries Accommodating Them' (Meetings Coverage, DEV/3375, 10 December 2018).

exclude examined shortly which were justified by the protection of Australia's sovereignty.

From 2000 to 2020, twelve immigration ministers worked with these prime ministers to pass through the Parliament amendments that kept out or removed noncitizens. Only Immigration Minister Philip Ruddock, serving in Howard's ministry, and Morrison as immigration minister and later prime minister, explicitly justified proposed legislative amendments in the Parliament by reference to sovereignty.

III The Function of Sovereignty in the Amendments to Exclude

This section examines how the amendments to exclude and the respective lawmaking debates defended against the threats to sovereignty that Howard identified and to which Morrison added. The laws urgently enacted against asylum seekers in 2001 have become the norm and the use of sovereignty to justify more than their exclusion has continued.[73] What emerges from this analysis is that the sovereignty asserted in 2001, which over the period in question was further broadened, had the function of defending against any interference with the power of the executive over migration law.

A *Keeping Out Unwelcome Noncitizens*

During the period 2000 to 2020 the Parliament passed ten amendments with the stated objective of preventing asylum seekers from arriving on Australian territory.[74] Three amendments using sovereignty as a justification were made from 2001 to 2006.[75] From 2008 to 2013 three further amendments

73 See Oren Gross and Fionnula ni Aolain for discussion of the normalising or emergency measures made in crisis in Oren Gross and Fionnula ni Aolain, *Law in Times of Crisis: Emergency Powers in Theory and Practice* (Cambridge University Press, 2006) 228–43. See also David Dyzenhaus, *The Constitution of Law: Legality in a Time of Emergency* (Cambridge University Press, 2006).

74 *Migration Amendment (Excision from Migration Zone) Act 2001* (Cth); *Migration Amendment (Excision from Migration Zone) (Consequential Provision) Act 2001* (Cth); *Border Protection (Validation and Enforcement Powers) Act 2001* (Cth); *Migration Legislation Amendment (Transitional Movement) Act 2002* (Cth); *Deterring People Smuggling Act 2011* (Cth); *Migration Legislation Amendment (Regional Processing and Other Measures) Act 2012* (Cth); *Migration Amendment (Unauthorised Maritime Arrivals and Other Measures) Act 2013* (Cth); *Migration and Maritime Powers Legislation Amendment (Resolving the Asylum Legacy Caseload) Act 2014* (Cth); *Migration Amendment (Protection and Other Measures) Act 2015* (Cth); *Migration Amendment (Regional Processing Arrangements) Act 2015* (Cth); *Migration Amendment (Repairing Medical Transfers) Act 2019* (Cth).

75 *Migration Amendment (Excision from Migration Zone) Act 2001* (Cth); *Migration Amendment (Excision from Migration Zone) (Consequential Provision) Act 2001* (Cth); *Border Protection (Validation and Enforcement Powers) Act 2001* (Cth).

were made which strengthened the policy direction that sovereignty had previously justified.[76] From 2014 to 2020, the strengthening of the 2001 policy direction continued and was once again explicitly justified as necessary to sovereignty.[77]

The ten amendments to exclude did two contradictory things. They simultaneously shrank the effective sovereign territorial border and expanded Australia's sovereign control[78] in a convoluted effort to assert sovereignty. While military-like terms such as Operation Sovereign Borders and Border Force, introduced from 2013, emphasised the threat at the territorial border, the amendments decoupled the concept of sovereignty from territorial borders, expanding sovereign control beyond the border. This process is analysed shortly.

1 2001–6: The Elastic Sovereign Border

The legislative process of these early amendments is examined in detail because the function that sovereignty played set a pattern that was followed over the period being examined. The amendments were positioned as defences against the same threats to sovereignty that Howard, the prime minister across this period, identified.

In 2001, calling on the Parliament to support three amendments to the *Migration Act 1958* (Cth),[79] Philip Ruddock, the Minister for Immigration and Multicultural Affairs (1996–2003) in the Howard Coalition government, framed the rationale for the three bills as a protection of the government's power: 'The Australian public has a clear expectation that Australian sovereignty, including in the matter of entry of people to Australia, will be protected by this parliament and the government'.[80]

The first of the three amendments shrank Australia's territory for certain purposes. Certain Australian islands were declared not to be part of Australia

76 *Deterring People Smuggling Act 2011* (Cth); *Migration Legislation Amendment (Regional Processing and Other Measures) Act 2012* (Cth); *Migration Amendment (Unauthorised Maritime Arrivals and Other Measures) Act 2013* (Cth).

77 *Migration and Maritime Powers Legislation Amendment (Resolving the Asylum Legacy Caseload) Act 2014* (Cth); *Migration Amendment (Protection and Other Measures) Act 2015* (Cth); *Migration Amendment (Regional Processing Arrangements) Act 2015* (Cth); *Migration Amendment (Repairing Medical Transfers) Act 2019* (Cth).

78 Commonwealth, *Parliamentary Debates*, House of Representatives, 18 September 2001, 30869 (Philip Ruddock). See also Explanatory Memorandum, Migration Amendment (Excision from Migration Zone) (Consequential Provisions) Bill 2001, 2.

79 Migration Amendment (Excision From Migration Zone) Bill 2001; Migration Amendment (Excision From Migration Zone) (Consequential Provisions) Bill 2001; Border Protection (Validation and Enforcement Powers) Bill 2001.

80 Commonwealth, *Parliamentary Debates*, House of Representatives, 18 September 2001, 30869 (Philip Ruddock).

for the purposes of applying for protection.[81] This shielded the government from certain obligations in international law, such as those in the 1951 *Convention Relating to the Status of Refugees* and the 1967 *Protocol Relating to the Status of Refugees* insofar as they had been transformed into provisions of the *Migration Act 1958* (Cth) at that time, and set out the agreed law for dealing with asylum claims made on shore.[82]

Ruddock repeated his rationale of sovereign choice when introducing the second bill: 'It is clearly up to Australia to determine who can cross our borders, who can stay in Australia, and under what conditions such people can remain'.[83] This was a statement of the government's view of the law, not a justification for change.[84] It was a statement of a Westphalian interpretation of sovereignty as absolute control of a territory and its people and did not take into account the commitments Australia had entered into under international law and those commitments that had been transformed into domestic law.[85]

To boost his justification Ruddock claimed that asylum seekers aided by 'people smugglers' were stealing the places of those 'who have the greatest need for protection'.[86] What Ruddock was choosing to do in the name of sovereign choice was to shield the executive from knowing whether any asylum seeker they were excluding by these amendments had a greater or lesser need for protection than others waiting in UNHCR camps. It also shielded him from the consequences of the *Migration Act 1958* (Cth), which set out a process of responding to claims for asylum. Just as keeping asylum seekers offshore on the *MV Tampa* shielded Howard, the prime minister, from

81 Commonwealth, *Parliamentary Debates*, House of Representatives, 18 September 2001, 30870 (Philip Ruddock).; Migration Amendment (Excision from Migration Zone) Bill 2001.

82 *Migration Act 1958* (Cth) compilation on 18 September 2001. See s 5(1) for definitions of Refugee Convention and Refugee Protocol and ss 36 and 411 for the process of responding to asylum seekers.

83 Commonwealth, *Parliamentary Debates*, House of Representatives, 18 September 2001, 30872 (Philip Ruddock).

84 *Robtelmes v Brenan* (1906) 4 CLR 395, 401, reiterated in *Ah Yin v Christie* (1907) 4 CLR 1428, 1431.

85 See Chapter 2 Section VI for a list of those commitments. See also IA Shearer, 'The Relationship Between International Law and Domestic Law', in Brian R Opeskin and Donald Rothwell (eds), *International Law and Australian Federalism* (Melbourne University Press, 1997) 34. Note as well that the *Migration Act 1958* (Cth) s 36(2) in force in 2001 specifically referenced the Refugee Convention and the Refugee Protocol. For further discussion see Hathaway (n 16); Mathews (n 31); Foster, *International Refugee Law* (n 16); Natalie Klein, 'Assessing Australia's Push Back the Boats Policy Under International Law: Legality and Accountability for Maritime Interceptions of Irregular Migrants' (2014) 15 *Melbourne Journal of International Law* 414; Susan Kneebone (ed), *Refugees, Asylum Seekers and the Rule of Law: Comparative Perspectives* (Cambridge University Press, 2009); Bostock (n 32) 294–7.

86 Commonwealth, *Parliamentary Debates*, House of Representatives, 18 September 2001, 30870 (Philip Ruddock).

knowing whether or not they were refugees, as discussed previously, the amendments would shield the immigration minister.[87]

In 2006 an attempt was made to further shrink the border to 'preserve Australia's sovereignty',[88] and because 'Border protection requires continued vigilance'.[89] This was a failed bill to excise all Australian territory from the migration zone.[90] The Opposition mocked the bill. Tony Burke, Labor Shadow Minister for Immigration, Integration and Citizenship, said 'in the name of border protection [the bill] abolishes our nation's border'.[91]

What the excision amendments did, or tried to do, was to avoid the consequences in Australian law of an onshore claim for asylum. Ruddock asserted that the processes used to identify refugees and the place in which claims were assessed were 'issues for sovereign states to settle'.[92] In 2002 Howard had declared the idea of excising all of Australia's territory 'ludicrous',[93] but four years later his immigration minister proposed it in the name of sovereignty.

The second and third 2001 amendments extended sovereign control beyond territorial borders. The second 2001 amendment created a new category of illegality, an 'offshore entry person' in the *Migration Act 1958* (Cth) s 198A.[94] Even though a person had not entered Australian territory, now redefined, this amendment gave power to 'officers including Defence Force personnel' to 'place the person [the offshore entry person] on a vehicle or vessel; restrain the person on a vehicle or vessel; remove the person from a vehicle or vessel; use such force as is necessary and reasonable'.[95]

The 'offshore entry person' was defined by Australian law but excluded from its protection. The amendment excluded the 'offshore entry person' from the protection of the court against this treatment, except the protection offered under the narrow criteria of judicial review by the High Court.[96] This

87 Howard, 'Interview with Prime Minister John Howard' (n 31).
88 Commonwealth, *Parliamentary Debates*, House of Representatives, 11 May 2006, 8 (Andrew Robb).
89 Commonwealth, *Parliamentary Debates*, House of Representatives, 11 May 2006, 7 (Andrew Robb).
90 Migration Amendment (Designated Unauthorised Arrivals) Bill 2006.
91 Commonwealth, *Parliamentary Debates*, House of Representatives, 9 August 2006, 18 (Tony Burke).
92 Commonwealth, *Parliamentary Debates*, House of Representatives, 11 May 2006, 8 (Andrew Robb).
93 Commonwealth, *Parliamentary Debates*, House of Representatives, 9 August 2006, 18 (Tony Burke).
94 Explanatory Memorandum, Migration Amendment (Excision from Migration Zone) (Consequential Provisions) Bill 2001, 6.
95 Explanatory Memorandum, Migration Amendment (Excision from Migration Zone) (Consequential Provisions) Bill 2001, 7.
96 Explanatory Memorandum, Migration Amendment (Excision from Migration Zone) (Consequential Provisions) Bill 2001, 7. Achieved by adding s 494AA(1)(d).

'offshore entry person' was placed outside the sovereign territory of Australia for asylum seeking but was still subjected to its sovereign power for the act of attempting to enter. Asylum seeking on this excluded territory was declared illegal, and the amendment allowed the asylum seeker to be bodily detained, restrained, removed and subjected to force.[97]

Finally, this second amendment purported to defend sovereignty by creating a temporary rather than permanent protection visa for those who made a successful claim for protection, explicitly denying these refugees family reunion.[98] This assertion of sovereignty was justified as a discouragement to others, the same logic that is applied to criminal penalties.[99] The impact on the mental and physical health of temporary protection on refugees has been well documented over the decades.[100]

The third of the three bills aimed to enhance the 'control' of Australia's maritime borders.[101] Retrospective in its effect, it made all the actions taken by Australia in the *MV Tampa* incident legal and gave power to 'move vessels carrying unauthorised arrivals and those on board'.[102] The minister justified this measure, too, as essential for the 'maintenance of Australia's sovereign right' to 'determine who would enter, or not'.[103] The bill authorised the executive action taken in the *MV Tampa* issue, asserted by the prime minister as a right, to ensure its legality and authorise future action. In debate the

97 Explanatory Memorandum, Migration Amendment (Excision from Migration Zone) (Consequential Provisions) Bill 2001, 7. Achieved by adding s 494AA(1)(d). Note this is the policy attempted by the Sunak Conservative government in the UK and admired by President Trump. 'PM Statement on the Stop the Boats Bill' (7 March 2023) <www.gov.uk>; Madeline Gleeson and Theodore Konstadinides, 'The UK's Rwanda Policy and Lessons from Australia', *UHCLA* (14 March 2024) <https://ukconstitutionallaw.org>; *SBS News* (4 August 2017) <www.sbs.com.au/news/article/you-are-worse-than-i-am-transcript-reveals-turnbull-told-trump-he-could-decide-not-to-take-asylum-seekers/pasw4h0t7>.

98 Commonwealth, *Parliamentary Debates*, House of Representatives, 18 September 2001, 30872 (Philip Ruddock).

99 Commonwealth, *Parliamentary Debates*, House of Representatives, 18 September 2001, 30872 (Philip Ruddock). See, eg, *Sentencing Act 2017* (SA) s 4(10)(d).

100 See, e.g., Nicholas Procter, 'Support for Temporary Protection Visa Holder: Partnering Individual Mental Health Support and Migration Law Consultation' (2004) 11(1) *Psychiatry, Psychology and Law* 110; Shakeh Momartin et al, 'A Comparison of the Mental Health of Refugees with Temporary Versus Permanent Protection Visas' (2006) 185(7) *Medical Journal of Australia* 357.

101 Commonwealth, *Parliamentary Debates*, House of Representatives, 18 September 2001, 308071 (Philip Ruddock).

102 Commonwealth, *Parliamentary Debates*, House of Representatives, 18 September 2001, 308073 (Philip Ruddock).

103 Commonwealth, *Parliamentary Debates*, House of Representatives, 18 September 2001, 308072–3 (Philip Ruddock).

immigration minister contrasted asylum seekers with 'settlers from all over the world who have come to Australia lawfully'.[104]

The legality of the executive actions in the *Tampa MV* incident were tested in *Victorian Council for Civil Liberties Inc v Minister for Immigration and Multicultural Affairs*,[105] which was overturned by *Ruddock v Vadarlis*.[106] The majority of the Federal Court found that executive power under s 61 of the Constitution, unless limited or changed by legislation, empowered the executive to prevent entry of noncitizens and effect their exclusion. However, in dissent Black CJ drew from English historical jurisprudence to argue that the prerogative powers of the executive under s 61 did not extend to excluding aliens in time of peace.[107] Therefore Black CJ concluded that the government went beyond their legal power in *MV Tampa*. However, the 'sovereign right to determine who will enter and reside in Australia' and the place of that right in the executive's power was confirmed by the majority.[108]

These bills were passed by the Parliament without amendment. The debate adopted a simplistic promotion of sovereignty that ignored the interdependencies of a globalised world and the international obligations to which Australia had explicitly committed.[109] The view of sovereignty promulgated was an unquestionable right to control the entry of people, a right purportedly threatened by asylum seekers who were not referred by the UNHCR.[110] The debate reveals the impotence or unwillingness of the Parliament to acknowledge the phenomena of globalisation that were drivers of the situation of unauthorised asylum seekers.[111] Instead both sides of Parliament agreed that border control was the problem. The government's solutions were excision and offshore processing in Nauru and temporary protection visas (TPVs). The Opposition

104 Commonwealth, *Parliamentary Debates*, House of Representatives, 18 September 2001, 30871 (Philip Ruddock).

105 (2001) 110 FCR 452.

106 (2001) 110 FCR 491.

107 (2001) 110 FCR 500.

108 Kim Rubenstein contests the use of sovereignty to justify the action and contests the use of the concept of absolute power to exclude aliens in Kim Rubenstein, 'Citizenship, Sovereignty and Migration: Australia's Exclusive Approach to Membership of the Community' (2002) 13(2) *Public Law Review* 102, 104. Michael Head warns that the High Court's reversal of the Federal Court decision in *MV Tampa Case* (n 4) gave licence to unfettered executive power and arbitrary detention, in Michael Head, 'The High Court and the Tampa Refugees' (2002) 11(1) *Griffith Law Review* 23, 32. The legal reasoning and constitutional interpretation of the majority judgment has been questioned. See, e.g., Bradley Selway, 'All at Sea – Constitutional Assumptions and "the Executive Power of the Commonwealth"' (2003) 31 *Federal Law Review* 495, 506. Selway concludes that s 61 executive power is still subject to legislative and judicial restraint. The nature of s 61 executive power continues to be investigated. See, e.g., Peta Stephenson, 'Statutory Displacement of the Prerogative in Australia', in Janina Boughey and Lisa Burton Crawford (eds), *Interpreting Executive Power* (Federation Press, 2020) 203.

109 See Chapter 2 Section VI.

110 Commonwealth, Parliamentary Debates, *House of Representatives*, 18 September 2001, 30869 (Philip Ruddock).

111 See Chapter 3 Section III B.

spokesperson, Con Sciacca, Labor Shadow Minister for Immigration from 1998 to 2001, claimed the history of TPVs had shown they are not an effective disincentive.[112] The Opposition proposed using the coastguard and international cooperation, which they explained meant working with Indonesia to stop people leaving on boats for Australia.[113]

The Opposition's comments reveal that their conceptualisation of the problem matched that of the government. The Opposition position put by Stephen Martin, Shadow Minister for Trade and Tourism, was: 'Labor believes we cannot be a soft touch [to people smugglers], but that means having a smart touch in gaining international cooperation'.[114] This international cooperation, the Opposition explained, would involve convincing Indonesia to manage these asylum seekers to avoid them travelling by boat to Australia. It did not address the broad globalised drivers of migration.[115] This narrow view is further revealed in the Opposition's other proposal of a 'coastguard' to be 'tough on illegals and crack down on boat people'.[116]

An anecdote recounted by a government member highlights, perhaps inadvertently, two phenomena of globalisation that the Parliament appeared to ignore but that were at the nexus of globalisation, sovereignty and migration law. It also reveals the function that the assertion of sovereignty played in the legislative process. During debate Bruce Billson, Liberal Member for Dunkley 1996–2016, recounted a discussion he had with Ruddock, at that time immigration minister:

> Philip, do you know what worries me? It is that the best advice I can give my local constituents [Afghans] is to save up their money and have their relatives arrive 'illegally'. I don't want to give my constituents that advice. I do not want to say that, somehow, they are infinitely advantaged, infinitely better off than people in refugee camps if they can cobble together the cash, pay a people smuggler $16,000 to $19,000 each and arrive on our shores illegally and that their prospects of being granted a refugee visa through the court system will be infinitely better than if the United Nations High Commissioner for Refugees, the dude who looks after this complicated problem, looks at their case and says, 'I'm sorry, there are others whose circumstances are more compelling'.[117]

112 Commonwealth, *Parliamentary Debates*, House of Representatives, 19 September 2001, 30956 (Con Sciacca).
113 Commonwealth, *Parliamentary Debates*, House of Representatives, 19 September 2001, 30956 (Con Sciacca).
114 Commonwealth, *Parliamentary Debates*, House of Representatives, 19 September 2001, 31013 (Stephen Martin).
115 See Chapter 3 Section III.
116 Commonwealth, *Parliamentary Debates*, House of Representatives, 19 September 2001, 31013 (Stephen Martin).
117 Commonwealth, *Parliamentary Debates*, House of Representatives, 19 September 2001, 30961 (Bruce Billson).

In this simple anecdote Billson raised two phenomena of globalisation that the amendments and Opposition proposals ignored. The first is the phenomenon of globalised communication technology. These technologies provide instant communication and financial transactions, making it possible to fund and organise the movement of a person across the world outside the frameworks of national sovereignty.[118] Known as a tool for terrorism,[119] this same technology facilitates aspirations by providing detailed information about the opportunities and freedoms in other places and maintains strong family ties.[120]

The second phenomenon that Billson raised is the inability or failure of international institutions of which Australia is a member to address unregulated migration. These Afghan relatives, he said,

> go to the United Nations High Commissioner for Refugees and they visit the Red Cross in northern Pakistan. My local community is frustrated that their relatives cannot gain entry. That frustration is often borne out of the simple fact that there are 23 million displaced refuge-seeking individuals under the supervision of the United Nations High Commissioner for Refugees. There is a handful of countries around the world that offer a haven for those people – for 23 million people seeking somewhere to resettle, seeking a refuge.[121]

While not recommending using people smugglers, he demonstrated in this anecdote the logic of doing so and the lack of viable alternatives.[122]

Failure to address the phenomena and consequences of globalisation allowed the Parliament to take a narrow view of the problem it faced against which it could successfully assert its sovereignty. Asylum seekers were characterised as 'illegals' and 'queue jumpers',[123] 'customers' of people smugglers,[124] and as not genuinely persecuted because they had enough money to pay a people smuggler.[125] The people smugglers were labelled as 'criminal gangs'

118 See Chapter 3 Section II C.
119 See Chapter 3 Section II C.
120 See Chapter 3 Section II B.
121 Commonwealth, *Parliamentary Debates*, House of Representatives, 19 September 2001, 30961 (Bruce Billson).
122 See Bostock (n 32) 299–300.
123 Commonwealth, *Parliamentary Debates*, House of Representatives, 19 September 2001, 31012 (Stephen Martin).
124 Commonwealth, *Parliamentary Debates*, House of Representatives, 18 September 2001, 30870 (Philip Ruddock).
125 Commonwealth, *Parliamentary Debates*, House of Representatives, 19 September 2001, 30962 (Bruce Billson); Commonwealth, *Parliamentary Debates*, House of Representatives, 19 September 2001, 30968 (Jackie Kelly).

and 'the real villains'.[126] Both asylum seekers and people smugglers were characterised as a threat to Australia's sovereignty because of their attempt to enter Australian territory in order to seek safety.[127]

This detailed examination of the early debates has been made because these debates set a precedent that was closely followed. The rationale of protecting or asserting sovereignty functioned in these amendments to enhance executive control, avoid the implications of Australian domestic law by retrospective legislation and offshore processing, minimise the scrutiny of the courts and avoid or minimise the impact of Australia's obligations under international law.[128] The assertion of sovereignty also allowed the drivers of the globalisation phenomenon of the increased movement of displaced people, forced migrants and asylum seekers and the inadequacy of the global response through international institutions, to be either ignored or represented as the enemy of sovereignty. The precedent that this 2001 legislative process set is not just one of political rhetoric. These early amendments established a framework of laws and justifications that has been followed as a template for further amendments.

2 *Exclusion Without the Language of Sovereignty: 2011–3 Amendments*

During the period 2011 to 2013 a Labor government was in office and the language of sovereignty was not used, but three of the four amendments in this period refined and extended the previous government's amendments that were justified at the time as an important expression of national sovereignty.[129]

Chris Bowen, Minister for Immigration in the Gillard Labor government 2010–3, made this consistency explicit in three ways. Firstly in his second reading speech for the Deterring People Smuggling Bill 2011 he emphasised

126 Commonwealth, *Parliamentary Debates*, House of Representatives, 19 September 2001, 30956 (Con Sciacca).

127 Commonwealth, *Parliamentary Debates*, House of Representatives, 18 September 2001, 30870 (Philip Ruddock); Commonwealth, *Parliamentary Debates*, House of Representatives, 19 September 2001, 30968 (Jackie Kelly).

128 McAdam and Chong argue that international law matters because it establishes a standard of 'dignity and fairness' to which Australia has voluntarily committed. She expresses concern that Howard implied that Australia could ignore these commitments and 'make our own moral judgments'. McAdam and Chong (n 16) 174–7, citing Sally Sara, 'Prime Minister Continues to Push for Regional Services', *AM, ABC Radio* (18 February 2000) <www.abc.net.au/am/storie/s101290.htm>. Note Howard made this statement before the *MV Tampa* incident and these amendments.

129 *Deterring People Smuggling Act 2011* (Cth); *Migration Legislation Amendment (Regional Processing and Other Measures) Act 2012* (Cth); Migration *Amendment (Unauthorised Maritime Arrivals and Other Measures) Act 2013* (Cth).

consistency with the previous government's policy and noted that the amendments 'do not affect the treatment of individuals seeking protection or asylum in Australia'.[130] Secondly, the aim of these amendments was to 'restore to the executive the power to manage one of a government's core functions'.[131] The consistency with the previous amendments justified as asserting sovereignty indicates that the sovereignty that the previous government had defended from the judiciary, international law and domestic law was the executive control of migration decisions. Thirdly, consistent with the previous government's amendments were the threats against which the amendments defended executive power. These threats were the scrutiny of the courts and the implications of international law.

The first amendment was the Deterring People Smuggling Bill 2011. In an earlier amendment, the *Border Protection Legislation Amendment Act 1999* (Cth), Ruddock, the Coalition immigration minister, introduced the phrase 'lawful right to come to Australia'.[132] This was in the context of defining and criminalising people smuggling. The Deterring People Smuggling Bill 2011 gave a legislative definition. 'No lawful right to come to Australia' meant that under Australian domestic law, with limited exceptions, a visa was necessary to lawfully enter Australia. This was made retrospective to 1999 and was passed just a day before an appeal by a young Indonesian person accused of people smuggling was heard in the Victorian Supreme Court.

Scott Morrison, Shadow Minister for Immigration and Citizenship 2009–13, justified the Opposition's support by characterising the bill as a limit on the courts and as justified under international law.[133] He echoed the threats to sovereignty Howard claimed. He said: 'Courts may have their opinions on these things – but what the parliament is saying here today is that this parliament has an opinion about these matters, and we are making it crystal clear what constitutes this unlawful act'.[134] While quoting the statement in art 31 of the Refugee Convention that 'Contracting States shall not impose penalties, on account of their illegal entry or presence', he asserted that 'Australia has different rules and systems for dealing with those who would seek to enter Australia illegally'.[135] In the debate he was not challenged

130 Commonwealth, *Parliamentary Debates*, House of Representatives, 1 November 2011, 12349 (Brendan O'Connor).

131 Commonwealth, *Parliamentary Debates*, House of Representatives, 21 September 2011, 10946 (Chris Bowen).

132 Explanatory Memorandum, Border Protection Legislation Amendment Bill 1999, 48.

133 Commonwealth, *Parliamentary Debates*, House of Representatives, 1 November 2011, 12353 (Scott Morrison).

134 Commonwealth, *Parliamentary Debates*, House of Representatives, 1 November 2011, 12353 (Scott Morrison).

135 Commonwealth, *Parliamentary Debates*, House of Representatives, 1 November 2011, 12353 (Scott Morrison).

on the ground that these different rules and systems could amount to 'penalties', which the international convention forbids.[136]

The second amendment introduced was the Migration Legislation Amendment (Regional Processing and Other Measures) Bill 2012. This continued the previous government's efforts to clarify and strengthen the executive power, already in place, and shield it from judicial interference. The amendment was a response to the High Court judgment in *Plaintiff M70/2011*.[137] In that case the court that found that two Afghan asylum seekers could not be removed by the immigration minister to Malaysia because it was a country whose laws did not provide the assurances necessary under the *Migration Act 1958* (Cth) to be processed and treated as asylum seekers according to international law.[138] Without using the specific language of sovereignty, Bowen positioned his amendment as 'restoring executive power to set Australia's border protection policies'.[139]

Also continued from previous debates was the narrow conceptualisation of globalisation. Bowen said:

> These amendments are designed to provide the government of the day with the flexibility to find practical solutions with regional partners to reduce the risk of the loss of life at sea, to combat people smuggling and to determine the border protection policy it determines to be in the national interest.[140]

He declared a belief, but provided no evidence, that offshore processing was a deterrent 'to those dangerous boat journeys'.[141] The separation of the policy goals of addressing people smugglers and asylum seekers was blurred. He aimed to 'remove the lure of probable settlement in Australia, the product that people smugglers are able to sell'.[142] Australia was characterised as an

136 See discussion in Guy S Goodwin-Gill, 'Article 31 of the 1951 Convention Relating to the Status of Refugees: Non-Penalization, Detention, and Protection', in Erika Feller, Volker Türk and Frances Nicholson (eds), *Refugee Protection in International Law: UNHCR's Global Consultations on International Protection* (Cambridge University Press, 2003) 185.

137 *Plaintiff M70/2011 v Minister for Immigration and Citizenship* and *Plaintiff M106/2011 v Minister for Immigration and Citizenship* [2011] HCA 32.

138 *Plaintiff M70/2011 v Minister for Immigration and Citizenship* and *Plaintiff M106/2011 v Minister for Immigration and Citizenship* [2011] HCA 32.

139 Commonwealth, *Parliamentary Debates*, House of Representatives, 21 September 2011, 10945 (Chris Bowen).

140 Commonwealth, *Parliamentary Debates*, House of Representatives, 21 September 2011, 10945 (Chris Bowen).

141 Commonwealth, *Parliamentary Debates*, House of Representatives, 21 September 2011, 10945 (Chris Bowen).

142 Commonwealth, *Parliamentary Debates*, House of Representatives, 21 September 2011, 10946 (Chris Bowen).

attractive country, drawing asylum seekers to its shore. The drivers for people arriving by boat continued to be largely unexamined in the debate. The practical solutions involved increasing the immigration minister's discretion to purchase the sovereignty of other nations. Bowen stated, 'the only condition for the designation of a country is that the minister thinks that it is in the national interest to make the designation'.[143]

Morrison confirmed that the bill was a return to what was in place under the previous Coalition government's policies, but he nevertheless negotiated an amendment to deny the executive the very broad discretion proposed.[144] The bill also ensured that unaccompanied minors could be involuntarily transferred to a third country.[145] Morrison expressed no concerns regarding this.[146]

The third amendment was the Migration Amendment (Unauthorised Maritime Arrivals and Other Measures) Bill 2013. This bill also sought to reinforce the measures put in place by the previous government, which that government had justified as asserting sovereignty. The bill echoed the failed Migration Amendment (Designated Unauthorised Arrivals) Bill 2006 and achieved a final decoupling of territory from sovereignty in migration law concerning asylum seekers. In his second reading speech Bowen explained that the objective of the amendment was to ensure that, even if a person managed to arrive on the mainland, the offshore processing legislation would apply to them. The bill also legislated an express public interest power for the immigration minister to revoke any determination that a person was not subject to regional processing.[147] Bowen noted what he called the 'safety valve' of s 198AE, giving the immigration minister discretion in the public interest to exempt an 'unauthorised maritime arrival' from regional processing.[148] The bill was passed with a Senate amendment that required reporting to the Parliament.

During this period, the only time in the decades of interest that a Labor government was in office, migration law continued to focus on the exclusion of asylum seekers and to defend against the threats that Howard had identified by increasing executive control of migration decisions and attempting

143 Commonwealth, *Parliamentary Debates*, House of Representatives, 21 September 2011, 10946 (Chris Bowen).

144 Commonwealth, *Parliamentary Debates*, House of Representatives, 22 September 2011, 11177 (Scott Morrison); Amendment BP256 2010 2011 2012, Migration Legislation Amendment (Offshore Processing and Other Measures) Bill 2011, 2.

145 Commonwealth, *Parliamentary Debates*, House of Representatives, 21 September 2011, 10947 (Chris Bowen).

146 Commonwealth, *Parliamentary Debates*, House of Representatives, 22 September 2011, 11177 (Scott Morrison).

147 Commonwealth, *Parliamentary Debates*, House of Representatives, 31 October 2012, 12739 (Chris Bowen).

148 Commonwealth, *Parliamentary Debates*, House of Representatives, 31 October 2012, 12738 (Chris Bowen).

to minimise the scrutiny of the judiciary and the implications of international law.[149]

However, there was one important and impactful exception to this policy direction. The fourth bill introduced in this period was aimed at inclusion, not exclusion, and was the only bill that moved out of the policy position established by the previous government and that limited the minister's discretion. The Migration Amendment (Complementary Protection) Bill 2011 transformed Australia's commitments under the *International Covenant on Civil and Political Rights* (ICCPR), the *Convention against Torture and Other Cruel, Inhuman or Degrading Treatment or Punishment* (CAT) and the *Convention on the Rights of the Child* (CROC) into the *Migration Act 1958* (Cth), making them Australian law and in that way obliging the consideration of other factors beyond conventional reasons for granting protection.[150] This meant that, even if an asylum seeker's claims for protection did not fit within the five Refugee Convention reasons of fearing persecution on the grounds of race, religion, nationality, political opinion or membership of a particular social group,[151] Australian domestic law required that the delegate consider other risks such as those set out in the CAT and the CROC. The espoused rationale for this change was efficiency but its effect was to broaden the statutory grounds for protection.[152]

The minister explained that the CAT and CROC included a commitment to not refoul those at serious risk of harm for reasons not covered under the Refugee Convention.[153] The situation which the bill addressed was that

149 Note that some of the asylum seeker exclusionary measures were reversed for a short time between 2008 and 2010.

150 *International Covenant on Civil and Political Rights*, opened for signature 16 December 1965, 999 UNTS 171 (entered into force 3 March 1976); *Optional Protocol to the International Covenant on Civil and Political Rights*, opened for signature 16 December 1966, 999 UNTS 171 (entered into force 23 March 1976); *Second Optional Protocol to the International Covenant on Civil and Political Rights*, opened for signature 15 December 1989 (entered into force 15 December 1989); *Convention Against Torture and Other Cruel, Inhuman or Degrading Treatment or Punishment,* opened for signature 10 December 1984, 1465 UNTS 85 (entered into force 26 June 1987); *Convention on the Rights of the Child,* opened for signature 20 November 1989, 1577 UNTS 3 (entered into force 2 September 1990).

151 Michelle Foster notes that the United Nations High Commissioner for Refugees recognises that 'the responsibility to protect in the context of refugee law is now understood to involve a wider set of obligations than those set out in the Refugee Convention alone'. Michelle Foster, 'Non-Refoulement, on the Basis of Socioeconomic Deprivation: The Scope of Complementary Protection in International Human Rights Law', in Mary Crock and Tom D Campbell (eds), *Refugees and Rights* (Taylor & Francis Group, 2015) 127, 129–31 ('Non-Refoulement').

152 Commonwealth, *Parliamentary Debates*, House of Representatives, 24 February 2011, 1356, 1359 (Chris Bowen).

153 Commonwealth, *Parliamentary Debates*, House of Representatives, 24 February 2011, 1357 (Chris Bowen).

people needing protection for these reasons could only be granted a protection visa by the personal intervention of the immigration minister.

Reliance on the non-compellable discretionary power of the immigration minister to ensure compliance with obligations to not refoul was inconsistent with Australia's international commitments.[154] The amendment expanded the reasons to grant a protection visa in the act to incorporate these other international instruments.[155]

Counter to the dominant policy direction, this amendment widened statutory grounds for inclusion, embraced international law obligations and limited the immigration minister's discretion. Writing contemporaneously with this amendment's enactment, Jane McAdam welcomed it because it transformed Australia's international commitments into domestic law.[156] She saw this amendment as heralding a 'new domestic protection paradigm' based on rights in law rather than, as previously, the immigration minister's discretion.[157]

3 An Affront to Sovereignty: 2014–8

With the return of a Coalition government the language of sovereignty also returned, and the direction of the laws put in place in 2001 was further strengthened. Four amendments were proposed and three were successful.

The first 'exclusion amendment' bill to be presented to the Parliament failed, but the debate reveals the government's objective, which was to restore ministerial discretion over asylum seeker protection decisions. The bill aimed to reverse the *Migration Amendment (Complementary Protection) Act 2011* (Cth). The title of the bill, the Migration Amendment (Regaining Control Over Australia's Protection Obligations) Bill 2013, summarised the intent. The justification for this bill from Scott Morrison, Minister for Immigration in the Abbott Coalition government 2013–4, made clear that the control to be regained was that of the immigration minister. Morrison justified the proposed reversal of the *Migration Amendment (Complementary Protection) Act 2011* (Cth) by criticising the courts, which he claimed had 'broadened the scope of the interpretation of these [non-Refugee Convention] obligations beyond that which is required under international law'.[158] Echoing his

154 Jane McAdam, 'From Humanitarian Discretion to Complementary Protection – Reflections on the Emergence of Human Rights-Based Refugee Protection in Australia' (2011) *Australian International law Journal* 53–4 ('From Humanitarian Discretion').

155 For a detailed analysis of the link between the Refugee Convention and international human rights norms see Hathaway (n 16).

156 McAdam, 'From Humanitarian Discretion' (n 154) 55.

157 McAdam, 'From Humanitarian Discretion' (n 154) 54–5.

158 Commonwealth, *Parliamentary Debates*, House of Representatives, 11 December 2013, 1522 (Scott Morrison).

prime minister's claim that asylum seekers were 'playing us for mugs',[159] he criticised the system of judicial review, claiming that it was vulnerable to asylum seekers attempting to 'make vexatious claims to try to game the system in the courts'.[160] What the bill would achieve was to shore up executive control by restoring the immigration minister's previous discretion to decide whether complementary protection was necessary to meet Australia's non-refoulement obligations. The Opposition claimed that Morrison's attack on the courts was without basis.[161] This bill was unsuccessful, but its aims were not abandoned.

The second of the three amendments was the Migration Amendment (Protection and Other Measures) Bill 2015. While otherwise successful, it did fail in one area, which was the attempt to reduce the judiciary's role and enhance the immigration minister's power. This was to be achieved by inserting a definition, a new s 6A in the *Migration Act 1958* (Cth), for assessing the real chance of an asylum seeker experiencing significant harm if returned to their country. This limitation on non-refoulement obligations under the ICCPR and CAT aimed to give the immigration minister more power over complementary protection, reducing the influence of international obligations and the interpretive scope for the judiciary.[162]

Having failed on the first attempt to return complementary protection to the immigration minister's personal discretion, the new amendment proposed a different strategy to reduce the scope of the protection that could be interpreted under the legislation.[163] The risk of significant harm, which included being 'arbitrarily deprived of [one's] life', the 'death penalty' and 'torture', was now to be assessed under the new standard of being 'more likely than not', meaning, as Morrison explained, 'greater than a 50 per cent chance'.[164] This meant that a delegate could assess country information and the individual's claims, and if it appeared there was less than a 50% chance they would be killed or tortured then they could be sent back to their country of origin.

159 Julian Drape and Lauren Farrow, 'Asylum Seekers Playing Us for Mugs: Abbott', *Sydney Morning Herald* (online, 9 June 2012) <www.smh.com.au/national/asylum-seekers-playing-us-for-mugs-abbott-20120609-202d4.html>.

160 Commonwealth, *Parliamentary Debates*, House of Representatives, 11 December 2013, 2345 (Scott Morrison). See Anthea Vogl and Elyse Methven, 'We Will Decide Who Comes to This Country, and How They Behave: A Critical Reading of the Asylum Seeker Code of Behaviour' (2015) 40(3) *Alternative Law Journal* 175. Their analysis of the Code of Behaviour demonstrates that it is framed by an argument that Australians need protecting from asylum seekers, rather than asylum seekers being the ones who need protection.

161 Commonwealth, *Parliamentary Debates*, House of Representatives, 11 December 2013, 2339 (Mark Dreyfus).

162 See Foster, 'Non-Refoulement' (n 151) 127.

163 Migration Amendment (Protection and Other Measures) Bill 2014; Commonwealth, *Parliamentary Debates*, House of Representatives, 25 June 2014, 7279 (Scott Morrison).

164 Migration Amendment (Protection and Other Measures) Bill 2014 item 6A.

This proposed change was in fact what seems to have already been departmental policy approved by the immigration minister but was challenged in *Minister for Immigration and Citizenship v SZQRB*.[165] The lawful standard was judged to be the same 'real chance' applied to assess refugee claims on the Refugee Convention grounds. The departmental policy had now been shown to be 'not in accordance with Australian law'.[166] This failed measure in the amendment tried unsuccessfully to make lawful this previously unlawful policy of a higher standard of proof. The human impact on failed asylum claims shown in retrospect to have been illegally assessed but which were not appealed has not been examined.[167]

These two failed attempts to shield migration decisions to exclude asylum seekers from judicial scrutiny and the influence of international law provide further insight into the nature and function of the sovereignty which justified these policy directions. The concept of sovereignty was used here to justify an attempt to legislate unfettered executive decision-making.

The third amendment passed in the Parliament was the Migration and Maritime Powers Legislation Amendment (Resolving the Asylum Legacy Caseload) Bill 2014. The rationale for this amendment was presented as delivering 'national security and economic prosperity'.[168] This was to be achieved through the bill by measures including banning any 'illegal maritime arrival' from gaining permanent protection and strengthening the minister's power to direct boat turn backs at sea.[169] Asylum seekers, people smugglers and the implications of Australia's obligations under international law were all targets of this amendment, and its goal was to exclude them or their influence from Australian territory. Asylum seekers were characterised as those 'who flagrantly disregard our laws and arrive illegally in Australia'.[170] They

165 [2013] FCAFC 33.

166 *Minister for Immigration and Citizenship v SZQRB* [2013] FCAFC 33, [247].

167 This is possibly a large number. After initial rejection by the departmental delegate the applicant for asylum needed first to have the merits of their claim reviewed by the Administrative Appeals Tribunal before they were eligible to appeal to the minister. While independent, the tribunal takes into account departmental policy and is bound by ministerial directions made under *Migration Act 1958* (Cth) s 499. For a discussion of the Administrative Appeals Tribunal's independence see Chantal Bostok, 'The Effect of Ministerial Directions on Tribunal Independence' (2011) 66 *AIAL Forum* 33.

168 Commonwealth, *Parliamentary Debates*, House of Representatives, 25 September 2014, 10545 (Scott Morrison).

169 Commonwealth, *Parliamentary Debates*, House of Representatives, 25 September 2014, 10545 (Scott Morrison). Note Ante Missbach and Wayne Palmer argue that boat turn backs are a form of people smuggling into Indonesia by the Australian government in Antje Missbach and Wayne Palmer, 'People Smuggling by a Different Name: Australia's "Turnbacks" of Asylum Seekers to Indonesia' (2020) 74(2) *Australian Journal of International Affairs* 185.

170 Commonwealth, *Parliamentary Debates*, House of Representatives, 25 September 2014, 10545 (Scott Morrison).

were not to be 'rewarded with a permanent protection visa'.[171] Permanent protection for Refugee Convention reasons was represented as a 'reward', presumably for those who waited in refugee camps and fitted under the cap on humanitarian intake that the immigration minister now sought the power to set in this new bill.[172]

Child asylum seekers and the influence of international jurisprudence were also targets of the bill. Morrison and Richard Marles, Shadow Minister for Immigration and Border Protection 2013–6, agreed that children 'inherit the immigration status of their parents'.[173] No mention was made of the situation of unaccompanied child asylum seekers.[174] The amendment also removed all references to the Refugee Convention in the *Migration Act 1958* (Cth), instead codifying an Australian interpretation. Morrison justified this as defending Australia against 'the interpretations of foreign courts or judicial bodies which seek to expand the scope of the refugee convention well beyond what was ever intended by this country or this parliament'.[175] Marles highlighted the impotence of such a measure as 'our courts will refer to them [interpretations of foreign courts] anyway, even if this were to pass the parliament'.[176]

Neither Morrison nor others in the Parliament, except one, addressed the global developments that created the problem they attempted to solve. The exception was Susan Lines, Western Australian Labor senator 2013–present, who commented on the narrowness of the debate: 'All the questions from government backbenchers to ministers, whether in the other place or in the Senate, are about stopping the boats. They are not about the world's global refugee issue'.[177] There was no response to this contribution to the debate.[178]

171 Commonwealth, *Parliamentary Debates*, House of Representatives, 25 September 2014, 10545 (Scott Morrison).
172 Commonwealth, *Parliamentary Debates*, House of Representatives, 25 September 2014, 10545 (Scott Morrison).
173 Commonwealth, *Parliamentary Debates*, House of Representatives, 22 October 2014, 11576 (Richard Marles); Commonwealth, *Parliamentary Debates*, House of Representatives, 25 September 2014, 10548 (Scott Morrison).
174 See Maria O'Sullivan's critique of the operation of the law on this issue even before this further amendment. O'Sullivan suggests a conflict of interest in the minister's roles as guardian and deporter of children and she notes the uneasy fit of this treatment of children with comparable countries' practice and with the *Convention on the Rights of the Child* in Maria O'Sullivan, 'The "Best Interests" of Asylum-Seeker Children: Who's Guarding the Guardian?' (2013) 38(4) *Alternative Law Journal* 224; see especially 227.
175 Commonwealth, *Parliamentary Debates*, House of Representatives, 25 September 2014, 10547 (Scott Morrison).
176 Commonwealth, *Parliamentary Debates*, House of Representatives, 22 October 2014, 11576 (Richard Marles).
177 Commonwealth, *Parliamentary Debates*, Senate, 4 December 2014, 10263 (Susan Lines).
178 See also Sharon Pickering and Leanne Weber, 'New Deterrence Scripts in Australia's Rejuvenated Offshore Detention Regime for Asylum Seekers' (2014) 39(4) *Law & Social Inquiry* 1006, 1007. Pickering and Weber comment on the narrow focus on deterrence of asylum seekers and unwelcome migrants rather than rights under international law.

Asylum seekers, under the framework of using sovereignty to justify exclusion, were positioned as a threat to Australian sovereignty.

The fourth amendment passed was the Migration Amendment (Regional Processing Arrangements) Bill 2015, and through this the power of the government to avoid sovereign responsibilities by purchasing the sovereignty of other states was legislated. Peter Dutton, Minister for Immigration and Border Protection 2014–8 in both the Abbott and Turnbull Coalition governments, stated that his rationale was to stop people smuggling and save the lives of people who might be drowned as they attempted to come to Australia by boat.[179] What the bill in fact proposed was to remove any possibility that the judiciary could find that the government did not have the power to operate regional processing, legislatively enabled to that point by the *Migration Legislation Amendment (Regional Processing and Other Measures) Act 2012* (Cth). The new amendment was to apply retrospectively from 18 August 2012 onward. It aimed to nullify any adverse outcome that might arise from the High Court's contemporary consideration of an appeal concerning the Commonwealth's 'securing, funding and participating' in the detention of a Bangladeshi asylum seeker in a Nauruan detention centre.[180] The amendment was passed, and the majority of the High Court found that the Commonwealth's actions in paying Nauru to detain asylum seekers were lawful under the *Migration Act 1958* (Cth) s198AHA, which had been inserted by the amendment. Only Gordon J dissented. Her dissent expressed the outcome that the government feared and that had motivated the amendment. That feared outcome was a diminution of the executive government's power to continue offshore detention. In her dissent Gordon J acknowledged that the 'Commonwealth has exercised its undoubted power to expel that alien from Australia or prevent entry by that alien into Australia'.[181] This had been since 1906 the established doctrine of the Commonwealth.[182] However, she argued that once the alien was expelled that right to expel expired. Applying *Chu Kheng Lim v Minister for Immigration, Local Government and Ethnic Affairs (Lim)*[183] she argued that s 198AHA did not support this further detention in immigration detention facilities.

179 Commonwealth, *Parliamentary Debates*, House of Representatives, 24 June 2015, 7508 (Peter Dutton). See Leanne Weber and Sharon Pickering, *Globalization and Borders: Death at the Global Frontier* (Palgrave Macmillan, 2011) 197–216 for a summary of a refutation of this rationale. Weber and Pickering argue that the conceptualisation of sovereignty as border control creates the conditions for these immigrant deaths.

180 *Plaintiff M68/2015 v Minister for Immigration and Border Protection and Others* (2016) 257 CLR 42–3.

181 *Plaintiff M68/2015 v Minister for Immigration and Border Protection and Others* (2016) 257 CLR 134.

182 See Chapter 4 Section II C, citing *Robtelmes v Brenan* (1906) 4 CLR 395; *Ah Yin v Christie* (1907) 4 CLR 1428.

183 (1992) 176 CLR 1.

Retrospective legislation was once again used to make legal what was potentially an illegal act of the executive justified as protecting and asserting sovereignty beyond territorial borders.[184]

In this debate the global phenomena of displaced people and forced migration were raised as a threat, and the response was deterrence.[185] No link was drawn between those phenomena and the opportunity they could provide for meeting the need in Australia for skilled migrant workers.[186] Government members supported the bill as the only alternative to open borders for a 'sovereign nation' at a time when 'probably 50 million or so people would qualify as refugees' and 'hundreds of millions of people would love to come and live in Australia'.[187] Both this speaker and others asserted the government's right to decide on entry by quoting Howard's 2001 election speech, which introduced into debate the link between sovereignty and refusing entry to asylum seekers.[188]

While recognising that there were 'more displaced people, more asylum seekers, more refugees, on the planet today than there have been at any time since the Second World War', and that the physical conditions on Nauru should be improved, the Opposition supported the bill on the basis that it would stop people coming by boat from Java to the Australian external territory of Christmas Island.[189] No evidence was presented in the debate to quantify the impact of offshore processing, compared to, for example, boat turn backs, or other factors influencing the flow of asylum seekers, on diminishing numbers of unauthorised maritime arrivals, but both major parties subscribed to this belief.

Those few who spoke against the bill criticised it as an attack on the judiciary.[190] Andrew Wilke, Independent Member for Clark, Tasmania from 2010 to present, complained that the bill was 'undermining our system of democracy' in response to a possible adverse High Court interpretation of

184 See Dastyari and Hirsch (n 50) 437–45 for the doubtful legality under international law of such arrangements of assisting another country to deter asylum seekers.

185 Pickering and Weber (n 178).

186 See Georgina Costello's argument that asylum seekers can become high-achieving Australians contributing to the national well-being in Georgina Costello, 'Winners and Losers in Australian Asylum Seeker Justice' (2014) 155 *Victorian Bar News* 44–5.

187 Commonwealth, *Parliamentary Debates*, House of Representatives, 24 June 2015, 7506 (Craig Kelly).

188 Commonwealth, *Parliamentary Debates*, House of Representatives, 24 June 2015, 7506 (Craig Kelly). See also Commonwealth, *Parliamentary Debates*, House of Representatives, 24 June 2015, 7501 (Luke Simpkins).

189 Commonwealth, *Parliamentary Debates*, House of Representatives, 24 June 2015, 7499 (Richard Marles).

190 Commonwealth, *Parliamentary Debates*, House of Representatives, 24 June 2015, 7507 (Parkes); Commonwealth, *Parliamentary Debates*, House of Representatives, 24 June 2015, 7505 (Andrew Wilke); Commonwealth, *Parliamentary Debates*, Senate, 24 June 2015, 7505 (Susan Lines).

current legislation. He claimed the term 'regional processing centre' was a misnomer as they were wholly funded and operated by Australia. He proposed the title 'offshore processing in another country'.[191]

However, the second reading speech claimed that regional processing would absolve Australia of any accusation that it breached a fundamental value by depriving asylum seekers of liberty. Dutton made clear this benefit of outsourcing sovereign responsibility:

> I wish to make it clear that Australia does not restrain the liberty of persons in regional processing countries. To the extent that the liberty of persons taken to regional processing countries is restrained in those countries, this is done by those countries under the respective laws of those countries. These amendments do not otherwise provide authority for any restraint over the liberty of persons. The lawful authority for any restraint over liberty arises under the law of the relevant regional processing country.[192]

This replicates Howard's use of the concept of sovereignty to absolve Australia of responsibility for placing children in detention when he said: 'Accommodation at an OPC [offshore processing centre] is not detention under Australian law . . . host countries are sovereign nations'.[193]

Ironically one government member spoke in favour of offshore processing but at the same time stated: 'No sovereign nation can subcontract out their migration policy to the people smugglers'.[194] His comment aligns poorly with Dutton's statement quoted previously, from which it can be inferred that the policy of the amendment was to outsource the issue of asylum seekers by purchasing the sovereignty of other nations.

4 2019 to the Present: Preserving the 'Government's Ultimate Discretion'[195]

The Migration Amendment (Repairing Medical Transfers) Bill 2019 is the final successful measure of the period, part of the elaborate effort to prevent the entry of asylum seekers but also to minimise the scrutiny of the judiciary and the impact of international law obligations while strengthening executive control and discretion.

191 Commonwealth, *Parliamentary Debates*, House of Representatives, 24 June 2015, 7505 (Andrew Wilke).

192 Commonwealth, *Parliamentary Debates*, House of Representatives, 24 June 2015, 7489 (Peter Dutton).

193 Howard, 'Offshore Processing' (n 42).

194 Commonwealth, *Parliamentary Debates*, House of Representatives, 24 June 2015, 7506 (Craig Kelly).

195 Commonwealth, *Parliamentary Debates*, House of Representatives, 4 July 2019, 296 (Peter Dutton).

During the debate Dutton, Minister for Home Affairs 2017 to 2021 in the Turnbull and Morrison Coalition governments, justified the repeal of the *Home Affairs Legislation Amendment (Miscellaneous Measures) Act 2019* (Cth) by echoing Howard's words of 2001:

> Any law which removes the government's ultimate discretion to decide who enters Australia's borders undermines our strong border protection policies. As a nation, it is imperative that we are able to determine who enters Australia and whether they should remain within our borders permanently.[196]

The immigration minister further justified the amendment by claiming that the medical care needs that had prompted the previous amendment were non-existent.[197] He also claimed that the asylum seekers had increased self-harm for the 'explicit purpose of manipulating the system and gaining access to our country'.[198] The Opposition opposed the bill on humanitarian grounds and the advice of the medical community.[199] Addressing the immigration minister's purported loss of power, the Opposition noted that the previous amendment had given veto power to the immigration minister on the basis of national security or serious character concerns. Only on health grounds could a ministerial decision be reviewed. The bill was passed by a government majority. An assertion of the critical importance to Australian sovereignty of preventing the entry of asylum seekers was the rationale for denying better access to medical care.

The analysis of these exclusion amendments with an objective to prevent the entry of asylum seekers reveals the function and nature of sovereignty in this legislative process. The sovereignty that was asserted was a Westphalian sovereignty of absolute control concentrated in the office of the immigration minister.[200] In the name of this sovereignty, the amendments attempted to shield migration decision-making from judicial scrutiny, the influence and

196 Commonwealth, *Parliamentary Debates*, House of Representatives, 4 July 2019, 296 (Peter Dutton).
197 Commonwealth, *Parliamentary Debates*, House of Representatives, 4 July 2019, 296 (Peter Dutton).
198 Commonwealth, *Parliamentary Debates*, House of Representatives, 4 July 2019, 296 (Peter Dutton). This response ignored the physical and psychological conditions of offshore detainees and their legal status. See discussion in Azadeh Dastyari and Maria O'Sullivan, 'Not For Export: The Failure of Australia's Extraterritorial Processing Regime in Papua New Guinea and the Decision of the PNG Supreme Court in Namah' (2016) 42(2) *Monash University Law Review* 308.
199 Commonwealth, *Parliamentary Debates*, House of Representatives, 4 December 2019, 296 (Kristina Keneally); Commonwealth, *Parliamentary Debates*, House of Representatives, 24 July 2019, 296 (Mark Dreyfus).
200 See Luigi Condorelli and Antonio Cassese, 'Is Leviathan Still Holding Sway Over International Dealings?', in Antonio Cassese (ed), *Realizing Utopia: The Future of International Law* (Oxford University Press, 2012) 14, 22; Brown, *Walled States* (n 7) 33–7.

obligations of international law and at times the implications of Australia's domestic law. The amendments achieved this by changing the definition of Australian territory and through this attempting to avoid the domestic and international legal implications of asylum claims made on shore and by outsourcing sovereign obligations. The removal of the reference to the Refugee Convention from the *Migration Act 1958* (Cth) asserted an independence from international law and a control over its interpretation, even though the obligations under the Refugee Convention were voluntarily assumed as an act by a sovereign narion.[201] Physically excluded from Australian territory but caught in the net of this assertion of sovereignty was a tiny percentage of the world's asylum seekers, refugees and forced migrants, who under Australian law were made 'illegal noncitizens' even though they might never have stood on Australian soil. They were caught in the net of an Australian sovereignty decoupled from territorial borders and asserted as defending sovereignty, understood as the concentration of discretionary power in the executive.

B 'Kicking Out'[202] the Unwelcome Noncitizen: Exclusion of Those Already in Australia

This section deals with the second group of amendments. These amendments had the objective of removing any unwanted noncitizen, not just asylum seekers, already on Australian territory.[203] While the ultimate objective was to remove individuals from the territory, the process to achieve this involved exclusion from economic and social participation in a range of ways.[204] Borrowing Anne McNiven's description of the irregular migrant in Europe, the unwelcome noncitizen is the 'immanent outsider',[205] within Australian territory but excluded.[206]

201 See McAdam and Chong (n 16).
202 Morrison, 'Until the Bell Rings' (n 14).
203 Note that a 'permanent resident' is defined in *Australian Citizenship Act 2007* (Cth) s 5. The category of noncitizen includes permanent residents. However a child born to a permanent resident and who remains from birth in Australia is considered a citizen after ten years: *Australian Citizenship Act 2007* s 12(1)(b).
204 It can also be argued that it has involved the exclusion from the protection of the rule of law and this is the subject of Chapter 7.
205 Anne McNevin applies Isin's concept of the 'immanent outsider' to the 'irregular migrant' in Anne McNevin, 'Political Belonging in a Neoliberal Era: The Struggle of the Sans-Papiers' (2006) 10(2) *Citizenship Studies* 135, 137. See the introduction of this term in E Isin, *Being Political: Genealogies of Citizenship* (University of Minnesota Press, 2002) 22. See also Paul Mundoon and Andrew Schaap, 'Aboriginal Sovereignty and the Politics of Reconciliation: The Constituent Power of the Aboriginal Embassy in Australia' (2012) 30 *Environment and Planning D: Society and Space* 548 applying this concept to Australian Indigenous people. See also Alice Barter, 'The "Other's" Encounters with the Australian Judiciary' (2017) 8 *Indigenous Law Bulletin* 15.
206 The issue of the noncitizen and the rule of law is taken up more fully in Chapters 7 and 8.

These amendments fit within the policy framework justified as protecting sovereignty established in 2001 and broadened in 2018, even though the language of sovereignty did not feature as prominently in these debates. Morrison, as prime minister, broadened the scope of sovereignty as a justification for exclusion to encompass 'kicking out', not just keeping out, the unwelcome noncitizen who was already in Australia.[207] These amendments can also be seen to align with the template Howard established because the lawmaking defends against the same kinds of threats to sovereignty that Howard identified in 2001 when he asserted sovereignty as the justification to exclude asylum seekers. In the same way as the amendments which aimed to keep out asylum seekers, these 'kicking out' amendments increased the immigration minister's control of decisions in migration law by warding off judicial scrutiny, attempting to minimise obligations under international law and the operation of Australia's own domestic law. The broad potential application of these 'kicking out' amendments to any noncitizen, justified as an expression of sovereignty, further extends the rationale of sovereignty from territorial border control and creates new borders within the community and new categories of exclusion.

An example is the set of amendments made to onshore immigration detention provisions.[208] Immigration detention is a step, sometimes lasting many years, toward physical exclusion of people already in the territory or a control mechanism while immigration status is determined. Detention excludes the noncitizen from social and economic participation in the community, including by separating families. By 2000 mandatory immigration detention was already in law,[209] but since then the immigration minister's discretion has been broadened,[210] the role of the judiciary limited[211] and the operation of the criminal law of the Australian states evaded.[212]

The objective of this part of immigration law is to remove. This is not new, but the process of removal is not as simple as it seemed in 1901 when

207 See Morrison, 'Until the Bell Rings' (n 14). See also his contribution to debate as Opposition spokesperson on immigration in which he linked changes to immigration detention and the character test to sovereignty. Commonwealth, *Parliamentary Debates*, House of Representatives, 30 May 2011, 5045 (Scott Morrison).

208 While the inmates of residential detention include 'illegal' maritime arrivals and visa 'overstayers', by June 2021 more than half were there because the minister had made a judgment that they were not of good character. The example of the character test amendments is discussed in Chapter 8.

209 *Migration Reform Act 1992* (Cth) introduced s 54W which made detention mandatory of those suspected by an officer to be an unlawful noncitizen.

210 Explanatory Memorandum, Migration Amendment (Detention Arrangements) Bill 2005, 2, 3.

211 Explanatory Memorandum, Migration Amendment (Duration of Detention) Bill 2003.

212 Commonwealth, *Parliamentary Debates*, House of Representatives, 14 May 2020, 3441 (Alan Tudge).

the Parliament debated the *Pacific Island Labourers Act 1901* (Cth) and the main issue of contention was the destination of the deported labourers.[213] Unwelcome noncitizens in the 21st century can spend extended periods in various forms of immigration detention while their legal status is disputed or their removal effected.[214] For example, on 30 June 2021, 1,492 people were held in immigration detention in Australia, 114 for more than 1,825 days, with the average period of detention 673 days.[215] Of these, approximately half were there because the immigration minister had made a judgment that they were not of good character and a quarter because they had arrived by boat without pre-authorisation, placing them in the category of 'illegal maritime arrival'.[216]

A brief background to immigration detention in Australia helps to illustrate that, since 2001, just as asylum seekers were positioned as an enemy to be kept out,[217] detainees have been increasingly represented as the enemy within, threatening sovereignty, a sovereignty which according to Morrison encompasses the concept of protecting the safety and welfare of the individual citizen from predators within.[218] Detention centres were first introduced in 1958 to distinguish migration detention from criminal detention. The immigration minister then described jails as 'depressing places'.[219] He justified the introduction of immigration detention centres by noting that 'Very often the deportee has a blameless record; his only offence is a statutory one against our immigration laws'.[220] In 1992 the immigration minis-

213 In the debate on 12 December 1901 the issues were where a Pacific Islander should be deported to and who should decide. The Parliament was asked to assume that the deportation would be conducted humanely. See, e.g., the exchange between Alfred Conroy, Member for Werriwa 1901–6, and Charles Kingston, Minister for Trade and Customs in the Barton Protectionist Party, in Commonwealth, *Parliamentary Debates*, House of Representatives, 12 December 2001, 8633.

214 *Migration Amendment (Clarifying International Obligations for Removal) Act 2021* (Cth). This act can be read as allowing ongoing administrative detention. See Sangeetha Pilau, 'The Migration Amendment (Clarifying International Obligations for Removal) Act 2021: A Case Study in the Importance of Proper Legislative Process', *Australian Public Law* (Web Page, 10 June 2021) <https://auspublaw.org/2021/06/the-migration-amendment-clarifying-international-obligations-for-removal-act-2021/>.

215 Department of Home Affairs, *Immigration Detention and Community Statistics Summary* (Report, 30 June 2021) 12.

216 Department of Home Affairs, *Immigration Detention and Community Statistics Summary* (Report, 30 June 2021) 7. For discussions of the character test under *Migration Act 1958* s 501 see Samuel C Duckett White, 'God-Like Powers: The Character Test and Unfettered Ministerial Discretion' (2020) 41 *Adelaide Law Review* 1; Rights Advocacy Project, *Playing God: The Immigration Minister's Unrestrained Power* (Report, Liberty Victoria, 2017).

217 See Section II for a discussion of Operation Sovereign Borders.

218 Morrison, 'Until the Bell Rings' (n 14).

219 Commonwealth, *Parliamentary Debates*, House of Representatives, 1 May 1958, 3 (Alexander Downer).

220 Commonwealth, *Parliamentary Debates*, House of Representatives, 1 May 1958, 3 (Alexander Downer).

ter complemented his introduction of mandatory detention with enhanced merit review processes and noted in his second reading speech, 'My primary responsibility is to make sure that asylum seekers [who were now to be kept in mandatory detention] are treated with dignity and fairness. They have a right to expect their cases to be handled fairly and quickly'.[221] However, the debate on the detention legislation of 2000–20 shifted from viewing the potential inmates as 'blameless' and deserving to be treated with 'dignity' to objects to be feared.

Under amendments in the 2000–20 period, offences in detention, including trying to escape, were made crimes.[222] Strip searching was authorised.[223] The duration of immigration detention was legislated to last until a court made a final determination, not an interlocutory order, that the detention was illegal or that the person was a lawful noncitizen.[224] The consequence of this later amendment shielded the immigration minister's discretion from judicial intervention. It meant that, even if the court considered that there were detrimental impacts of being in detention, or that the risk to the community of the person was low, the judicial discretion to allow the person liberty in the community was removed until a final judgment was made.[225] The immigration minister's discretion was broadened to allow some detainees to leave detention but on reporting conditions similar to criminal parole or bail, such as a requirement to be at a certain address at a certain time and to report regularly in person to authorities.[226] From 2013 time in immigration detention was to count towards a prison sentence for those convicted of people smuggling.[227]

This process of demonising immigration detainees continued. In 2017, and after rejection by the Parliament and some reworking again in 2020, the Parliament was asked to consider the Migration Amendment (Prohibiting Items in Immigration Detention Facilities) Bill.[228] That bill continued the shift toward characterising those in administrative detention as criminals. In 2017 the amendment was justified on the basis that 'more than half

221 Commonwealth, *Parliamentary Debates*, House of Representatives, 4 November 1992, 2620 (Gerry Hand).

222 *Migration Legislation Amendment (Immigration Detainees) Act 2001* (Cth).

223 *Migration Legislation Amendment (Immigration Detainees) Act (No 2) 2001* (Cth).

224 Explanatory Memorandum, Migration Amendment (Duration of Detention) Bill 2003.

225 Explanatory Memorandum, Migration Amendment (Duration of Detention) Bill 2003.

226 Explanatory Memorandum, Migration Amendment (Detention Arrangements) Bill 2005, 2, 3. For a medical assessment of the impact of community detention on mental health see Nicholas Procter, 'Engaging Refugees and Asylum Seekers in Suicidal Crisis' (2013) 20(9) *Australian Nursing Journal* 44.

227 *Crimes Legislation Amendment (Law Enforcement Integrity, Vulnerable Witness Protection and Other Measures) Act 2013* (Cth). This implies that detention is viewed as a punishment.

228 Migration Amendment (Prohibiting Items in Immigration Detention Facilities) Bill 2017; Migration Amendment (Prohibiting Items in Immigration Detention Facilities) Bill 2020.

of the detainee population consists of high-risk cohorts'.[229] That bill aimed to ban mobile phone usage by detainees, introduce detection dogs and further broaden the immigration minister's discretion to control activity in detention centres.[230] In 2020, justifying the reworked bill, Alan Tudge, Acting Minister for Immigration, Citizenship, Migrant Services and Multicultural Affairs in the Morrison Coalition government (2019–20), noted that 'some of the detainees have a history of child sex offences or violent crimes' and that the government 'would not tolerate behaviour that is illegal or behaviour that threatens the stability of immigration'.[231] The reworked bill allowed the use of detector dogs, without a warrant, to sniff facilities, but not, as in the 2017 bill, detainees or visitors. In addition, under the new bill, staff would not be able to remove 'certain medications and healthcare supplements' in certain circumstances as previously proposed.[232] Mobile phones were not to be completely banned but staff could still 'seize phones from certain categories of detainees' and search for mobile phones in other circumstances.[233]

When the bill was first debated in 2017 the lack of substantial need for the bill and the demonisation of the detainees were both reasons for its failure. For example Anne Aly, then Labor Member for Cowan 2016, noted that the immigration minister had provided

> no substantial justification for the measures that are proposed in this bill, and those measures do not come on advice of either Serco or International Health and Medical Services – both of the main providers of services in detention centres and detention facilities – which begs the question: why is this bill even necessary?[234]

Cathy McGowan, Independent Member for Indi 2013–9, neatly summarised the Parliament's view and the reason for the failure of the 2017 bill to proceed. She said, 'Why say that we as a nation need to be almost bullying

229 Commonwealth, *Parliamentary Debates*, House of Representatives, 13 September 2017, 10180 (Peter Dutton). See Chapter 8 for a discussion of risk and the character test.
230 Migration Amendment (Prohibiting Items in Immigration Detention Facilities) Bill 2017.
231 Commonwealth, *Parliamentary Debates*, House of Representatives, 14 May 2020, 3441 (Alan Tudge). This rationale bypasses the operation of states' criminal law such as sentencing and parole and rehabilitation goals.
232 Commonwealth, *Parliamentary Debates*, House of Representatives, 14 May 2020, 3442 (Alan Tudge). This rationale bypasses the operation of states' criminal law such as sentencing and parole and rehabilitation goals.
233 Commonwealth, *Parliamentary Debates*, House of Representatives, 14 May 2020, 3442 (Alan Tudge). This rationale bypasses the operation of states' criminal law such as sentencing and parole and rehabilitation goals.
234 Commonwealth, *Parliamentary Debates*, House of Representatives, 7 February 2018, 511 (Anne Aly).

to get the point of view across?'[235] These measures would have shifted the detention population further toward the category of the criminal and do this outside the criminal law processes. McGowan hinted at this purpose when she noted

> the subtlety of changing the names of the transition accommodation centres. We're now going to call them all 'immigration detention facilities'. I think it is from that name alone that we get a sense of what the government is trying to do here.[236]

The Commonwealth Ombudsman made this point more overtly.[237] He was concerned that detention should not be viewed as punitive, noting that the people subject to these measures are not in immigration detention to be punished for committing a crime but there because they do not have a valid visa. The ombudsman noted that the importance of principles such as fairness, transparency, proportionality, the right to seek review or to complain and the availability of independent oversight. The ombudsman noted that 'There is a risk, however, that its administration could take on a punitive character if the principles mentioned above are not upheld'.[238]

There was also concern from senate committees. The Senate Standing Committee for the Scrutiny of Bills was concerned that 'the broad discretionary nature of the powers conferred on authorised officers to search for and seize prohibited things' risked arbitrary use of this power especially where officers can also use force including strip searching and sniffer dogs.[239] The committee was also concerned that, except for prescribed medication, the bill placed 'no limit on the type of things that the immigration minister may determine to be prohibited'.[240] The committee suggested that such a substantial policy decision should be stated in the act and not left to the discretion of the immigration minister and their authorised officers through a delegated instrument.[241] The Senate Legal and Constitutional Affairs Legislation Committee reported in 2020 and could not agree on the bill, producing a main

235 Commonwealth, *Parliamentary Debates*, House of Representatives, 7 February 2018, 515 (Cathy McGowan).
236 Commonwealth, *Parliamentary Debates*, House of Representatives, 7 February 2018, 515 (Cathy McGowan).
237 Commonwealth Ombudsman, Submission to Senate Legal and Constitutional Affairs Committee (July 2020) 2.
238 Commonwealth Ombudsman, Submission to Senate Legal and Constitutional Affairs Committee (July 2020) 2.
239 Senate Standing Committee for the Scrutiny of Bills, Scrutiny Digest 7 of 2020.
240 Senate Standing Committee for the Scrutiny of Bills, Scrutiny Digest 7 of 2020.
241 Senate Standing Committee for the Scrutiny of Bills, Scrutiny Digest 7 of 2020.

report from the Coalition members and dissenting reports from Labor and the Australian Greens.[242] The bill did not pass into law.

In summary this account of the amendments traces the representation of detention centre inmates from 'largely blameless' in 1958 to an 'unacceptable risk to the Australian community', in Dutton's and Tudge's words, by 2020.[243] The policy framework enacted into migration law justified as the assertion and protection of sovereignty has justified these apparently punitive measures by positioning people subject to these measures not as criminals being punished, which is not a legally valid purpose of detention unless it is pursuant to an exercise of judicial power by the judiciary,[244] but as enemies of sovereignty. They had become 'predators'.[245] The detainee had become the enemy to be excluded.

The validity of legislation that gives power to detain the noncitizen in immigration detention has been tested over many years. A majority in the High Court has consistently found that this validity rests on the purpose of the detention. In *Commonwealth v AJL20*[246] the majority held that, even though the executive had failed to be diligent in executing the duty to act within a reasonable time frame, the power to detain had not expired. Gordon and Gleeson JJ in dissent argued that it had. The majority applied *NAES v Minister for Immigration and Multicultural and Indigenous Affairs.*[247] In that case Beaumont J found that:

> Even if inexcusable delay on the part of the Department had been demonstrated . . . the only appropriate remedy, in my view, would have been an application for mandamus compelling 'the officer' upon whom is placed the statutory duty prescribed by s 198 to remove the applicant 'as soon as [is] reasonably practicable' in the circumstances of the applicant's case.[248]

242 Kim Carr and Anthony Chisholm, *Labor Party Senators' Dissenting Report* (Report, 2020) <www.aph.gov.au/Parliamentary_Business/Committees/Senate/Legal_and_Constitutional_Affairs/ProhibitedItems/Report/section?id=committees%2freportsen%2f024483%2f73518>; Nick McKim, *Australian Greens Dissenting Report* (Report, 2020) <www.aph.gov.au/Parliamentary_Business/Committees/Senate/Legal_and_Constitutional_Affairs/ProhibitedItems/Report/section?id=committees%2freportsen%2f024483%2f73521>.

243 Commonwealth, *Parliamentary Debates*, House of Representatives, 14 May 2020, 3441 (Alan Tudge).

244 *Chu Kheng Lim v Minister for Immigration* (1992) 176 CLR 1. See Peter Billings, 'Whither Indefinite Immigration Detention in Australia? Rethinking Legal Constraints on the Detention of Non-citizens' (2015) 38(4) *University of New South Wales Law Journal* 1386.

245 Morrison, 'Until the Bell Rings' (n 14).

246 [2021] HCA 21, 567, 568. See also cases such as *Al-Kateb v Godwin* (2004) 219 CLR 562; *Graham v Minister for Immigration and Border Protection* (2017) 263 CLR 1, 91.

247 [2003] FCA 2, 1.

248 [2003] FCA 6–7.

It remains law, with one exception, that if the purpose of immigration detention is to remove the person, the law is nonpunitive and is therefore not an encroachment on the role of the judiciary. This indefinite detention for a nonpunitive purpose is valid despite it appearing, as the ombudsman feared, to have a punitive character.[249] The exception was the result of a 2023 High Court judgment ruling that for a certain group of detainees who could not be returned to their own country because they had been found to be refugees, detention was unconstitutional if there was 'no real prospect of removing them[from Australia to anywhere else] in the reasonably foreseeable future'.[250] However, apart from this group the decision on who remains in detention or is released into community detention is solely at the discretion of the immigration minister, who has the personal, non-compellable power to make an order to grant a visa, even if it has not been requested, to those in detention[251] and to 'make, vary or revoke' permission to reside in community detention rather than a detention centre.[252] This power remains as ruled in the subsequent case of *ASF17 v Commonwealth of Australia* .[253] In that case a man with no criminal history has been in immigration detention for more than a decade.

A noncitizen can remain in immigration detention as long as the immigration minister intends to deport that person.[254] The small number who fit into the exception remain on temporary visas under conditions of surveillance similar to criminal parole.

249 Commonwealth Ombudsman (n 237). See also Peter Billings' (n 244) discussion of the punitive nature of prolonged detention, the high level of discretion of the minister, the lack of transparency for decisions on who should be in detention and the inconsistency with Australia's international human rights commitments. In his 2015 article he was hopeful that the High Court was increasing scrutiny on the legality of this detention. As the cases noted previously show, this is not the majority view up to the time of writing.

250 *NZYQ v Minister for Immigration, Citizenship and Multicultural Affairs* [2023] HCA 37 [2].

251 S 195A(2).

252 Explanatory Memorandum, Migration Amendment (Detention Arrangements) Bill 2005; *Migration Act 1958* (Cth) ss197AE, 197AF. See also Rosalind Croucher, *QA v Commonwealth (Department of Home Affairs) [2021] Report into Arbitrary Detention and the Best Interests of Children* (Report, Australian Human Rights Commission, February 2021) 4–5. Croucher found that the minister breached his own guidelines by keeping minors in detention for two years and eight months, that the detention breached Australia's obligations under the ICCPR and articles 3 and 37(b) of the *Convention on the Rights of the Child* and that the father, who was kept in detention for a total of eight years before being granted a temporary protection visa, should not have had to wait for such an extended period.

253 [2024] HCA 19; 98 ALJR 782.

254 *Al-Kateb v Godwin* (2004) 219 CLR 562.

IV Hypersovereignty or Stunted Sovereignty?

Drawing on both theory and history, this survey of the exclusion amendments shows that they can be understood as both an expression of hypersovereignty and a stunted anachronistic version of sovereignty.

Wendy Brown's theorising of wall building positions the expression of sovereignty as exclusion. She names the walls built to exclude 'poor people, workers, or asylum seekers' as hypersovereignty: the performance of exclusion as a demonstration of sovereign power that simultaneously signals the waning capacity to wield Westphalian sovereignty. She sees this exclusion as an anachronistic expression of a Westphalian sovereignty of unfettered power, enfeebled by globalisation, out of place in a globalised world where the internal sovereignty of states has been tempered by their commitment to international agreements.[255] It is a reversion to Westphalian sovereignty but ineffective against the globalised neoliberal logic of the global market.

As Australia embraced economic globalisation and accepted the consequent vulnerabilities and interdependencies as the price of economic gain,[256] Howard, the first prime minister of the period under consideration, established a legacy of migration legislation and policy that treated the exclusion of certain asylum seekers and other unwelcome immigrants as an issue of existential importance. The Australian Parliament responded to the unwelcome phenomena of globalisation such as the increased global movement of asylum seekers and forced migrants,[257] along with the difficulty of ensuring strict compliance with migration law requirements, with extensive legislation to exclude the asylum seeker and the unwanted noncitizen.[258] In this way the exclusion amendments give some support to a characterisation of this legislation as a site of hypersovereignty, an assertion of power in a globalised world where boundaries between nations are blurred and traditional areas of sovereign control are lost or traded away.

One of the features of these exclusion amendments was the concentration of sovereign authority over migration decisions in the executive government in the person of the immigration minister. The philosophies of sovereignty proposed by Carl Schmitt and Georgio Agamben, introduced in Chapter 1, are useful in further understanding the nature of this sovereignty, which concentrated power and focussed on exclusion through migration law.

Schmitt placed the sovereign outside the legal order, deciding in a situation of conflict what constitutes 'the public interest or interest of the state,

255 See Chapter 3 Section III; See Chapter 2 Section VI and n 174. Antonio Cassese, *International Law in a Divided World* (Oxford University Press, 1986) 13–14.

256 See Chapter 5.

257 See Chapter 3 Section III B.

258 See a similar response in the example of the international student visa in Chapter 5 Section IV.

public safety and order' and whether the constitution should be suspended.[259] For Schmitt, the threat to the state is the enemy.[260] There are parallels with this conception of sovereignty and the use of sovereignty to justify the exclusion amendments to Australian migration law. By inserting measures in the amendments that shielded executive power from interference, the executive can be seen as asserting itself as a kind of Schmittian unified sovereign, identifying the enemy and defending the state against it. From 2001 asylum seekers arriving at the border in boats were characterised as a threat to sovereignty. Asylum seekers and noncitizens were not directly named as the enemy, but this can be inferred from the use of sovereignty as a rationale for this exclusion. It can also be inferred from the military language for migration programs such as Operation Sovereign Borders and the use of the defence forces in this initiative. In Schmitt's sense of being an enemy, an enemy of a way of life,[261] it can also be seen in Morrison's use of sovereignty in his speech on pandemic measures.[262]

The positioning of the excluded as an enemy and the sovereign as the identifier of this enemy is also the logic of using sovereignty to justify immigration detention, both onshore and offshore. Through the series of amendments to immigration detention laws, detainees experienced the deprivation of liberty at the non-compellable, nonaccountable discretion of a single person, the immigration minister, not a member of the judiciary. However, unlike Schmitt's theory, which positions the wielding of sovereign power as necessarily outside the law, the exclusion amendments are part of the normal law through which the immigration minister has the discretion to make these sovereign decisions.

Critiquing Schmitt, Agamben theorised that Schmitt's categorical pairing of friend/enemy of the state should be replaced with the pairing of inclusion/exclusion.[263] This understanding of sovereignty also helps to explain the nature of sovereignty that justified the different kinds of exclusion achieved by the amendments.

Firstly, in 2001 the rationale of sovereignty was represented as a defence against a breach of the territorial physical border by asylum seekers, to which the exclusion amendments were a response. However, a part of this exclusion from territory was the system of offshore immigration detention, which placed the excluded asylum seekers outside Australian territorial sovereign

259 Schmitt, *Political Theology* (n 5) 6–7.

260 Schmitt, *The Concept of the Political* (n 5) 26–7. Note Schmitt defines the enemy as the stranger with whom it is possible to be in conflict if there is a threat to one's way of life.

261 Schmitt, *The Concept of the Political* (n 5) 26–7. Note Schmitt defines the enemy as the stranger with whom it is possible to be in conflict if there is a threat to one's way of life.

262 Commonwealth, *Parliamentary Debates*, House of Representatives, 8 April 2020, 2909 (Scott Morrison). See also Chapter 5 Section III.

263 Agamben (n 6) 8.

borders but, like Agamben's bandit, still captured by Australian sovereignty through laws that declared them illegal, facilitated their incarceration and banned them forever from the full life of the sovereign space.[264] In this way, even with amendments with the stated objective of preventing entry to territory, the border of exclusion is not the territorial border. It is the border of sovereign power which moves outside Australia's own territorial boundaries to establish offshore processing but shrinks back again when the implications of this sovereignty are unwanted. This expanding and contracting of sovereignty is illustrated in the debate and legislation on regional processing in 2015 and on children in offshore immigration detention in 2001.[265] In 2001 Prime Minister Howard declared that children in offshore processing were not Australia's responsibility.[266] In 2015 the immigration minister declared that the treatment of asylum seekers in offshore detention was the responsibility of another sovereign nation.[267] At the same time he sponsored an amendment that inserted into the *Migration Act 1958* (Cth) the power of the Commonwealth to 'take, or cause to be taken, any action in relation to the arrangement or the regional processing functions of the country' and defined action as including '(a) exercising restraint over the liberty of a person; and (b) action in a regional processing country or another country'.[268] The amendments allowed the government to retain the power to exclude but not the sovereign responsibility under its own domestic law. Agamben's description of the edge of sovereignty as the place where 'the law applies in no longer applying'[269] seems to apply.

A second category of exclusion makes a reality out of Agamben's metaphors of the bandit, the comatose patient and the concentration camp inmate.[270] Exclusion in onshore detention for asylum seekers or other noncitizens, such as those who have overstayed their visa or are deemed to be not of good character, places a border between the community and those detained. In all cases since 2005 that border between inclusion and exclusion has only been crossed at the discretion of the immigration minister.[271] It is at the immigration minister's absolute and non-compellable discretion to decide who will remain in detention and who will be allowed to live in the community and under what conditions.[272] Just like Agamben's concentration

264 Agamben (n 6) 127.
265 Commonwealth, *Parliamentary Debates*, House of Representatives, 24 June 2015, 7508 (Peter Dutton).
266 Howard, 'Offshore Processing' (n 41).
267 Commonwealth, *Parliamentary Debates*, House of Representatives, 24 June 2015, 7489 (Peter Dutton).
268 *Migration Act 1958* (Cth) s198AHA.
269 Agamben (n 6) 8.
270 Agamben (n 6) 183–6.
271 *Migration Amendment (Detention Arrangements) Act 2005* (Cth).
272 *Migration Act 1958* (Cth) ss 197AA–197AG.

camp inmate, the detainee is present on Australian territory but excluded from the full life of the community, relegated to the 'bare life' at the edge of sovereign power that also affirms the existence of that power of sovereignty to exclude.[273]

The third form of exclusion achieved by the amendments is less tangible. Agamben theorised that, rather than sovereignty being outside the law, as in Schmitt's theory, the edge of sovereignty was the place of exclusion, the place where 'the law applies in no longer applying'.[274] This exclusion achieved in the amendments is the creation of a legal framework that encompasses the legal, illegal and potentially illegal noncitizen.[275] This subjects the noncitizen to administrative power and ministerial discretion, which this thesis argues excludes noncitizens from the full benefit of what Gleeson J described as the 'basic guarantee of the rule of law'.[276] No tangible border or distinguishing feature identifies these 'bandits' or 'comatose patients' or 'concentration camp' inmates, to borrow Agamben's metaphors. Just like the comatose patient their status is defined by law. Their existence as a noncitizen, as opposed to a citizen enjoying the full life of the community, is a legal status which can change, and just as with the comatose patient this can occur without the agency of the noncitizen. The law can change and allow the medical team to turn off life support. The legislation gives the immigration minister personal power to decide inclusion or exclusion. Across the two decades in question this decision and the concentration of this power in the immigration minister have been justified on the ground of protecting or asserting sovereignty.

This use of sovereignty, a hypersovereignty signalling waning sovereignty, can be also understood in the context of the historical benchmarks of 1901, 1958 and 1978,[277] as stunted sovereignty. In Australian migration law for more than half the 20th century the policy priority was the exclusion of non-white people. The legality of their exclusion was derived from sovereignty but the justification for these laws was a policy of racial discrimination.[278] Only when such a policy was abandoned did asserting or protecting sovereignty become a policy goal of migration law, as demonstrated in the 1978 historical benchmark.[279] Only from 2001 was this policy goal elevated to an issue of national significance and importance. In 2001, faced with

273 Agamben (n 6) 185.

274 Agamben (n 6) 28–9.

275 James Hathaway notes that, while the definition of lawful presence in a state is left to states, this is not unlimited. States are obliged to comply with the 'normative requirements of the Refugee Convention'. In essence there appears to be an expectation to abide by the spirit not just the letter of the law. See Hathaway (n 16) 177–8.

276 Murray Gleeson, *The Rule of Law and the Constitution* (ABC, 2000) 6. This least tangible exclusion is discussed further in Chapters 7 and 8.

277 See Chapter 4.

278 See Chapter 4.

279 See Chapter 4.

asylum seekers arriving on boats, Howard deployed the rationale of sovereignty to justify the policy framework of exclusion that was achieved through the amendments discussed previously. In doing so Howard paraphrased and repurposed the High Court judgment of *Robtelmes v Brennan* 1906 and *Ah Yin Christie* in 1907.[280] In 1906 the judgement confirmed the Federation's constitutional authority to pass laws to prevent entry, and to remove people from Australian territory, and through this the court confirmed the legality of pursuing the policy vision of a white Australia. In 2001 in a second reading speech to Parliament, the prime minister raised the exclusion of asylum seekers to an issue of sovereignty, marking it as an issue of national importance.[281] In 1901 the national vision of a white Australia was expressed and embraced by the Parliament. It was delivered by legislating a high level of discretion for the immigration minister. In 1901 the reason for this discretion was to achieve the Parliament's purpose while managing the dependency and vulnerability of the new Federation. Ministerial discretion allowed the Parliament to pass laws in which they could mean 'a lot more than we say'.[282] This policy goal and legislative technique of avoiding putting the White Australia policy clearly in legislation and instead legislating discretion for the immigration minister to deliver the policy continued in the lawmaking leading to the new *Migration Act 1958* (Cth). With the abandonment of the White Australia policy no national vision was proposed for this policy. In the debates from 2001 to 2020 sovereignty was the openly declared justification. Exclusion itself was the vision and the increasing discretion of the immigration minister had no comparable rationale to 1901. It was merely asserted and fought for.

From an application of Schmitt, Agamben and Brown and a comparison with history, the concept of sovereignty that functioned to justify these amendments can be seen both as hypersovereignty and as a stunted version of sovereignty. What may have been fit for purpose in 1901 is an ill fit when applied to the realities of a wealthy liberal democracy in the globalised world of the 21st century. This expression of hypersovereignty has made enemies and dangerous outsiders of asylum seekers and noncitizens in order to demonstrate sovereign power concentrated in the executive government.

280 See Chapter 4, citing *Robtelmes v Brenan* (1906) 4 CLR 395, 401; *Ah Yin v Christie* (1907) 4 CLR 1428, 1431.

281 Commonwealth, *Parliamentary Debates*, House of Representatives, 29 August 2001, 30569 (John Howard).

282 See Chapter 4 Section II, citing Commonwealth, *Parliamentary Debates*, House of Representatives, 20 September 1901, 5075 (Allan McLean).

V Conclusion

From 2001 to 2020 Australian prime ministers established a policy framework in which their government's amendments to prevent entry of unwanted migrants and to remove noncitizens were represented as issues of sovereignty. The debates on the amendments made within this framework demonstrate the function and nature of the sovereignty asserted. From an examination of the threats which the legislation defends against, it emerges that the function of sovereignty was to shield the executive government's actions from the influence or opprobrium of international law, the implications of Australia's own domestic law, the scrutiny of the judiciary and at times even the Parliament. Later, under Morrison's prime ministership, asserting sovereignty was represented as protecting the safety of the vulnerable from the threat of the noncitizen predator and finally the preservation of the lifestyle of Australians. Sovereignty characterised in these ways was used to justify the exclusion of asylum seekers, refugees and those noncitizens already in Australia who breached visa conditions.

The theories of sovereignty of Schmitt, Agamben, Brown and Dauvergne give further insight into the nature and function of the sovereignty expressed as exclusion and give some support to characterising the exclusion amendments as hypersovereignty. For Schmitt it is a sovereign act to identify the enemy. For Agamben the excluded define the edge of sovereignty. For Brown, 21st-century wall building to exclude the poor and the refugee is a site of hypersovereignty, anachronistic Westphalian sovereignty asserted against waning sovereignty. Together applied to the exclusion amendments these theories demonstrate the unlinking of sovereignty and exclusion from any physical border, in contrast to the purported objectives of the amendments and language such as Operation Sovereign Borders. The amendments and the threats against which they shielded executive decision-making reveal that the sovereignty asserted was the demonstration of executive power.

The comparison of the exclusion amendments with historical benchmarks from the 20th century supports a view that these exclusion amendments made between 2000 and 2020 are an expression of a hypersovereignty, a turning to migration law as the 'new last bastion of sovereignty in a globalising world'.[283] In 1901 exclusionary amendments and the legislative techniques utilised aimed to achieve a policy goal of a white Australia. In 2001–20 the exclusion of refugees and other unwanted noncitizens was characterised as an expression of sovereignty with no overt link to a national purpose or an acknowledgement of Australia's sovereign power or responsibility.

What the making of these amendments reveals about the values underlying the sovereignty used as the justification to exclude is the subject of the next chapter.

283 Dauvergne (n 8) 588.

Chapter 7

Values Revealed

Australian Values and Amendments to the Migration Act 1958, 2000–20

I Introduction

The previous chapter discussed the use of sovereignty as a justification for amendments to the *Migration Act 1958* (Cth) made between 2000 and 2020. The chapter concluded that this use of sovereignty can be understood in two ways: a hypersovereignty, an outdated Westphalian sovereignty in the face of waning sovereignty in a globalising world;[1] and a stunted sovereignty that continued the traditional use of migration legislation to urgently exclude by replacing a policy of racial discrimination with a policy of sovereign necessity.[2]

Catherine Dauvergne argues that a nation's values are revealed by those it excludes.[3] Following this lead and in order to further investigate the nature of sovereignty used as a justification for the amendments, the purpose of this chapter is to identify the Australian values embedded in these amendments in order to more thoroughly define the sovereignty that has functioned as their overarching policy rationale.[4] Literature on Australian migration law includes the argument that the treatment of asylum seekers and other unwelcome noncitizens is at odds with international human rights law and values.[5]

1 Wendy Brown, *Walled States, Waning Sovereignty* (Zone Books, 2010) 19–20 ('*Walled States*'). See Chapter 2 Section III. See also Chapter 5 especially Section V regarding the competition of the philosophies of neoliberalism and Westphalian sovereignty in the amendments to the student visa legislation which had the objective of economic gain not exclusion. See also Catherine Dauvergne, 'Sovereignty, Migration and the Rule of Law in Global Times' (2004) 67(4) *Modern Law Review* 588 ('Sovereignty, Migration').

2 See Chapter 4 especially Section V.

3 Dauvergne, 'Sovereignty, Migration' (n 1).

4 See Chapter 6.

5 See, e.g., Australian Human Rights Commission, *Lives on Hold: Refugees and Asylum Seekers in the 'Legacy Caseload'* (Report, 2019); Azadeh Dastyari and Asher Hirsch, 'The Ring of Steel: Extraterritorial Migration Controls in Indonesia and Libya and the Complicity of Australia and Italy' (2019) 19 *Human Rights Law Review* 435; Tania Penovic and Azadeh Dastyari, 'Boatloads of Incongruity: The Evolution of Australia's Offshore Processing Regime' (2007) 13(1) *Australian Journal of Human Rights* 33; Tania Penovic and Adiva

DOI: 10.4324/9781003515852-9

This chapter adds to this examination of values by assessing the amendments against Australia's own espoused values as incorporated into migration regulations. For this purpose 'values' are defined as 'principles or moral standards held by a person or social group . . . a generally accepted or personally held judgement of what is valuable and important in life'.[6] This dictionary definition is relevant on the basis of the statutory interpretative assumption that the Parliament intended the ordinary meaning of the word as the starting point to derive the parliamentary purpose.[7]

The chapter begins by introducing these espoused values and outlining their development and purpose. Next, the chapter traces how three of the enacted values were used in the Parliament's amendment debates and how far their representation in these debates drifted from their ordinary meaning.

The chapter argues that these values were emptied of ordinary meaning and repurposed to justify amendments aimed to exclude. The first value, 'compassion for those in need', is chosen because of its prominent function in the debates. The second, 'fair play', is chosen because of the centrality of the concept of a 'fair go' as an Australian cultural value[8] and the centrality of procedural fairness to equality before the law.[9] Thirdly, the value 'the English language as the national language' is chosen because of the historical significance of language testing as an exclusionary device in Australian migration

Sifris, 'Children's Rights Through the Lens of Immigration Detention' (2006) 20 *Australian Journal of Family Law* 12; Satvinder Juss, 'Detention and Delusion in Australia's Kafkaesque Refugee Law' (2017) 36 *Refugee Survey Quarterly* 146, 161; Jane McAdam, 'From Humanitarian Discretion to Complementary Protection – Reflections on the Emergence of Human Rights-Based Refugee Protection in Australia' (2011) 18 *Australian International Law Journal* 53–4; Eve Lester, *Making Migration Law: The Foreigner, Sovereignty and the Case of Australia* (Cambridge University Press, 2018).

6 'Value' (def 5d), *Oxford English Dictionary* (online, 1 June 2022).

7 See, e.g., Keifel CJ, Nettle and Gordon JJ in *SZTAL v Minister For Immigration* (2017) 262 CLR 362. Note also that this dictionary definition aligns in a schematisation of values discourse with the category of 'good', a moral category denoting an ethical judgment. See Tony Bennett, Lawrence Grossberg and Meaghan Morris, *New Keywords: A Revised Vocabulary of Culture and Society* (John Wiley and Sons, 2005) 370–1.

8 John Howard, 'Melbourne Press Club Address', *PM Transcripts* (Speech, 22 November 2000) <https://pmtranscripts.pmc.gov.au/release/transcript-11678>. For a discussion of a fair go see Peter Saunders, 'What Is Fair About a "Fair Go"? [There are Many Different Types of Fairness]' (2014) 20 *Journal of Public Policy and Ideas* 3; Greg Martin, 'Stop the Boats! Moral Panic in Australia over Asylum Seekers' (2015) 29(3) *Continuum* 304, 312, 316; Frank Brennan, 'What's Lost in Translation', *The Age* (online, 23 January 2007) <www.theage.com.au/national/whats-lost-in-translation-20070123-ge41op.html>. Note that Brennan defines a fair go as follows: 'A fair go for all is guaranteed when we who are not politicians know that our moral sense matters, able to affect law and policy for the good of the nation'.

9 *Re Minister for Immigration and Multicultural Affairs and Another Ex Parte Miah* (2001) 206 CLR 57, 86; James Allsop, 'Values in Law: How They Influence and Shape Rules and the Application of Law' (Speech, Centre for Comparative and Public Law, University of Hong Kong, 20 October 2016) 49.

law.[10] The chapter examines the function of these espoused values in this law-making. Through this examination, it identifies the actual Australian values that underpin the assertion of sovereignty that justified the amendments. This chapter does not make a values-based assessment by introducing values from international human rights norms or from the purported values of liberal democratic institutions.[11] Nor is this judgment based on a sense of moral indignation.[12] The values-based assessment is invited by the executive's incorporation of an explicit statement of Australian values in migration legislation.[13]

II The Espoused Australian Values

The relevance to the analysis of law, of identifying which values underpin the amendments to the *Migration Act 1958* (Cth) justified by sovereignty, was neatly summarised in a speech in 2016 by James Allsop, chief justice of the Federal Court. He stated, 'Law is life and life is infused with values'.[14] To thoroughly examine the nature and function of sovereignty it is therefore important to examine the values enacted through these amendments. Allsop went on to argue that in law there are 'essential human values' which must be balanced with rules because 'law is not value free'.[15] Relevant to exercises of public power, which include migration law, these 'essential human values' are 'a rejection of unfairness and an insistence on essential equality; respect for the integrity and dignity of the individual; and mercy'.[16] Allsop asserted that the 'defining character' of the constitutional power of the judiciary, distinct from executive power, is the requirement that the judiciary exercise these values.[17]

10 See Chapter 4. See legislation establishing the White Australia policy 'education test', commonly known as the dictation test, at *Immigration Restriction Act 1901* s 3. See a parliamentary comment when abolishing the education test at Commonwealth, *Parliamentary Debates*, House of Representatives, 1 May 1958, 1396–7 (Alexander Downer). For a discussion of the testing of English competence as part of the test process see, e.g., Dominic Npoanlari Dagbanja, 'The Invisible Border Wall in Australia' (2019) 23(2) *UCLA Journal of International and Foreign Affairs* 221.

11 See, e.g., Jane McAdam, 'An Intellectual History of Freedom of Movement in International Law: The Right to Leave as a Personal Liberty', in Mary Crock and Tom D Campbell (eds), *Refugees and Rights* (Taylor & Francis Group, 2015) 3; Catherine Dauvergne, *Humanitarianism, Identity and Nation: Migration Laws in Canada and Australia* (ProQuest Ebook Central, 2004) 7 ('*Humanitarianism*').

12 See, e.g., Lester (n 5) 288–9.

13 The first Australian Values Statement enabled by *Migration Regulations 1994* (Cth) r 1.03 sch 4, pt 3 cl 3.1 can be found at <www.legislation.gov.au/Details/F2007L03959> (Australian Values Statement 2007–2019). The statement from 2020 is at <www.legislation.gov.au/Details/F2020L01305> ('Australian Values Statement 2020').

14 Allsop (n 9) 49, 51.

15 Allsop (n 9) 49, 53–4. See also Chapter 7 for a discussion of values and the rule of law.

16 Allsop (n 9) 49. See also *Hands v Minister for Immigration and Border Protection* [2018] 225 FCAFC 628, 630.

17 Allsop (n 9) 49–50.

In the same way globalisation is not value free. Wendy Brown argues that the neoliberal market logic of globalisation 'displaces legal and political principles (especially liberal commitments to universal inclusion, equality, liberty, and the rule of law) with market criteria'.[18] Brown argues that, despite the attempts to exclude through the wall building she theorises, the underlying value of globalisation, which is neoliberalism, is not excluded.[19] Martin Krygier and Paul O'Connell make similar arguments about the impact of globalised neoliberal values.[20] There is also a range of literature theorising the expression of Australian values in immigration and citizenship legislation and policy.[21]

Within this context of values, as an underpinning factor in law, globalisation and political and social discourse, the enactment of a statement of values in the regulations under the *Migration Act 1958* (Cth) is noteworthy. It is against these espoused values, found in the Australian Values Statement and in this way given a status beyond any political rhetoric, that the chapter assesses the values expressed in the amendments and justified as asserting or protecting sovereignty.

A The Creation of the Australian Value Statement

In 2006 the Australian government introduced an Australian citizenship test and accompanying this test was the Australian Values Statement.[22] The statement was enacted as a legislative instrument not requiring parliamentary approval. It is not disallowable by Parliament and does not need a statement

18 Brown, *Walled States* (n 1) 34. See also Wendy Brown, *Undoing the Demos: Neo Liberalism's Stealth Revolution* (Zone Books, 2015) ('*Undoing the Demos*'). See also discussion of the student visa in Chapter 4 Section II D and Section III.

19 Brown, *Undoing the Demos* (n 18).

20 See discussion in Chapter 3 Section II D; Martin Krygier, 'Transformations of the Rule of Law: Legal, Liberal and Neo', in Ben Golder and Daniel McLoughlin (eds), *The Politics of Legality in a Neoliberal Age* (Routledge, 2018) 19; Paul O'Connell, 'On Reconciling Irreconcilables: Neo-Liberal Globalisation and Human Rights' (2007) 7 *Human Rights Law Review* 483, 485. See also Samuel Moyn, 'A Powerless Companion: Human Rights in the Age of Neoliberalism' (2014) 77 *Law and Contemporary Problems* 147–8.

21 See, e.g., Maria Chisari, 'Testing Citizen Identities: Australian Migrants and the Australian Values Debate' (2015) 21(6) *Social Identities* 573; Stefano Gulmanelli, 'John Howard and the "Anglospherist" Reshaping of Australia' (2014) 49(4) *Australian Journal of Political Science* 581; Mary Walsh and Alexander C Karolis, 'Being Australian, Australian Nationalism and Australian Values' (2008) 43(4) *Australian Journal of Political Science* 719; Christian Joppke, 'Through the European Looking Glass: Citizenship Tests in the USA, Australia, and Canada' (2013) 17(1) *Citizenship Studies* 1, 6–7. See also Danielle Every on discourses of racism in the parliamentary debate on the Border Protection Bill 2001: Danielle Every, 'A Reasonable, Practical and Moderate Humanitarianism: The Co-Option of Humanitarianism in the Australian Asylum Seeker Debates' (2008) 21(2) *Journal of Refugee Studies* 210. For a discussion on the values of humanitarianism in migration law see Dauvergne, *Humanitarianism* (n 11) 7.

22 John Howard, 'Joint Press Conference with Mr Andrew Robb Parliamentary Secretary to the Minister for Immigration and Multicultural Affairs Phillip Street, Sydney', *PM Transcripts* (11 December 2006) <pmtranscripts.pmc.gov.au>.

of compatibility with human rights,[23] as almost all legislation and disallowable instruments require.[24] The regulation enacting the statement authorises the immigration minister to 'approve one or more values statements for the subclasses of visas specified in the instrument'.[25] The regulation gives the immigration minister wide discretion regarding the content of the statement. The only limit is that the statement must include 'values that are important to Australian society' and comply with Australian law, but the immigration minister is also given discretion to 'include other provisions'.[26] The declared purpose of the citizenship test which included the statement was to speed up the integration of migrants.[27] It was 'about cohesion and integration . . . not about discrimination and exclusion'.[28]

Launching the test, Andrew Robb, Parliamentary Secretary for Immigration and Multicultural Affairs 2006–7 in the Howard Coalition government, explained to his audience that certain visa applicants would also be required to sign a commitment to respect 'our values'.[29] These were applicants for permanent visas, or visas which could lead to permanent visas, or temporary visas which allowed more than twelve months' residence. Robb told his audience that there had been extensive consultation on the values and that the final list had received 93% support.[30] When introducing the statement to the Parliament, Kevin Andrews, Minister for Immigration and Citizenship 2007 in the Howard Coalition government, declared that 'these are the values that guide us'.[31]

The statement, communicating Australian values to the noncitizen,[32] was set out in legislation and is replicated here.

1. Australian society values respect for the freedom and dignity of the individual, freedom of religion, commitment to the rule of law, parliamentary democracy, equality of men and women and a spirit of egalitarianism that embraces mutual respect, tolerance, fair play and compassion for those in need and pursuit of the public good;

23 Australian Values Statement 2007–2019 (n 13) [2], [8].

24 See Attorney-General's Department, 'Statements of Compatibility' (Web Page) <www.ag.gov.au/rights-and-protections/human-rights-and-anti-discrimination/human-rights-scrutiny/statements-compatibility>.

25 *Migration Regulations 1994* (Cth) reg 1.03, sch 4, pt 1, 4019, pt 3, 3.1.

26 *Migration Regulations 1994* (Cth).

27 Howard, 'Joint Press Conference' (n 22).

28 Howard, 'Joint Press Conference' (n 22).

29 Howard, 'Joint Press Conference' (n 22).

30 Howard, 'Joint Press Conference' (n 22).

31 Commonwealth, *Parliamentary Debates*, House of Representatives, 17 September 2007, 39 (Kevin Andrews).

32 The term noncitizen is a statutory concept meaning those who do not meet the definition of citizen in the *Migration Act 1958* (Cth) s 5, and the *Australian Citizenship Act 2007* s 4. Note Edelman J in the majority distinguishes between noncitizen and non-alien in *Love v Commonwealth of Australia* (2020) 270 CLR 152–3.

2. Australian society values equality of opportunity for individuals, regardless of their race, religion or ethnic background;
3. the English language, as the national language, is an important unifying element of Australian society.
4. I undertake to respect these values of Australian society during my stay in Australia and to obey the laws of Australia.[33]

The stated rationale for applying the statement to visa applicants as well as citizenship applicants breaks down when it is also applied to temporary visa holders who are not on a pathway to permanency or citizenship. However, the inclusion even at its introduction of such a wide group of visa applicants demonstrates the shared policy values and directions which underlie these two areas of law to which all noncitizens are subject.[34] Because of this the discussion of the statement and its development includes reference to citizenship issues, but this is only to provide the context.

B *The Purpose of the Australian Values Statement: Integration or Exclusion?*

The government's rationale for the elevation of a statement of Australian values to the status of formal regulation under the *Migration Act 1958* (Cth) can only be inferred. If the goal was to provide information, enacting legislation was unnecessary. If the goal was to enforce compliance, why are there no legal consequences for not conforming to the values?

Enactment suggests other unstated priorities. Stefano Gulmanelli argues that across this period in which John Howard was prime minister, 1996–2007, he used the concept of shared values to refocus the multiculturalism that had been promoted by the previous governments.[35] Under Howard, a new Australian multiculturalism that placed Anglo-Celtic culture at the centre and ethnic cultures at the periphery was promoted. Gulmanelli views the introduction of the citizenship test and its Australian values as the final act in reinstating a traditional Anglocentric understanding of Australia.[36] This refocussing began as a 'denied agenda' which, as Howard gained power, became more explicitly expressed.[37] In this way Howard's declaration that the new citizenship test and the values were introduced to unite, not exclude,[38] has internal logic.

33 Australian Values Statement 2007–2019 (n 13).
34 The two areas of law are *Migration Act 1958* (Cth) and the *Australian Citizenship Act 2007* (Cth).
35 Gulmanelli (n 21) 582–9.
36 Gulmanelli (n 21) 585–6, 589. See also Carol Johnson, 'John Howard's "Values" and Australian Identity' (2007) 42(2) *Australian Journal of Political Science* 195, 197–9.
37 Gulmanelli (n 21) 582.
38 Howard, 'Joint Press Conference' (n 22).

Applying Gulmanelli's analysis, the values are an invitation to the new version of multiculturalism, which is closer to versions of assimilation.[39] Howard's declared purpose to unite can in this way be understood as an invitation to become more like 'us'. Howard's own words seem to confirm this analysis. For example at the end of his period in office, Howard responded to a question about the Muslim population of Australia by saying:

> Well there's every reason to try and assimilate, and I unapologetically use that word, assimilate a section of the community, a tiny minority of whose members have caused concern and after all once somebody's become a citizen of this country the best thing we can do is to absorb them into the mainstream.[40]

The statement's purported aim of accelerating integration was not explained when introduced, only declared. The extent to which knowledge of the values in the statement accelerated integration of noncitizens was not measured. Establishing such a statement with such a purpose suggests that those visa applicants from other English-speaking Western liberal democracies who espouse similar values and Anglo-Celtic heritage, such as New Zealand, Canada, the United States and the United Kingdom, would be preferred, as being more likely to achieve the swift integration the government declared to be a community benefit, while applicants from other countries might not.[41]

While the efficacy of the statement in promoting integration has not been shown,[42] there is some indication that the statement has increasingly become a weapon to exclude, both symbolically for the visa applicant as a form of 'ideological assimilation'[43] and tangibly for the citizenship applicant. Two examples illustrate this escalation.[44]

The first example is from 2015. Prior to this point, as Christian Joppke argued in 2013, there was evidence in Australia of political rhetoric 'at the level of the political elite' that access to citizenship should be more tightly

39 Gulmanelli (n 21) 593; Johnson (n 36) 205.

40 John Howard, 'Interview with Neil Mitchell Radio 3AW, Melbourne', *PM Transcripts* (Radio interview, 11 May 2007) <pmtranscripts@pmc.gov.au>.

41 Dagbanja (n 10) 222 argues this policy intent is apparent in the different application of English competency testing for certain visas depending on nationality.

42 See, e.g., Louise Pratt, *Dissenting Report by Labor Senators* (Report, 2017) [1.23] <www.aph.gov.au/Parliamentary_Business/Committees/Senate/Legal_and_Constitutional_Affairs/Citize nshipBill2017/Report/d01>.

43 Johnson (n 36) 205.

44 Note the use of the statement as an instrument of exclusion has not been widely discussed. Dagbanja (n 10) 225 for example references the Australian Values Statement to support his argument on the inappropriateness of the use of English proficiency to exclude on the basis of nationality, but this is incidental to his argument.

restricted, but the polices and legislation remained inclusive.[45] This began to change when Tony Abbott, Coalition prime minister 2013–5, launched a national consultation with the aim 'to improve understanding of the privileges and responsibilities of Australian citizenship'.[46] The idea of citizenship as a privilege was raised earlier in 2006 when Howard launched the new citizenship test.[47] However, Howard had talked of privileges and opportunities, not responsibilities.[48] The use of the term 'responsibilities' signals that obligations will be imposed.

On coming to office Abbott's government had already introduced the Asylum Seeker Code of Behaviour, which applied to asylum seekers on bridging visas who were living in the community.[49] This Code of Behaviour represents asylum seekers as a potential threat, reversing the reality that it was the asylum seekers who needed protection.[50] Launching the consultation on citizenship in 2015, Abbott can be seen to broaden this representation of threat to all noncitizens. Abbott began with a warning about the 'threat from those, including those in our midst, who would do us harm'.[51] He linked the consultation process to a new measure previously announced to enable the government to 'strip dual citizens involved in terrorism of their Australian citizenship'.[52] In this way the government represented the border between the

45 Joppke (n 21).

46 Department of Home Affairs, *Australian Citizenship: Your Right, Your Responsibility. The National Consultation on Citizenship Final Report* (Report, Undated) 6 <www.homeaffairs.gov.au/reports-and-pubs/files/australian-citizenship-report.pdf>.

47 Howard, 'Joint Press Conference' (n 22).

48 Howard, 'Joint Press Conference' (n 22).

49 Code of Behaviour for Subclass 050 Bridging (General) Visa Holders. For an analysis of the enforcement and operation of the code see Meg Randolph et al., 'Australia's Asylum Seeker Code of Behaviour: A Statistical Analysis' (Border Crossing Research Brief No 15, Border Crossing Observatory, Monash University, July 2019) <www.monash.edu/data/assets/pdf_file/0007/1872061/research-brief-15-FINAL-MR.pdf>.

50 Anthea Vogl and Elyse Methven, 'We Will Decide Who Comes to This Country, and How They Behave: A Critical Reading of the Asylum Seeker Code of Behaviour' (2015) 40(3) *Alternative Law Journal* 175.

51 Tony Abbott, 'Joint Press Conference', *PM Transcripts* (26 May 2015) <https://pmtranscripts.pmc.gov.au/release/transcript-24499>. For a discussion on the victimisation of certain immigrant groups see, e.g., Scott Poynting and Barbara Perry, 'Climates of Hate: Media and State Inspired Victimisation of Muslims in Canada and Australia Since 9/11' (2007) 19(2) *Current Issues in Criminal Justice* 151; Waqas Tufail and Scott Poynting, 'A Common "Outlawness": Criminalisation of Muslim Minorities in the UK and Australia' (2013) 2(3) *International Journal for Crime Justice and Social Democracy* 43.

52 Tony Abbott, 'Joint Press Conference', *PM Transcripts* (26 May 2015) <https://pmtranscripts.pmc.gov.au/release/transcript-24499>. For a discussion on the victimisation of certain immigrant groups see, e.g., Poynting and Perry, 'Climates of Hate: Media and State Inspired Victimisation of Muslims in Canada and Australia Since 9/11' (2007) 19(2) *Current Issues in Criminal Justice* 151; Waqas Tufail and Scott Poynting, 'A Common "Outlawness": Criminalisation of Muslim Minorities in the UK and Australia' (2013) 2(3) *International Journal for Crime Justice and Social Democracy* 43.

migrant and entry to citizenship as a vulnerable entry point to be guarded from a threat from the noncitizen.

The consultation process continued this representation. It positioned a list of what were presented as Australian values (a slightly different list to those already enacted) with questions designed to seek the public's views on 'how to promote the value of Australian citizenship and deter Australians from becoming involved in terrorism'.[53] The final report of the consultation was based on responses which could be categorised as positive, negative or ambivalent to the questions posed. The quantum of ambivalent responses was not reported.[54]

The final report found that Australians were acutely concerned that citizenship was undervalued, especially by those 'who by their conduct have chosen to break with the values inherent in being an Australian citizen'.[55] It recommended that the waiting period for applying for citizenship should be increased from four years lawfully present in Australia to four years of permanent residence, 'so that a person's word and deed across this time' could be considered.[56] This was a judgment upon applicants and those who had acquired citizenship by conferral, as distinct from those acquiring it by birth.[57] They were to have an increased 'probationary period' to monitor whether they lived up to core Australian values.[58] The consultation process appears to position Australian values as a scorecard to highlight difference and promote suspicion of the noncitizen, not as an instrument of integration, unless integration is understood as conformity to an idealised Anglo-Celtic norm as Gulmanelli and Johnson describe.[59] The government's response to this consultation was a failed amendment which attempted to insert into the citizenship test an assessment of conduct contrary to Australian values, echoing the process already in place for certain asylum seekers.[60] While espousing the purpose of integration, the Australian values were to be positioned as a hurdle to citizenship.[61]

53 Department of Home Affairs, *Australian Citizenship: Your Right* (n 46) 6.
54 Department of Home Affairs, *Australian Citizenship: Your Right* (n 46) 23.
55 Department of Home Affairs, *Australian Citizenship: Your Right* (n 46) 3.
56 Department of Home Affairs, *Australian Citizenship: Your Right* (n 46) 4.
57 Citizenship by conferral, also termed naturalisation, is the process through which a noncitizen most commonly acquires citizenship. See *Australian Citizenship Act 2007* (Cth) s 2A. See also *Love v Commonwealth of Australia* (2020) 270 CLR 152 for the status of Indigenous Australians.
58 Department of Home Affairs, *Australian Citizenship: Your Right* (n 46) 4, 10.
59 Gulmanelli (n 21); Johnson (n 36).
60 Australian Citizenship Legislation Amendment (Strengthening the Requirements for Australian Citizenship and Other Measures) Bill 2017; Commonwealth, *Parliamentary Debates*, House of Representatives, 15 June 2017, 6610 (Peter Dutton). This followed a failed 2014 bill with comparable requirements: Australian Citizenship and Other Legislation Amendment Bill 2014.
61 Heli Askola, 'Copying Europe? Integration as a Citizenship Requirement in Australia' (2021) 55(1) *International Migration Review* 4, 22. He argues that up to that point the citizenship requirements in Australia remained 'liberal and inclusive'.

The second example that demonstrates the values as a weapon of exclusion is from 2020, when the exclusionary use of the statement was further entrenched and became more tangible. A new statement published in October 2020 changed the content for the first time since 2007 and also changed the obligations it imposed on visa applicants and citizenship applicants.[62] The purpose of the statement was also broadened.

The change in content included the addition of 'freedom of speech'. No rationale was given for this addition. A second content change was that definitions for some values were provided. The rule of law was defined as meaning that 'all people are subject to the law and should obey it'. Parliamentary democracy was defined as meaning that 'laws are determined by parliaments elected by the people, those laws being paramount and overriding any other inconsistent religious or secular "laws"'. Omitted from this definition is any sense of protection under the rule of law from arbitrary power,[63] or the constitutional role of the judiciary in the formation of the law or the rule of law.[64] A third significant change in content was achieved by a subtle change in the wording of the English language sentence which previously read, 'The English language, as the national language, is an important unifying element of Australian society'.[65] After the 2020 change it read 'the English language as the national language, and as an important unifying element of Australian society'.[66] The wording change ('is' changed to 'and as') has positioned the English language as a value in itself.

There was also a notable omission. The 'spirit of egalitarianism' was omitted, as were two of the attributes it was said to embrace: 'fair play' and the 'pursuit of the public good'.[67] In its place is a 'fair go', said to embrace 'mutual respect; tolerance; compassion for those in need; equality of opportunity for all'.[68] Fairness, which encompasses equal treatment as well as opportunity as captured in egalitarianism and fair play, is only partially represented.

The obligations imposed were also strengthened. Firstly, while previously framed in terms of 'respect', the obligation is now expressed as one of 'conduct': 'I undertake to conduct myself in accordance with these values of Australian society during my stay in Australia and to obey the laws of Australia'.[69] This added obligation of conduct implies an expectation that

62 Australian Values Statement 2020 (n 13).

63 See further discussion in Chapter 8. See Martin Krieger's discussion of the original purpose of the rule of law in Martin Krygier, 'Rule of Law: Pasts, Presents, and Two Possible Futures' (2016) 12 *Annual Review of Law and Social Science* 199, 203.

64 See also Hon Murray Gleeson's discussion in Murray Gleeson, *The Rule of Law and the Constitution* (ABC, 2000) 67, quoting Owen Dixon, 'The Law and the Constitution' (1936) 51 *Law Quarterly Review* 590.

65 Australian Values Statement 2007–19 (n 13).

66 Australian Values Statement 2020 (n 13).

67 Australian Values Statement 2007–19 (n 13).

68 Australian Values Statement 2020 (n 13).

69 Australian Values Statement 2020 (n 13).

the visa applicant's usual behaviour might need to be modified to fit the Australian standard.

Secondly, an obligation regarding the English language is now included: 'I undertake to make reasonable efforts to learn the English language if it is not my native language'.[70]

Finally, the purpose of the statement for the citizenship applicant was also changed. The original stated purpose of the introduction of the statement was to provide helpful information for the new migrant, but in 2020 knowledge of the values and the definition of these values were given a tangible exclusionary use. This exclusion was not from entering or remaining in Australia. It was exclusion from the privileges of citizenship. Announcing an updated citizenship test, Alan Tudge, Acting Minister for Immigration, Citizenship, Migrant Services and Multicultural Affairs in the Howard Coalition government 2019–20, said:

> Our Australian values are important. They have helped shape our country and they are the reason why so many people want to become Australian citizens.
>
> The updated citizenship test will have new and more meaningful questions that require potential citizens to understand and commit to our values like freedom of speech, mutual respect, equality of opportunity, the importance of democracy and the rule of law.[71]

Since November 2020, the values in the statement comprise 20% of the citizenship test, and answering each values question correctly is mandatory. For example, the mandatory test question on values could include this sample question, drawn from the practice test published on the Department of Home Affairs website on 19 November 2020:

Should people in Australia make an effort to learn English?

a. People in Australia should speak whichever language is most commonly spoken in their local neighbourhood
b. There is no expectation to learn any particular language in Australia
c. Yes, English is the national language of Australia, and it helps to get an education, a job, and to integrate into the community.[72]

70 Australian Values Statement 2020 (n 13).

71 Alan Tudge, 'Focus on Values in Updated Australian Citizenship Test' (Media Release, Commonwealth Department of Home Affairs, 17 September 2020) ('Focus on Values'). This can be seen as a step toward achieving the failed attempts of 2014 and 2017 to test conduct. See discussion at n 60.

72 Department of Home Affairs, *Australian Citizenship: Our Common Bond* (Practice Test, 2020) 46 <https://immi.homeaffairs.gov.au/citizenship-subsite/files/our-common-bond-testable.pdf>.

To choose option a or b is a mistake that would lead to failure of the whole test and the requirement to re-sit the test.[73]

The origin, development and use of the statement hints at a purpose that was not openly declared. Viewed in the light of Gulmanelli's argument about Howard's increasingly bold Anglocentric agenda, the statement, delivered at the end of Howard's ten years as prime minister, could be viewed as an attempt to secure that agenda. Whatever Howard's purpose, the use of the statement in migration and citizenship administration has not been abandoned, only given additional uses.

The discussion now turns to the values that make up the statement. Immigration ministers have declared these values to be 'the values that guide us',[74] the values that 'have helped shape our country'[75] and values that are 'inherent in being an Australian citizen'.[76] The following discussion of three of the 'Australian values' in the statement compares these values and their representation with the use of the values in the debates on exclusionary amendments. Through this analysis the chapter aims to further reveal the nature of the sovereignty that justified these amendments. The chapter argues that these three values have been repurposed and redefined when used in parliamentary debate on the amendments.

Within the policy framework of asserting and protecting sovereignty,[77] values such as compassion and fairness were stripped of their ordinary meaning and used to justify an expression of sovereign control that was neither compassionate nor fair in any ordinary sense.[78] An examination of the 2020 elevation of the English language to the status of a value in the statement and the concurrent changes to visa requirements suggest that, in reality, values not apparent in the ordinary meaning of 'the English language as the national language, and as an important unifying element of Australian society' are being promoted.[79]

To analyse these enacted values and their use in the debates, the 'ordinary meaning of words'[80] will be used as a reference point, as it is for statutory interpretation.

73 The policy at the time of writing is that the test can be sat again if failed. Department of Home Affairs, 'Citizenship Test and Interview' (Web Page, 15 June 2022) <https://immi.homeaffairs.gov.au/citizenship/test-and-interview/learn-about-citizenship-interview-and-test>.

74 Commonwealth, *Parliamentary Debates*, House of Representatives, 17 September 2007, 39 (Kevin Andrews).

75 Tudge, 'Focus on Values' (n 71).

76 Commonwealth, *Parliamentary Debates*, House of Representatives, 17 September 2007, 39 (Kevin Andrews).

77 See Chapter 6.

78 Every (n 21) argues similarly that in 2001 the Howard government reconstructed the term 'humanitarian' within a liberal discourse, and this allowed Australia to claim to be humanitarian while enacting the 2001 legislation against asylum seekers.

79 Australian Values Statement 2020 (n 13).

80 See n 7 and accompanying text.

III The Value of 'Compassion for Those in Need'

The first value to be considered is 'compassion for those in need'.[81] This value has remained listed in the statement since 2007 and is incorporated into the 2020 version as an aspect of the 'fair go'. The ordinary meaning of compassion is 'the feeling or emotion, when a person is moved by the suffering or distress of another, and by the desire to relieve it; pity that inclines one to spare or to succour'.[82] It overlaps in definition with the term 'mercy', used by Allsop.[83] Mercy is defined as 'clemency and compassion shown to a person who is in a position of powerlessness or subjection or to a person with no right or claim to receive kindness'.[84]

The first issue to address before an analysis of the use of compassion in the debates is why the Australian Parliament needed to address the value of 'compassion for those in need' in debates framed by a policy about using its sovereign exclusionary power declared by the High Court as early as 1906.[85] As discussed previously, when introducing this sovereignty discourse to justify exclusion, Howard claimed 'a right to control borders' and asserted that 'they [the asylum seekers] don't have any legal right to be in Australia'.[86] Compassion for those in need is not required of the Parliament by Australian law.[87] Despite this, analysis of parliamentary debates about exclusionary legislation since 2000 shows that parliamentarians accepted that the value of compassion needed to be addressed. There is no specific mention in debate of the statement or the obligations it places on visa applicants. Nevertheless, even before the introduction of the statement, compassion was an

81 Australian Values Statement 2007–19 (n 13); Australian Values Statement 2020 (n 13).

82 'Compassion' (def 2a), *Oxford English Dictionary* (online, 1 June 2022). See also Michelle Peterie's discussion of how the concept of compassion is used in government and Opposition ministerial press statements concerning refugees and asylum seekers, 2001 to 2016. She concludes through this analysis that governments have denied compassion by casting doubt on this group's innocence, suffering and affinity to Australians. Michelle Peterie, 'Docility and Desert: Government Discourses of Compassion in Australia's Asylum Seeker Debate' (2017) 53(2) *Journal of Sociology* 351, 361.

83 Allsop (n 9).

84 Mercy can be defined as 'Clemency and compassion shown to a person who is in a position of powerlessness or subjection, or to a person with no right or claim to receive kindness; kind and compassionate treatment in a case where severity is merited or expected, esp. in giving legal judgment or passing sentence'. 'Compassion' (def 1a), *Oxford English Dictionary* (online, 1 June 2022).

85 *Robtelmes v Brenan* (1906) 4 CLR 395.

86 John Howard, 'Interview with Prime Minister John Howard, Neil Mitchell', *Radio 3AW* (31 August 2001).

87 Note however the opportunity for the court to show compassion where a statute allows judicial discretion: Tom Bingham, *The Rule of Law* (Penguin Books, 2011) 51; Murray Gleeson, 'Outcome, Process and the Rule of Law' (2006) 65(3) *Australian Journal of Public Administration* 5, 127. See also Allsop (n 9).

issue in debate and was co-opted as part of the justification for legislation to exclude.

One reason for Parliament to address the issue of compassion might be, as Catherine Dauvergne suggests, that the humanitarian intake of refugees is an expression of the national identity of the liberal state.[88] According to this logic a claim of compassion for refugees would mark Australia as belonging to the West.[89] The debate shows some evidence of this. For example, Australian government members speaking in the debates on the legislation boasted of what they termed a proud history of compassion for refugees, claiming that compassionate heritage as part of Australia's identity.[90] The reason for addressing compassion in the debate could also be more pragmatic. Acknowledging the issue of compassion might have been prompted, at least partially, by the need to address the concerns of Australian citizens whose families remained in refugee camps.[91]

Whatever prompted this decision to address the value of compassion, the result was a problem that the Parliament tried to solve: how to reconcile the value 'compassion for those in need', which the Parliament espoused as an Australian valued and which, since 2007, had been enshrined in migration regulations, with exclusionary measures aimed at those who, on any ordinary understanding, were in need. How the Parliament attempted to solve this problem was demonstrated in the debates. Compassion for those in need was carefully interpreted and prioritised against other values, and the pity that prompts compassion was channelled towards certain objects and away from others. The following discussion shows four ways that the Parliament dealt with this problem of the value of 'compassion for those in need' in debates concerning exclusion.

Firstly, the compassion of Australia was commended in order to justify the assertion of exclusionary sovereignty by characterising that act as a necessary exception to the central characteristic value of Australia. The Parliament justified support for the migration exclusionary legislation, explicitly and implicitly, as a balance struck by a 'good hearted country'[92] that is decent

88 Dauvergne, *Humanitarianism* (n 11).

89 See Harald Bauder, 'State of Exemption: Migration Policy and the Enactment of Sovereignty' (2021) 9(5) *Territory, Politics, Governance* 675. Bauder argues that Western democracies, with a case study of the USA, exempt themselves from 'prevailing liberal norms' when forming migration policy.

90 See, e.g., Commonwealth, *Parliamentary Debates*, House of Representatives, 18 September 2001, 30871 (Philip Ruddock).

91 See, e.g., Commonwealth, *Parliamentary Debates*, House of Representatives, 19 September 2001, 30961 (Bruce Billson). See also Chapter 6 Section III A, quoting Bruce Billson's electorate concerns.

92 Commonwealth, *Parliamentary Debates*, House of Representatives, 19 September 2001, 30956 (Con Sciacca).

and humane,[93] generous,[94] compassionate and 'leading the world' on its acceptance of refugees.[95] Australia's post-World War II migration, driven by defence and economic needs, as expressed in the first Minister for Immigration Arthur Calwell's 'populate or perish' slogan,[96] was reinterpreted in the debate as an act of generosity and compassion.[97] For example, one government member claimed that 'the almost 5.7 million people [who] have come to Australia from other countries, with almost 600,000 of those under refugee and other humanitarian programs' since 1945, evidenced Australia's compassion.[98]

The second way that compassion was used was to justify exclusion as an act of compassion. For example, legislation such as the *Migration and Maritime Powers Legislation Amendment (Resolving the Asylum Legacy Caseload) Act 2014* (Cth), promoted as delivering 'national security and economic prosperity', was also justified as stopping 'tragedy', narrowly defined as death during sea travel to Australia from Indonesia.[99] Another example is a speech to the Parliament by Malcolm Turnbull, Coalition prime minister 2015–8, on the establishment of the new Home Affairs portfolio, whose mission was to focus on 'counterterrorism and violent extremism, counter foreign interference, serious and organised crime, cybersecurity, border security, immigration and social cohesion'.[100] That speech also included the justification of compassion. Turnbull claimed that strengthening national security and law enforcement would prevent asylum seekers dying at sea, implying

93 Commonwealth, *Parliamentary Debates*, House of Representatives, 9 September 2001, 30960 (Bruce Billson).

94 Commonwealth, *Parliamentary Debates*, House of Representatives, 18 September 2001, 30871 (Philip Ruddock).

95 Commonwealth, *Parliamentary Debates*, House of Representatives, 19 September 2001, 30968 (Jackie Kelly).

96 Katrina Stats, 'Characteristically Generous? Australian Responses to Refugees Prior to 1951' (2014) 60(2) *Australian Journal of Politics and History* 177, 184.

97 Commonwealth, *Parliamentary Debates*, House of Representatives, 19 September 2001, 30968 (Jackie Kelly).

98 Commonwealth, *Parliamentary Debates*, House of Representatives, 19 September 2001, 30968 (Jackie Kelly). For discussions on policy goals and the postwar refugee intake see Graeme Hugo, 'From Compassion to Compliance? Trends in Refugee and Humanitarian Migration in Australia' (2001) 55 *GeoJournal* 27, 36; Juliet Pietsch, 'Immigration and Refugees: Punctuations in the Commonwealth Policy Agenda' (2013) 72(2) *Australian Journal of Public Administration* 143; Peter Waxman, 'The Shaping of Australia's Immigration and Refugee Policy' (2000) *19 Immigrants and Minorities* 53. For a history see Katrina Stats' critique of the narrative that Australia's history pre-Federation to 1951 was characteristically humanitarian at Stats (n 96).

99 Commonwealth, *Parliamentary Debates*, House of Representatives, 25 September 2014, 10545 (Scott Morrison).

100 Commonwealth, *Parliamentary Debates*, House of Representatives, 7 December 2017, 1315 (Malcolm Turnbull).

a compassionate rationale.[101] In later debates, Peter Dutton, Home Affairs Minister in the Turnbull and later Morrison Coalition governments 2017–21, claimed that one benefit of the repeal of the 'Medevac law'[102] was that it would remove the motivation for 'transferees', meaning asylum seekers in offshore detention, from self-harming.[103] The repealed law had prioritised medical assessment for asylum seekers in offshore detention who needed to be transferred to Australia for urgent medical treatment. Compassion was used to justify reversal of that humane policy.

These examples show that compassion in the debate was focussed locally, not globally. It is only those, for example, who might die on a boat from Indonesia attempting to reach Christmas Island or suffer in other carefully defined ways that were the focus of compassion.

The third way that the concept of compassion was used in the debate was to directly challenge the meaning of compassion in the context of migration. For example, in 2012 Scott Morrison, Coalition Shadow Minister for Immigration and Citizenship, attacked the government's claim to compassion: 'It is one thing to sound compassionate; it is another thing to be compassionate and to have policies that deal with the problem'.[104]

The fourth way and arguably the most common way that compassion was used in the debate was to demonise the object of compassion. Those asylum seekers who purportedly refuse to wait in refugee camps for an offer of a place were scorned.[105] For example, in 2012 Opposition Leader Tony Abbott claimed asylum seekers were 'playing us for mugs'.[106] In effect he tried to refocus pity from asylum seekers to Australians whose compassion he claimed was being abused.[107] At the same time, people smugglers were demonised as people lacking compassion for the same asylum seekers who were scorned in the parliamentary debate. People smugglers, it was claimed, are 'not motivated by any desire to help others, but by base motives

101 Commonwealth, *Parliamentary Debates*, House of Representatives, 7 December 2017, 1315 (Malcolm Turnbull).

102 Migration Amendment (Urgent Medical Treatment Bill) 2018, enacted as *Home Affairs Legislation Amendment (Miscellaneous Measures) Act 2019*.

103 Commonwealth, *Parliamentary Debates*, House of Representatives, 4 July 2019, 296 (Peter Dutton).

104 Commonwealth, *Parliamentary Debates*, House of Representatives, 27 November 2012, 13430 (Scott Morrison).

105 Commonwealth, *Parliamentary Debates*, House of Representatives, 18 September 2001, 30869 (Philip Ruddock).

106 Julian Drape and Lauren Farrow, 'Asylum Seekers Playing Us for Mugs: Abbott', *Sydney Morning Herald* (online, 9 June 2012) <www.smh.com.au/national/asylum-seekers-playing-us-for-mugs-abbott-20120609-202d4.html>.

107 Vogl and Methven (n 50) find a similar reversal in their discussion of the Asylum Seeker Code of Behaviour.

of greed'.[108] Within three weeks of the interview quoted previously, after the drowning of some asylum seekers, Abbott, by that time the prime minister, referred in Parliament to these asylum seekers as 'desperate people . . . [with] a desire for a better life'.[109] These comments reveal the difficulty of maintaining both positions – demonising living asylum seekers and showing compassion for drowned asylum seekers.

Also illustrative of this process of the demonising of a potential object of pity is the shift in the parliamentary debate, across the decades, about legislation concerning immigration detention centres where noncitizens without a valid visa are placed, pending their removal from Australia.[110] That series of debates demonstrates the government's escalating attempts to redirect pity away from these detention centre inmates.[111]

Repurposing the concept of compassion as part of the justification for measures designed to exclude has not gone unchallenged. Some members and senators have countered government claims to compassion, pointing out, for example, that there is 'horrific' sexual and physical abuse in offshore detention centres established by Australia[112] and that Australia's claim to lead the world in compassion for refugees is based on a misleading statistic which does not count the thousands of refugees being settled in countries with land borders that provide easier access for asylum seekers.[113] However, such contributions were largely ignored in the debate. For example, the statistics presented by Susan Lines, Western Australian Labor senator, to dismantle what she termed the 'myth' of Australia's compassion and generosity, drew no response from Scott Morrison, Minister for Immigration and Border

108 Commonwealth, *Parliamentary Debates*, House of Representatives, 18 September 2001, 30869 (Philip Ruddock).

109 Commonwealth, *Parliamentary Debates*, House of Representatives, 25 June 2012, 13430 (Tony Abbott).

110 *Migration Act 1958* (Cth) s 189. For further discussion of Australia's immigration detention as an exclusionary mechanism of the state see Amy Nethery, 'A Modern-Day Concentration Camp: Using History to Make Sense of Australian Immigration Detention Centres', in Klaus Neumann and Gwenda Tavan (eds), *Does History Matter? Making and Debating Citizenship* (ANU Press, 2009) 65, 72.

111 See Chapter 6 Section III.

112 Commonwealth, *Parliamentary Debates*, Senate, 24 September 2001, 27702 (Natasha Stott Despoja); Commonwealth, *Parliamentary Debates*, Senate, 25 June 2015, 4572 (Robert Di Natale). For a recent report on detention conditions see Australian Human Rights Commission, *Inspections of Australia's Immigration Detention Facilities 2019* (Report, 2020). For discussion of the regulation of body searching of migrants see Marinella Marmo, 'Strip Searching: Seeking the Truth "in" and "on" the Regular Migrant's Body', in Peter Billings (ed), *Crimmigration in Australia* (Springer, 2019) 197.

113 Commonwealth, *Parliamentary Debates*, Senate, 4 December 2014, 10263 (Susan Lines). For a further discussion on Australia's refugee intake in a global context see Mary Crock, Ben Saul and Azadeh Dastyari, *Future Seekers II: Refugees and Irregular Migration in Australia* (Federation Press, 2006) 15–7, 27–35.

Protection in the Abbott Coalition government 2013–4, who presented the bill. Lines said:

> Australia does not host a large number of refugees. By comparison, Pakistan, a country that does not have the wealth that Australia has, hosts over 1.6 million refugees. Iran hosts almost 900,000 refugees. Chad has almost half a million. And Australia? Just 13,750 refugees are granted permanency residency by Australia each year – a tiny, tiny drop in the ocean. Per $1 billion of GDP, we take in less than 35 refugees. By comparison, Pakistan takes 2,811.[114]

Arguments using the value of compassion as a rationale for exclusion become difficult to sustain in the face of evidence such as that which Senator Lines presented or when Australians are tempted to rescue their relatives by paying a people smuggler instead of leaving them waiting for years in a refugee camp.[115] The debate did not resolve the tension between asserting the right to 'decide who will come to this country'[116] and compassion for the millions of asylum seekers escaping persecution or driven out of their countries by war or poverty.[117] Bruce Billson, Liberal Member for Dunkley, Victoria 1996–2016, seemed to sum up this lack of resolution. He excused his support for exclusionary legislation as being 'with a heavy heart'.[118] Other speakers' attempts to resolve this tension between espoused compassion and policies of exclusion of asylum seekers point to efforts at international cooperation, but even this most often concerned the problem of stopping demands on Australia's hospitality, not addressing the global needs of asylum seekers.[119]

Challenges to the idea that Australian asylum seeker legislation is consistent with a view of Australia as compassionate, such as that made by Senator

114 Commonwealth, *Parliamentary Debates*, Senate, 4 December 2014, 10263 (Susan Lines).

115 Commonwealth, *Parliamentary Debates*, House of Representatives, 19 September 2001, 30961 (Bruce Billson).

116 Scott Morrison, 'Until the Bell Rings', *Prime Minister Media Centre* (Speech, Menzies Research Centre, 6 September 2018) <www.pm.gov.au/media/until-bell-rings-address-menzies-research-centre>.

117 Note the numbers of asylum seekers quoted by Billson in 2001 (n 115) and Lines in 2014 (n 113) and the UN statement in 2016 that there is a 'growing global phenomenon of large movements of refugees and migrants' in 'unprecedented' numbers: 244 million moving from their birth country in 2015 of whom 65 million were forcibly displaced, driven by the effects of climate change, poverty, violence or persecution or a combination of these factors. *New York Declaration for Refugees and Migrants*, UN Doc A/RES/71/1 (3 October 2016).

118 Commonwealth, *Parliamentary Debates*, House of Representatives, 19 September 2001, 30961 (Bruce Billson).

119 See, e.g., Commonwealth, *Parliamentary Debates*, House of Representatives, 21 September 2011, 10945 (Chris Bowen); Commonwealth, *Parliamentary Debates*, House of Representatives, 19 September 2001, 30956 (Con Sciacca) and discussion in Chapter 5.

Lines,[120] introduced to the debate a global perspective on compassion. However, this did not prompt a policy change or even an acknowledgment from the government. The debate remained domestically focussed. For example, in 2011 the Opposition criticised the government's claim of compassion with reference to whom the government had allowed to fill the humanitarian places allocated in the budget, in that year 8,000. The Opposition represented the problem as the wrong choice of refugee, not an inadequate response to the global need. The arbitrary number 8,000 shows that compassion in the migration context is a carefully measured quantity of humanitarianism.[121]

What emerges from the analysis of the debates is the narrow repertoire of policy responses proposed to address the escalating challenge of the global movement of people driven by war, famine and poverty as well as persecution.[122] In 2001, confronted with the new phenomenon of direct demands for asylum from a proportionally tiny but increasing number of individuals arriving onshore, the response was the assertion of sovereignty as a right to exclude, and the apparent need to further justify these amendments to exclude as compassionate. Boat turn backs, excision of Australian territory from the migration zone, effectively unlimited offshore and onshore immigration detention of both adults and children, proposals to improve the national coastguard, and improving relationships with Indonesia to keep asylum seekers away are all difficult to justify as compassionate.[123]

The value 'compassion for those in need' and the amendments to exclude are an uneasy fit. The debate on the legislation stripped the value 'compassion for those in need' of any ordinary meaning. Compassion was repurposed in the debate to justify exclusion, rather than to show mercy or ameliorate suffering.

IV The Value of Fair Play and a Fair Go

The second value to be considered is fairness. In contrast to 'compassion for those in need', the value of fairness has long been recognised as a fundamental value of the common law and of public law administrative decision-making.[124] The concept of the fair go is also recognised as a quin-

120 Commonwealth, *Parliamentary Debates*, Senate, 4 December 2014, 10263 (Susan Lines).

121 See Every's discussion of humanitarianism which she analyses, in the context of asylum seeker policy, as a balancing of an often exagerrated cost to the nation with a duty to assist. Every (n 21) 211–14.

122 *New York Declaration for Refugees and Migrants*, UN Doc A/RES/71/1 (3 October 2016).

123 See Chapter 6 Section III.

124 Allsop (n 9) 49; John Basten, 'Conferring Statutes Conferring Powers – A Process of Implication or Applying Values?', in Janine Boughey and Lisa Burton Crawford (eds), *Interpreting Executive Power* (Federation Press, 2020) 54, 65.

tessential Australian cultural value.[125] It is therefore not surprising that the Parliament would see the need to address the issue of fairness.

The ordinary meaning of fairness is 'honesty; impartiality, equitableness, justness; fair dealing'.[126] The value of fairness was included in the statement as 'fair play' up until October 2020.[127] The ordinary meaning of 'fair play' is 'respect for the fair or equal treatment of all concerned, or respect for the rules of a game or sport; just or honest conduct'.[128] The concept of equal treatment as a value was also included in the statement with the phrase 'a spirit of egalitarianism'. Neither fair play nor egalitarianism remained in the statement after October 2020.

Fairness arose in debate on exclusionary legislation in three contexts. The first was procedural fairness, a concept that focusses on the fairness of a process, not on the outcome of that process.[129] The second was fairness in the sense of playing by the rules. The third context concerned Australia's role internationally. In each debate the ordinary meaning of fairness was narrowed or redefined to justify the proposed exclusionary measure.

The first context, procedural fairness, has been described as a right. When Chief Justice French characterised the common law as 'a repository of rights and freedoms', he declared as one of those rights 'the right to procedural fairness when affected by the exercise of public power'.[130] However, this right, the common law presumption of procedural fairness, is vulnerable when there is clear legislative intent to modify or even abolish it.[131] Three examples of the Parliament's attempt to legislate to dilute the standard of procedural fairness that certain noncitizens would be afforded are discussed shortly.[132]

125 Brennan (n 8).
126 'Fairness' (def 6), *Oxford English Dictionary* (online, 1 June 2022).
127 Australian Values Statement 2007–19 (n 13).
128 'Fair Play' (def A), *Oxford English Dictionary* (online, 1 June 2022).
129 For a discussion on procedural fairness in the migration context see, e.g., Robyn Creyke, 'Procedural Fairness in Tribunals and Commissions of Inquiry' (2019) 150 *Precedent* 4; Emily McDonald and Maria O'Sullivan, 'Protecting Vulnerable Refugees: Procedural Fairness in the Australian Fast Track Regime' (2018) 41(3) *University of New South Wales Law Journal* 1003; Matthew Groves, 'Interpreters and Fairness in Administrative Hearings' (2016) 40 *Melbourne University Law Review* 506. See also a tracing of High Court interpretations of fairness in Mathew Groves, 'The Unfolding Purpose of Fairness' (2017) 45(4) *Federal Law Review* 653.
130 Robert French, 'Protecting Human Rights Without a Bill of Rights' (2010) 43 *John Marshall Law Review* 769, 786, quoting *Wik Peoples v Queensland* (1996) 187 CLR 1, 182.
131 Susan Kiefel, 'Social Justice and the Constitution – Freedoms and Protections' (Mayo Lecture, James Cook University, 24 May 2013). See Justice John Basten's summary of the factors the High Court has taken into consideration regarding a denial of procedural fairness in Basten (n 124) 61–2.
132 For an analysis of the extent to which these and other attempts at codification have been effective see Grant Hooper, 'Three Decades of Tension: From the Codification of Migration Decision-Making to an Overarching Framework for Judicial Review' (2020) 48(3) *Federal Law Review* 401, 431.

The debates reveal how the Parliament dealt with the value of fairness in this context.

The first debate concerns the government's response to an adverse High Court ruling in an asylum seeker case, *Re Minister for Immigration and Multicultural Affairs and another Ex parte Miah*.[133] The court found that that 'the *Migration Act* did not exclude the application of the common law rules of natural justice, that is procedural fairness, to the Minister or the Minister's delegate'.[134] This judgment, confirming that the court had a role in assessing the fairness of the decision-making process, was viewed by the government as a problem it needed to solve.

The Migration Legislation Amendment (Procedural Fairness) Bill 2002 introduced in response aimed to ensure that 'the common law requirements of natural justice or the procedural hearing rule' were excluded in cases of granting or cancelling visas and replaced by procedures set out in legislation.[135] The bill attempted to remove the possibility of an appeal to the judiciary on the basis that the applicant had not had a fair hearing, as might be judged by the standard of the common law.[136]

Criticisms of the bill compared the common-law standards of fairness to the measures in the bill. Those criticisms reveal an awareness of the ordinary meaning of fairness and its history as a common-law value. Those members objecting positioned fairness as a right. The bill, they said, was a 'roll back of rights'.[137] Fairness required accountability and transparency of process and decisions based on the particular facts of an individual case,[138] and 'fairness and equality before the law'.[139] The objectors also labelled the bill as un-Australian. The bill failed the test, it was said, of the 'fair go'.[140] Independent Member for Calare, New South Wales Peter Andren, 1996–2007, summed up the concerns: 'rather than prevent the "bad decisions" happening, this bill just removes a further avenue of recourse in having such decisions reviewed'.[141]

133 (2001) 206 CLR 57. Now the *Migration Legislation Amendment (Procedural Fairness) Act 2002*.

134 (2001) 206 CLR 57. Now the *Migration Legislation Amendment (Procedural Fairness) Act 2002*.

135 Commonwealth, *Parliamentary Debates*, House of Representatives, 13 March 2002, 1106 (Philip Ruddock).

136 Commonwealth, *Parliamentary Debates*, House of Representatives, 13 March 2002, 1106 (Philip Ruddock).

137 Commonwealth, *Parliamentary Debates*, House of Representatives, 26 June 2002, 4420 (Carmen Lawrence).

138 Commonwealth, *Parliamentary Debates*, House of Representatives, 26 June 2002, 4422 (Carmen Lawrence).

139 Commonwealth, *Parliamentary Debates*, House of Representatives, 26 June 2002, 4422 (Carmen Lawrence).

140 Commonwealth, *Parliamentary Debates*, House of Representatives, 26 June 2002, 4480 (Peter Andren).

141 Commonwealth, *Parliamentary Debates*, House of Representatives, 26 June 2002, 4480 (Peter Andren).

Philip Ruddock, Minister for Immigration in the Howard Coalition government 1996–2003, justified the bill on the grounds that codifying procedural fairness would allow migration officials 'to confidently discharge their duties without having to decipher what the common law natural justice or procedural fairness rules may require in each particular case'.[142] The bill, he claimed, would reinstate procedures aimed to be fair, efficient and quick.[143] Ruddock argued in favour of the fairness of the bill by even questioning the justice of the common law, which as noted previously is the source of rights and freedoms. He asked, 'What is so magic about the common law system . . . ?'[144] He claimed fairness, but his objective was efficiency. The bill was passed and remains in force.

By 2014, fairness as a right and an Australian value was no longer asserted by the Opposition despite the previous objections about the fairness of such measures.[145] A broader application of the codified procedures for offshore applicants as well as those onshore was agreed to achieve a necessary 'consistency'.[146] Only the Australian Greens argued that the bill was unfair. They claimed that the measures in the bill would impact disproportionately on a 'high-vulnerability group' such as minors and women and would 'undermine access to fair, just and due process'.[147] However, the majority prioritised the consistency of the fairness rules, not the content of that fairness compared to a common-law standard.

These examples demonstrate that the ordinary meaning of fairness in the context of procedural fairness was not unknown to the Parliament. The Parliament heard, for example, the detailed objections to the 2002 bill. They heard the Australian Greens' objection in 2014. However, this standard of fairness, which has been understood as a right and a value under the common law, was judged a lower priority than administrative efficiency when dealing with the noncitizen. The common law standard of procedural fairness was a problem to be solved by encoding rules in an attempt to remove any judicial oversight of what the immigration ministers or their delegates might consider to be fair.

A second context where the value of fairness arose concerned the narrowing of the value of fairness to mean merely playing by the minister's arbitrary

142 Commonwealth, *Parliamentary Debates*, House of Representatives, 26 June 2002, 4483 (Philip Ruddock).

143 Commonwealth, *Parliamentary Debates*, House of Representatives, 13 March 2002, 1106 (Philip Ruddock).

144 Commonwealth, *Parliamentary Debates*, House of Representatives, 13 March 2002, 4482 (Philip Ruddock).

145 See, e.g., Commonwealth, *Parliamentary Debates*, House of Representatives, 26 June 2002, 4420 (Carmen Lawrence).

146 Commonwealth, *Parliamentary Debates*, House of Representatives, 16 June 2014, 5997 (Richard Marles) debating Migration Legislation Amendment Bill (No 1) 2014.

147 Commonwealth, *Parliamentary Debates*, Senate, 3 September 2014, 6322 (Sarah Hanson-Young).

rules. It was a justification that conflated the making of a rule with fairness and narrowed the concept of equal treatment to equality only with others in an arbitrarily defined group. This approach to fairness was used to justify the different treatment of asylum seekers depending on how they arrived in Australia and, from 2014, their date of arrival.

How an asylum seeker arrived and whether that complied with Australian immigration entry rules was used as the single criterion of the fairness of treating different groups of asylum seekers differently.[148] In 2001, for example, Prime Minister Howard explained how it would not be fair to allow people arriving on a boat to be given preference to people waiting in other parts of the world who had UNHCR clearance.[149] This accusation that asylum seekers arriving by boat were 'queue jumping' was first directed at Vietnamese people arriving on boats in the 1970s and has been repeated across the decades since.[150] This rationale is based on a false premise that there is an accessible orderly queue which an asylum seeker could join.[151] The other implication of this justification for different rules for different groups is that illegal entrants are supposedly acting unfairly. It implies that the standard of fairness expected of the asylum seeker is that they consider the plight of other asylum seekers ahead of their own.

Despite the factual dubiousness, the justification is entrenched. In a speech supporting the *Deterring People Smuggling Act 2011* (Cth), Morrison, from Opposition, demonstrated his sense that fairness was about respect for the rules, not equal treatment for all concerned. In support of the law at that time, he said: 'Australia has different rules and systems for dealing with those who would seek to enter Australia illegally'.[152] This statement was presented as a declaration of the legitimacy of these rules and systems and the policy of legislating differentiated treatment between legal and illegal entrants. The argument on this occasion, while not directly referencing fairness, implied that having different rules for different groups of asylum seekers was not

148 Commonwealth, *Parliamentary Debates*, House of Representatives, 19 September 2001, 30964 (Bruce Billson); Commonwealth, *Parliamentary Debates*, House of Representatives, 1 November 2011, 12353 (Scott Morrison).

149 John Howard, 'Interview on Radio 3AW, Melbourne', *PM Transcripts* (Radio interview, 31 August 2001) <https://pmtranscripts.pmc.gov.au/release/transcript-12043>.

150 See, e.g., Commonwealth, *Parliamentary Debates*, House of Representatives, 19 September 2001, 31012 (Martin). For more on queue jumping see Catherine Ann Martin, 'Jumping the Queue? The Queue-Jumping Metaphor in Australian Press Discourse on Asylum Seekers' (2021) 57(2) *Journal of Sociology* 343.

151 See contrary arguments to the concept of an orderly queue at Commonwealth, *Parliamentary Debates*, Senate, 24 September 2001, 27702 (Natasha Stott Despoja); Commonwealth, *Parliamentary Debates*, Senate, 26 November 2014, 27816 (Meg Lees).

152 Commonwealth, *Parliamentary Debates*, House of Representatives, 1 November 2011, 12353 (Scott Morrison).

unfair. Again in 2018 David Coleman, Immigration Minister in the Turnbull and Morrison Coalition governments 2018–20, distinguished fairness from what he termed 'faux fairness', which he explained was 'spending money or empowering people who seek to abuse the immigration system', a reference to asylum seekers applying directly to Australia for protection, rather than those processed offshore and resettled.[153] Coleman through this was questioning the validity of domestic law.

The process of conflating rulemaking with fairness was escalated in 2014 when Scott Morrison, as immigration minister, sponsored the successful *Migration Amendment (Resolving the Asylum Seeker Caseload) Act 2014* (Cth). This legislation established a different system for the assessment of protection claims and protection visa conditions, depending on the date and mode of arrival onto Australian territory, and limited merits review.[154] Morrison was unapologetic about differentiating between asylum seekers on this basis: 'The government is of the view that a "one size fits all" approach to responding to the spectrum of asylum claims made under Australia's protection framework is inconsistent with a robust protection system that promotes efficiency and integrity'.[155]

The 'spectrum of asylum claims' on which the logic of the bill was based was a spectrum of time of arrival and mode of arrival, not the strength of protection claims. Ending his second reading speech, Morrison declared this new system would enable the government to deal with claims 'efficiently, quickly, fairly and with integrity'.[156] It was the only time in the speech that he mentioned fairness. Speed and efficiency were the prioritised values.[157]

By conflating rulemaking and fairness in these ways, any ordinary meaning of fairness was lost. Equality of treatment, part of the ordinary meaning of fair play,[158] was narrowed to mean equality of treatment only with

153 David Coleman, 'Sydney Institute Address' (Speech, 13 August 2019) <https://minister.homeaffairs.gov.au/davidcoleman/Pages/sydney-institute-address.aspx>.

154 The level of success of the government's efforts to dilute the standard of merits review from the Administrative Appeals Tribunal standard under the Fast Track scheme of limited review is thoroughly examined in Joel Townsend and Hollie Kerwin, 'Erasing the Vision Splendid? Unpacking the Formative Responses of the Federal Courts to the Fast Track Processing Regime and the "Limited Review" of the Immigration Assessment Authority' (2021) 49(2) *Federal Law Review* 185.

155 Commonwealth, *Parliamentary Debates*, House of Representatives, 25 September 2014, 10545 (Scott Morrison).

156 Commonwealth, *Parliamentary Debates*, House of Representatives, 25 September 2014, 10545 (Scott Morrison).

157 For a further discussion of the introduction of contrasting migration provisions for offshore and onshore refugees and asylum seekers see Crock, Saul and Dastyari (n 113) 18; Hugo (n 98) 36.

158 'Fair play' (n 128).

other people in an arbitrarily defined group based on date or mode of arrival. The second reading speech did not address the content of that treatment or the fairness of the criteria for this grouping. In light of Chief Justice Allsop's discussion of the limits of rules in seeking to establish fairness, this debate appeared to redefine fairness more than to embed it in legislation. Allsop noted that, while rules are necessary, 'a rule for everything is to invite incoherence', and that rules and what Allsop terms 'human values' must be balanced.[159] The expansion of categories and rules discussed previously represents an incoherent fairness cut adrift from its ordinary meaning.

The third reference to fairness in the debates on exclusionary legislation concerns the contested concept of burden sharing. Burden sharing in this context is a concept that carries with it the notion of each nation taking its fair share of the economic and social burden of asylum seekers.[160] The focus of burden sharing is beyond the nation's own borders. It requires attention not only to the impact of a burden on the state but also to the burden itself and the capacity of other nations. Two examples from the debate demonstrate how this concept of taking one's fair share of the burden was used to justify limiting Australia's humanitarian intake and establishing offshore processing.

Firstly, the claim that Australia was doing more for refugees than was proportionate or fair was used in 2020 by Tudge, the immigration minister, to justify a policy of reducing the humanitarian intake. Tudge repeated the dubious claim that 'we'll still be the third most generous country in the world on an absolute basis, in terms of our humanitarian intake, and it will still be a slight increase on what it was last year'.[161] The assertion of Australia as a fair country taking more than its fair share was juxtaposed with the assertion of a sovereign right. Tudge ignored the global context. He ignored the fact that the identified pool of refugees available through the UNHCR to be resettled in the Humanitarian Program was a tiny fraction of the world's asylum seekers.[162]

Secondly, burden sharing was used to justify the offshore processing of asylum seekers. In the second reading speech of the Migration Legislation Amendment (Offshore Processing and Other Measures) Bill 2011, which was designed to 'restore executive power to set Australia's border protection

159 Allsop (n 9) 49–51.
160 For a global perspective on sharing the burden of refugees see Arie Afriansyah and Angky Banggaditya, 'Refugee Burden Sharing: An Evolving Refugee Protection Concept?' (2017) 10(3) *Arena Hukum* 333; Meltem Ineli-Ciger, 'The Global Compact on Refugees and Burden Sharing: Will the Compact Address the Normative Gap Concerning Burden Sharing?' (2019) 38 *Refugee Survey Quarterly* 115.
161 Alan Tudge, 'Interview with Fran Kelly RN Breakfast' (Interview, 12 October 2020).
162 Note resettled refugees globally were less than 0.45% of the estimated total refugee population in the 2018 calendar year. Refugee Council of Australia, 'How Generous Is Australia's Refugee Program Compared to Other Countries?' (Web Page, 9 May 2020) <www.refugeecouncil.org.au/2018-global-trends/>.

policies', Chris Bowen, Minister for Immigration and Citizenship in the Gillard Labor government 2010–3, quoted the following comment from the United Nations High Commissioner for Refugees:

> under certain circumstances, the processing of international protection claims outside the intercepting State could be an alternative to standard 'in country' procedures.
>
> Notably, this could be the case when extraterritorial processing is used as part of a burden-sharing arrangement to more fairly distribute responsibilities and enhance available protection space.[163]

Bowen implied by his use of this quotation that offshore processing in countries such as Nauru or Papua New Guinea, notably less wealthy than Australia,[164] would be a fair distribution of the burden of asylum seekers.

In October 2020, the value 'fair play' was omitted from the statement. The only mention of fairness that remains is a 'fair go', which is now defined without mentioning fairness in broader terms. It could be argued that such a change is merely a politically motivated rebranding to co-opt a quintessential Australian term for expressing egalitarianism, a 'fair go' being often touted as the universal Australian value.[165] Whatever the motivation, the ordinary meaning of fairness is no longer espoused as one of 'the values that guide us'.[166] Perhaps this is fitting. The exclusionary legislation, despite government claims, does not accord with the ordinary meaning of fairness or fair play.

V The English Language as the National Language

The third value used as an example in this discussion is 'the English language as the national language and an important unifying element', which is now included in the statement as a value rather than an accompanying declaration. This value does not share the moral dimension of other values in the statement, such as compassion or fairness. Neither does it allude to rights or freedoms such as 'the freedom and dignity of the individual'.[167] Unlike the other values in the statement, it includes a purpose, unity, and is accompanied with a new obligation on the visa applicant to commit to attempt to learn

163 Commonwealth, *Parliamentary Debates*, House of Representatives, 21 September 2011, 10945 (Chris Bowen).

164 In 2011 the World Bank calculated the GDP per capita of Papua New Guinea as USD \$2,406.91, the GDP per capita of Nauru as USD \$6,568.103 and the GDP per capita of Australia as USD \$62,517.83. World Bank, 'GDP Per Capita (Current US\$)' (Website, 2022) <https://data.worldbank.org/indicator/NY.GDP.PCAP.CD?view=chart>.

165 Howard, 'Melbourne Press Club Address' (n 8).

166 Commonwealth, *Parliamentary Debates*, House of Representatives, 17 September 2007, 39 (Kevin Andrews).

167 Australian Values Statement 2020 (n 13).

English while in Australian territory. The elevation of the English language to the status of a value could appear merely cosmetic. Compliance with the commitment that the visa applicant is required to make is not monitored. There is no penalty for not conducting oneself according to the value 'a fair go', for example, and there is no penalty for not learning English. These obligations on the visa applicant appear to have no tangible impact. However, by examining the context of this change and the historical context of what is now declared an Australian value, one can speculate about two alternative rationales for this elevation, which speak to a more significant purpose.

Firstly, this elevation could signal that the economic value of each non-citizen, whether visa applicant or applicant for citizenship, is now elevated to an Australian value reflecting the priorities of the current government. This would suggest that the logic of neoliberalism, which values the migrant as a market factor, has become dominant even in family reunion and other migration amendments that do not have an overt economic objective.[168] Evidence for this hypothesis is found in the statements of immigration ministers. In 2000 Ruddock was inviting young mobile workers with good English to bridge Australia's skill gaps.[169] In 2019 Coleman emphasised that economic benefit to Australia was central to his migration decision-making, and that meant, he said, that workers with the ability to speak English were most desirable.[170] In 2020 Tudge noted the importance of English to 'getting a job'.[171]

This economic hypothesis is also supported by the context of Tudge's announcement of changes to the statement in 2020. Concurrent with his announcement, he introduced two other changes concerning English language competence for visa holders. The first was increased funding for English language training for visa applicants and citizens by conferral. In his second reading speech, he outlined a list of practical benefits of English competence which prioritised 'getting a job'.[172] The second change announced was the imposition of a language test on partner visa applicants and their sponsors. In the budget 2020/2021 the treasurer announced: 'The Government will introduce English language requirements for Partner visa applicants and their permanent resident sponsors. These changes will help support

168 See discussion in Chapter 6 Section III D and Section IV.

169 Philip Ruddock, 'Australian Immigration: Grasping the New Reality' (Speech, Nation Skilling: Migration Labour and the Law Symposium, 23 November 2000) <https://parlinfo.aph.gov.au/parlInfo/search/display/display.w3p;query=Id:%22media/pressrel/UY836%22>.

170 David Coleman, 'Address to the Migration Institute of Australia Conference' (Speech, Migration Institute of Australia, 19 October 2018).

171 Commonwealth, *Parliamentary Debates*, House of Representatives, 29 October 2020, 8829 (Alan Tudge).

172 Commonwealth, *Parliamentary Debates*, House of Representatives, 29 October 2020, 8829 (Alan Tudge).

English language acquisition and enhance social cohesion and economic participation outcomes'.[173]

Tudge's press release following this announcement was headed 'New requirement to learn English to maximise job prospects'. It stated that 'from late 2021, new partner visa applicants and permanent resident sponsors will be required to have functional level English or to demonstrate that they have made reasonable efforts to learn English'.[174] Previously only work visas had English language requirements and priorities.

The espoused rationale for both these changes was economic benefit. They provide further support to the hypothesis that the characterisation of the English language as an Australian value reflects the value of economic prosperity and independence.[175] Because the link between English competence and economic prosperity is so frequently made, the value might more accurately be entitled 'economic prosperity'.

A second alternative hypothesis for the rationale for elevating the English language to an Australian value is that it is a next step in an escalation of the official national status and dominance of the English language, history and culture of Australia over competing languages, histories and cultures. This hypothesis suggests that the English language is used as a weapon of exclusion.[176] Support for this alternative hypothesis can be found in both the history of this element of the statement and the context of the 2020 announcement.

The history can be traced back to 2006, when a sentence declaring English as the national language was included in the first statement. In that form it could be understood as information for the prospective citizen or visa applicant about the pervasive use of the English language, including by the government and the courts in Australia. It would be misleading if it implied that Parliament had legislated or the courts had declared English as a national language. The Constitution does not impose a national language either. However, in 2006, when Howard launched the new citizenship test which included the statement, he said not only that English was the national

173 Josh Frydenberg and Matthias Corman, *Budget 2020–21: Budget Paper No 2* (6 October 2020) 10 <https://archive.budget.gov.au/2020-21/bp2/download/bp2_complete.pdf>.

174 Alan Tudge, 'New Requirement to Learn English to Maximise Job Prospects' (Media Release, 8 October 2020).

175 See Chapter 5 on the neoliberalism expressed in the student visa amendments.

176 See, e.g., Tim McNamara and Kerry Ryan, 'Fairness Versus Justice in Language Testing: The Place of English Literacy in the Australian Citizenship Test' (2011) 8(2) *Language Assessment Quarterly* 161; Gwenda Tavan, 'Testing Times: The Problem of "History" in the Howard Government's Australian Citizenship Test', in Klaus Neumann and Gwenda Tavan (eds), *Does History Matter? Making and Debating Citizenship* (ANU Press, 2009) 125, 138–41.

language but also, 'Nothing unites a country more than its common language, because from a language comes a history and a culture'.[177]

This is a claim for the English language that is beyond the practical purposes of gaining skills, a job or being able to communicate in society. This claim for the English language is an example of what Aileen Moreton-Robinson terms 'possessive logics'.[178] She defines this concept as a 'mode of rationalization . . . that is underpinned by an excessive desire to invest in reproducing and reaffirming the nation-state's ownership, control and domination'.[179] This 'possessive logic' can be seen in Howard's claim for the English language by noting what he excludes and what he diminishes. As Gulmanelli and Johnson argue, Howard placed Anglo-Celtic culture at the centre and pushed other cultures to the periphery.[180]

Howard's statement linking English language, culture and history excludes any acknowledgment of First Nations languages or the role of First Nations history and culture in shaping Australia.[181] Nor does it acknowledge that Australian citizenship has been conferred on people of more than two hundred nationalities.[182] In a speech at a citizenship ceremony contemporaneous with the launch of the statement, Howard observed only that migrants becoming citizens will retain 'a special place in your hearts for the country in which you were born'.[183] Their language, culture and history were characterised as a private emotional bond and not part of the Australian historical and cultural fabric. Howard's later comments regarding assimilating Muslim Australians supports this interpretation.[184]

Support for this alternative hypothesis that the English language is used to exclude can also be found in 2020 in the announcement of changes to the statement made by Tudge. While making no direct mention of the English language, Tudge echoed Howard's reference to history and culture in his announcement of changes to the statement: 'Our Australian values are

177 John Howard, 'Press Conference', *PM Transcripts* (11 December 2006) <https://pmtranscripts.pmc.gov.au/release/transcript-22626>.

178 Aileen Moreton-Robinson, *White Possessive: Property, Power and Indigenous Sovereignty* (University of Minnesota Press, 2014) xii.

179 Aileen Moreton-Robinson, *White Possessive: Property, Power and Indigenous Sovereignty* (University of Minnesota Press, 2014) xii.

180 See Gulmanelli (n 21) 585–6, 589; Johnson (n 36).

181 For a discussion of the centrality of Australian First Nations language, law, history and culture see Irene Watson, 'Re-Centring First Nations Knowledge and Places in a Terra Nullius Space' (2014) 10(5) *AlterNative* 508.

182 In 1949 Australian citizenship was conferred on people of thirty-five nationalities. By 2019/2020 this was two hundred nationalities. Department of Home Affairs, 'Australian Citizenship Statistics' (Web Page, 9 August 2022) <www.homeaffairs.gov.au/research-and-statistics/statistics/citizenship-statistics>.

183 John Howard, 'Address at Australia Day Citizenship Ceremony Commonwealth Park, Canberra', *PM Transcripts* (Speech, 26 January 2007) <https://pmtranscripts.pmc.gov.au/release/transcript-15152>.

184 Howard, 'Interview with Neil Mitchell' (n 40).

important. They have helped shape our country'.[185] Along with this reflection Tudge introduced tangible exclusionary policies contemporaneously with the 2020 elevation of English to a value. He imposed a language requirement on partner visa applicants and their sponsors, which it is reasonable to predict will have a significant impact on now ex-refugee applicants. Before a permanent partner visa could be granted, English competence to a vocational standard had to be demonstrated by both sponsor and partner.[186] A sponsor and partner from an English-speaking country would be unaffected. A sponsor and partner from a country such as Afghanistan or Pakistan would now have a new and for some a burdensome obligation.[187]

Howard's and Tudge's words and actions in 2020 support an understanding that the elevation of the English language to a value is an elevation of more than the language itself. What is elevated to an espoused Australian value is a version of history that includes colonisation and the imposition of Anglo-Celtic culture and that excludes the contribution of First Nations and non-English-speaking migrants. This change to the status of the English language, enacted as a value in a regulation under the *Migration Act 1958* (Cth), along with the new obligation on visa applicants to attempt to learn English and the English language requirements for applicants for partner visas, not just work visas, demonstrates the use of the English language value as a message of exclusion to all but those of Anglo-Celtic heritage.

These changes also echo Australia's history of the use of language competence as a tool of exclusion in Australian migration law.[188] Nowhere in the *Immigration Restriction Act 1901* was the Parliament's declared preference for 'purely British stock'[189] stated, and nowhere was a ban on certain migrants based on their appearance or ethnicity explicitly enacted.

Opposing the use of the education test, but not the goal, one member called it a 'miserable subterfuge' and argued that the Parliament should in a 'manly fashion' declare that 'the coloured races must go'.[190] In an attempt to persuade his parliamentary colleagues to vote for this technique, a government member at the time admitted the test was a 'sidewind' and assured the Parliament that 'we mean a great deal more than we say'.[191]

185 Tudge, 'Focus on Values' (n 71).

186 Tudge, 'New Requirement' (n 174).

187 The requirement, which is at the minister's discretion, is to reach the competency level or demonstrate attendance at five hundred hours of English classes. Tudge, 'New Requirement' (n 174). This was announced in Frydenberg and Corman (n 173) 10.

188 See Chapter 4 Section II.

189 Commonwealth, *Parliamentary Debates*, House of Representatives, 6 September 1901, 4625–6 (William McMillan).

190 Commonwealth, *Parliamentary Debates*, Senate, 15 November 1901, 7332 (James Stewart).

191 Commonwealth, *Parliamentary Debates*, House of Representatives, 20 September 1901, 5075 (Allan McLean).

This alternative hypothesis argues that the elevation of English to an Australian value means a great deal more than is said in the words themselves. It is significant both symbolically and tangibly. Symbolically it is another step toward making into law Howard's declaration of English as the national language and British history and culture as the national history and culture and in that way excluding both those who were already in Australia before colonisation and many of those who came after. In 2020 the government claimed that English competence would enhance social cohesion, the 'unity' that is the purpose accompanying this new value.[192] A logical conclusion is that social cohesion would be achieved by cultural and tangible exclusion. The imposition of an English language requirement on partner visa applicants and spouses has the potential to be a hurdle to family reunion only for certain groups. Through these changes the government, like those introducing the 1901 education test, can be seen to 'mean a great deal more than we say'.[193] The cultural 'denied agenda' Howard is argued to have prosecuted is continued by stealth.[194]

VI Conclusion

The incorporation of an explicit statement of Australian values in migration legislation invites an assessment of how these values were expressed in the parliamentary debates and legislative techniques to make migration amendments. Such an assessment demonstrates a wide gap between the ordinary meaning of terms such as compassion and fairness and how these terms were used in debate. The assertion of sovereignty or the purported need to protect it justified amendments to the *Migration Act 1958* (Cth) that were an ill fit with the values espoused. If a nation's values are revealed by those it excludes, the debates on the amendments do not show Australia as compassionate or fair. The values that underpin the amendments with the objective to exclude are not those espoused in either of the versions of the Australian Values Statement, nor are they consistent with the government's characterisation of Australian migration decisions as compassionate or as guided by a fair go or fair play. It can be argued that the introduction of the statement itself had an unstated exclusionary purpose. There is no evidence that the statement has assisted integration, its stated purpose, but there is some evidence that it has been used symbolically and tangibly to exclude. Its introduction and development of obligations, which includes the declaration of English as the national language, can be analysed as an escalation of the centrality of

192 Australian Values Statement 2020 (n 13).

193 Commonwealth, *Parliamentary Debates*, House of Representatives, 20 September 1901, 5075 (Allan McLean).

194 Gulmanelli (n 21) 582.

an idealised Anglo-Celtic culture and the minimisation of the importance of other ethnicities and cultures.

When used in debate on the amendments that enacted laws that prioritised the values of executive control, efficiency and economic gain, the value 'compassion for those in need' was emptied of any ordinary meaning. The ordinary meaning of fairness was reduced in these amendments to consistency with a set of arbitrary rules and the balance between these rules and values was lost.[195] The common-law value of natural justice and procedural fairness was diminished. A constrained interpretation of burden sharing allowed the ongoing outsourcing of sovereign responsibility for asylum seekers to be represented as fairness. Each of these claims to fairness allowed an increase of executive control over decision-making and an attempt to narrow the scrutiny of the judiciary.

The elevation of the English language to the status of a value in the statement with the stated purpose of promoting unity can be understood in two ways. There is some evidence, in ministerial statements and in the concurrent application of English testing for family reunion visas, that this elevation represents an expansion of the neoliberal logic of the market which is argued to be an underpinning value of globalisation. There is also evidence in ministerial statements and in the expansion of English testing to partner visas that the value is a further entrenchment of Anglo-Celtic cultural centrality that seeks to exclude other languages, histories and cultures from what is valued as Australian.

The next chapter examines the impact of these amendments on what is meant by the rule of law, another value in the statement which has been consistently espoused by the executive as an Australian value across the period 2000–20.

195 See Allsop (n 9) 49–51.

Part Three

The Anachronism of a Sovereignty That Justifies Exclusion

Chapter 8

Sovereignty of Exclusion and the Rule of Law

I Introduction

As argued in the previous chapters the amendments to the *Migration Act 1958* (Cth) made between 2000 and 2020, espoused by governments as fair and as made by a compassionate nation, were justified as necessary to assert or protect Australian sovereignty. To this end the amendments increased executive control over migration decisions by shielding them from the implications of international human rights law, domestic law and judicial scrutiny.[1] The purpose of this chapter is to examine the consequences of this for the rule of law experienced by the noncitizen, subject to these amendments. This examination will complete the inquiry into the nature of the sovereignty that has justified the amendments to the *Migration Act 1958* (Cth) made between 2000 and 2020 with the objective to exclude.

The chapter begins by briefly surveying the history and current contested meaning of the rule of law, placing the definition of the concept, now enacted in the Australian Values Statement in the formulation 'that all people are subject to the law and should obey it',[2] in this context. Secondly, the chapter examines the role of the Australian judiciary as guardians of the rule of law through the work of interpreting both the law and the Constitution.[3] Thirdly, through an examination of commentary and key judgments in migration case law, the chapter examines the content of judicial review and what this means for the rule of law for the noncitizen. Finally, by drawing on the example of the amendments to the character test in *Migration Act 1958* (Cth) s 501 and judgments concerning the test, the chapter finds that the constitutionally guaranteed 'rule of law' for the noncitizen, even the permanent resident, is almost indistinguishable from the rule of the immigration minister.

1 See Chapter 6.
2 See Chapter 7 Section II.
3 Wendy Lacey refers to the judiciary in this way in Wendy Lacey, 'Restoring the Rule of Law Through a National Bill of Rights' (2008) 84 *Precedent* 28.

DOI: 10.4324/9781003515852-11

This inquiry has significance beyond the treatment of the noncitizen under the *Migration Act 1958* (Cth) and the integrity of the law expressing Australia's sovereignty in a globalising world. This is because it is at the interface of migration legislation and judicial scrutiny that the meaning of 'the rule of law' in Australia is being worked out. The content of the rule of law for the noncitizen demonstrates the possibilities of what the rule of law could mean for any person confronted with the power of the Australian state.

II The Contested Meaning of the Rule of Law

A A Brief History

In the late 19th century British jurist AV Dicey influentially stated that the rule of law contains three essential meanings. Firstly, 'no man is punishable or can be lawfully made to suffer in body or goods except for a distinct breach of law established in the ordinary legal manner before the ordinary courts of the land'.[4] Secondly, all are equally subject to the law.[5] Thirdly the British constitution is 'pervaded by the rule of law' because its principles, such as 'the right to personal liberty', have been developed through the common-law process of 'decisions determining the rights of private persons in particular cases brought before the courts'.[6] More than a century later the *Constitutional Reform Act 2005* (UK) affirmed the 'existing constitutional principle of the rule of law'.[7]

Scholars since Dicey have elaborated and debated the meaning of the rule of law. Martin Krygier notes that the concept is now 'part of old and ongoing moral and political arguments about fundamental matters of political organization, concerns, and ideals, much affirmed and much contested'.[8] He sounds a warning about its current use. He suggests that the concept of the rule of law has been harnessed for so many purposes that it has been virtually emptied of an agreed meaning. Tamanaha makes a similar point.[9]

4 AV Dicey, *An Introduction to the Study of the Law of the Constitution*, ed ECS Wade (Macmillan, 10th ed, 1959) 187–8.
5 AV Dicey, *An Introduction to the Study of the Law of the Constitution*, ed ECS Wade (Macmillan, 10th ed, 1959) 193.
6 AV Dicey, *An Introduction to the Study of the Law of the Constitution*, ed ECS Wade (Macmillan, 10th ed, 1959) 195.
7 *Constitutional Reform Act 2005* (UK) s 1(a).
8 Martin Krygier, 'Rule of Law: Pasts, Presents, and Two Possible Futures' (2016) 12 *Annual Review of Law and Social Science* 199, 202.
9 Brian Tamanaha, *On the Rule of Law: History, Politics, Theory* (Cambridge University Press, 2004) 114.

B *Theories of the Rule of Law: Thick or Thin?*

One way to make sense of the various approaches to the concept of the rule of law is to place them on a continuum from thin to thick.[10] Such a continuum is largely cumulative, with versions of the rule for law at the thick end containing elements of the thinner interpretations.

At the thin or 'minimalist' end of this continuum the rule of law is defined by a primary focus on the source of power and processes.[11] It is a formal legality. Dicey's essence is captured as 'a system where law is supreme and protects people against the arbitrary power of individuals and the state'.[12] John Finnis identifies eight characteristics that constitute a thinner understanding of the rule of law. These emphasise stable, clear and coherent law that is not retrospective, enabling the law to be a guide to behaviour. Included is the accountability of those administering the law.[13]

Critics of this thin definition say it reduces the meaning to merely law as rule by government.[14] The rule of law, it is argued, in its thinnest definition becomes almost indistinguishable from the 'rule of man'.[15] It might better be described as 'rule *by* law' because it fails to deliver the core meaning of the rule of law which is 'meaningful restraints on the state and individual members of the ruling elite'.[16] The government of China has interpreted the rule of law in this thinnest of ways.[17] Tamanaha highlights the deficiencies

10 Brian Tamanaha, *On the Rule of Law: History, Politics, Theory* (Cambridge University Press, 2004) 91. See also Michael J Trebilcock and Ronald J Daniels, *Rule of Law Reform and Development* (Edward Elgar Publishing, 2008) 12–4, 16–20, 23–9.

11 Randall Peerenboom, *China's Long March Toward Rule of Law* (Cambridge University Press, 2006) 3–5.

12 Hossein Esmaeili, 'On a Slow Boat Towards the Rule of Law: The Nature of Law in the Saudi Arabian Legal System' (2009) 26 *Arizona Journal of International & Comparative Law* 1, 3. See also Dyson Heydon, 'Judicial Activism and the Death of the Rule of Law' (2004) 10(4) *Otago Law Review* 493, 494–5.

13 John Finnis, *Natural Law and Natural Rights* (Clarendon Press, 1980) 270–1. See also Lon L Fuller, *The Morality of Law* (Yale University Press, rev ed, 1977) 39. Note also Robert S Summers, 'A Formal Theory of the Rule of Law' (1993) 6(2) *Ratio Juris* 127, 127–34. Summers proposes an institutional component to his formal version of the rule of law matching Finnis and Fuller. He also adds an axiological component of values that the rule of law should serve which include the values of liberalism such as private autonomy and respect for the dignity of the individual. Joseph Raz also has eight principles. He summarises that these should be able to guide behaviour and that the enforcement of the law should conform with these principles and be effective. Joseph Raz, 'The Rule of Law and Its Virtues', in Aileen Kavanagh and John Oberdiek (eds), *Arguing About Law* (Routledge, 2009) 181, 183–6.

14 Tamanaha (n 9) 96.

15 Tamanaha (n 9) 96.

16 Peerenboom, *China's Long March* (n 11) 8. See also Randall Peerenboom, 'Varieties of Rule of Law', in Randall Peerenboom (ed), *Asian Discourses of Rule of Law* (Routledge, 2004).

17 Peerenboom, *China's Long March* (n 11) 8. See also Randall Peerenboom, 'Varieties of Rule of Law', in Randall Peerenboom (ed), *Asian Discourses of Rule of Law* (Routledge, 2004).

of a 'formal legality' that is not concerned with the content of the law, only its formality and process.[18] He notes that without content this version of the rule of law can still produce 'evil laws'.[19] Unfranchised minorities can be oppressed. The more faithfully an oppressive law such as slavery is adhered to, the worse is the effect.[20]

At the other end of the continuum are thick or substantive definitions of the rule of law. These thick versions incorporate formal legality but add substantive elements. A very thick definition incorporates equality, welfare and preservation of community.[21] Tamanaha suggests that to the extent a common meaning of the rule of law exists within Western societies, it encompasses the 'formal legality' that Finnis describes but includes the substantive elements of 'individual rights and democracy'.[22] Tom Bingham ascribes to an even thicker version. He proposes eight principles that build on Finnis' formal legality by adding protection of human rights, practical access to justice and compliance with international law.[23] These more substantive definitions of the rule of law have been described as common-law constitutionalism.[24] This theory ascribes norms to the common law against which a particular law can be judged.[25] Dyzenhaus warns that without such a thick understanding of the rule of law there is no way to judge when 'rule by law ceases to be in accordance with the rule of law'.[26] For example, without an agreed standard of fairness, as a substantive element of the rule of law, on what basis is a law to be judged to be fair?[27] The reader might ask this question when reviewing the use of the concept of fairness in parliamentary debates on migration law.[28]

The thick definitions of the rule of law also have critics. These criticisms fall into three categories. Firstly, their overreach: Raz, for example, argues that the rule of law is a necessary and useful value, but it is limited to this: 'Conformity to the rule of law is not the ultimate goal'.[29] Raz describes the rule

18 Tamanaha (n 9) 96.
19 Tamanaha (n 9) 100.
20 Tamanaha (n 9) 95.
21 Tamanaha (n 9) 112.
22 Tamanaha (n 9) 111.
23 Tom Bingham, *The Rule of Law* (Penguin Books, 2011) 37–129.
24 Thomas Poole, 'Dogmatic Liberalism – T.R.S. Allan and the Common Law Constitution' (2002) 65(3) *Modern Law Review* 463; Paul Craig, 'The Common Law, Shared Power and Judicial Review' (2004) 24(2) *Oxford Journal of Legal Studies* 237, 250.
25 Poole (n 24) 464.
26 David Dyzenhaus, *The Constitution of Law: Legality in a Time of Emergency* (Cambridge University Press, 2006) 42; See also TRS Allan, *The Sovereignty of Law: Freedom, Constitution and Common Law* (Oxford University Press, 2013); M Loughlin, *Public Law and Political Theory* (Clarendon Press, 1992).
27 Tamanaha (n 9) 94. See also Chapter 7 Section IV.
28 See Chapter 7.
29 Raz (n 13) 191–2.

of law as a 'negative value', its strength being to minimise harm.[30] It must be balanced with other values, not stretched to the point of being prioritised over other goals.[31] His approach admits that the rule of law might mean the rule of evil laws, as Tamanaha warns.[32] He compares the rule of law with a sharp knife, useful for good or bad purposes. For Raz, conformity to the rule of law is an essential prerequisite to achieving any other purpose, but those purposes are not part of the rule of law.[33] Secondly, critics note the difficulty of defining and prioritising the substantive elements and the extent to which these should take priority over the will of a democratically elected government.[34] Thirdly, adding substantive elements to formal legality is argued to undermine the certainty and predictability of the law which formal legality gives.[35]

The definitions on this continuum of thin to thick can also be evaluated according to their connection to the original 'mischief' that the concept was developed to address, that of arbitrary and unaccountable use of power. Krygier suggests that the 'rule of law' should be the answer to the question, 'How might it [power] be rendered at least safe and then, more positively, helpful for those subject to it, rather than loom as a perennial source of threat and fear?'[36] TRS Allan makes a similar point. He describes the law as 'shielding the individual from hostile discrimination on the part of those with political power'.[37] Using this framework the thin definitions of the rule of law can be viewed more as the answer to the problem of chaos. The thicker definitions of the rule of law incorporate substantive elements that to various degrees address the problem of power as a source of 'threat and fear'[38] and provide a protective shield.[39]

Despite the ongoing criticism and debate, the concept of the rule of law, in a similar way to the concept of sovereignty, remains present in modern

30 Raz (n 13) 191.
31 Raz (n 13) 191. See also Lisa Burton Crawford's critique of TRS Allan's theories in Lisa Burton Crawford, *The Rule of Law and the Australian Constitution* (Federation Press, 2017) 158–71 ('*Rule of Law*').
32 Tamanaha (n 9) 100.
33 Raz (n 13) 189.
34 James Allan, 'Reasonable Disagreement and the Diminution of Democracy: Joseph's Morally Laden Understanding of the Rule of Law', in Richard Elkins (ed), *Modern Challenges to the Rule of Law* (LexisNexis NZ, 2011) 85; Poole (n 24).
35 James Allan, 'Reasonable Disagreement and the Diminution of Democracy: Joseph's Morally Laden Understanding of the Rule of Law' in Richard Elkins (ed), *Modern Challenges to the Rule of Law* (LexisNexis NZ, 2011) 91; Poole (n 24); Trebilcock (n 10) 23–41. See the discussion of the comparative merits and issues of either end of the rule of law continuum in the context of international development.
36 Krygier (n 8) 203.
37 TRS Allan, *Constitutional Justice: A Liberal Theory of the Rule of Law* (Oxford University Press, 1993) 22.
38 Krygier (n 8).
39 Allan, *Constitutional Justice* (n 36).

discourse.[40] The enactment of it as a value in the Australian Values Statement is such an example. Brian Tamanaha notes the difficulties with the concept but responds that the concept of the rule of law is 'too important to contemporary affairs to be left in confusion'.[41] Lord Bingham argues that the use of the concept in modern discourse is not casual: the judges and lawmakers in the United Kingdom and internationally use the term with purpose and meaning.[42] He suggests three reasons for not abandoning the concept in the United Kingdom: it is referenced in case law, it is written into statute and in 2004 the UN Secretary-General named the rule of law as a foundational concept of the United Nations and a force to implement 'international human rights norms and standards'.[43]

Against this range of rule of law definitions, the definition given to this value in the Australian Values Statement can be characterised as a thin interpretation of the rule of law, concerned as it is with the formal legality of institutions and processes.[44] The rule of law in the statement is defined as 'all people are subject to the law and should obey it'.[45] The source of that law is also defined as parliamentary democracy, meaning 'our laws are determined by parliaments elected by the people, those laws being paramount and overriding any other inconsistent religious or secular "laws"'.[46] Missing in the definition is any sense of the protective power of the rule of law for the individual against the power of the state.[47] Also ignored is the role of the judiciary.

III The Judiciary as Guardians of the Rule of Law

Contrary to the immigration minister's omission in his definitions in the statement, the judiciary is an institution of lawmaking under the Constitution.[48] With colonisation of Australia came the common-law tradition and the British 'theory of the supremacy of the law'.[49] At Federation the concept of the rule of law became foundational to the Australian Constitution, as it is in the United Kingdom.[50] Despite its origins Australian constitutional arrangements differ from the United Kingdom. As Gleeson CJ noted in his

40 Bingham (n 23) 6. See also Chapter 2 Section III A on the theories of the relationship between law and sovereignty.
41 Tamanaha (n 9) 4.
42 Bingham (n 23) 6–8.
43 Bingham (n 23) 6–7.
44 See Peerenboom, *China's Long March* (n 11).
45 See Chapter 7 Section II.
46 See Chapter 7 Section II.
47 Krygier (n 8) 203.
48 See Chapter 2 Section IV.
49 Murray Gleeson, *The Rule of Law and the Constitution* (ABC, 2000) 6, quoting Owen Dixon, 'The Law and the Constitution' (1936) 51 *Law Quarterly Review* 590.
50 JJ Spigelman, 'Public Law and the Executive' (2010) 34 *Australian Bar Review* 10, 20; Bingham (n 23) 6–7.

judgement in *Attorney-General (Western Australia) v Marquet*, 'Unlike Britain in the nineteenth century, the constitutional norms which apply in this country are more complex than an unadorned Diceyan precept of parliamentary sovereignty'.[51]

In Australia, in contrast to the UK, the power of the Parliament is limited by a written Constitution.[52] The Constitution establishes the three arms of government and 'limits the legislative, executive and judicial power' that they can wield.[53] It gives the Australian people the supreme power to change the 'basic law of the Australian nation', that is the written Constitution, through referenda.[54] How the three arms of government work together has been simply stated as 'the legislature makes, the executive executes, and the judiciary construes the law'.[55] The following discussion surveys the views that the judiciary has expressed concerning the content of the rule of law.

A Views on the Rule of Law

Members of the High Court and other senior members of the judiciary in the 2000–20 period expressed a range of views about the concept of the rule of law both in their judgments and in extra-curial comment. This section of the chapter examines these views by firstly attempting to place the explicit references to the rule of law on the thick to thin continuum and secondly by examining the level of substantive content members of the High Court ascribed to the work of statutory interpretation.

At what could be described at the thinner end,[56] Heydon J emphasised the rule of law values of 'certainty' and 'non-retrospectivity'.[57] He criticised the Victorian Charter of Human Rights for threatening these values.[58] His position reflected Professor George Winterton's remark that 'The rule of law and the integrity of judicial interpretation of the Constitution should not be sacrificed for anything – even a result which, on a particular occasion, may promote human or civil rights'.[59]

The Hon Murray Gleeson's definition is further toward the centre of the continuum. He states that it is through the Constitution that the rule of law delivers to the Australian people 'a predictable and ordered society . . . [and]

51 (2003) 217 CLR 545, 565.
52 *Momcilovic v The Queen* (2011) 245 CLR 1, 88.
53 Gleeson (n 48) 6.
54 Gleeson (n 48) 6.
55 *Momcilovic v The Queen* (2011) 245 CLR 1, 155–6, quoting Isaacs J in *New South Wales v Commonwealth* (1915) 20 CLR 54, 90, quoting *Wayman v Southard* 23 US 1, 46 (1825).
56 Murray Gleeson, 'Outcome, Process and the Rule of Law' (2006) 65(3) *Australian Journal of Public Administration* 5 ('Outcome, Process').
57 *Momcilovic v The Queen* (2011) 245 CLR 1, 152.
58 *Momcilovic v The Queen* (2011) 245 CLR 1, 152.
59 George Winterton, 'Justice Kirby's Coda in Durham Holdings' (2002) 13 *Public Law Review* 165, 170.

a shield for individuals from arbitrary state action'.[60] The rule of law, he said, means that 'the law is supreme over the acts of government and private persons' and 'requires the creation and maintenance of an actual order of positive laws'[61] and that 'the exercise of public power must find its ultimate source in a legal rule'.[62] Adding a slightly thicker element, Gleeson suggests that the citizen's right to demand a justification of the use of public power 'in terms of rationality and fairness' is an aspect of the rule of law. His view is that the judiciary, with its 'inherited values favouring the rule of law',[63] may use common-law interpretative principles to 'show compassion, human understanding, and fairness' and to presume that Parliament would not infringe an individual's rights.[64] Gleeson advises, however, that if the statue is unambiguous no judge has the power to disobey the law.[65]

Arguing for an even more substantive definition, closer to that of Bingham's,[66] and standing somewhat apart from his fellow judges, Hon Michael Kirby defines the rule of law as 'more than obedience to the law that exists in the books'.[67] To him a law that is contrary to universal human rights is a breach of the rule of law.[68] He cites examples under Australian law where formal legality led to 'seriously unjust and unfair outcomes'.[69] These examples include the indefinite administrative immigration detention of the stateless Mr Al-Kateb, which was found to be lawful in a judgment which remains law today except for a small group.[70] In *Al-Kateb* the majority found that under the *Migration Act 1958* (Cth) ss 189, 196 and 198, as long as the purpose of detention was 'removal of non-citizens from Australia and their separation from the Australian community until that occurred' a noncitizen could be held in detention even if that removal 'was not reasonably practicable

60 Gleeson, *The Rule of Law* (n 49) 4, quoting *Reference re Secession of Quebec* [1998] 2 SCR 217, 257–8.
61 Gleeson, *The Rule of Law* (n 49) 4, quoting *Reference re Secession of Quebec* [1998] 2 SCR 217, 257–8.
62 Gleeson, *The Rule of Law* (n 49) 4, quoting *Reference re Secession of Quebec* [1998] 2 SCR 217, 257–8.
63 Matthew Smith, 'The Constitutional Right to Judicial Review of Administrative Action: Reflections on Bodruddaza' (2008) 84 *Precedent* 38, 42.
64 Gleeson, *The Rule of Law* (n 49) 127.
65 Gleeson, *The Rule of Law* (n 49) 127–8.
66 Bingham (n 23).
67 Michael Kirby, 'The Rule of Law Beyond the Law of Rules' (2010) 33 *Australian Bar Review* 195, 210.
68 Michael Kirby, 'The Rule of Law Beyond the Law of Rules' (2010) 33 *Australian Bar Review* 195, 210.
69 Michael Kirby, 'The Rule of Law Beyond the Law of Rules' (2010) 33 *Australian Bar Review* 204.
70 Michael Kirby, 'The Rule of Law Beyond the Law of Rules' (2010) 33 *Australian Bar Review* 205, citing *Al-Kateb v Godwin* (2004) 219 CLR 562. Kirby's judgment was a dissent from the majority. See *NZYQ v Minister for Immigration, Citizenship and Multicultural Affairs* [2023] HCA 37 [2] and discussion of this in Chapter 6.

in the foreseeable future'.[71] Mr Al-Kateb had already spent four years in detention by the date of the judgment.[72]

By contrast, Edelman J, in his dissenting judgment in *Graham*, eschews any role for the judiciary to give normative weight to the values, thick or thin, that are embedded in the concept of the rule of law.[73] In extra-curial comment, he has suggested that such terms as 'the rule of law' and the 'principle of legality' 'serve only to conceal reasoning and invite questions'.[74]

B Statutory Interpretation

Another way to discern the range of views about the content of the rule of law is to examine how members of the High Court and other senior members of the judiciary describe their work of statutory interpretation. By examining the statements of judges discussing both their interpretative role and the relevance of the common law even in an era of increased codification of Australian law, it is possible to infer a view. For example, while noting that in the Constitution there is no comprehensive statement of individual human rights, Chief Justice Susan Keifel, in an extra-curial speech, has stated that it is through the process of interpretation that implied rights and freedoms in the Constitution are recognised.[75] Keifel sees the lack of express rights protection in the Constitution as deliberate, to allow a flexible and adaptive interpretation, what she terms a 'flesh[ing] out'.[76] The work of the judiciary, she says, is 'revealing or uncovering' these implications.[77] This work of interpretation is guided by the common-law rights and freedoms which underpin the principles of statutory interpretation that have developed.[78] As found in *Wik*, it is through the application of the common law that the boundary between judicial and legislative functions is identified.[79] In this way the common law is the 'ultimate constitutional foundation in Australia'.[80]

71 *Al-Kateb v Godwin* (2004) 219 CLR 562, 563.

72 See also discussion of this case in Juliet Curtin, '"Never Say Never": Al-Kateb v Godwin' (2005) 27(2) *Sydney Law Review* 355.

73 *Graham v Minister for Immigration and Border Protection* [2017] HCA 33 [106]–[107] ('*Graham*').

74 James Edelman, 'Foreword', in Janina Boughey and Lisa Burton Crawford (eds), *Interpreting Executive Power* (Federation Press, 2020) v–vi.

75 Susan Kiefel, 'Social Justice and the Constitution – Freedoms and Protections' (Mayo Lecture, James Cook University, 24 May 2013); Enid Campbell and Matthew Groves, 'Privative Clauses and the Australian Constitution' (2004) 4 *Oxford University Commonwealth Law Journal* 51, 76.

76 Kiefel (n 75).

77 Kiefel (n 75), quoting *Victoria v Commonwealth* (1971) 122 CLR 353, 401–2 (Windeyer J).

78 Kiefel (n 75), quoting *Victoria v Commonwealth* (1971) 122 CLR 353, 401–2 (Windeyer J).

79 In *Wik Peoples v Queensland* (1996) 187 CLR 1 the High Court found that pastoral leases did not in all cases extinguish native title. For a discussion of this case see Maureen Tehan, 'The Wik Peoples v Queensland; the Thayorre People v Queensland' (1997) 21(1) *Melbourne University Law Review* 343.

80 Kiefel (n 75), citing *Wik Peoples v Queensland* (1996) 187 CLR 1, [182] (Gummow J).

The Hon James Spigelman argues that the role of statutory interpretation is to preserve the common law:

> Statutory interpretation is not merely a collection of maxims. It is a distinct body of law. Its significance is emphasised by the fact that the protection which the common law affords to the preservation of fundamental rights and liberties is, to a substantial extent, secreted within the law of statutory interpretation.[81]

Chief Justice Allsop is clear that the values of the common law are not overtaken by statute but inform its interpretation. In an extra-curial speech, he noted the link between interpretation and societal morality. The statute and its words do not exist in a vacuum. The role of interpretation is to apply the values in new circumstances:

> The proper balance to be struck must recognise the requirement that rule and principle conform to moral standards as the gauge of the law's flexibility and as its avenue for growth, and in order to accommodate changes in society's conceptions of the application of unchanged values. The balance must also recognise the danger of absence of adequate rules that may confound law by a drift into a formless void of sentiment and intuition.[82]

Keifel's predecessor, Chief Justice Robert French, calls the common law a source of rights protection, a 'repository of rights and freedoms'.[83] French suggests these rights include:

> The right of access to the courts, immunity from deprivation of property without compensation, legal professional privilege, privilege against self-incrimination, immunity from the extension of the scope of a penal statute by a court, immunity from interference from vested property rights, immunity from interference with equality of religion, and the right to access legal counsel when accused of a serious crime,[84] no deprivation of liberty except by law; the right to procedural fairness when affected by the exercise of public power, and freedom of speech and of movement.[85]

81 Spigelman (n 50).

82 James Allsop, 'Values in Law: How They Influence and Shape Rules and the Application of Law' (Speech, Centre for Comparative and Public Law, University of Hong Kong, 20 October 2016) 49, 50.

83 Robert French, 'Protecting Human Rights Without a Bill of Rights' (2010) 43 *John Marshall Law Review* 769, 786.

84 Robert French, 'Protecting Human Rights Without a Bill of Rights' (2010) 43 *John Marshall Law Review* 769, 786, citing Jennifer Corrin, 'Australia: Country Report on Human Rights' (2009) 40 *Victoria University of Wellington Law Review* 37, 41–2.

85 French (n 83) 786.

At the juncture between this interpretative role of the courts and the Parliament's power to pass laws is the 'principle of legality', the most wide ranging of the interpretive principles.[86] This is the principle to which Gleeson referred:[87] that the Parliament should not be presumed to intend to 'remove or affect fundamental rights or freedoms' unless such an intention is expressed with 'irresistible clarity'.[88] The principle protects the rights that French lists.[89] It means that in the absence of express language to the contrary the courts must presume Parliament intended that the words of a statute 'be subject to the basic rights of the individual'.[90] However, even two decades before the time of writing, McHugh J questioned the continuing utility of this presumption.[91] He noted that 'nearly every session of Parliament produces laws which infringe the existing rights of individuals'.[92] He suggested that because of this 'it is now difficult to assume that the legislature would not infringe rights or interfere with the general system of law'.[93]

In the same case Kirby J warned against abandoning the presumption of legality despite agreeing with the trend in legislation that McHugh J highlighted. Kirby J observed that deciding whether a right is fundamental is key to applying the presumption.[94] He proposed that the *Universal Declaration of Human Rights* and the *International Covenant on Civil and Political Rights* can aid in defining a 'fundamental' right.[95] These rights extend beyond French's list to include such rights as the following:

> Everyone is entitled to all the rights and freedoms set forth in this Declaration, without distinction of any kind, such as race, colour, sex, language, religion, political or other opinion, national or social origin, property, birth or other status. Furthermore, no distinction shall be made on the basis of the political, jurisdictional or international status of the country or territory to which a person belongs, whether it be independent, trust, non-self-governing or under any other limitation of sovereignty.[96]

86 Anthony Mason, 'The Interaction of Statute Law and Common Law' (2015) 27 *Judicial Officers Bulletin* 87, 90, citing *Coco v The Queen* (1994) 179 CLR 427, 446; *Electrolux Home Products Pty Ltd v Australian Workers' Union* (2004) 221 CLR 309, [21] (Gleeson CJ, dissenting).
87 Gleeson, *The Rule of Law* (n 49).
88 Kiefel (n 75).
89 French (n 83).
90 French (n 83).
91 *Malika Holdings Pty Ltd v Stretton* (2001) 204 CLR 290, 298 [28].
92 *Malika Holdings Pty Ltd v Stretton* (2001) 204 CLR 290, 298 [28].
93 *Malika Holdings Pty Ltd v Stretton* (2001) 204 CLR 290, 298 [28].
94 *Malika Holdings Pty Ltd v Stretton* (2001) 204 CLR 328 [121].
95 *Malika Holdings Pty Ltd v Stretton* (2001) 204 CLR 328 [121]; UN General Assembly, *Universal Declaration of Human Rights*, GA Res 217 A (111) (10 December 1948); *International Covenant on Civil and Political Rights*, opened for signature 16 December 1965, 999 UNTS 171 (entered into force 3 March 1976).
96 UN General Assembly, *Universal Declaration of Human Rights* (n 95) art 2.

The work of the judiciary in discovering new rights continues. French notes that the presumption that a statute should be interpreted subject to basic human rights can be used to recognise new rights, not just those that have historically been accepted. He cites the recognition of native title rights as an example and explains that in that decision 'the seriousness of the consequences to indigenous inhabitants of extinguishing their traditional rights and interests in land' was a consideration of the court.[97]

In summary, the judiciary has expressed a range of views from thin to thick about the concept of the rule of law, and one member has questioned whether the courts have any normative role in this debate. However, a logical conclusion that can be drawn from statements about the interpretative role of the judiciary and the values and rights variously expressed in the common law, which are considered when legislation is interpreted, is that the rule of law under the Australian Constitution has a more nuanced and contested meaning, and for some a much more substantive meaning, than the espoused definition of obedience to laws made by the Parliament which Alan Tudge, Acting Minister for Immigration, Citizenship, Migrant Services and Multicultural Affairs in the Morrison Coalition government (2019–20), inserted into the statement in 2020.

IV The Rule of Law and Judicial Review of Migration Decisions

All decisions made under the *Migration Act 1958* (Cth), whether made by the immigration minister acting personally or by a delegate, are subject to judicial review of executive action under s 75(v) of the *Constitution*. The extent of this review in almost all migration cases that come before either the High Court or Federal Courts, is constrained by the privative clause, *Migration Act 1958* (Cth) s 474.[98] Through this judicial review the High Court can direct officers of the Commonwealth, including immigration ministers,

97 French (n 83) 789 citing *Mabo v. Queensland (No 2)* (1992) 175 CLR 1, 64.

98 Note that under the privative clause (s 474) no Chapter III court can review the merits of a decision, although some decisions made by a delegate, but not by the minister personally, may be reviewed by an administrative, not judicial, tribunal or assessment authority. For discussions of the role and limits of reviews of migration decisions see Chantal Bostock, 'The Effect of Ministerial Directions on Tribunal Independence' (2011) 66 *AIAL Forum* 33; Peter Billings and Khanh Hoang, 'Characters of Concern, or Concerning Character Tests? Regulating Risk Through Visa Cancellation, Containment and Removal from Australia', in Peter Billings (ed), *Crimmigration in Australia: Law, Politics, and Society* (Springer, 2019) 119, 128–43; Grant Hooper, 'Three Decades of Tension: From the Codification of Migration Decision-Making to an Overarching Framework for Judicial Review' (2020) 48(3) *Federal Law Review* 401. See Philip Ruddock's paper setting out his reasons as Minister for Immigration for introducing a privative clause in Philip Ruddock, 'Narrowing of Judicial Review in the Migration Context' (1997) 15 *AIAL Forum* 13.

to obey the law. The precise meaning of that law is finally determined by the judiciary in its role as interpreter of legislation and of the Constitution.[99]

The significance of this judicial role and the working out of its relationship to the migration legislation is surveyed shortly.

A The 'Basic Guarantee of the Rule of Law': Judicial Review

In 2000, writing extra-curially, the Hon Murray Gleeson characterised s 75(v) of the *Constitution* as a 'basic guarantee of the rule of law'.[100] This basic guarantee of the rule of law has the potential to protect the individual, whether citizen or noncitizen, from the arbitrary use of power by those wielding political power. This is an attribute at the core of even the thinnest definitions of the rule of law.[101] Gleeson warned:

> Working out the principles according to which the will of an elected Parliament that is responsive to popular opinion must bend to the law, as enforced by unelected and independent judges, is one of the most important and difficult issues of current debate.[102]

At stake, Gleeson said, was the extent to which human rights will be prioritised over other political interests.[103]

The principles that govern the interface between political and judicial power remain contested. In *S157/2002 v The Commonwealth*[104] the High Court read down an attempt to block judicial scrutiny of migration cases through a privative clause. In *Bodruddaza v Minister for Immigration and Multicultural Affairs*,[105] the High Court found

> s 486A of the *Migration Act* was invalid because it curtailed or limited the right or ability of the applicant to seek relief under s 75(v) as to be inconsistent with the place of that provision in the constitutional structure.[106]

99 See Lisa Burton Crawford's elaboration of this role and of the limits of the judicial review of executive decisions in Crawford, *Rule of Law* (n 31) 103–33.
100 Gleeson, *The Rule of Law* (n 49) 67. Note Lisa Burton Crawford argues that a constitutional guarantee of the rule of law cannot be achieved because one cannot have a rule that anyone, officials or members of the community, will in fact obey the rules. Crawford, *Rule of Law* (n 31) 194–7.
101 Krygier (n 8) 203.
102 Gleeson, *The Rule of Law* (n 49) 63.
103 Gleeson, *The Rule of Law* (n 49) 63.
104 (2003) 211 CLR 476 (S157/2002).
105 (2007) 228 CLR 651 ('*Bodruddaza*').
106 (2007) 228 CLR 652 ('*Bodruddaza*').

Judicial review was in this way positioned as a constitutional right.[107]

Alan Freckelton has surveyed statutory attempts up to 2015 to curtail the application and extent of s 75 judicial review, such as the insertion of a privative clause, which was the issue in *S157/2002*, time limits on applications to the court and constraints on procedural fairness.[108] Freckelton argues that these legislative attempts to constrain judicial review have been largely ineffectual, as the court has retained its power of legislative and constitutional interpretation. His analysis is that, because the judiciary retains its interpretative power to decide what is or is not the content of an error of law in a particular case, the content and the breadth of judicial review have not been successfully constrained by the legislature.[109]

Lisa Burton Crawford has a different view. She argues that the Parliament does constrain judicial review.[110] Citing *Minister for Immigration and Citizenship v Li*[111] and *Minister for Immigration and Border Protection v Singh*,[112] she notes that the standard of reasonableness of an executive decision in a particular case is based on the statutory context. In this way, Crawford argues, it is the Parliament that decides the limits of review.[113]

This interface is critical to all who are subject to an administrative decision. It is even more critical to the noncitizen. This is because administrative decisions made under the *Migration Act 1958* (Cth) have a fundamental impact on the liberty, safety and well-being of every noncitizen.[114] Other administrative decisions do not generally deprive a person of their liberty for an indeterminate period.[115] A high proportion of cases where this interface between judicial and legislative power is being worked out concerning migration law. In the area of migration law the appellant workload of the judiciary has dramatically accelerated since 2000.[116] Migration appeals were 8% of Federal Court appellant

107 See also Smith (n 63) 39.

108 Alan Freckelton, *Administrative Decision Making in Australian Migration Law* (ANU Press, 2015) 228. See also Jeremy Kirk, 'The Entrenched Minimum Provision of Judicial Review' (2004) 12(1) *Australian Journal of Administrative Law* 64; Leighton McDonald, 'The Entrenched Minimum Provision of Judicial Review and the Rule of Law' (2010) 21(1) *Public Law Review* 14; Will Bateman, 'The Constitution and the Substantive Principles of Judicial Review: The Full Scope of The Entrenched Minimum Provision of Judicial Review' (2011) 39(3) *Federal Law Review* 463.

109 Freckelton (n 108). Hooper (n 98) makes a similar argument.

110 Lisa Burton Crawford, 'The Entrenched Minimum Provision of Judicial Review and the Limits of "Law"' (2017) 45 *Federal Law Review* 569, 574 ('Entrenched Minimum').

111 (2013) 249 CLR 332, 362 [63], 369 [86] (Hayne, Keifel and Bell JJ); 371 [92] (Gageler J).

112 (2014) 231 FCR 437, 445 [43].

113 Crawford, 'Entrenched Minimum' (n 110), citing *A-G (NSW) v Quin* (1990) 170 CLR 1, 35–6 (Brennan J).

114 See Chapters 5 and 6 for examples of this.

115 See Chapter 6 Section III.

116 Federal Court of Australia, *Annual Report 1999–2000* (Report, 2000) 13.

work in 1995/96.[117] This rose to 35% in 1999/2000.[118] Currently 72.3% of the Federal Court's entire appellate workload is taken up by the task of identifying the lawful boundaries of executive decision-making in migration appeals for judicial review, as noted previously.[119] The human rights that Gleeson views as at stake are those of noncitizens, and their families and communities.[120]

B *The Judgment in Graham: The Content of Judicial Review*

The relationship between the expression of the will of the Parliament and the judiciary's defence of the 'basic guarantee of the rule of law' through judicial review is illustrated in the migration case of *Graham*.[121] This case gives further definition to what the basic guarantee of the rule of law might mean for the noncitizen.

In *Graham* the majority found that s 503A(2) of the *Migration Act 1958* was invalid but only to the extent that it shielded the immigration minister from disclosing information to the High Court or to the Federal Court under s 476A(1)(c) and (2) when they exercise jurisdiction to review the immigration minister's decision under the character test provisions.[122] The majority found that the Parliament cannot pass a law that denies the court, under s 75(v) of the *Constitution*, the 'ability to enforce the legislated limits of a [Commonwealth] officer's power'.[123] Citing *Plaintiff S157/2002 v The Commonwealth*,[124] the majority of the court found that s 75(v) of the *Constitution* 'secures a basic element of the rule of law'.[125] It found:

> The question whether or not a law transgresses that constitutional limitation is one of substance, and therefore of degree. To answer it requires an examination not only of the legal operation of the law but also of the practical impact of the law on the ability of a court, through the application of judicial process, to discern and declare whether or not the conditions of and constraints on the lawful exercise of the power conferred on an officer have been observed in a particular case.[126]

117 Federal Court of Australia, *Annual Report 1999–2000* (Report, 2000) 13.
118 Federal Court of Australia, *Annual Report 1999–2000* (Report, 2000) 13.
119 Federal Court of Australia, *Annual Report 2019–2020* (Report, 2020) 24. Note also that 63.44% of all filings in the Federal Circuit Court were migration matters. Federal Circuit Court, *Annual Report 2019–2020* (Report, 2020) 37.
120 Gleeson, *The Rule of Law* (n 49) 63. For an example of the impact on the community see Allsop J in *Hands v Minister for Immigration and Border Protection* [2018] 225 FCAFC 628 ('*Hands*').
121 *Graham* (n 73).
122 *Graham* (n 73) 2.
123 *Graham* (n 73) 3.
124 (2003) 211 CLR 476, 482 [5], cited in *Graham* (n 73) 25.
125 *Graham* (n 73) 25.
126 *Graham* (n 73) 27.

The judgment noted that the court cannot carry out its function of discerning whether the immigration minister exercised statutory discretion reasonably (for example, 'according to the rules of reason and justice, not according to private opinion; according to law, and not humour, and within those limits within which an honest man, competent to discharge the duties of his office, ought to confine himself'[127]) unless the court can view the material on which a decision was based.[128] In summary, the majority judgment emphasised the court's pivotal role in the 'rule of law' under the Australian Constitution and that this is carried out by applying, case by case, the interpretative process. Implied is that the court will not accede to legislative attempts to distance a 'particular case' from the scrutiny of the court.[129]

While such a decision can be seen as an assertion of the judicial role against the attempts at encroachment of executive power, much was left unsaid. Their honours found in *Graham* that there was a minimum content to judicial review and that this was a matter of 'substance and therefore of degree'.[130] However, their Honours did not specify what this substance or degree might encompass. To what extent that substance might include bringing to bear the common-law values that, for example, former Chief Justice Robert French or Chief Justice Allsop expounded is uncertain.[131] As a guarantee of the rule of law for the noncitizen who is subject to the *Migration Act 1958* (Cth), it appears a guarantee of the thinnest of versions of the rule of law, including a guarantee, as Tamanaha notes, of the enforcement of 'evil laws'.[132] Kirby's view on the majority judgment in *Al Kateb* was that it was an example of this kind of enforcement.[133] In summary, while the judgment in *Graham* maintains that the basic guarantee of the rule of law through judicial review has

127 *Graham* (n 73) 30, quoting *R v Anderson; Ex parte Ipec-Air Pty Ltd* (1965) 113 CLR 177, 189, citing *Sharp v Wakefield* [1891] AC 173, 179. The judgment also made references to recent migration cases *Minister for Immigration and Border Protection v Stretton* (2016) 237 FCR 1; *Minister for Immigration and Border Protection v Eden* (2016) 240 FCR 158.

128 *Graham* (n 73) 2.

129 For detailed discussion of *Graham* see Leighton McDonald, 'Graham and the Constitutionalisation of Australian Administrative Law' (2018) 91 *AIAL Forum* 47; Greg Weeks and Matthew Groves, 'Legislative Limitations on Judicial Review: The High Court in Graham' (2018) 24 *Australian Journal of Administrative Law* 209. Note that even before the judgment was made in *Graham* the government anticipated a negative result. It proposed the Migration Amendment (Validation of Decisions) Bill 2017, which was passed days before the final judgment in Graham. It preserved possibly invalid decisions. Another amendment attempting to restore the government's purpose defeated in *Graham* was proposed in Migration and Citizenship Legislation Amendment (Strengthening Information Provisions) Bill 2020. This lapsed on the dissolution of Parliament in April 2022.

130 *Graham* (n 73) 3.

131 French (n 83); Allsop (n 82).

132 Tamanaha (n 9) 100. Note Crawford agrees with Raz that this is all the rule of law can be. See Crawford, *Rule of Law* (n 31) 180; Raz (n 13) 191–2.

133 Kirby (n 67).

some content, it could not be described as a judgment made in favour of a substantive definition of the rule of law. At most, bringing together the range of judicial interpretations of the rule of law and some of the aspects of statutory interpretation discussed previously, it can be inferred from the judgment that in a future case there might be an opportunity for a more substantive understanding of the rule of law to be applied.

C *Legislative Techniques That Constrain Judicial Review: A Significant Judgment in Dissent*

As well as demonstrating these continued attempts to limit the judiciary's role and the judiciary's insistence on both the importance of its constitutional role and the power to define its content, *Graham* is also important because of an argument made in dissent and the issues it raises about the meaning of the rule of law for the noncitizen. The dissenting argument by Edelman J aligns with the thinner definitions of the rule of law, such as those propounded by Raz,[134] and what Tamanaha referred to as 'rule by government' and Randall Peerenboom as 'rule *by* law'.[135] It is also an argument for political accountability.

Edelman J argued against the majority view that there was a minimal content to judicial review.[136] He noted that nothing had been presented in *Graham* that dissuaded him of the 'vital constructional role' of pre-Federation history when considering the implications of s 75(v). Drawing on that history, he was persuaded that the framers of the Constitution intended s 75(v) to have no more than a limited accountability function.[137] He argued that to define the content of judicial review was to purport to give normative weight to values, thick or thin, underlying the concept of the rule of law.[138] Such a role would 'require the Court simply to make unmediated policy decisions' based on either 'the policy views of the individual members of the Court or the alleged perceptions of the public or some section of it'.[139] These normative judgments, he argued, are for the Parliament alone. Parliament legislates and 'must squarely confront what it is doing and accept the political cost'.[140]

134 Raz (n 13) 191–2.
135 Tamanaha (n 9) 96; Peerenboom, *China's Long March* (n 11) 8.
136 Weeks and Groves note the significance of Edelman J's dissenting judgment. They note Justice Edelman's comparative youth and suggest that his views could gain orthodoxy as other more experienced members of the High Court retire. Weeks and Groves (n 129) 210.
137 *Graham* (n 73) 47 [104].
138 *Graham* (n 73) 49 [106].
139 *Graham* (n 73) 49 [108].
140 *Graham* (n 73) 39, quoting *R v Home Secretary; Ex parte Simms* [2000] 2 AC 115, 131 (Lord Hoffmann) and noting it is 'described as "frequently cited" by this Court' in *Lee v NSW Crime Commission* (2013) 251 CLR 196, 309 [311].

Supporting this position, he argued that there was long historic precedent for the validity of statutes that use strategies to limit judicial scrutiny of executive decisions. He added that since before Federation there had been accepted techniques that parliaments had used to constrain judicial review.[141] These techniques, he said, are privative clauses, and he alluded to 'giving powers to Ministers and other statutory bodies in terms so broad that it becomes difficult for a court ever to hold that they have been exceeded'.[142] He noted with approval Crawford's questioning of the judgment in *Plaintiff S157/2002* (reading down the privative clause in s 474), which relied on an understanding of the rule of law.[143] The logic of this argument in dissent is that what the majority of the High Court in *Bodruddaza* described as a right,[144] and what Gleeson called the basic guarantee of the rule of law,[145] can be rendered by the Parliament to be little more than a symbolic day in court.

Edelman J interpreted the right in *Bodruddaza* as guaranteeing only that Parliament could not legislate to preclude a claim based on s 75 (v) but the judgment allowed regulation of access to s 75(v) through such provisions as time limits.[146] Edelman J's view would in practice place decisions on the 'legislated limits of a decision maker's power' to which the majority in *Graham* referred beyond the power of the High Court.[147] This would depart from the view of the majority in *Graham*, who saw this limit as theirs to discern. The common-law values which other members of the judiciary have described as informing the performance of the judicial role would have no substantive opportunity to be applied.[148]

D *The Content of the Basic Guarantee of the Rule of Law for the Noncitizen*

In *Graham* the majority judgment guarantees the substance of judicial review but not what that substance is. The dissent found the power to decide the substance of judicial review to lie firmly with the Parliament and, subject to legislation, with the executive. If judicial review is the basic guarantee of the rule of law for the noncitizen in Australia, that guarantee appears to align

141 *Graham* (n 73) 52 [116].
142 *Graham* (n 73) 52 [116].
143 *Graham* (n 73) 48 [106], citing Crawford, *The Rule of Law* (n 31) 110. Note that in Australia the privative clause in *Migration Act 1958* (Cth) s 474 was read down in *Plaintiff S157/2002 v Commonwealth* (2003) 211 CLR 476, 506. The privative clause was found to apply only to decisions made lawfully. The power of judicial review under s 75(v) of the *Constitution* remained to discern whether a purported decision was made unlawfully.
144 *Bodruddaza* (n 105) 652.
145 Gleeson, *The Rule of Law* (n 49) 67.
146 *Graham* (n 73) 50 [110].
147 *Graham* (n 73) 2–3.
148 See Section III for those values and judicial comment.

closely with the thinner versions of the rule of law. It is a guarantee of the process of review and a guarantee that, if the statute can be so interpreted, some of the various rights, freedoms and values identified as part of the common law by members of the judiciary may be applied to that process.

In his dissent Edelman J described the accepted legislative technique of drafting 'in terms so broad that it becomes difficult for a court ever to hold that they [the legal limits of the legislated power] have been exceeded'.[149] The next section of this chapter examines how this technique is used in the character test provision, *Migration Act 1958* (Cth) s 501, and its impact on the meaning of the rule of law for the noncitizen.

V The Rule of Law and the Character Test

One reason that character test cases are used as an example in this inquiry into the rule of law is captured in a statement by Chief Justice Allsop. In his judgment in *Hands v Minister for Immigration and Border Protection*,[150] he said, 'the question of the consequences of a failure to pass the character test not infrequently raise important questions about the exercise of Executive power'.[151] These questions and how they are resolved in cases inform the understanding of the meaning of the rule of law for the noncitizen. These cases are an example of the consequences for the noncitizen of the shielding of executive power from effective scrutiny in migration cases which, as argued previously, was done through the amendments justified by sovereignty.

This section begins by introducing the character test. By drawing on the research of David Dyzenhaus, it explains in broad terms how the test creates a state of rule of the immigration minister, as opposed to any of the versions of the rule of law discussed previously. Secondly this section outlines how the breadth of application of this discretion was achieved and why this aspect of migration law is particularly relevant to the situation of the noncitizen under the rule of law. Thirdly this section examines two provisions of the test and the judiciary's response in order to demonstrate the extent of the immigration minister's discretion and how this this legislation fits Edelman J's description of a provision that 'makes [it] difficult for a court ever to hold that they [the legislated limits of a decision-maker's power] have been exceeded'.[152]

149 *Graham* (n 73) 52 [116].
150 *Hands* (n 120).
151 *Hands* (n 120) 630.
152 *Graham* (n 73) 52 [116].

A Legislating 'Terms so Broad'[153]

The following outline of some key features of the test provides a context for this discussion. The character test, *Migration Act 1958* (Cth) s 501, was introduced in its current form in 1998 and further amended in *Migration Amendment (Character and General Visa Cancellation) Act 2014* (Cth) and *Migration Amendment (Character Cancellation Consequential Provisions) Act 2017* (Cth).[154] The test is a decisive factor in administrative decision-making in any matter concerning the noncitizen.[155] This is because to be granted a visa or retain a current visa the applicant must pass the test. This is achieved by allaying any suspicions that the immigration minister might reasonably have that the applicant is not of good character.[156] To inform this decision the test sets out a list of criteria.[157] If the immigration minister is making the decision personally the test criteria and national interest are considered.[158] The criteria include but extend beyond the objective criterion of a criminal conviction.[159] For example, a person can fail the test if the immigration minister has a reasonable suspicion that a person with no criminal record has 'conduct past and present' that the immigration minister judges to be unsatisfactory.[160] The immigration minister might also suspect that the noncitizen has an association with a person who 'is or has been involved in criminal conduct',[161] or that there is a risk that in the future

153 *Graham* (n 73) 52 [116].

154 *Migration Legislation Amendment (Strengthening of Provisions Relating to Character and Conduct) Act 1998*. Note that Australian migration legislation has always included some kind of character provision. See *Immigration Restriction Act 1901* s 3(e). See a discussion of this history in Michael Grewcock, 'Reinventing "the Stain": Bad Character and Criminal Deportation in Contemporary Australia', in Sharon Pickering and Julie Ham (eds), *The Routledge Handbook on Crime and International Migration* (Taylor & Francis Group, 2014) 121 ('Reinventing'). See also Samuel C Duckett White, 'God-Like Powers: The Character Test and Unfettered Ministerial Discretion' (2020) 41(1) *Adelaide Law Review* 1–3.

155 Note that character considerations are also made in citizenship decisions, but the *Australian Citizenship Act 2007* does not contain a test.

156 *Migration Act 1958* (Cth) s 501(1)–(2).

157 *Migration Act 1958* (Cth) s 501(6). Definitions relating to a substantial criminal record are at s 501(7), (7A), (8)–(11).

158 *Migration Act 1958* (Cth) s 501(6). Definitions relating to a substantial criminal record are at s 501(3).

159 See Michael Grewcock's comment on the double punishment of this provision in Michael Grewcock, 'Punishment, Deportation and Parole: The Detention and Removal of Former Prisoners Under Section 501 Migration Act 1958' (2011) 44(1) *Australian & New Zealand Journal of Criminology* 56.

160 *Migration Act 1958* (Cth) s 501(6)(c) (ii). See *Godley v Minister for Immigration and Multicultural and Indigenous Affairs* (2004) 83 ALD 411, [56] (Lee J), approved on appeal in *Minister for Immigration and Multicultural and Indigenous Affairs v Godley* (2005) 141 FCR 552, [34]. In that case good character was interpreted as an enduring moral quality.

161 *Migration Act 1958* (Cth) s 501(6)(b)(i)–(ii).

the noncitizen, with or without a criminal record, might commit a crime or a risk that they might be 'liable to become involved in activities that are disruptive' to some part of the community.[162] This includes risks defined by national security concerns.[163] Decisions made by a delegate can be reviewed under the natural justice provision of administrative merits review.[164] Decisions made by the immigration minister personally are not subject to merits review.[165] The immigration minister also has the power, acting personally and without merits review, to change a decision to an adverse one, that is one that finds that a person does not pass the test, or to remake the adverse decisions of a delegate, whatever that decision was, and even if the decision is already under the review of the Administrative Appeals Tribunal. In that way the immigration minister has the power to ensure any decision avoids merits review.[166]

The decisions made personally by the immigration minister are only subject to judicial review under s 75(v) of the *Constitution*. However, even the opportunity for this judicial review has been narrowed by the combination of provisions in the 2014 amendment and the 2017 amendment.[167] The result is that, if the immigration minister under s 501BA had decided not to revoke the cancellation of a visa that was cancelled under s 501(3A) (inserted in 2014), the noncitizen could be removed from Australia before that noncitizen had the opportunity to seek judicial review, the only review available.

In 2003 the Commonwealth Ombudsman said that the discretion given to the immigration minister by this legislation was 'an outstanding example of what we call an unconfined discretion. In theoretical terms, there can be no broader discretion than that'.[168] Chris Evans, immigration minister 2007 to 2010 in the Rudd Labor government, gave a more colourful description. On coming to office from Opposition, he expressed discomfort 'about playing God . . . and the lack of transparency and accountability' in making character

162 *Migration Act 1958* (Cth) 501(6)(d)(v).

163 Susan Rimmer describes the impact of this in Susan Harris Rimmer, 'The Dangers of Character Tests: Dr Haneef and Other Cautionary Tales' (Discussion Paper No 101, Australia Institute, 2008). See *Minister for Immigration & Citizenship v Haneef* [2007] FCAFC 203, [44]. For a discussion of the counter-terrorism policing approach in this case see Sharon Pickering and Jude McCulloch, 'The Haneef Case and Counter-Terrorism Policing in Australia' (2010) 20(1) *Policing & Society* 21.

164 *Migration Act 1958* (Cth) s 501(1)–(2).

165 *Migration Act 1958* (Cth) s 501(3).

166 *Migration Act 1958* (Cth) ss 501a, 501b.

167 See details of this amendment in Khanh Hoang, 'Migration Amendment (Character Cancellation Consequential Provisions) Act 2017' (Legislative Brief, Andrew & Renata Kaldor Centre for International Refugee Law, 2019).

168 Evidence to Senate Committee on Ministerial Discretion in Migration Matters, Parliament of Australia, Canberra, 18 November 2003, 14 (Commonwealth Ombudsman).

decisions.[169] However, after this assessment the 'unconfined discretion' was extended, by Coalition governments, even further.[170]

Dyzenhaus describes this kind of law as a grey hole and explains how it is constructed.[171] The grey hole is not a 'lawless void'.[172] The legislation which creates the grey hole has the appearance of formal legality, but the constraints on executive action under the test 'are so insubstantial that they pretty well permit the executive government to do as it pleases'.[173] It is unfettered executive discretion masked by the outward formalities of law.

Dyzenhaus' solution is not to abolish discretion, which has a recognised place in the administration of the law. Some level of discretion is accepted as integral to the operation of complex administrative systems.[174] Dicey's position, that discretion for public officials administering the law is inconsistent with the rule of law, has been overtaken.[175] Law is interpreted and applied by individuals, making discretion an inevitable feature of any legal system.[176] Discretion is also seen by some commentators as necessary to allow the law to respond to individual circumstances and to show fairness and compassion.[177] Dyzenhaus' view is that executive discretion creates the grey hole when decisions are not open to effective legal challenge.[178] It is the extent of ministerial discretion, not discretion itself, that creates the grey hole.

Dyzenhaus argues that the grey hole is more damaging to the preservation of the rule of law than for the executive to act outside the law, because

169 Evidence to Standing Committee on Legal and Constitutional Affairs Estimates (Additional Budget Estimates), Senate, Canberra, 19 February 2008 (Chris Evans). Note that during his period in office he did not seek to alter the scope of his discretion.
170 See Section D.
171 Note that Dyzenhaus was focussed on laws made in times of emergency, not specifically on migration law. Dyzenhaus (n 26).
172 Dyzenhaus (n 26) 50.
173 Dyzenhaus (n 26) 42.
174 Tamanaha (n 9) 126.
175 Bingham (n 23) 50. See Carol Harlow and Richard Rawlings, *Law and Administration* (Cambridge University Press, 3rd ed, 2009) 17; Greg Weeks, *Soft Law and Public Authorities: Remedies and Reform* (Hart Publishing, 2016) 26; Greg Weeks, 'Soft Law and Public Liability: Beyond the Separation of Powers?' (2018) 39 *Adelaide Law Review* 303, 305.
176 Bingham (n 23) 50. See Carol Harlow and Richard Rawlings, *Law and Administration* (Cambridge University Press, 3rd ed, 2009) 17; Greg Weeks, *Soft Law and Public Authorities: Remedies and Reform* (Hart Publishing, 2016) 26; Greg Weeks, 'Soft Law and Public Liability: Beyond the Separation of Powers?' (2018) 39 *Adelaide Law Review* 303, 305.
177 Bingham (n 23) 51; Gleeson, 'Outcome, Process' (n 56).
178 Tamanaha (n 9) 126. For further discussion on the use of statute to shield executive power from judicial scrutiny see Dominique Dalla-Pozza and Greg Weeks, 'A Statutory Shield of the Executive: To What Extent Does Legislation Help Administrative Action Evade Judicial Scrutiny?', in Janina Boughey and Lisa Crawford (eds), *Interpreting Executive Power* (Federation Press, 2020) 184, especially 187–90. Also see Mathew Groves, 'The Return of the Almost Absolute Statutory Discretion', in Janina Boughey and Lisa Crawford (eds), *Interpreting Executive Power* (Federation Press, 2020) 129, 136–47.

it allows a 'rule by law', a minimalist rule of law, to be normalised.[179] Such legislation appears as democratically made law approved by the judiciary. Gross and Aolain identify how this normalisation occurs. They explain that the dichotomy established between normalcy and emergency, the urgent need that is used as a rationale for the grey hole, masks the process by which during a prolonged declared emergency the law is so changed that identifying the normal might be no longer possible.[180] What began as an acceptable measure to respond to an emergency becomes the norm.[181]

The 'emergency' which prompted the *Migration Legislation Amendment (Strengthening of Provisions Relating to Character and Conduct) Act 1998* (Cth) and established the 'unfettered discretion' of the character test was not comparable to the states of emergency that Dyzenhaus and Gross and Aolain discuss. The 1998 amendment was a response to the government's concern over the independence of the Administrative Appeals Tribunal merits review of migration decisions, which had been dramatically demonstrated in the case of *Jia v Minister of Immigration & Multicultural Affairs*.[182] Philip Ruddock, Minister for Immigration and Multicultural Affairs 1996–2003 in the Howard Coalition government, made this purpose clear. In his second reading speech introducing the character test, Ruddock asserted that 'discretion should be in the hands of the minister . . . [not] unelected judges or tribunal members who are intent on creative decision making which puts them in the position where they are making laws'.[183] The discretion granted to the immigration minister by the legislation is only limited by judicial review under s 75(v) of the Constitution. This move to increase executive control and diminish the role of the judiciary was justified as being in the national interest. It was only after Scott Morrison became Coalition prime minister (2018–22) that character test matters were brought under the broad policy

179 Dyzenhaus (n 26) 42–51.

180 Oren Gross and Fionnula ni Aolain, *Law in Times of Crisis: Emergency Powers in Theory and Practice* (Cambridge University Press, 2006) 220–43.

181 Oren Gross and Fionnula ni Aolain, *Law in Times of Crisis: Emergency Powers in Theory and Practice* (Cambridge University Press, 2006) 220–43.

182 [1996] AATA 236. This was a case in which a noncitizen who had a past criminal conviction for rape was found to be of good character. See Alan Freckelton, 'The Benefit of Law, the Devil and the Jia Litigation' (2015) 23 *Australian Journal of Administrative Law* 37.

183 Commonwealth, *Parliamentary Debates*, House of Representatives, 2 December 1998, 1247 (Philip Ruddock). See the later comments of Immigration Minister Peter Dutton referring in similar language to the judiciary. Amy Remeikis and Ben Doherty, 'Dutton Says Australia Won't "Surrender our Sovereignty" by Signing UN Migration Deal', *The Guardian* (online, 25 July 2018) <www.theguardian.com/australia-news/2018/jul/25/dutton-says-australia-wont-surrender-our-sovereignty-by-signing-un-migration-deal>. See also Chapter 6 for the range of ways the amendments attempted to block judicial scrutiny.

rationale of protecting or asserting sovereignty.[184] This justification was used to even further concentrate executive control in a similar way to the national interest.

B The Character Test: Breadth of Application

The unfettered discretion available to the immigration minister under the *Migration Act 1958* (Cth) is not confined to the character test. There are many other examples in migration legislation.[185] But one reason why the test is an important example in a discussion of the rule of law is because of its breadth of application as well as the extent of the immigration minister's discretion.

Every noncitizen is subject to the 'unfettered discretion' in the character test at any time. This includes the visa applicant attempting to enter Australian territory, the asylum seeker, the refugee, the 'absorbed person' and the permanent resident, even those who have lived in Australia for decades since infancy.[186] Under the *Migration Act 1958* (Cth) s 501 the immigration minister can decide that any noncitizen fails the 'character test', resulting in their becoming an 'unlawful non-citizen',[187] vulnerable to removal and deportation.[188]

The origin of this broad application of the test is traced by Gummow and Hayne JJ in *Minister for Immigration and Multicultural and Indigenous Affairs v Nystrom*.[189] A character test with limited application and scope for discretion was introduced in 1992.[190] This test became applicable to all noncitizens in 1994 as one of the unintended implications of the universal visa system.[191]

It was only when the major reforms of the character provisions were made by Ruddock in 1998 that the choice to use this test to deport any

184 Scott Morrison, 'Until the Bell Rings', *Prime Minister Media Centre* (Speech, Menzies Research Centre, 6 September 2018) <pm.gov.au/media>.

185 See Chapters 5 and 6 for examples of this. For an account of the range of discretions the minister has in asylum seeker matters in the *Migration Act 1958* (Cth) see Rights Advocacy Project, *Playing God: The Immigration Minister's Unrestrained Power* (Report, Liberty Victoria, 2017).

186 See, e.g., *Minister for Immigration and Multicultural and Indigenous Affairs v Nystrom* (2006) 228 CLR 566, 572; *Falzon v Minister for Immigration and Border Protection* [2018] HCA 2, [1] ('*Falzon*'); *Caric v Minister for Immigration and Border Protection* [2017] FCA 1391, [19], [21].

187 *Migration Act 1958* (Cth) ss 13, 14. Note since *Love v Commonwealth of Australia* (2020) 270 CLR 152 this excludes Indigenous Australians.

188 *Migration Act 1958* (Cth) s 4(c). Note since *Love v Commonwealth of Australia* (2020) 270 CLR 152 this excludes Indigenous Australians. Note the introduction of the citizenship test in 2007 and the extension of waiting periods for citizenship prolongs the vulnerability to this test even for the noncitizen on a pathway visa to citizenship.

189 [2006] HCA 50, 566.

190 *Migration (Offences and Undesirable Persons) Amendment Act 1992* (Cth).

191 *Migration Reform Act 1994* (Cth).

noncitizen was placed at the immigration minister's discretion.[192] This was achieved by strengthening the immigration minister's power over delegated decision-makers. The 1998 amendment authorised the immigration minister under an amended s 499 of the *Migration Act 1958* (Cth) to give binding directions, not as previously just 'general advice',[193] to delegated decision-makers, including to 'require a person or body to exercise the power under section 501 [the character test] instead of the power under sections 200 and 201 [the deportation power] in circumstances where both powers apply'.[194] There are no stated criteria for how the immigration minister should choose between the powers which bestow different levels of discretion.

However, there is a significant difference in the consequences of that choice for the noncitizen. The vulnerability to deportation under sections 200–1 is time limited, while exclusion under the character test is not. A noncitizen is only vulnerable to deportation if a criminal offence was committed before they had been in Australia for ten years cumulatively. The criteria for deportation concern criminal conviction. The character test has much broader criteria involving suspicion and conduct, not just conviction.[195] The decisions under s 200 can be reviewed on merit by the Administrative Appeals Tribunal. Under s 501 only a delegate's decision, not the immigration minister's, can be merits reviewed.[196]

The implication of the interaction of the amended s 501 with the deportation power in s 200 was not discussed in the 1998 amendment's explanatory memorandum or the second reading speech. In parliamentary debate about the 1998 amendment Ruddock brushed away an Opposition member's comment that 'cancelling the visa of a person who is already here . . . concerns issues of deportation' by saying: 'This [the amendment] was dealing with character issues in the broad. It was not dealing with criminal deportation. . . . When you bring in a migration bill, of course you are asked to deal with other issues.'[197] The issue was not pursued in debate despite what could be inferred of Ruddock's unstated intentions: that s 501 had a different

192 *Migration Legislation Amendment (Strengthening of Provisions Relating to Character and Conduct) Act 1998* (Cth). As Grewcock notes this restored the situation to the pre-1983 status when any person considered an alien could be deported under the deportation power. This was changed by the *Migration Amendment Act 1983* (Cth), which placed a ten-year residency limit on those who could be deported. Grewcock, 'Reinventing' (n 154) 125.

193 *Migration Legislation Amendment (Strengthening of Provisions in Relation to Character and Conduct) Act 1998* (Cth) s 16.

194 *Migration Legislation Amendment (Strengthening of Provisions in Relation to Character and Conduct) Act 1998* (Cth) s 16(1A).

195 *Migration Act 1958* (Cth) s 501(6).

196 *Migration Act 1958* (Cth) s 499(4)(1)(a)–(ba).

197 Commonwealth, *Parliamentary Debates*, House of Representatives, 2 December 1998, 1244–7 (Philip Ruddock).

scope from the deportation power and would be used to deport residents on grounds much broader than those of the deportation power.

The impact of these changes became apparent. In 2006 the Commonwealth Ombudsman noted that s 501 was increasingly being used to cancel the visas of long-term residents and that these cancellations were made by the immigration minister personally, avoiding merits review.[198] The ombudsman's recommendation that the government consider raising the threshold for cancellation under s 501 in relation to permanent residents has not been acted upon.[199] The 2006 ombudsman's investigation found that 'long-term residents [who] had arrived as babies or small children . . . often assumed they were, in fact, Australian citizens'.[200] The department responsible for administering the *Migration Act 1958* (Cth) when the 1998 amendment was enacted did not inform noncitizens that 'the new part of the chapter 501 provisions could be applied to them'.[201] To support his recommendation the ombudsman noted that the intention to use the amended s 501 to cancel the visas of those who could not be removed under the deportation power was not made explicit to the Parliament when the amendment was enacted.[202]

When this broad application was tested in *Nystrom*, the High Court confirmed the legality of the immigration minister's use of the character test on a long-term resident who was no longer vulnerable to deportation, on the basis that

> The provisions [s 201 and s 501] have a different legislative history and a different relationship to the constitutional sources of power in s 51(xix) and (xxvii) as already explained. The Act contains two separate but consonant statutory systems for deportation and removal which operate differently.[203]

198 Commonwealth Ombudsman, *Department of Immigration and Multicultural Affairs: Administration of s 501 of the Migration Act 1958 as It Applies to Long Term Residents* (2006).

199 Commonwealth Ombudsman, *Department of Immigration and Multicultural Affairs: Administration of s 501 of the Migration Act 1958 as It Applies to Long Term Residents* (2006) [2.2] Recommendation 7.

200 Commonwealth Ombudsman, *Department of Immigration and Multicultural Affairs: Administration of s 501 of the Migration Act 1958 as It Applies to Long Term Residents* (2006) [3.4].

201 Commonwealth Ombudsman, *Department of Immigration and Multicultural Affairs: Administration of s 501 of the Migration Act 1958 as It Applies to Long Term Residents* (2006) [3.4].

202 *Migration Act 1958* (Cth) ss 200–1.

203 *Minister for Immigration and Multicultural and Indigenous Affairs v Nystrom* (2006) 228 CLR 566, 616.

Critiquing the judgment in *Nystrom*, Michelle Foster makes a similar point to the ombudsman.[204] She suggests that the use of s 501 to remove long-term residents is the government's way of 'circumventing the protection of long-term residents intrinsic in s 201 of the Migration Act' and of retaining the reach of the discretion that s 501 provides.[205] She observes that the Parliament's purpose for the ten-year residency limit on deportation was to recognise that the group of long-term residents (that the character test can now remove) had a right not to be expelled and that Australia had a responsibility for them.[206] If that was so, this right and responsibility has been removed by the Parliament and replaced through s 501 with the immigration minister's discretion.

The ruling in *Nystrom* means that there is no time limit to the vulnerability of the noncitizen, even a long-term resident, to removal under the character test at the immigration minister's discretion.[207] It should be noted that, since *Nystrom*, the High Court found in *Love v Commonwealth of Australia* that one group of noncitizens, Indigenous Australians, are not subject to the character test on the basis that they are not aliens.[208] Up until that case and based on the ruling in *Nystrom*, it was the case that under the character test and the related provisions regarding its use, a limit to its breadth of application could only come from a change in legislation. Such a change to legislation would not be novel. As Michael Grewcock notes in his history, it was a High Court finding that deportation of a resident of twenty years was lawful which prompted the Hawke Labor government to legislate the ten-year limitation[209] on deportation which the ombudsman has recommend be applied to the character test.[210]

It could be, and has been, speculated that a person brought to Australia as a child could claim a degree of connection to Australia, but the High Court has not yet recognised this group.[211] In *Love v Commonwealth of Australia*[212] Kiefel CJ argued in dissent that from Federation the Parliament had

204 Michelle Foster, 'An "Alien" by the Barest of Threads: The Legality of the Deportation of Long Term Residents from Australia' (2009) 33 *Melbourne University Law Review* 483.
205 Michelle Foster, 'An "Alien" by the Barest of Threads: The Legality of the Deportation of Long Term Residents from Australia' (2009) 33 *Melbourne University Law Review* 484–5.
206 Michelle Foster, 'An "Alien" by the Barest of Threads: The Legality of the Deportation of Long Term Residents from Australia' (2009) 33 *Melbourne University Law Review* 483, 507.
207 Michelle Foster, 'An "Alien" by the Barest of Threads: The Legality of the Deportation of Long Term Residents from Australia' (2009) 33 *Melbourne University Law Review* 514.
208 *Love v Commonwealth* (2020) 270 CLR 152.
209 Grewcock, 'Reinventing' (n 154) 125. This changed the wording of s 501(6)(d) from 'significant risk' to 'risk'.
210 *Pochi and MacPhee and Another* (1982) 151 CLR 101.
211 *Pochi and MacPhee and Another* (1982) 151 CLR 101.
212 (2020) 270 CLR 152.

the power to decide who was an alien and that it was only the case of *Pochi* that imposed the limit that alienage could not be attributed to someone who 'could not possibly answer that description'.[213] She rejected the contention that s 51(xix) of the Constitution did not include Aboriginal persons.[214] On the basis of her dissent, a change to the law applying to applicants such as Mr Nystrom could only come through statutes. However, in the same case Edelman J, also drawing on Federation history, came to the majority conclusion that Indigenous Australians are not aliens.[215]

Until the law changes, by statutory change or a change in interpretation, all noncitizens, with the exception of Indigenous Australians, remain subject to the grey hole in the law that is the character test. The next section examines two criteria in the test that epitomise the grey hole in law. These are the consideration of risk and national interest. They have the appearance of legality but allow rule by the immigration minister.

C *Avoiding Risk of Harm*

The underlying logic of the character test is the avoidance of the risk of harm. The importance of the task of evaluating the risk of harm in decision-making under the character test was emphasised by Rangiah J in *Moana v Minister for Immigration and Border Protection*.[216] He found that the 'common thread that underlies each of the criteria in s 501(6) [the character test] is the risk of harm posed' to the Australian community.[217] An evaluation of risk of harm is 'centrally relevant to the exercise of the Minister's discretion in most cases'.[218] Decisions which ignore this evaluation will be vulnerable to jurisdictional error.[219] This is the reason why the issue of risk dealt with in the 2014 amendment is so central to the discretion in the character test.

Before the 2014 amendment the test already contained the broadest discretion, but in 2014 it was broadened even further.[220] One of the changes made by the amendments was the simple removal of the word 'significant' from the description of risk in the test criteria.[221] Since 2014 the immigration minister or a delegate has had the discretion to cancel a visa if there is any

213 (2020) 270 CLR 171.
214 (2020) 270 CLR 181–2.
215 (2020) 270 CLR 153, 290–321, especially 293–9.
216 [2015] FCAFC 54, [50].
217 [2015] FCAFC 54, [50].
218 [2015] FCAFC 383, [74].
219 [2015] FCAFC 383, [74].
220 See a summary of these measures in Explanatory Memorandum, Migration Amendment (Character and General Visa Cancellation) Bill 2014.
221 *Migration Amendment (Character and General Visa Cancellation) Act 2014* (Cth).

risk that the person might, for example, 'engage in criminal conduct', 'harass, molest, intimidate or stalk', vilify, incite discord or 'represent a danger in any other way'.[222] Ian Coyle and Patrick Keyzer draw on research on recidivism to argue that an assessment of likelihood of repeated criminal conduct is meaningless.[223] Assessing the likelihood of future unsatisfactory conduct appears even more difficult. The immigration minister gives the instruction, for example, that delegated decision-makers must have regard to 'acts of family violence, regardless of whether there is a conviction for an offence'.[224] The standard of proof is not specified.[225] It is the work of the decision-maker to assess the risk of whether in the future an alleged action might be repeated. Ministerial directions give binding direction to how this assessment should be made, but the content of these directions is made and altered at the discretion of the immigration minister.[226] In summary it is difficult to see how a judgment could be made that these statutory limits are exceeded. The response of the judiciary confirms this.

Under the character test the only constraint on the immigration minister's discretion is that the immigration minister's suspicion that a person does not pass the character test must be reasonable.[227] The High Court most recently summarised the condition of reasonableness in *ABT17 v Minister for Immigration* (*ABT17*),[228] a case concerning the review of an asylum seeker protection claim. The summary combines the principles of Wednesbury unreasonableness and the judgment in *Minister for Immigration and Citizenship v Li*[229] that a reasonable decision needs an 'evident and intelligible justification'.[230] The High Court in *ABT17* applied these to both the process of decision-making and the conclusion. Citing precedents, the majority judgment defined reasonableness by stating:

> The answer is to be found in recognising that '[t]he implied condition of reasonableness is not confined to why a statutory decision is made; it extends to how a statutory decision is made' such that '[j]ust as a power is exercised in an improper manner if it is, upon the material before the

222 *Migration Act 1958* (Cth) s 501(6)(d).
223 Ian Coyle and Patrick Keyzer, 'The Removal of Convicted Noncitizens from Australia – Is There Only a "Minimal and Remote" Chance of Getting It Right?' (2016) 41(2) *Alternative Law Journal* 86–7.
224 Ministerial Direction 90, para 8.1.1(1)(a)(iii).
225 Note that being the defendant in an intervention order is not the same as being a defendant to a criminal charge.
226 *Migration Act 1958* (Cth) s 499.
227 *Migration Act 1958* (Cth) s 501.
228 (2020) 269 CLR 439 ('*ABT17*').
229 (2013) 249 CLR 332.
230 (2013) 249 CLR 332 [76].

decision-maker, a decision to which no reasonable person could come, so it is exercised in an improper manner if the decision-maker makes his or her decision in a manner so devoid of plausible justification that no reasonable person could have taken that course'.[231]

Judicial review of decisions concerning the assessment of risk under the character test can be seen in the cases of *Stretton v Minister for Immigration and Border Protection (No 2)*[232] and *Falzon v Minister for Immigration and Border Protection*.[233] They show the high bar set for a finding of unreasonableness.

In *Stretton* Allsop CJ overturned the finding of unreasonableness by the original judge, whose reasoning was that the decision to deport was unnecessary for the purpose of protecting the community.[234] Allsop CJ found that, while a different immigration minister might have been 'prepared, on the community's behalf, to take the low risk of the possibility of the non-citizen's reoffending to avoid the harshness inflicted by the removal', it was not legally unreasonable for the immigration minister to decide to cancel his visa.[235] In *Falzon*[236] the High Court confirmed that it was not the court's role to find that 'the criteria of deportation are overly harsh or unduly burdensome or otherwise disproportionate to the risk to the safety and welfare of the nation posed'.[237] Mr Falzon was a sixty-one-year-old man who had arrived from Malta as a three-year-old.[238]

However, in *Hands v Minister for Immigration and Border Protection*[239] unreasonableness was found. Allsop CJ found that the lack of real consideration of the material by the immigration minister and those in the department who had provided him with a draft decision led to an unreasonable

231 *ABT17* (n 228) 450–1, citing *Minister for Immigration and Citizenship v Li* (2013) 249 CLR 332, 371 [91]; *Minister for Immigration and Ethnic Affairs v Teoh* (1995) 183 CLR 273, 290, citing *Prasad v Minister for Immigration and Ethnic Affairs* (1985) 6 FCR 155, 169–70. Cf *Minister for Immigration and Citizenship v SZIAI* (2009) 83 ALJR 1123, 1128–9 [20]–[25]; 259 ALR 429, 434–6. Note Crawford, 'Entrenched Minimum (n 110), argues that the extent and nature of this requirement is shaped by the statute and so is a constraint placed by the legislation, not the judiciary. See also Michael Barker and Alice Nagel, 'Legal Unreasonableness: Life After Li' (2015) 79 *AIAL Forum* 1; Leighton McDonald, 'Reasons, Reasonableness and Intelligible Justification in Judicial Review' (2015) 37 *Sydney Law Review* 467.

232 [2016] FCAC 11, [20].

233 [2018] HCA 2, [95].

234 *Minister for Immigration and Border Protection v Stretton* [2016] FCAC 11, [20].

235 *Minister for Immigration and Border Protection v Stretton* [2016] FCAC 7, [17].

236 [2018] HCA 2.

237 *Falzon* (n 186).

238 *Falzon* (n 186) [1].

239 *Hands* (n 120).

conclusion based on a 'central finding of fact . . . without any probative foundation'.[240] In his judgment he stated:

> Public power, the source of which is in statute, must conform to the requirements of its statutory source and to the limitations imposed by the requirement of legality.
>
> Legality in this context takes its form and shape from the terms, scope and policy of the statute and fundamental values anchored in the common law: *Minister for Immigration and Border Protection v Stretton* (2016) 237 FCR 1 at [9]; *Minister for Immigration and Border Protection v SZVFW* (2018) 264 CLR 541 at [59]. The consequences of these considerations are that where decisions might have devastating consequences visited upon people, the obligation of real consideration of the circumstances of the people affected must be approached confronting what is being done to people.[241]

Allsop CJ's judgment echoes in some ways Edelman J's statement in *Graham* that Parliament legislates and Parliament 'must squarely confront what it is doing and accept the political cost'.[242] In *Hands* Allsop CJ is not warning of a political cost but rather a human cost. This human cost is the consequence of the immigration minister, the decision-maker, ignoring the fundamental values of the common law, which Allsop CJ expressed in this instance as requiring the immigration minister to give full consideration to the human cost of how the legislated discretionary power is deployed. However, despite this win in court for Mr Hands, the reality for him and other noncitizens is that the discretion to cancel again, even after such a finding, remains with the immigration minister. The court's power is to declare the decision illegal and require the immigration minister to make a legal decision. It remains open to the immigration minister to reconsider the case and come to a legally reasonable decision that might still be against the applicant. For example in *Caric v Minister for Immigration and Border Protection*,[243] the court found that the decision to deport Ms Caric was not lawful because the Parliamentary Secretary had failed to consider the legal consequence of her 'possible indefinite detention' in Australia if the visa cancellation was not revoked.[244] The matter was returned to the decision-maker, but the court acknowledged that it was likely the same decision would be made by the immigration minister

240 *Hands* (n 120) 640–1.
241 *Hands* (n 120) 630.
242 *Graham* (n 73) 39.
243 [2017] FCA 1391.
244 [2017] FCA 1391 [19], [21]. Note despite *NZYQ v Minister for Immigration, Citizenship and Multicultural Affairs* [2023] HCA 37 this remains the law at the time of writing. See discussion in Chapter 6.

even after the necessary inquiry. Just as the court noted in *Stretton*[245] and in *Falzon*,[246] the disproportionate impact of exclusion from Australia relative to the low risk to the community is not an aspect of the immigration minister's decision that is open to review. The discretion to assess risk is so broad it is difficult to see how it can be exceeded.

D National Interest

The second provision in the character test that is critical to the unfettered nature of the discretion the test provides is the criterion of 'national interest'. The immigration minister has personal unreviewable power to refuse or cancel a visa in the national interest.[247] This criterion is an example of the grey hole in its starkest form.[248] Under the character test since 1998, the immigration minister acting personally[249] and outside the rules of natural justice[250] has had power to refuse or cancel a visa if the immigration minister 'reasonably suspects' that the person fails the character test and 'the minister is satisfied the refusal or cancellation is in the national interest'.[251] When first introduced in 1998 the level of discretion created by this measure was noted by Lawrie Ferguson, a member of the Opposition shadow Labor ministry from 1997 to 2007. He said in debate:

> We have to put a degree of faith in the current Minister for Immigration and Multicultural Affairs and his long-term commitment to Amnesty International and human rights. We have a person in the job who would, on balance, be responsible in these matters.[252]

He warned that 'a person with less concern for human rights than the current immigration minister' could use the discretion in the character test for political ends.[253] This concern appears justified, as the case law shows.

245 *Stretton* (n 234).
246 *Falzon* (n 186).
247 *Migration Act 1958* (Cth) s 501(3)(d).
248 See Gabrielle Appleby and Alexander Reilly for discussion of public and national interest and proposed limits to this discretion in Gabrielle Appleby and Alexander Reilly, 'Unveiling the Public Interest: The Parameters of Executive Discretion in Australian Migration Legislation' (2017) 28(4) *Public Law Review* 293.
249 *Migration Act 1958* (Cth) s 501(4).
250 *Migration Act 1958* (Cth) 501(5).
251 *Migration Act 1958* (Cth) 501(3)(d).
252 Commonwealth, *Parliamentary Debates*, House of Representatives, 2 December 1998, 1241 (Lawrie Ferguson).
253 Commonwealth, *Parliamentary Debates*, House of Representatives, 2 December 1998, 1238 (Lawrie Ferguson).

In *Re Patterson; Ex Parte Taylor*[254] Kirby J argued that the use of this criterion should be limited. He noted that the immigration minister had explained in the second reading speech that, 'in exceptional or emergency circumstances, the immigration minister, acting personally will be given powers to act decisively on matters of visa cancellation', and that the use of national interest was limited to those emergency circumstances.[255] The minister had argued that only such exceptional circumstances could justify the suspension of natural justice.[256] However, Kirby J's view was not the majority's and not reflected in the text of the statute. Kirby J identified the making of the choice between the cancellation power in s 501(2) (over which natural justice applied) and s 501(3) (over which it did not) as a decision and held that that decision needed to be open to judicial scrutiny. But his argument did not win majority support, and one of Dyzenhaus' grey holes in the law was created.

In one line of cases continuing up to the present, the use of the immigration minister's national interest power in s 501(3)(d) has not been limited to emergency cases.[257] The Federal Court found in 2018 that 'the matters that the Minister may take into account in determining the national interest are matters for the Immigration minister.'[258] The High Court in *S297/2013 v Minister for Immigration*[259] validated political accountability as an influence on decisions about national interest. It found that the object of placing a power into the hands of the immigration minister 'is that he may exercise it according to government policy' and in doing so

> may properly have regard to a wide range of considerations of which some may be seen as bearing upon such matters as the political fortunes of the government of which the Minister is a member and, thus, affect the Minister's continuance in office.[260]

Kinslor and English suggest that the result is that the national interest is 'a very wide term supporting a diversity of views – so long as they are held by the minister'.[261]

254 (2001) 207 CLR 391.
255 (2001) 207 CLR 500 [326].
256 (2001) 207 CLR 504–5, [335]–[340].
257 *Madafferi v Minister for Immigration and Multicultural Affairs* [2002] FCAFC 220 [89]; *Anaki v Minister for Immigration and Border Protection* [2018] FCA 195, [21].
258 *Anaki v Minister for Immigration and Border Protection* [2018] FCA 195, [21].
259 (2015) 255 CLR 231.
260 (2015) 255 CLR 242 [18], quoting *Hot Holdings Pty Ltd v Creasy* (2002) 210 CLR 438, 455 [50].
261 Joanne Kinslor and James English, 'Decision Making in the National Interest?' (2015) 79 *AIAL Forum* 35, 47.

VI Conclusion

The definition of the value 'the rule of law' in the Australian Values Statement and the operation of that value for the noncitizen subject to the *Migration Act 1958* (Cth) reflects a thin conception of the rule of law. It is cut adrift from the origins of the concept as a shield from arbitrary power by laws which confer a broad discretion on the immigration minister. A series of statutes have largely stripped the noncitizen of the opportunity for a decision concerning their liberty and well-being to be scrutinised by the courts in a way that fully applies the rights and freedoms of the common law. Common-law natural justice is codified, and for the immigration minister acting personally even this code might not apply. The basic guarantee of the rule of law, judicial review, is substantially reduced to the formality of a day in court. The role of the courts at most is to require the immigration minister to make a lawful decision, but that decision can still be harsh and vastly disproportionate to the risk of harm. The example of the character test in s 501 demonstrates how the statute constructs what Dyzenhaus calls a grey hole in the law: unfettered discretion, cloaked in legal formalities and opaque concepts such as national interest is introduced as an emergency measure but quickly becomes part of the normal operation of migration law.

The consequence for the noncitizen subject to the *Migration Act 1958* (Cth) is that they are subject to a rule of law that is indistinguishable from the personal rule of the immigration minister. The amendments made between 2000 and 2020 justified this increase in executive control as a protection or assertion of sovereignty. For the noncitizen this has been at the cost of living under a rule of law that 'loom[s] as a perennial source of [potential] threat and fear'.[262]

262 Krygier (n 8) 203.

Chapter 9

Conclusion

What can be concluded about the nature of the sovereignty that was used to justify exclusionary amendments to the *Migration Act 1958* (Cth) between 2000 and 2020, an era of increasing opportunity, interdependency and vulnerability brought about by globalisation? It is submitted that this sovereignty was narrowly conceived as the Australian executive government's unfettered power to exclude the unwanted migrant who was characterised as an existential threat. This final chapter of the book draws five conclusions based on the arguments made in this thesis which together led to this overarching conclusion.

The first conclusion about the nature of the sovereignty that justified the amendments is that this sovereignty aligns more closely with a Westphalian conception of sovereignty as unfettered supreme authority over a territory and its people than with a more nuanced 21st-century conception, such as the view of James Crawford and others that sovereignty simply means 'the totality of powers a state may have under international law' which is therefore subject to international commitments.[1] It is a conception of sovereignty that confers a right to decide who can be excluded without regard to those international commitments. It is a conception of sovereignty which has ignored the challenge made by Indigenous claims to sovereignty. It is a conception of sovereignty narrowly focussed on exclusion and which overlooks how economic globalisation has driven forced migration and asylum seeking.

Secondly, it can be concluded that this expression of Australian sovereign power to exclude the unwanted migrant can only be partially explained by the theories of Wendy Brown and Catherine Dauvergne, who see the exclusion of the unwanted migrant as a marker of the waning sovereignty brought about by globalisation. Instances from Australia's first century as a

1 James Crawford, *The Creation of States in International Law* (Oxford University Press, 2006) 32–3. See also Stephen Hall, *Principles of International Law* (Lexis Nexis, 7th ed, 2019) 3–4; Hans Kelsen, 'Sovereignty and International Law' (1960) 48(4) *Georgetown Law Journal* 627.

DOI: 10.4324/9781003515852-12

federation challenge the application of this theory to the migration amendments made between 2000 and 2020. They demonstrate that, despite economic, defence and diplomatic dependencies and vulnerabilities, excluding the unwanted migrant has featured prominently in the way Australia has used sovereign power since Federation. From 1901 until several years beyond 1958, the unwanted migrant was openly identified in parliamentary debate as the non-white migrant. This policy of exclusion, known as the White Australia policy, was prioritised even where it caused economic loss. However, for reasons of defence and diplomacy the racial discrimination underlying the White Australia policy was never explicitly legislated. By 1978 it had been officially abandoned. The justification for exclusion was no longer overt racial discrimination. The Parliament was told by the government that the first principle of migration policy was now to be sovereignty, which was impliedly to be located in the Australian government, the executive. Before 2001 this migration policy principle was alluded to in parliamentary debate on only two more occasions, both in 1986.[2] This history gives support to a view that, at a time when the sources and limits of the sovereign power of the newly formed federation of colonies were somewhat uncertain, the Parliament prioritised the exclusion of the unwanted non-white person as an assertion of power. In that way, the way the migration power was wielded to exclude in 1901 can be understood as foundational to the expression of sovereignty in Australian policy and law, which demonstrates that more recent amendments are not a new response to globalisation.

Supporting this conclusion is the example of the international student visa. In debates about amendments to the law on that topic, the Parliament wrestled with two competing philosophies: the neoliberalism that underpins the current wave of globalisation and a version of the Westphalian sovereignty of unfettered control demonstrated in the earliest migration legislation of 1901. The student visa amendments established the hybrid status of the international student. Students were welcome, lucrative consumers, but under the amendments they could automatically, and sometimes even without notice, become illegal noncitizens who could be placed in detention and deported if reported as breaking prescriptive codes of conduct. Even given the reality of what had quickly become a major export industry, priority was given to expressing a Westphalian sovereignty that emphasised absolute authority over people who entered Australia and the individual circumstances and behaviour which allowed them to remain. Migration policy was characterised in debate as a cornerstone of Australian society, not just a market tool. Neoliberalism and sovereignty as exclusion were in tension.

2 Commonwealth, *Parliamentary Debates*, House of Representatives, 20 February 1986, 952 Chris (Hurford); Commonwealth, *Parliamentary Debates*, House of Representatives, 10 April 1986, 1969 (Chris Hurford).

The third conclusion that can be drawn about the nature of the sovereignty used to justify exclusionary amendments is based on the conceptualisation of the threats to sovereignty that these amendments were purportedly addressing. The elevation of sovereignty from a policy principle in 1978 to a prime ministerial justification for the exclusion amendments from 2001 gives some support to Brown's and Dauvergne's theories about the nexus of sovereignty, globalisation and migration law. In the period 2000–20, the Australian government embraced economic globalisation despite interdependencies and vulnerabilities that could be seen as a threat to sovereign control. Concurrent with this, it represented the admission of uninvited asylum seekers to Australian territory or the presence of those deemed to have a character flaw as a threat to sovereignty of national significance. From 2001, successive governments enacted sometimes elaborate and convoluted migration amendments to address this threat.

These were justified in Parliament and in ministerial comment as necessary to assert and protect Australia's sovereignty, in this way characterising the noncitizen as a potential or actual existential threat. These amendments detained and excluded asylum seekers, detained other unwelcome noncitizens for sometimes years, and deported any noncitizen deemed by the immigration minister to be a risk. In these efforts to exclude, sovereignty was disconnected from territory and disconnected from achieving a national objective such as a white population, as had been the case under the White Australia policy.

This assertion of sovereignty as a justification functioned to exclude more than the unwanted migrant. The amendments further concentrated sovereign power in the executive government by attempting to shield the executive government's actions from the influence or opprobrium of international law, the implications of Australia's own domestic law, the scrutiny of the judiciary and at times even the Parliament. At the end of this period, under Scott Morrison's prime ministership, asserting sovereignty was represented as protecting the safety of the vulnerable from the threat of the noncitizen predator and the preservation of the lifestyle of Australians. This elevation of a small number of unwelcome migrants to the level of an existential threat can be analysed as an exercise of hypersovereignty: the performance of exclusion as a demonstration of sovereign power that simultaneously signals the waning capacity to wield Westphalian sovereignty.

Fourthly, what can be concluded about the nature of this sovereignty is that it is underpinned by a mixture of the values of neoliberalism and Anglo-Celtic ethnocentrism and not by the espoused Australian values of successive governments. The language of Australian values such as compassion and fairness and the importance of speaking English was instead weaponised to exclude the unwanted migrant. It was used to justify the further strengthening of executive control.

Finally, it can be concluded that the conception of the rule of law asserted and protected by this sovereignty is indistinguishable from the rule of the immigration minister. The amendments designed to exclude have shielded migration decisions from the scrutiny of the judiciary to such an extent that the harshness of decisions that are disproportionate to any risk of harm is unable to be legally challenged. The consequence is that unwanted migrants can be deprived of their liberty for an undefined period, sometimes lasting many years. The final decision on whether or not to exclude a noncitizen from Australia's territory, from economic or community participation, or from the enjoyment of liberty is enshrined in legislation as being at the immigration minister's non-compellable, most often non-reviewable discretion. Successive governments have justified this as a necessary assertion of a sovereign right or a protection of sovereignty. For the noncitizen this sovereignty is concentrated in the person of the immigration minister. The nature of this sovereignty for the noncitizen resembles Jean Bodin's voice of God.[3]

And the future?

In 2022 Australia had a change of government and in 2023 a change to the leadership of the High Court. The new immigration minister inherited and has retained the broad discretionary power, his 'voice of God', and has used it to be more inclusive to refugees by modifying migration regulations and ministerial directions and raising humanitarian visa numbers at 20,000.[4]

However, under the leadership of the new chief justice, the High Court has made a small encroachment on this discretion. The High Court has overturned the 2004 precedent set in *Al-Kateb v Godwin*.[5] The court found in *NZYQ v Minister for Immigration, Citizenship and Multicultural Affairs*[6] (2023) that detaining the applicant, who had completed a sentence for child sex offences,[7] was unconstitutional. This was because of 'no real prospect of the removal of the plaintiff from Australia becoming practicable in the reasonably foreseeable future'.[8] The implication of this ruling was that a cohort of immigration detainees who had previously been found to be refugees were released into the community. The government responded with legislation that amended the temporary visa conditions for this cohort to include electronic monitoring and curfews and other restrictions not unlike criminal parole.[9]

3 Jean Bodin, *Six Books of the Commonwealth*, tr and abridged MJ Tooley (Basil Blackwell, 1955) 25–30.

4 Migration Amendment (Resolution of Status Visa) Regulations 2023. On 9 February 2023, the Australian government revoked Ministerial Direction 80 – order for considering and disposing of family visa applications and replaced it with Ministerial Direction 102 – order for considering and disposing of family visa applications. Budget 2025–2025 <https://budget.gov.au>.

5 (2004) 219 CLR 562.

6 [2023] HCA 37.

7 [2023] HCA 37 [2].

8 *NZYQ v Minister for Immigration, Citizenship and Multicultural Affairs* [2023] HCA37.

9 *Migration Amendment (Bridging Visa Conditions) Act* 2023 ss 76B, 76C,76D.

Despite these changes of government policy and High Court precedent, there is yet no strong indication of change to the overarching policy framework of sovereignty as a justification for exclusionary migration amendments, which from 2000 to 2020 operated to exclude the unwanted migrant, as well as to diminish the scrutiny of the judiciary and the obligations of international law, and to repurpose espoused Australian values.

And the world takes note.[10] In 2017 Professor Juss from King's College London advised 'we should take Australia seriously quite simply because what Australia does in border controls today, the rest of the world might do tomorrow. We ignore it at our peril'.[11] And the UK government did not ignore it.[12] It copied it.[13] Europe too has also taken note.[14] The impact on migration policy in the USA is also documented.[15] In a transcript of a conversation between then Australian prime minister Turnbull and President Trump concerning the US taking offshore asylum seekers from Australia, Turnbull said 'Even if we think you are the best person in the world, even if you are a Nobel Prize-winning genius, we will not let you in'. Mr Trump replied: 'That is a good idea. We should do that too. You are worse than I am'.[16]

10 Satvinder Juss, 'Detention and Delusion in Australia's Kafkaesque Refugee Law' (2017) 36 *Refugee Survey Quarterly* 146, 161. Prof Juss is a leading academic at Dickson Poon School of Law, King's College London.

11 Professor Juss is a leading academic at Dickson Poon School of Law, King's College London.

12 Madeline Gleeson and Theodore Konstadinides, 'The UK's Rwanda Policy and Lessons from Australia', *UHCLA* (14 March 2024) <https://ukconstitutionallaw.org>.

13 'PM Statement on the Stop the Boats Bill' (7 March 2023) <www.gov.uk>.

14 Sasha Polakow-Suransky, 'How Europe Fell in Love with Australia's Immigration Policy', *The Guardian* (12 October 2017) <www.theguardian.com/world/2017/oct/12/how-europes-far-right-fell-in-love-with-australias-immigration-policy>.

15 Jason Wilson, 'The USA Is Imprisoning People It Finds Undesirable: Australia Has Already Lived This Nightmare', *The Guardian* (27 June 2019); Daniel Ghezelbash, *Refugee Lost: Asylum Law in an Interdependent World* (Cambridge University Press, 2018).

16 Quoted in *SBS News* (4 August 2017) <www.sbs.com.au/news/article/you-are-worse-than-i-am-transcript-reveals-turnbull-told-trump-he-could-decide-not-to-take-asylum-seekers/pasw4h0t7>.

Index